THE S. S. HUEBNER FOUNDATION
FOR INSURANCE EDUCATION

LECTURES

LIFE INSURANCE TRENDS AND PROBLEMS
LIFE INSURANCE TRENDS AT MID-CENTURY
INVESTMENT OF LIFE INSURANCE FUNDS
ACCIDENT AND SICKNESS INSURANCE
PENSIONS: PROBLEMS AND TRENDS
THE BENEFICIARY IN LIFE INSURANCE
LIFE INSURANCE SALES MANAGEMENT
ALL LINES INSURANCE
RISK MANAGEMENT
INSURANCE, GOVERNMENT, AND SOCIAL POLICY: STUDIES IN INSURANCE
    REGULATION

STUDIES

AN ANALYSIS OF GOVERNMENT LIFE INSURANCE
GROUP LIFE INSURANCE
GROUP HEALTH INSURANCE
GROUP ANNUITIES
THE ECONOMIC THEORY OF RISK AND INSURANCE
LIFE INSURANCE HOUSING PROJECTS
LIFE INSURANCE INVESTMENT IN COMMERCIAL REAL ESTATE
TOTAL DISABILITY PROVISIONS IN LIFE INSURANCE CONTRACTS
INSURANCE AND ECONOMIC THEORY
TRANSITION TO MULTIPLE-LINE INSURANCE COMPANIES
COMPULSORY TEMPORARY DISABILITY INSURANCE IN THE UNITED STATES
DEVELOPMENT OF COMPREHENSIVE INSURANCE FOR THE HOUSEHOLD
SAVINGS BANK LIFE INSURANCE
RIGHTS OF CREDITORS IN LIFE INSURANCE POLICIES
REGULATION OF BLUE CROSS AND BLUE SHIELD PLANS
SUBROGATION IN INSURANCE THEORY AND PRACTICE
PARTICIPATING LIFE INSURANCE SOLD BY STOCK COMPANIES
CORPORATE SELF-INSURANCE AND RISK RETENTION PLANS
RATEMAKING FOR HOMEOWNERS INSURANCE
THE REGULATION OF RECIPROCAL INSURANCE EXCHANGES
AUTOMOBILE LIABILITY CLAIMS: INSURANCE COMPANY PHILOSOPHIES AND
    PRACTICES
UNSATISFIED JUDGMENT FUNDS

Insurance, Government, and Social Policy

STUDIES IN INSURANCE REGULATION

edited by

SPENCER L. KIMBALL

Dean and Professor of Law
University of Wisconsin

and

HERBERT S. DENENBERG

Harry J. Loman Professor of Insurance
Wharton School of Finance and Commerce
University of Pennsylvania

Published for

THE S. S. HUEBNER FOUNDATION FOR INSURANCE EDUCATION

University of Pennsylvania

by

Richard D. Irwin, Inc., Homewood, Illinois
Irwin-Dorsey Limited, Georgetown, Ontario

© 1969

THE S. S. HUEBNER FOUNDATION FOR INSURANCE EDUCATION

University of Pennsylvania

First Printing, July, 1969

Library of Congress Catalog Card No. 77–83125

Printed in the United States of America

THE S. S. HUEBNER FOUNDATION
FOR INSURANCE EDUCATION

The S. S. Huebner Foundation for Insurance Education was created in 1940, under the sponsorship of the American Life Convention, the Life Insurance Association of America (then the Association of Life Insurance Presidents), and the Institute of Life Insurance, and operated under a deed of trust until 1955 at which time it was incorporated as a Pennsylvania nonprofit corporation. Its primary purpose is to strengthen and encourage insurance education at the collegiate level. Its activities take three principal forms:

a) The providing of fellowships to teachers in accredited colleges and universities of the United States and Canada, or persons who are contemplating a teaching career in such colleges and universities, in order that they may secure preparation at the graduate level for insurance teaching and research.

b) The publication of research theses and other studies which constitute a distinct contribution directly or indirectly to insurance knowledge.

c) The collection and maintenance of an insurance library and other research materials which are made available through circulating privileges to teachers in accredited colleges and universities desirous of conducting research in the insurance field.

Financial support for the Foundation is provided by contributions from more than one hundred and twenty life insurance companies and proceeds from the sale of Foundation publications.

The program of activities is under the general direction of a Board of Trustees representing the life insurance institution. Actual operation of the Foundation has been delegated to the University of Pennsylvania under an administrative plan submitted by the University and approved by the Board of Trustees. The University discharges its responsibilities through an Administrative Board consisting of five officers and faculty members of the University of Pennsylvania and four academic persons associated with other institutions. Active management of the Foundation is entrusted to an Executive Director, appointed by the University of Pennsylvania.

vii

Foreword

INTEREST in insurance regulation has reached an intensity and scope unprecedented in this country and perhaps any other part of the world. Dialogue on the subject is taking place in all sections of the country and at all levels of government. Numerous Congressional and state legislative investigations are underway, all looking toward statutory resolution of the problems at which they are directed. It can truly be said that "insurance is in the midst of a legislative avalanche."

Current regulatory proposals dealing with such issues as insurance for urban cores, reparation to victims of automobile accidents, medical care reimbursement, the holding company phenomenon, credit insurance, rate regulation, and the financial soundness of private pension plans go beyond the professional concerns of the insurance business, having obvious implications for society in general. While the social problems of our times cannot be solved by insurance alone, many of them cannot be solved without insurance. For better or for worse, new legislative initiatives are likely to be launched—and perhaps consummated—to deal with those social ills believed to lend themselves to insurance remedies. These efforts have profound economic, political, and social significance.

Despite the importance of insurance regulation, there is only a handful of scholarly books on the subject and most of these are out of date. In an attempt to help rectify this deficiency in insurance literature, the Huebner Foundation asked two leading academic authorities on insurance regulation, Professor Herbert S. Denenberg and Professor Spencer L. Kimball, to arrange a series of lectures on the subject to be given at the University of Pennsylvania, in accordance with a long-standing custom of the Foundation. Professors Denenberg and Kimball developed an imaginative sequence of lectures and persuaded a distinguished group of academic, legal, and regulatory authorities to prepare papers on the various topics thought to be relevant to the current scene. They also searched existing literature on the general subject and selected a few "nuggets" that would enrich and round out the published record. In addition, they exercised their editorial prerogative to include some of their own perceptive writings on the subject. The result is a book that should be enthusiastically received by all who have an interest in the insurance institution. This book deserves a prominent place on the library shelf of any serious student of insurance and especially of those who have regulatory and legislative responsibilities.

The editors were uniquely qualified for this undertaking. Dr. Denenberg, a native of Nebraska, is a graduate of Johns Hopkins University. He holds a Ph.D. degree from the University of Pennsylvania, a J.D. degree from Creighton University, and an LL.M. from Harvard University. He is the coauthor of four books and the author or coauthor of over 40 articles. With Dr. Juan Aponte of the University of Puerto Rico, he carried out a study of the automobile accident problem in Puerto Rico that led to the legislative prescription of a new system, called the Social Protection Plan, for indemnifying the victims of automobile accidents. He served as Research Director and Special Counsel for the President's National Advisory Panel on Insurance in Riot-Affected Areas. For the last several years he has been working with Professor Kimball in a thoroughgoing revision of the insurance laws of Wisconsin. Since 1962 he has been on the Insurance faculty of the Wharton School and currently occupies the Harry J. Loman Chair for Property and Liability Insurance.

Professor Kimball is a native of Arizona and a Phi Beta Kappa graduate from the University of Arizona with a major in mathematics. He attended Oxford University as a Rhodes Scholar, receiving a B.C.L. (Bachelor of Civil Law) with First Class Honors. He received an S.J.D. degree from the University of Wisconsin. He became Dean of the University of Utah College of Law at the age of 31. He later joined the University of Michigan Law School faculty and a year ago was appointed Dean of the Law School at the University of Wisconsin. He is author of *Insurance and Public Policy* (which won the Elizur Wright Award for 1961), three other books, and a host of articles in law journals and other scholarly publications. Since 1966 he has been Staff Director of the Insurance Laws Revision Committee of the Legislative Council of the State of Wisconsin, an undertaking that is having a major impact on insurance codes throughout the country.

The Foundation is profoundly grateful to Professors Denenberg and Kimball for putting together what promises to be a highly significant addition to insurance literature. It is also grateful to the many authorities who contributed papers for inclusion in the volume. They have made an enduring contribution to insurance education.

Philadelphia
June, 1969

DAN M. McGILL
Executive Director

Preface

I

THIS BOOK began with a series of lectures on insurance regulation organized by the editors and presented at the University of Pennsylvania during the 1966–68 academic years under the auspices of the S. S. Huebner Foundation for Insurance Education. The idea for the series of lectures was in turn inspired by the involvement of the editors in the current revision of the insurance laws of Wisconsin. The need for such lectures and other research is too obvious for comment. There is relatively little serious research being done in insurance and the least adequately researched field of all is insurance regulation. Any additional serious investigations that could be stimulated would help to fill a gaping hole in the literature, a hole that is especially obvious to the editors because of their efforts to revise the regulatory laws of Wisconsin.

In order to provide somewhat more comprehensive treatment of the subject than the lectures alone provided, the editors have also included essays that were not part of the lecture series, including both previously unpublished and some already published materials. Although a truly comprehensive treatment of insurance regulation would be impossible in a single volume, and difficult except in the form of a systematic treatise, the editors have attempted to build a framework for analysis affording a treatment of the covered subject matter that is as unified and integrated as possible in independently prepared essays.

The editors are indebted to the Huebner Foundation for financing the lecture series. They are also indebted to the Insurance Laws Revision Committee of the Legislative Council of the State of Wisconsin—on whose staff they serve as Director and Associate Director—for having enabled them to study at first hand the issues of insurance regulation in connection with the revision of the in-

surance laws of Wisconsin begun in 1966 and still going on. Some
of the papers in this book are directly adapted from work done in
connection with that revision.

Many, in addition to those named in this preface and in the
lectures printed herein, contributed to the creation of this volume.
We cannot name them all, but feel we should mention: Dr. Dan M.
McGill, Executive Director of the S. S. Huebner Foundation, who
worked with us on behalf of the Foundation; some members of the
secretarial staffs associated with the project who do much work and
get little official credit—Judy Moran, Louise Morrison, Elaine Gross;
and Mildred A. Brill, Administrative Assistant of the Huebner
Foundation.

II

A fundamental principle of the Wisconsin revision is that sound
draftsmanship is dependent upon thorough research. The editors,
therefore, view the research initiated and stimulated during this
project, at the universities and elsewhere, as an integral part of the
revision process itself, and such cooperation between universities
and state governments as essential to the success of the revision.
Close cooperation between university and government is sometimes
referred to as the "Wisconsin idea." The editors submit that the
cooperative effort evidenced by the lecture series and this volume
is in the best tradition of the "Wisconsin idea."

It should not need to be stated, although it is customary to so
state, that the editors do not necessarily espouse the views reflected
in these papers, except those they wrote themselves; and they are
not free from doubts about the latter. Nevertheless, the editors
value the efforts and respect the views of the authors of the papers
included here, and believe their views deserve careful attention and
study.

We submit this volume as an effort to fill an important gap in
the literature of insurance and hope that it will be useful to many
people.

June, 1969   SPENCER L. KIMBALL
                               HERBERT S. DENENBERG

Table of Contents

PART IV. RATE REGULATION IN PROPERTY AND LIABILITY INSURANCE

PART VI.   FEDERAL INTEREST IN INSURANCE REGULATION

EPILOGUE

PART I

The Purposes of Insurance Regulation

chapter 1

An Approach to a General Theory of Insurance Regulation

THE FOLLOWING SELECTION provides some answers to the questions: "Why is it that we do what we do in insurance regulation" and "Where is it that we are trying to go?" The emphasis here is on the fundamental questions to which the myriad technical problems of insurance regulation are subordinate.

THE REGULATION OF INSURANCE*

Spencer L. Kimball
Dean and Professor of Law
University of Wisconsin

What I wish to contribute in this paper is a general or theoretical approach to the subject of insurance regulation. It is intended to provide a framework for thinking about—a method of approach to —problems of insurance regulation. A theoretical approach like this tends to be derided by practical men, sometimes gently and sometimes not. They should be told that a good distinction between what is practical and what is theoretical in law is this: What is practical is what happens in your office, and what is theoretical is what happens in someone else's office!

Oliver Wendell Holmes, Jr. also once had a useful remark to make on the subject.[1] He said that what he meant by theory was

---

* This paper is an edited version of an address presented July 17, 1967, and July 8, 1968, to the First and Second Annual Insurance Seminars, developed jointly by the National Association of Insurance Commissioners and the College of Insurance of New York. It was published by the National Insurance Law Service in pamphlet form in 1967 and distributed to the Service's subscribers.

[1] Oliver Wendell Holmes, Jr., "The Path of the Law," *Harvard Law Review*, Vol. 10 (1897), pp. 457, 473–78.

simply getting to the bottom of his subject. It seems to me that one of the things that is wrong in insurance regulation, generally, is a lack of theory. There is no sense of a framework, of a carefully thought-out basis for deciding what it is we want to do, no reflection upon the question where we are going, and why, no getting to the bottom of the subject. What we have is a dynamic going system which tends to expand to the outermost limits of its logic without ever stopping to ask the basic questions: "Why is it that we do what we do" and "Where is it that we are trying to go?"

SHOULD INSURANCE BE REGULATED?

The first question that can be asked is: "What need is there for regulation at all?" Various reasons have been given for the regulation of insurance. One is the fact that large amounts of money are involved. If we are speaking of aggregates, this would lead, I suppose, to intensive regulation of the oil business. If we are talking about large amounts of money on individual transactions, it certainly would be more sensible to regulate the prices of houses than of the fire insurance that covers them after they are sold.

The length or duration of the contract is another reason often given for regulation. This, of course, is hardly justification, for except in the field of life insurance most insurance contracts are of relatively short duration. The complexity of the transaction is also given as a reason for regulation, but that is not a clear reason, either. Buying a car or a house or entering into a construction contract is a far more complicated transaction for most of us, about which we understand a great deal less.

Another reason given is that the money involved belongs to the policyholder in some sense. It is true that there is a kind of quasi-trust idea floating around the insurance world. But this is the result of, not the justification for, insurance regulation. Moreover, as every lawyer knows, there is no technical "trust" in insurance. There is nothing but an ordinary debtor-creditor relationship, just as in most contractual relationships.

One comes back then to the basic question: "Why regulate at all, or why regulate with the peculiar intensity and comprehensiveness with which the insurance business is now regulated?" This is a question that ought to be asked regularly in every insurance department in the country. It might fairly be asked whether we should not leave all of insurance, or large parts of insurance, or many aspects of insurance, to the marketplace to regulate rather than involving ourselves in the comprehensive kind of control in which we engage?

None of the considerations that I suggested a few moments ago would seem to justify the comprehensive regulation that now exists. Taken together they may come somewhat closer to justifying it, but even then the question is a fair one, to be asked repeatedly. Perhaps it would be better for us to abandon the notion that insurance deserves comprehensive and general regulation, and simply ask the question: "What particular branches of the insurance business, or what particular aspects of it, need for special reasons to be regulated?"

Of course, if one concludes, as perhaps one must conclude, that on the basis of historical considerations we are stuck with a system much like the system we have and that we cannot depart very far from it in any single generation, we ought at least to ask these questions repeatedly in very concrete and specific terms: "What is it explicitly that we are trying to do" and "How can we best go about it?"

THE PURPOSES OF REGULATION

This leads to the next questions: "What are the purposes or objectives of regulation" and "What is the public policy that is involved in the field of insurance?" I would suggest that one should divide the objectives of regulation into two groups, one of which we might call the internal and the other the external goals of insurance regulation.

The internal objectives are those that relate directly to the operation of the insurance business—attainment of which make the institution operate successfully. Basically they are twofold: The first is preservation and enhancement of the solvency or, as I prefer to call it, the *solidity*, of the insurance enterprise, or assurance that the enterprise is not only technically solvent but also is solid and sound so that it can properly perform its job in the community. The second is a related complex of things. In an article I wrote some years ago,[2] I gave it a Latin title, for want of anything better:

---

[2] S. Kimball, "The Purpose of Insurance Regulation: A Preliminary Inquiry in the Theory of Insurance Law," *Minnesota Law Review*, Vol. 45 (1961), p. 471, reprinted in part in S. Kimball, *Essays in Insurance Regulation* (1966). This article has a more elaborate treatment of objectives than can be included here.

aequum et bonum—those things that are good and equitable, and equal and fair. If you prefer to attach some English nouns to this group of objectives, one could say that the objective is to ensure fairness, and equity, and reasonableness in the insurance market.

How far should each of these be pressed? There are countries in the world, such as some of the European countries, in which insurance regulation has as its only internal goal, or almost its only internal goal, that of ensuring the solidity of the insurance enterprise. In these systems the regulatory apparatus concerns itself almost not at all with fairness, or equity, or reasonableness in the market. The difficulty is that by seeking fairness, equity, and reasonableness, we are not simply adding to the objective of solidity some other objectives that are completely consistent with it. The trouble is that fairness, reasonableness, and equity may in many instances conflict or at least present difficulties of reconciliation not only among themselves but also with the objective of solidity or solvency. A good example of this is in the field of rate regulation. The objective of solidity would do nothing more than press rates up and make them redundant. It would encourage, in addition, over-reserving. On the other hand, reasonableness presses downward on the rates and suggests or leads to accurate reserving. Can the objectives be reconciled? I return to that question later.

In addition to these internal objectives of insurance regulation, there are some external ones that are not relevant to the successful operation of the insurance business but nonetheless are important because they are general public policies of our society that cannot be ignored. A serious mistake is made if they are not taken into account in thinking about the regulatory enterprise, for they are there all the time and they constantly press in upon the insurance regulatory apparatus. There are many of them. I shall merely suggest two or three that are extremely important in the working out of the system.

Some are political in nature. For example, there is a libertarian objective—a view that liberty, i.e., freedom from governmental restraint, is a very important thing. This objective leads to both substantive and procedural restraints on official action of various kinds, appearing as constitutional limitations, statutory limitations, and common-law limitations. This is a very basic and very important value of our society that seriously limits the effectiveness of regulation. It is a goal we cannot overcome nor ignore, and do not want to overcome or ignore. The problem is how to reconcile the objectives of solidity, of fairness, reasonableness, and equity with the objective of preserving a meaningful degree of liberty to the regulated entrepreneur and other persons involved in the system?

The second political objective is one that we should avoid as far as we can, but that is always present in our system. I have elsewhere called this "local protectionism," something that you can recognize all over in the statutes if you look at their underlying purposes. They range from countersignature laws for agents to discriminatory tax structures. All of these things are manifestations of a kind of parochialism in our economy that as farsighted and nationally oriented individuals, we want to resist and overcome if we can.

A third political objective one might call "federalism," which can be described as expressing the very important value of wide dispersion of decision-making power in the community, particularly through geographical decentralization. I do not suppose there is much question but that a national regulatory system would be a good deal more efficient than 50 conflicting and varying regulatory agencies in the states. One can say this despite the existence of prime examples of inefficiency on the Potomac, because such multiplicity could hardly be anything other than an inefficient device. Yet there are important values in our society that are greater than, or at least must be balanced with, efficiency and one of them is the value of wide dispersion of decision-making power. It is worth paying something of a price for a dispersion of power for many good reasons.

We now move to some other external objectives that have relation to our insurance apparatus, even though they are not involved in the operation of the insurance enterprise itself. We might talk about various economic and social policies, such as one that might be termed socialization of risk, by which I mean a compulsory or quasi-compulsory extension of insurance coverage without necessarily involving an equitable distribution of cost on purely social grounds rather than economic ones.[3] In the automobile liability field one sees tremendous pressures of this kind toward the socialization of risk by provision of insurance for everyone at a price that is reasonable in terms of what the people in question can afford

---

[3] The author has discussed this development more fully in *Insurance and the Evolution of Public Policy* in The Annals of the Society of Chartered Property & Casualty Underwriters (Summer 1962), pp. 127–43.

to pay, or think they can afford to pay, and not in terms of the burdens imposed on society by their driving of cars.

Another important economic objective is freedom of entrepreneurs to form new units and enter the market. We might also call this goal one of freedom of access to the market. In some European countries, this objective of insurance regulation is rejected—it simply does not exist. Some European countries thus have a "need" test for the admission of new enterprises to the market, a kind of "certificate of convenience and necessity" applied to the insurance field. We have resisted this in this country and have regarded as an important value accessibility of the insurance market to new enterprisers. There are, of course, some indirect methods of restricting access to the market, such as the creation of high capital and surplus requirements as a barrier to entry. The much greater concern that we now have for the qualifications of organizers of new companies, adding to the procedural inconveniences of organization, some rules of accounting, to which I shall return shortly, all tend to restrict freedom of enterprise indirectly.

Finally, in this general area, insurance regulation has taken into account at some levels various objectives that are related to capital accumulation. It is not always clear what public policy is on these questions, and yet it plays on this field regularly. Investment control, for example, has many facets, and not all of them are simply concerned with the preservation of solidity in the insurance enterprise. They have other objectives as well. For example, insurers may be asked, or forced, to provide capital for special social needs. Thus, in the immediate postwar period, there was great pressure from the German government for German insurers to invest in housing, irrespective of the economic considerations that would have governed insurance investment. Public bond market support is another such capital accumulation objective that has currency from time to time.[4]

I have gone on at such length about these objectives, none of which is entirely novel, because it is extremely difficult in any particular situation to answer the question: what it is that you are trying to do in the process of regulation. It seems to me that at least in the important problems with which regulators concern them-

---

[4] For an interesting illustration of public bond market support as such a goal, see S. Kimball, *Insurance and Public Policy* (1960), pp. 272–75.

selves, it would be helpful for them to think through the question what it is that they are trying to do, or the law they are administering is trying to do, against a checklist, mental or written, of these objectives.

CONFLICT OF OBJECTIVES

The complexity of these objectives leads to the need to balance them. This is a problem familiar to every lawyer who has graduated from an American law school in the last generation or so, where the favorite activity of the law professor is to ask students to balance conflicting considerations. The objectives of insurance regulation are frequently in irreconcilable conflict, and they must be added up and weighed and a decision made how far to press this one and how far to relax that one.

One example of the kind of conflict that has to be solved will suffice. It is one that I have already mentioned—the conflict that exists between freedom of access to the market or freedom of enterprise and the solidity of the insurance companies that make up the market. It has been a fundamental principle of our free enterprise economy that no unnecessary burden should be placed upon entry into the market. But this collides directly and immediately with the objective of solidity. The specific problems this creates for the insurance regulatory apparatus are easily illustrated. How much capital and surplus should be required, for example? If the regulator were concerned only with solidity, he would immediately increase the requirements for starting any kind of insurance company up to many millions of dollars. Yet, at every turn, the importance of leaving some room for new enterprises forces him to reconsider and to limit his quest for solidity. The experience, competence, and character of the organizers is another place where solidity would demand very stringent controls. A distinguished insurance executive from the midwest recently expressed shock at New York insistence that he be fingerprinted when he wanted to organize a company in New York. Here are conflicting objectives to be weighed and balanced: the maintenance of solidity on the one side, and on the other the importance of freedom from harrassing government investigation and the value of permitting people freely to enter the insurance business, unless they have proved themselves to be incapable of it. Again, promoters' benefits in the organization of an insurance company can be severely limited. This is a way to help ensure the solidity of insurers. It is also a way to limit freedom of access to the market.

Another important factor is the accounting procedures that have become traditional in the insurance market and constitute artificial ways of preserving solidity. An example is the refusal to permit the capitalization of prepaid expenses and let them be run off over the life of the policy. Both property and life insurance have essentially the same phenomonen. The result is that the more business is written, the less solid the company appears to be, which places a severe handicap upon the new entrepreneur trying to expand rapidly.

THE CAPACITY TO REGULATE

There is another basic consideration in regulation that is important to consider regularly. That is the capacity or the resources of the department as a limitation upon what can be done and achieved. The willingness of the legislature to place added burdens on the insurance department is matched only by its reluctance to provide the money to do the job properly. This can be observed historically as well as in almost any given year. New jobs constantly come in to the office, but the money to do them is always hard to get.

The presence of enough warm bodies around the shop to do the job is only one aspect of the problem. It is not sufficiently recognized that even if you have enough warm bodies, there are serious limitations on human capacities, upon the intellectual, physical, and even moral competence of the regulator. The problem is one of knowing enough about what it is that we are doing to be confident that we do good and not harm. Consequently, I suggest as a sound principle of operation in the regulation of insurance that there should be no interference, no intervention, in the operation of the economy, unless we are reasonably sure what it is that we are doing. This is not because of the slightest ideological objection to intensive and extensive intervention in the business, but I think the experience of the last several decades has shown us that our early confidence in our capacity to regulate wisely was misplaced. We simply do not know enough about what we are doing, nor do individual human beings have the requisite competence and capacity to justify interference, unless the problem with which they are dealing is a serious one. Not only may we make errors about the nature and extent of the problem but we will surely fail to see all the side effects produced by the regulatory activity.

Some interesting points in Peter Drucker's little article, "How to Manage Your Time" are worth calling to the attention of regulators.[5] One of his suggestions about how to make life more efficient is this: one should ask himself the question "What am I doing that really does not need to be done at all, by me or anyone else?" Probably there are a good many such things, including a good many that are being done in the name of regulation of insurance. His second point is: "Which of the actions on my time log could be handled by somebody else just as well, if not better?" To list these is to suggest that one of the ways to extend the capacity and resources of the department and make the problem seem less unmanageable is wherever possible to unload the burden on somebody else, such as the trade associations or the companies. Regulation should certainly involve as much self-regulation as possible. Every time I suggest this, I hear cries of anguish from sources in the business that say, "It is the regulator's job, the insurance commissioner's job, to do this or that." It seems to me that it is a sound principle for the insurance commissioner to make regulation the insurance company's job wherever he can possibly do so, simply unloading the job on the industry. If you ask "How?" the answer, simply but abstractedly stated, is that the law should be so structured as to motivate people to do things in the proper way. I will illustrate this later.

There are innumerable illustrations of the way limited capacity and resources of the department and its people limit regulation. The approval of policy forms, at least in the way in which it is set up in the American statutes, is an illustration of work that is generally not done well. Perhaps it should not be done at all, or if you do have adequate resources should be done quite differently. As an example take an insurance department of medium size that approves tens of thousands of policy forms annually without a lawyer ever seeing any of them. This is true in more than one medium-sized and important insurance department in this country. I had occasion once to go to such a department to try to find out what was happening in the business with respect to a certain clause that was

---

[5] The article was available to the Seminar as one of the general reading assignments.

beginning to show up in litigation. The regulator, a fine and able person, had no idea of what was happening with respect to the clause. He was simply unaware whether it was being inserted or not, and seemed almost oblivious of its very existence. It is an absurd kind of regulation in which the regulator does not even know that much.

This suggests that we are dealing here with a problem in which the mechanics are extremely cumbersome and difficult. A different approach is called for, though surely standard policies are not the answer. That would create problems of a different kind. We might try to simplify the job and even say that certain parts of it are not worth doing, such as where commercial buyers of insurance are concerned. Why should we bother with the regulation of forms for the commercial buyer? For the mass market, it might be possible to go farther than we now do to produce a reasonable amount of standardization. This would channel the competition into a few places where it could be clearly understood, such as in price or the grosser aspects of coverage. We would then be seeking to make the market "transparent," to use the German phrase, so that the ordinary citizen could see better what he is doing when he buys a product.

Another illustration of the limitations of capacity and resources of the department is the problem of handling rate regulation with inadequate personnel. Many medium-sized departments, and most of the small departments, do not have available a trained casualty actuary to deal with the regulation of rates. That leads inevitably either to excessive reliance of the regulatory body upon the regulated entrepreneur for information, or else to instinctive and uninformed resistance to entreprenurial demands. This is one argument, though by no means a conclusive one, for either abandoning or changing drastically the rate regulatory method in American insurance law.

Another place where the inadequacy of human resources shows up is in the examination of insurance companies. Not only is there a shortage of qualified people for this purpose available in the department but there seem to be vacancies in technical organizations everywhere, and it is hard to know what to do in this area.

It happens that this coincides in time with the obsolescence of the traditional methods of examination and of the traditional accountant's learning. Companies do not have books any more. They have tapes, and drums, and other data processing devices. They can, of course, create books by printing out the information, but it is a serious question whether they should be asked to. This may be the moment to move very rapidly in a new direction, of trying to accommodate resources to needs by using the new communication devices that are available, and to abandon, over a short generation, the traditional system of examinations, and the annual reports too, for that matter. There is now—there has been for a long time, but we are beginning to realize it now—the possibility of relying to a very considerable extent on independent people outside of or not connected with the department. There is also, perhaps, an increasing awareness of the possibility of spot-checking instead of examining comprehensively. The computer people tell me that it is possible to work out with computers scientific strategies for examinations that enable one by random sampling to cover all of the things he is interested in by spot-checking. The company's own equipment can be used to do the job of control wherever the company is sufficiently mechanized in its accounting procedures. I am talking far beyond my knowledge of the subject, but after a good deal of briefing from company experts in the field. Some of them think we are at the beginning of a development that could completely revolutionize the process of examination. In achieving this it may be possible to make a virtue out of necessity and get along with fewer people in the department while doing a better job at the same time.

THE SIDE EFFECTS OF REGULATORY ACTIVITY

We need to consider in the regulatory process the interrelationships among various activities and aspects of the business, and particularly the side effects that result from regulatory activity. High-risk automobile insurance might be chosen as an illustration of the problems that exist.

How did it come about in the first place? Without meaning to foreclose all alternative explanations, nor to suggest an exhaustive explanation, I would suggest that rigidity in rates and forms produced by prior approval laws may have had a good deal to do with the necessity for development of the high-risk automobile business. One might compare, for example, the Lloyd's situation, where in an almost completely flexible and unregulated market, most risks can be placed at some price. This is subject to some absolute capacity limits in that market. In our system, naturally, the companies have to underwrite from filed rates, in relation to their rate structure. To some extent, they can improve their position by elaboration of the classification structure, but within limits. In any case, there are always people who present risks below that certain level that underwriters think will produce a reasonable margin of profit to the company. At some point the companies cut off the bottom risks. Consequently, a separate or supplemental market has to develop for part or all of the remaining risks in the form of special high-risk, high-priced automobile writers whose coverage is sometimes limited and whose price is fairly arbitrary and often quite high.

The problem as it now exists, and as it is seen from the point of view of the legislator, is essentially this. There are many decent citizens without a particularly bad record who have to pay high premiums that they do not think they can afford to pay, and may be subject to fairly arbitrary cancellation or nonrenewal, or other harsh treatment by insurance companies. This problem is an extremely difficult one, and I do not pretend to know the full answer. But I think it is clearly not the solution simply to assume that insurers are bad boys who can be taught good manners by a hard spanking, and whose arbitrariness will therefore or thereafter disappear. If you forbid nonwriting, cancellation, nonrenewal, and thus require the companies to take all comers, quite apart from what this does to the fundamental presuppositions of our legal system, you may eventually drive the companies out of the line altogether, or out of the state altogether. This is something of a problem. If a company is operating in a free enterprise economy, its management is crazy if it chooses to operate at a loss for very long over a very large section of its business. Profit is the name of the game. The position is not really different if it operates at a profit that is not as good as it could make through the application of its capital to competing lines of endeavor. What I am trying to suggest is not a definitive solution but the great importance of resisting stringent measures without deliberate and mature thought on the subject. There may not be any complete solution to this problem. It would not be surprising if there were left some remaining applicants for whom there was no adequate market at a price they could afford to pay. But one of the things we should expect in a complex society is that there will be some problems left that cannot be fully, or at least neatly, solved.

They can sometimes best be approached from an altogether different direction.

IMPLEMENTATION OF THE LAW

The last point in my general treatment has to do with the effective implementation of the insurance laws. Roscoe Pound made a statement a good many years ago to the effect that: "[T]he means of making legal rules effective . . . has been neglected almost entirely in the past. We have studied the making of law sedulously. It seems to have been assumed that, when made, law will enforce itself. . . . But the life of the law is in its enforcement."[6] In insurance we have considered ad nauseam, for example, the question "What practices shall be considered criminal rebating" etc., but have given inadequate consideration to the question "How can they be prevented most effectively?"

Perhaps this is truer in insurance than in other fields. There has been a very unsystematic and fragmentary treatment of the subject. The tradition here, as in most parts of our legal system, has been (1) to decide what conduct should be proscribed, (2) to make it criminal, and (3) to assume that the problem was solved. Ordinarily you would make it a misdemeanor, or if you were expecting trouble enforcing it and wanted to increase the sanctions, you would make it a felony. It is sometimes a felony, for example, to aid in any way in the operation of an unauthorized insurance business. I suppose it would then be a felony for a doctor to examine an applicant for an unauthorized life insurer, which seems to me to be the height of or, better, the depth of absurdity. Alternative to making something criminal and assuming that it will therefore be enforced, is to provide for revocation of a license, which is perhaps a very effective way to punish the company if at the same time you don't mind harming the policyholder, too.

This brings me to the crucial importance of relating means to ends in the regulation of insurance. Rate regulation, for example, seems to me to be the classic case of this problem. Rarely has anyone taken the trouble to ask what it is we are trying to do with

---

[6] Roscoe Pound, "The Scope and Purpose of Sociological Jurisprudence" (pt. 3), *Harvard Law Review*, Vol. 25 (1912), pp. 489, 514.

rate regulation. We talk glibly about rates not being inadequate, nor excessive, nor unfairly discriminatory, without asking what the meaning of these terms may be. But what is it that we are really trying to do when we seek "adequacy of the rates?" Obviously, we are attempting to ensure solidity of the company, though no explicit attention is given to this ultimate objective when one asks how to go about regulating rates. Adequate rates have only an indirect connection with solvency. You can have adequate rates and still go bankrupt in a hurry. Lots of other things can go wrong with the operation. It is very important to ask the question: "If rates are to be adequate, then adequate for what?" Similarly, if they are to be nonexcessive, "Nonexcessive with respect to what criteria?"

This is an area that badly needs rethinking. You will find a further discussion of the problem as applied to rates in an essay entitled "Goals of Insurance Laws—Means versus Ends," which is reprinted in part in my book, *Essays in Insurance Regulation.*[7]

SUMMARY

If I could make only a single point in this paper, it should be clear by now what it is that I should like to emphasize. We do not ask often enough, nor persistently enough, what it is we are trying to seek in insurance regulation, and how we can best achieve what we want without unfortunate side effects. Very little consideration is given to the relationship of ends and means, and very little effort is made to be sure that the things at which we aim and for which we struggle are truly ends and not merely means that have become invested with an air of sanctity by virtue of long acceptance. It should be clear that I think we have often mistaken means for ends and have often been misled into pursuit of the wrong things. A catalog of the things about which we have been wrong in insurance regulation would probably be longer than of the things about which we have been right. Insurance regulation could profit much by having officials far more cognizant than they are now, not only of the technical problems with which they deal but also of their obligation constantly to ask the fundamental questions, and of the nature of the fundamental questions.

---

[7] The essay was first printed in *Journal of Insurance,* Vol. 29 (1962), p. 19.

chapter 2

A Basic Formulation of the Purposes of Insurance Regulation: 1914

UNTIL RECENTLY, the literature of insurance has been remarkably free of fundamental discussion of the purposes of insurance regulation. Both the regulators and the regulated have seemed to be caught up in day-to-day problems and details so much that they could not take the long view and ask the basic questions.

The outsider to the regulatory process and the regulated industry, in a position to observe more objectively, is more likely to succeed in asking and sometimes even in answering the basic questions. In view of the paucity of discussion within the profession then and now, the early formulation of the purposes of insurance regulation by William Jennings Bryan seems remarkably prescient.

THE PURPOSES OF INSURANCE
REGULATIONS*

William Jennings Bryan
Secretary of State of the United States
Friday, September 18th, 10 A.M.

The President called the Convention to order at 10 A.M.

THE PRESIDENT: Gentlemen of the Convention, Ladies and Gentlemen: It gives me pleasure in calling the Convention to order this morning, to say to you that among other pleasures, we have the pleasure this morning to listen to the foremost American citizen, the great Commoner, a man that needs no introduction to any audience

---

* Taken from 1914 Proceedings, National Convention of Insurance Commissioners, pp. 64–67.

in the United States, so I take pleasure in presenting to you the Hon. W. J. Bryan, Secretary of State.

MR. BRYAN: I am not going to say I am glad to see you. I am a little in the position of a man who made a speech to the convicts in the penitentiary. He said he couldn't say he was glad to see them there, because it would be a reflection upon them, and then he couldn't say he was sorry to see them there, for that would be bad for the community from which they came. I can't say I am glad to see you, because I tried to keep from seeing you. I came down here to get a little rest, and my experience is that if I am going to rest I must go where I cannot see people, for if I get where there are people there are two things which prevent my resting; one is that there may be some one among them who has voted for me and he feels that he ought to tell me so, or some one who has not voted for me and is ashamed of it, and wants to make a confession, and, of course, either one has a claim upon my time. And if I do not find one of either class, there is sure to be some of another class to which I belong, that is that I want to see them. So when I want to rest I go as far away from the people as I can, so that I will not have to yield to the temptation, which is generally overpowering, to spend my time conversing with them.

I suppose if there is any one subject further from my particular work than another, it would be your subject. I am dealing with things external, and insurance is an internal matter. It is not even a national matter, except in the sense that every citizen is interested in everything that goes on in this country. You are the representatives of the various States and you are the representatives of the States in the work of controlling insurance, and it would be very presumptuous in me to assume that I could come and tell you anything about your business, and I am not going to try to. I am going to mention just one thing, that to my mind is the controlling matter in insurance.

When I was a young man I heard a minister, in the course of a sermon, use an illustration, and it has not only lingered in my mind, but it has affected my method of thought. He said if you wanted to pull a tree through a gate it all depended on how you went about it; if you took the trunk of a tree and pulled that through first, the branches could be pressed in against the trunk and you could get the tree through, but if you took a branch and tried to pull that through first, the other branches would spread out against the post and you could not get it through. In the consideration of any subject the important thing is to get control of the fundamental principles, and so in arguing questions I have tried to take that which was fundamental, and having established first the fundamental proposition, proceeded to those that are less important. You will find that in every subject there is a fundamental proposition. If you go into the irrigation districts and consider the important subject of irrigation, you will find that there is one fundamental principle that underlies irrigation; it is that water runs down hill. The man who tries to establish an irrigation plant without knowing that, is going to have difficulty.

There is a principle in insurance that is just as fundamental as that experienced in irrigation, and that is that security is the one thing that is important above all others. It is suggested by the word itself—*insured*. All the efforts of the State are directed toward the security of the insured. If you have absolute security it is insurance; if you have not, it is gambling. Gambling is the antithesis of security, and the efforts of legislation and administration is to take insurance out of the gambling class and put it into the certainty class. That is all there is to it. There are some other things to be considered incidentally. For instance, there is the expense of administration. Of course, the law takes that into question, but that is of less importance than the matter of security. The expense is important in two ways; if the expense is too large, it may cause bankruptcy and thus destroy security, and if it is not carried to the point where it causes bankruptcy, it still increases the expense of insurance, and the two things the insured has in mind are, first, security, and, second, the cost at which it is to be furnished, but the security comes first.

You will find that the sentiment of the country is overwhelmingly in favor of private enterprise. Some people are very much afraid of socialism, but if you will examine you will find that socialism is never suggested where private enterprise will do the thing that needs to be done.

We have a postal savings bank. We got it because the bankers of the country would not secure depositors. They would oppose and fight any proposition that was intended to secure the depositor. They would favor any proposition that would increase dividends, but they not only opposed the security of the depositor, but in a national assembly they denounced both. But the bankers will not control the country when they are speaking for themselves. Nobody can control the country who speaks for himself. The moment a man speaks for himself he loses his influence; when he speaks for others he has power. The people got tired of putting their money under an old carpet. And yet we found money going to Europe to be deposited in government saving banks in Europe rather than risk it in this country and finally the government took charge of it, and we have a savings bank, and we have it simply because the bankers would not protect the depositor. And gentlemen who believe in insurance and who want insurance in private companies, ought to learn a lesson from the past, and that is that every law that adds to security is a law in favor of the concern and not against it, and the last man, if he be intelligent, to oppose laws that give absolute security ought to be an insurance man, because it is the hope of continuing his business.

Insurance is a growing thing; insurance is illustrative of the idea of co-operation. The people bear together, and by distributing it over a period of years, it is less of a burden. The same rules that lead people to insure a house lead them to insure life, and it is wise. I am ashamed of myself when I think that I got married without carrying any life insurance, and the more I think of my folly the more I appreciate the sublime confidence of the woman who took me on faith. You know the marriage ceremony says, and sometimes it seems like a mockery, "With all my worldly goods I thee endow." In my case it was more like the preacher who got the words mixed and had the bridegroom say, "With all my goodly words I thee endow." That was about all I had to endow my wife with, and I repeat that I feel ashamed when I look back and think that with almost nothing in the way of property I invited the young lady to risk her future with me, and to depend on what I could earn. But I had not been married long before I took out insurance in a fraternal organization, and I want to say to you who represent what we call the old line companies, the old line company is no better company than the fraternal, for the fraternal company teaches men the value of insurance, and I venture the assertion that very few men who carry old line insurance did not commence with fraternal insurance. I am so anxious to be neutral, not only in war, but in peace, that I carry both, and I am in favor of all kinds, and I am in favor of anything and everything that contributes toward absolute security and toward the reduction in the cost of insurance.

I said that when you departed from security you entered the sphere of gambling. We found it necessary by law to regulate the insurance company in order that the man might not lose his investment. Can any of you tell me what percentage of insurance policies lapse after the first payment?

MR. SULLIVAN: About 70 percent, to the end, in fraternals.

A MEMBER: In the old line companies, from 19 to 34 percent.

MR. BRYAN: The fact that so many go out after the payment of the first premium is attributive to the skill of the solicitor. It shows that a great many come in because of the personality of the agent. Possibly some men insure as the woman marries—to get rid of the man. Sometimes they take the insurance because they are persuaded to take it, and then after the first payment they drop out, but the fact that the people drop out before they get the benefit of the insurance have led the States to make regulations in order to protect these people.

My only excuse for speaking is the excuse that John Allen gave when he asked to speak in Congress one day. He said, "Mr. Speaker, I want five minutes; it doesn't matter about what I have to talk nor what I have to say, but I have some constituents in the gallery who have come to hear me speak, and so I want to talk." So that is the reason I am here. I ought to be out walking, and I am going now, but as I had to talk to you I thought I would try to call your attention to what I believe is the most important thing in insurance, and to tell you that my sympathy is with you just in proportion as you make insurance sure and as you reduce the expense of it to the insured.

chapter 3

A Specific Implementation of the Basic Formulation: 1968

WILLIAM JENNINGS BRYAN, in the 1914 speech reprinted in Chapter 2, told the insurance regulators: "[M]y sympathy is with you just in proportion as you make insurance sure and as you reduce the expense of it to the insured."

Fifty-four years later, the Superintendent of Insurance of New York attempted to implement Bryan's stated purpose of insurance regulation in a series of specific proposals contained in the following paper.

RITUAL AND REALITY IN INSURANCE REGULATION*

Richard E. Stewart
Superintendent of Insurance of New York

In recent months, we have seen one after another of our great institutions—public and private, national and local—come under siege; and the siege was usually laid down by people the institution was created to serve—its students, its citizens, or its customers.

These events do not mean that our institutions have suddenly gone bad, but only that different things are now expected of them and that when rigorously measured against new expectations, the institutions are found wanting. The events dramatize how difficult it is for an institution, especially a large and complex one, to adapt to the changing expectations of its constituents.

---

* Address at the 1968 Joint Convention of the National Association of Casualty and Surety Agents and the National Association of Casualty and Surety Executives, at the Greenbrier, White Sulphur Springs, West Virginia, October 7, 1968.

If institutions generally are not good at adapting to changes in their environment, government regulatory institutions may have special difficulty and be in special danger, for the regulatory process may bring out those traits that are most resistant to change.

In most regulation, the public is only fitfully interested, and the regulator is insulated from public scrutiny by the complexity and obscurity of the regulatory process, just as the industry is insulated by the mere existence of the regulator.

Left alone with each other, the regulator and his industry unconsciously find a mutual interest in ritualizing their relationship. The regulator must emphasize law and regularity against the day he is challenged in court or denounced in public. He thus must look to form and detail, and he may look away from the operating realities of the industry and from the expectations of the public. The industry relies on the rituals of regulation to make government behavior predictable and to keep the regulator occupied in areas where interference can be tolerated. Inevitably, both regulator and regulated come to measure their effectiveness by their impact on each other; and they come to live, often quite comfortably, within a closed system.

To what areas do the rituals of regulation tend to confine the attention of government? Often to matters internal to the regulated industry, such as restricting entry to the market, attenuating competition, preserving the institutional structure of the industry, and balancing competitive advantage among entities of different form, sponsorship, or regional allegiance. As a result, too much regulatory energy is diverted into policing the status quo in the regulated industry and into refereeing contests within it.

These tendencies—to quarantine itself, to exalt ritual and detail, and to become distracted with internal problems of the industry—are, on the record, discernible in regulation of many kinds. It does not seem to matter what is being regulated or by whom or, in a narrow sense, how well. For the competent regulator the snare is not error; it is irrelevance.

If we confine our minds to the rituals of regulation, we will resist change. But we will not prevent it. All we will achieve is to make certain that when change comes—and eventually change always comes—it will be dictated by the rebuffed and the frustrated, and not by us who would honor our institution, share its assumptions, and value its continuity.

For any institution, the alternative to intelligent change is not permanence; it is extinction. For an industry regulated in the public interest, the alternative to regulation is not freedom; it is replacement.

To recognize the need for change, and to welcome it, is a sign of strength, not of weakness. An institution that can justify evolution only by invoking the specter of imminent disaster is likely to be an institution incapable of renewing itself from within. Better that we plan our changes calmly and without waiting for crises. In that spirit, I will propose today some changes for my own institution. I like to think they indicate that the New York Insurance Department—whose professional staff is the equal in competence, honor, and dedication of any other body of civil servants anywhere—is capable of adapting and renewing even its most basic functions.

THE FUNDAMENTAL PURPOSE OF REGULATION

Obviously, we are not concerned with change for its own sake, but only with change for the sake of helping the institution of insurance regulation do its job better. A good starting point is to identify the job, the purpose of our enterprise. Only if we have a clear idea of our overall mission can we have a standard for testing the usefulness of our specific activities.

Should we not try to express simply what we are about? Is it beneath our dignity to compress and weed out the complexities so that we tell people what is worth their attention?

In simple words, what is the public purpose of insurance regulation? What is government trying to accomplish that justifies all this activity?

A good, simple answer is that government is trying to help people get the most insurance for their money. This simple formulation does not tell all, but it contains some reminders of the purpose of regulation and some standards for determining whether our priorities are right—whether we are doing the things, and only the things, that further our public purpose.

Helping people get the most insurance for their money begins with helping people. We are reminded that regulation, as a government activity, should serve people. Putting it that way makes it sound obvious, but we have been discussing tendencies in the regulatory relationship that insulate the regulator from outside ideas and that tend to preoccupy him with ritual and with the internal problems of the industry—all of which can lead the regulator to forget whom he was put in office to serve.

The public-spirited regulator needs continuous infusions of the public spirit. If he recognizes the danger that regulation will become a closed system, he must seek out ways to keep it open. In New York, we have been trying to go out to meet with the insurance-buying public and especially to seek out those people who are most disaffected with the institutions of insurance and insurance regulation. This is not easy, and certainly it is not always pleasant. But tranquility is not the ultimate value in the public service, and it is part of the work of the regulator to welcome, on a continuous and constructive basis, the fresh thinking of those whose only connection with insurance is being the people insurance is supposed to serve.

The phrase "helping people get the most insurance for their money" contains a number of other ideas, and I would like to take them up one at a time and suggest ways of furthering each of these aspects of our public purpose in the regulation of property and liability insurance.

AVAILABILITY OF INSURANCE

First, helping people get the most insurance for their money concerns, among other things, a person's ability to get insurance.

The availability of insurance has great economic and social value. The accepted loss ratios in much of property and liability insurance indicate that people so value the ability to transfer certain risks of living that they will contribute a third to a half of their premium dollar to the operating expenses of the risk distribution system. It is no wonder that a public which is willing to pay that much to spread certain risks will react forcefully against what it regards as an unacceptable curtailment of its ability to spread those risks.

Generally, government can be expected to act to strengthen or replace the private insurance mechanism when the shortage of insurance is serious enough and the social cost of not acting—that is, of leaving the individual to take his chances alone—is too high. When government decides it must act—as it has done in auto assigned risk plans, fire insurance pools, catastrophe reinsurance, Medicare, workmen's compensation funds, and bans on racial discrimination in underwriting—it can anticipate strong support from the public, for the public encourages government to look beyond insurance as a private contract to insurance as a public function.

Residual markets change, and the work of the industry and government in strengthening those that are socially intolerable is a work that is never finished. It is in the interest of the industry, just as it is the duty of government to identify and act on those problems early and forthrightly enough that they can be solved with the minimum of suffering and ill will and with the minimum disruption of the private insurance mechanism.

We have such a situation today in auto liability insurance. Auto liability underwriting leaves as residual risks many people who on their individual merits may present no special hazard and who—because they are young or old or poor—may be least able to sustain a liability in excess of their insurance protection.

We already have a mechanism for strengthening the market, but it is out of date. The New York Automobile Assigned Risk Plan provides only the limits required by our compulsory insurance law. While it is logical that the Assigned Risk Plan can supply no less, there is no reason why it cannot supply more. In New York today, 10/20/5 protection is so inadequate as to be foolhardy for the driver and cruel to the victim. We simply need to keep our institution up-to-date, and we can do so by

—substantially increasing the amounts of liability insurance available through the Assigned Risk Plan; and
—providing auto physical damage insurance through the plan, at a rate based on experience in the plan.

QUALITY AND RELIABILITY OF INSURANCE

Helping people get the most insurance for their money contains a second idea—that of getting the most insurance, or of making sure that the insurance product is of high quality and reliability.

Experience in many fields has shown, not surprisingly, that where a promise of future performance is sold for present dollars, the buyer is at the seller's mercy. Where, as in insurance, the promise is complex and the seller is more powerful than the buyer, the disparity between the two parties' abilities to look out for themselves is marked. So for a long time government has stood with the buyer in helping assure the quality of the product. Examples are in the regulation of policy provisions, to see that they are clear and fair; in regulation for solvency or its equivalent, to see that the promise can be performed when it comes due; in regulation of the relationship between insurer and policyholder, to see that the promise is indeed performed fairly and that the buyer's reasonable expectations as to what he bought are not too rudely disappointed.

What the buyer of insurance is paying for is protection against a certain kind of economic loss for a certain time. Much of the value of the protection comes from the buyer's ability to plan on the basis of it, to use it in enduring commercial relations, and to draw from it peace of mind.

All these values are undermined if the insurer cancels at midterm, through no fault of the policyholder. Statutory policy forms have indeed long provided that the insurer may cancel at any time and for any reason. Yet underwriting techniques and management controls have improved to the point that companies should not suddenly wake up to find themselves overcommitted—or at least should no longer have the luxury of rectifying their error at the sole expense of those to whom they have sold their word.

In auto liability insurance, a public outcry against cancellations brought swift enactment of anticancellation laws in many states, including New York, often with broad industry support.

Events of the past year make it appropriate now to extend reasonable protection against cancellation to policyholders in the other personal property and liability lines. It is now clear that only law can establish those uniform minimum standards of conduct which will remove from susceptible managements the temptation to economize in ways that alienate the public from the institution of insurance. Such standards of conduct are in the interest not only of the public but of the vast majority of insurers who underwrite carefully and then stick by their policyholders. A business that sells promises depends, in the long run, on the trust of its buyers.

Another aspect of the reliability of the insurance product is the guarantee against loss due to insolvency of an insurer. Vigilant regulation can reduce company failures, but no government or private agency has ever devised a foolproof way of insulating any financial institution from insolvency.

Recognizing that despite everyone's best efforts there will be insolvencies, the federal government (for banks and savings and loan associations) and New York State (for life, workmen's compensation, and auto liability insurance), among other jurisdictions, have set up devices for spreading across the industry the cost of saving harmless those citizens who were owed something by the fallen brother.

Is this fair? Are you your brother's keeper? Sometimes in a competitive economy, he who asks the question slew his brother, and the voice of his brother's dependents cries out unmistakably. But regardless of fault, society has only three places to let the loss fall—on the policyholder, on government, and on the entire industry. Of the three the policyholder is probably most innocent and least able to shoulder the misfortune. The general revenues of government would be a fair target, at least for those insolvencies traceable to defects in government regulation, but it is unlikely that the public would accept the exposure without exacting minute control of the day-to-day operations of every company. From society's point of view, then, simple elimination suggests that the industry or, rather, the policyholders of all companies should share the cost.

The cost of protection, spread among the many, is small; the cost to the individual of having trusted in a worthless policy can be catastrophic.

In New York, we can extend insolvency protection by building upon an existing institution. Our Motor Vehicle Liability Security Fund contains $125 million. Interest alone adds $4.5 million a year, and each year our motorists contribute another $7 million. Yet in the Fund's 21-year existence only $6 million has been drawn out of it, and all indications are that the frequency and magnitude of insolvencies do not increase in proportion to overall premium volume.

The motorists have paid enough, and without diminishing their protection, we can build upon this unique security fund to extend similar protection to other policies held by these same people and by others. Auto insurance as now written is no more a threat to company solvency than are other lines. A person is no less deserving of insolvency protection behind his general liability policy or his homeowners policy than behind his auto policy.

By simply discontinuing assessments on auto insurance policies, commencing assessments on other lines, and broadening the Security Fund to cover all personal and small commercial lines, we can make an immediate improvement in the reliability of the promises sold by insurers to the people of New York State. By providing for all assessments to cease when the Security Fund has reached a specified dollar amount, we can achieve equity as among insurers and can guard against the sterile accumulation of funds in excess of the public need. By providing for assessments to resume if the Security Fund is ever drawn down below a specified amount, we can assure that all our policyholders are as fully protected against loss due to company insolvency, at any time in the future, as our auto insurance policyholders are now.

PRICE OF INSURANCE

The third part of helping people get the most insurance for their money concerns their money, that is, the price they have to pay for the insurance protection they buy.

In a national economy that looks to the market to set prices and to allocate resources, property and liability insurance has long enjoyed, or suffered from, a separate existence. Not too long ago, the paradigm of the property insurance pricing system was the cartel. Competition, such as existed, was assuredly not price competition at the consumer level, and elaborate private governments were maintained to make sure it stayed that way.

Like other institutions that rested immobile while the mores of the national economy and the expectations of the public changed about them, these private governments and the cartelized insurance market were overthrown.

The cartels may be dead, but they still rule us from their graves. Our present rating laws were enacted partly to insulate pricing cartels from antitrust attack, partly to impose social control over the practices of those cartels, and partly to preserve inviolate the regulatory jurisdiction of the states.

Government activity which was relevant to conditions 20 years ago may not be relevant to conditions today. If the institution of insurance regulation is to be able to renew itself from within, we must evaluate what government now does with respect to insurance prices in the light of current market conditions and in the light of the current needs of the buying public.

Since the prevailing rate regulatory laws were enacted, the property and liability insurance business has refined its pricing and underwriting methods, has grown and become more sophisticated, is exhibiting more diversity in price and distribution, and manifests a real willingness to compete in price. While much is still to be learned about insurance market structure and conduct, the structure is propitious for real competition—entry to the industry is easy, concentration is low, sellers are numerous, the product is largely undifferentiated, and total sales are expanding rapidly.

The public has an immense stake in the results of the insurance pricing and rate regulatory mechanisms, but it would seem to have no stake in the form of rate regulation apart from wanting that which yields the best result. What are the results desired of any system of rate regulation? To the buyer, the best pricing system would seem to be the one that yields prices as low as possible; stable prices not subject to large and sudden changes; and prices that are fair as among policyholders. The buyer also gains if the chosen system of rate regulation furthers other public objectives; if it increases rather than decreases the likelihood that insurance will be available and reliable.

The system should fit the current realities of the market and should direct our regulatory energies at what actually happens rather than into rituals that bear no clear relationship to reality. Finally, unless it is impractical or against the public interest, our insurance rate regulation should harmonize with general norms for conduct in the economy.

In my judgment and that of my top colleagues in the New York Insurance Department, the present needs of the people of the state of New York would be better served by a rating law which would not prescribe that rates be filed for the approval of the Superintendent. The watchfulness of our skilled examining staff would be directed at what was actually being charged in the field rather than only at the ritual assertion, in a rate filing, of what a company proposed to charge.

Under this system the forces of competition would be allowed to keep rates down. When cost decreases called for lower rates, the rates could be reduced at once. When cost increases called for higher rates, the rates could be adjusted without delay and hence without even temporary restriction of the availability of insurance. In all cases of aberration—where a rate was excessive, inadequate, discriminatory, or destructive of competition—the Department would have full power to suspend or disapprove the rate.

A system of regulation that relies on competition is valid only where competition exists. In any area or kind of insurance in which price competition at the consumer level was insufficient to assure that rates would be neither inadequate nor excessive, the Department should be able temporarily to reimpose prior approval. Such a power would be especially helpful in minimizing dislocations during a transition period and in protecting residual markets. It would also protect the insurance-buying public against any failure of resolve by those in the insurance industry who now profess a desire to compete but who may merely wish to stabilize their condition on a different and more congenial basis.

In New York, we can expect that a change to more competitive insurance rates will cause some rates to go up and some to go down. We should not anticipate any overall change in rate level as a result of the change in regulatory procedures. The important difference is that rates would be responsive to current costs and markets instead of being excessive for some risks, which are then overly courted, and inadequate for others, which are shunned and fall into the residual markets.

Those who do not wish to compete in price have conjured many possible evils of open competition. For example, will it lead to rate wars? During the past 50 years, there has been no evidence in California (where rate filings are not required) or in any other jurisdiction that rate competition leads to destructive rate wars. Their memory haunted the Merritt Committee a half century ago, but our own experience and the findings of the most recent congressional study should lay the specter to rest.

Similarly, there is no correlation between kind of rating law and the incidence of insolvency, and certainly no evidence that competition leads to insolvencies. If anything, one can infer from recent episodes that rate inflexibility creates pockets of unmet demand that invite the creation of marginal companies prone to fail.

Nor is there any indication that rate competition, given strict antitrust and examination safeguards, leads to higher rates than a prior approval law responsibly administered. Quantitative comparisons between different markets are far from conclusive, but a comparison of loss ratios of like companies in California and New York suggests that rates are similar.

Equally important, experience suggests that more competitively responsive rates lead to greater availability of insurance and to greater public satisfaction with its quality.

We are not limited to a counterfeit choice between regulation alone and competition alone to protect the public. Both are available, and we should use them in combination. To make competition and regulation reinforce each other best in ways relevant to current realities, it is now time to let competition work with less restraint upon the market price of insurance.

PROPOSED LEGISLATIVE CHANGE

These four changes—easier access to needed auto insurance, protection against cancellation, security in case of company insolvency, and open competition in rating—will help the property and liability insurance industry serve the public better and will focus our regulatory energies on real current problems.

By the end of the year, the New York Insurance Department will issue a report, refining these four proposals and setting out the documentation for them, so they may be considered at the 1969 session of our state legislature. Meanwhile, we will seek the views and technical advice of the public, other government agencies and all segments of the insurance industry.

These four proposed changes in the institution of insurance regulation are part of an attempt to keep that institution responsive to current public needs and to current realities within the regulated industry. Even if sound today, the four proposals should be looked upon as adaptations and not as permanent improvements, for that which is devised to be permanent is often, in the long run, no improvement at all.

Regulation is the process of bringing current values of society to bear on current practices of an essential industry, and hence regulation must seek relevance more than permanence. If we in government keep in mind, in simplest terms, what our real goals are, we will be best able to pursue those goals relentlessly.

If the limited resources of public attention and government power are to do the most good in insurance regulation, they should be directed at helping people get the most insurance for their money. Our efforts can be measured by how they affect the availability, reliability, and price of insurance. If we can orient our complex and venerable institutions to these simple, current goals, we will renew them from within, and they will endure—and deserve to endure—when their rituals are forgotten.

chapter 4

The Social Responsibilty of Insurance Regulation

THE PURPOSES of insurance regulation, stated on the most funda-mental level, have changed little in this century. But the more specific goals and methods by which government seeks to attain these general purposes are undergoing constant and occasionally dramatic revision. Some of these mid-20th-century trends are traced in the following discussion of the social responsibility of insurance regulation, which argues that government now has responsibility to encourage and guide and, if necessary, even require regulated indus-try to respond to the current needs of society. It then applies this responsibility to a discussion of emerging insurance problems.

THE SOCIAL RESPONSIBILITY OF
INSURANCE REGULATION*

Richard E. Stewart
Superintendent of Insurance of New York

A few miles north of here, on Morningside Heights, people long thought to have the habit of obedience are in revolt against an institution felt to control them but to be beyond their control.[1] It is hardly an isolated incident, and this is a good season for many another institution to measure itself against the present expectations of those it was created to serve.

What goes for other institutions goes for insurance, and now is a good time to look anew at the social responsibility of government as regulator of insurance.

---

* Adapted from remarks at the American Management Association Spring Conference on Government and Insurance, New York City, May 15, 1968.

[1] This talk was delivered at the time of the student riots at Columbia University of Morningside Heights in New York City.

33

Much of the literature on government regulation of business comments on the tendency of the regulator gradually to adopt a view of the world similar to the view held by the regulated industry. It is a natural consequence of similar training, similar tasks, similar data, and similar techniques. It has nothing to do with whether the regulator is disposed to be friendly to the industry or hostile to it. It certainly does not mean that the industry and the regulator will agree on the answers. It does mean they are likely to agree on the questions.

Regulation of any business can easily become for both sides a closed system whose values are established by reference to other parts of the same system. If the industry can measure its civic performance by how often it secures the approval of government, then its representatives have a clear measure of how well they are doing. If the government regulator can measure his thoroughness or independence or wisdom by how hard a time he gives the industry or by how often he says no, then he too has a clear and comfortable rule to live by. Such a system can be busy and effective within its own frame of reference and can even be quite congenial to both industry and government; but it leaves little room for questions to intrude from outside. Having quarantined itself, such a system can stay still while the outside world moves. More and more it can fail, through unawareness, to do what the rest of society, having changed in structure and expectations, needs and wants done in the regulated area.

This drift toward similar views of the world or toward a closed system is reinforced by a characteristic of institutional behavior that occurs far beyond the field of regulation. It is the tendency of the large organization—especially one with technical competence and a strong professional tradition—to do today what yesterday it did without incident. We can trace this tendency partly to the quasi-judicial character of some operations, with their emphasis on regular procedure and consistent decision. We can trace it partly to the disposition of technique to elaborate itself, to increase its momentum within the decision-making process, and to foreclose consideration of new objectives that develop outside the technical system. Finally, we can trace it pretty deeply into human nature—change is disquieting.

If we acknowledge that regulation can become a closed system and that any large organization can build up momentum in a straight line, inertia, then we are in a good position to talk about the social responsibility of government in insurance regulation.

Insurance has too important a public role not to be affected by changes in the surrounding society. The distribution of risk on a fair and stable basis is essential to personal and commercial financing, to an efficient disposition of resources, to the ability to plan ahead, and to simple peace of mind. Many of the functions of private insurance in the United States can be, and in other countries are, performed by government, and the stakes for the industry in staying responsive to changing public demands are obviously high.

Similarly, it is appropriate for government to define its role with some concern for the social importance of what is being regulated. Whatever may be the case in other industries, it is fairly clear that in insurance, government regulation is no longer simply the application of countervailing power against a dominant economic group that might otherwise abuse its own power. Today government has an additional responsibility to encourage and guide and to require the regulated industry to respond to the current needs of society at large where it is important and necessary. To do this, government has to exercise an informed judgment as to what the evolving public needs are, and should develop its own position early enough and on a sufficient scale. To succeed, the government regulator has consciously to overcome his own natural tendencies to operate a closed system and to keep going in a straight line.

The social responsibility of insurance regulation, then, is to recognize that changes in and out of insurance are constantly altering the social responsibility of insurance regulation; that its goals should change accordingly; that sometimes it falls to government to lead the industry toward change; and that it always falls to government to make the conscious effort to order its own house by current thought and not by habit.

In our own work in the New York Insurance Department, we have been trying to meet this responsibility. Examples of the effort are in our proposals on a pool for fire insurance in central cities,[2] on flexible interest rates on life insurance policy loans,[3] and on insur-

---

[2] Ch. 131 (1968), N.Y. Laws; background reports are reprinted in the 109th *Annual Report of the Superintendent of Insurance* (New York).

[3] N.Y. S. Bill 4344S (1968), N.Y. A. Bill 6360A (1968); not passed; background materials are set out in the 109th *Annual Report of the Superintendent of Insurance*.

ance holding companies and diversification,[4] as well as our participation with others on universal health insurance[5] and the Governor's study of the auto liability system.[6]

But reexamining one's own goals and one's own relevance to a
changing external situation is a job that is never completed. We
must continue to ask where the evolving social responsibility of
insurance and of insurance regulation is likely to lead. Are the
conventional goals still the only ones by which history will judge
us?

Consider, for example, the deep and durable belief that the sole
purpose of regulation is to protect the policyholder. Not surprisingly, this maxim places the regulator in exactly the same world as
the industry; his constituents, as it were, are those people already in
a contractual relationship with insurers.

But is the maxim a reliable guide to our evolving social responsibility? Recent government action to make property insurance more
readily available in the central city would suggest that we are also
trying to help some people who are not policyholders—whose
problem, indeed, is that they cannot become policyholders. The
movement toward universal health insurance suggests that government will act out of a sense of duty to people who neither are
policyholders nor want to be policyholders. Freedom of contract
and freedom of underwriting are obviously being subordinated to
other goals. It is not the first time; analogies already exist in
workmen's compensation and automobile insurance. But these steps
are being taken more and more by government as regulator—
thereby improving the technical product, increasing the participation of private industry, and giving the regulatory agency new
vigor. The facts of this new social responsibility of insurance regulation are becoming clear. The slogan will catch up later.

A second place to look for possibly changing goals is in rate
regulation of property and liability insurance. It is now 20 years

---

[4] *Report of the Special Committee on Insurance Holding Companies* (New
York, February 15, 1968).

[5] Governor Rockefeller of New York proposed universal health insurance
legislation in 1967 (N.Y. S.Bill 4268S, N.Y. A. Bill 5876A, Pr. 6215) and in
1968 (N.Y. S. Bill 5417S, N.Y. A. Bill 6816A); the measures were not passed;
background materials will be reprinted in the *Public Papers of the Governor* for
those years.

[6] A Committee on Compensating Victims of Automobile Accidents was
appointed by Governor Rockefeller on November 29, 1968.

since the prevailing rate regulatory laws were enacted, and it is common knowledge that they were enacted for a large number of reasons, some of which were better than others and some of which do not persist today. The law sets forth standards for rate review, but these should not be taken as fully expressing the philosophy or reason underlying the law. What, indeed, are the objectives of a modern rating law? Is the objective to keep rates down, or to keep rates up to preserve the institutional structure of the industry, or to promote uniformity of rate or predictability of rate? Is it to help the consumer evaluate the price and quality of the insurance product he is buying? Is it to encourage competition, and does competition mean the same thing to all of us? Is it to attract capital to the insurance operation, or to maintain continuous markets, or to make up for the lack of antitrust standards, or to balance the traditional freedom of underwriting? Several of these, and others, are legitimate objectives. Each kind of rating law and each way of administering it will give a different set of objectives precedence over the others, and it is our responsibility to keep our priorities abreast of changes in the regulated industry and in the expectations of the public.

A third example of the value of reexamining our thinking about what we do is in regulation for solvency. Sometimes we have indulged ourselves in the view that solvency—that is, the absence of failures of insurance companies—was entirely dependent on the quality of regulation. Vigilant regulation, some thought, could entirely prevent insolvencies. Certainly it helps; and when reinforced by high standards for entry to the business, regulated rates, conservative underwriting, and a rising stock market, it can achieve a very high percentage of success, as, indeed, it has done and will continue to do in New York. But we should not delude ourselves with the notion that insolvencies can't happen here. They can happen here, over the years they have happened here, and in the last two months we have put one company into rehabilitation on that ground and are moving to rehabilitate another. No one in any jurisdiction has ever figured out a foolproof method of regulating any kind of financial institution against insolvency, just as no one has ever figured out a foolproof way to prevent men from being dishonest, making mistakes, losing money, or having bad luck. All we can do, realistically, is require adequate capitalization, guard against management activities that threaten the financial condition of the company, and try to detect deterioration quickly and help in its repair. That is a lot, and new techniques for handling data will enable us to do it better than ever. But it is our responsibility to accept fully the fact that all these steps will sometimes not be enough. Any balanced system of regulation has to provide, in ways consonant with the changing expectations of society, for distress situations, where the stranded policyholder needs government strongly on his side.

These are just three of many areas where the evolution of thinking in and outside the field of insurance impresses on us the social responsibility to be sure that what we are doing is a relevant and desirable contribution to the well-being of society as a whole. The abiding question is whether we are doing what is important now and not distracting ourselves with what is not important any longer. The main social responsibility of insurance regulation may be the willingness to keep asking that question and to act on the answers.

PART II

The Process of Legislative Reform: from General Purposes to Specific Statutes

chapter 5

Problems of Comprehensive Insurance Revision Programs

THE GOALS of insurance regulation must be translated into legislative enactment. General statements of purpose may be formulated and are of central importance. But meaningfully assimilating these purposes into precise statutory language is something else again.

The following selection discusses the process of translation of purpose to statute and some of the problems involved. Both the philosophy and procedures of the Wisconsin insurance law revision program are explained in detail.

MODERN INSURANCE CODE REVISION: REFLECTIONS ON THE ART OF LEGISLATIVE REFORM*

Spencer L. Kimball
Dean and Professor of Law
University of Wisconsin

Herbert S. Denenberg
Harry J. Loman Professor of Insurance
Wharton School of Finance and Commerce
University of Pennsylvania

An insurance code, like other statutes, should be made to say "the right thing in the right way, in language that is as clear, simple, and accessible as possible,"[1] despite the great complexity of insurance as

---

* Reprinted with slight modification with permission, from the *Journal of the American Society of Chartered Life Underwriters*, Vol. 21, No. 4 (October, 1967). Copyright 1967 by the American Society of Chartered Life Underwriters.

[1] Reed Dickerson, *Legislative Drafting* (Boston: Little, Brown & Co., 1954), p. 3.

a contract, as a technique, as a business and as an instrument of
social planning, and the diversity of pressures that play upon the
legislature. This is the basic dilemma of the insurance law revisor.
The problem is all but insoluble.

This article seeks to describe the principles and procedures we are
trying to follow in the current Wisconsin revision of the insurance
laws. It should both illustrate the difficulties of the enterprise and
provide the staff's preliminary thinking about ways to surmount
them and to solve the problem. Despite emphasis on the concrete
Wisconsin experience, the ideas presented should be suggestive, and
if valid should be equally useful in any other state.

Wisconsin is only one of about a dozen states now actively
engaged in Code Revision.[2] But unlike the legislatures of many
other states, that of Wisconsin was not content with a mere "paste-
and-scissors" revision. For reasons partly resulting from Wisconsin's
peculiar history,[3] and partly from the accident that some Wisconsin
people of clearer-than-ordinary vision happen to become involved
with the conception and planning of this enterprise, the terms of
reference of the committee and the staff assigned to it are extremely
broad, making possible an unusually venturesome revision. In a
statute passed in 1965, the Wisconsin legislature found that the
public welfare and interest could only be protected by a "thorough,

---

[2] Alabama, Connecticut, Delaware, Kentucky, Maine, Michigan, Minnesota,
Nevada, New Jersey, Pennsylvania, Vermont, Wisconsin, and the Virgin Islands
are believed to be either now revising or on the verge of revising their insurance
statutes on a more-or-less systematic basis. Unless a much more precise and
limited statement were devised, an exact count would be meaningless and has
not been attempted. About fifteen other states have in some sense "revised" their
insurance statutes in the past decade. Many of the latter follow similar patterns
—they are "Williams codes," a reference to Mr. Robert D. Williams, who has
been actively engaged in insurance statutory revision as a practicing lawyer for
some years now. At a very early stage in his activity, Mr. Williams published his
thoughts on the nature of his task, in Robert D. Williams, *Modern Insurance
Code Revision* (1946), reprinted from the June, July, August, and September
1946 issues of *The Insurance Index*. No later pronouncement of his views has
come to our attention.

[3] Close cooperation between the State University and the State Government
dates in Wisconsin from the turn of the century and is sometimes referred to as
the "Wisconsin idea." See *Encyclopaedia Brittanica,* under title "Wisconsin."

It has led to much better than ordinary supporting services for the state
legislature, including an active and productive Legislative Council, an excellent
Legislative Reference Library and Bureau and, most important of all, an attitude
of receptivity to quality performance in legislative drafting and an understanding that quality is not cheaply bought.

careful study and modernization, revision and codification of the insurance laws to reflect the expansion of the insurance field and its increased competitive nature under present conditions," and called for a "unified, comprehensive study of the state insurance laws."[4] To accomplish this study an Insurance Laws Revision Committee was appointed, and staff employed. The Committee reports to the Wisconsin Legislative Council, which in turn is an arm of the Wisconsin Legislature. The Council is charged with broad responsibility relating to legislative investigations and recommendations, and making recommendations to the legislature on the insurance code revision is only one of its assigned tasks. It will base the recommendations on insurance on the work of the Insurance Laws Revision Committee and its staff.

The revision is not the responsibility of the Wisconsin Insurance Department. The staff is directly responsible to the Insurance Laws Revision Committee appointed under the statute. Nevertheless, the staff has attempted to keep the Wisconsin Insurance Department fully advised at each stage of this study. In return, the Insurance Department has also cooperated with the staff in every way, and has generously supplied information and ideas, and has criticized drafts. Its expertise has been invaluable to the revision.

The comprehensive revision of the insurance laws is now under way. The authors of this article are serving, respectively, as Director and Associate Director of the staff of the Insurance Laws Revision Committee. The legislature has already passed one substantial chapter, on the subject of "Delinquency Proceedings in Insurance," based on the staff recommendations in a document containing a chapter of sixty-one sections and extensive commentary.[5] It was unanimously passed by the Committee, the Council and the Legislature, with almost no change in the process. Additional chapters have been circulated in draft form. After considerable revision they, too, will go to the Committee as the staff's recommendation, and eventually to the Legislature. An additional bill on the *Administration of the Insurance Code* was before the 1967 Legislature[6] but

---

[4] Ch. 406, sec. 1 (1965), Wis. Laws 657.

[5] Ch. 89 (1967), Wis. Laws 220 is based on S. Kimball, H. Denenberg, and R. Bertrand, *Delinquency Proceedings in Insurance* (3d draft; Wisconsin Legislative Council, 1967). The slightly altered preface to that draft is printed in 1967 *Insurance Law Journal*, pp. 79–86.

[6] Wis. S. Bill 558S (1967).

was lost in the end-of-session log jam. There was little controversy respecting it, and it is likely to pass without difficulty in the 1969 session.

HISTORY OF WISCONSIN INSURANCE LAW

The principles and procedures used in the revision by the staff can only be understood in the light provided by a sketch of the history and nature of the present insurance code of Wisconsin and of other states. The insurance laws of Wisconsin have developed in large part in the twentieth century,[7] but are already antiquated. The insurance laws have shared in the common course of development of statute law in our legal system. As new problems were perceived, special statutes were passed to deal with them, leading to a vast accumulation of inadequately integrated *ad hoc* provisions.

This general pattern of development is most easily illustrated by using something much simpler than insurance law, like the development of the crime of embezzlement in the eighteenth century.[8] Before 1742 it was not a crime for a servant or employee to appropriate for himself personal property which he received from a third person for his master or employer. This rule resulted from a narrow definition of the medieval crime of larceny, which was based on a taking of property out of someone's possession.[9] The restricted rule was increasingly inconvenient as the development of banking in England made such non-trespassory taking more common and more harmful. In 1742, Parliament made it a crime to take banknotes under such circumstances, but *only if the defendant worked for the Bank of England.*[10] A few years later a separate statute made it a crime under similar circumstances to take banknotes paid in to

---

[7] For a general view of the historical development of Wisconsin insurance law, see S. Kimball, *Insurance and Public Policy* (1960).

[8] See generally J. Hall, *Theft, Law and Society* (1952), and see especially pp. 34–79. For a briefer treatment, see S. Kimball, *Historical Introduction to the Legal System* (1966), pp. 244–62.

[9] Bracton defined larceny as "the fraudulent dealing with another man's property with the intention of stealing, against the will of the lord whose property it is." H. de Bracton, *De Legibus et Consuetudinibus Angliae*, Vol. 2 (Twiss ed. 1879), p. 507. The word "contrectatio," here translated as "dealing," has the basic meaning of "touching" and thus the dealing meant by Bracton was the transfer of physical possession from the person entitled to it to the thief.

[10] 15 Geo. II, ch. 13, sec. 12 (1742).

an employee of the South Sea Company.[11] Still later, the Post Office was similarly protected.[12] It was not until 1799 that a statute protected all banks,[13] and not until the 1850's that the crime of embezzlement was fully developed along modern lines.[14]

The most important reason for this fragmentary and gradual development was that Parliament reacted only as specific problems came up, and reacted strictly in terms of the way it perceived the problem at the moment. Banks were relatively uncommon until the last decades of the eighteenth century.[15] Parliament could deal only with what it could see; what seems obvious to us now was invisible then.[16] Only as the economy grew did the full dimensions of the problem become evident. In the 1790's approximately four hundred banks were organized in England. Thus, by the end of the century Parliament could see the problem in larger terms, i.e., in terms of the entire banking institution. Even then, however, only *banks* were protected. The crime of embezzlement only became fully developed —so it protected all persons alike—in the mid-nineteenth century.[17]

In addition to the limitations on its perception of the problem, Parliament dealt with matters in the traditional pattern of the common law, by moving from specific case to specific case, rarely trying to anticipate larger problems by a more general treatment, and staying as far as possible from the abstract generalizations with which continental law is replete.

The development of insurance law has been similar to that of the law relating to embezzlement, except that insurance is far more complex, making the resulting development even more unsystematic if not also more irrational. For well over a century American legislatures have been feverishly grinding out insurance laws, a new

---

[11] 24 Geo. II, ch. 11, sec. 3 (1751).

[12] 5 Geo. III, ch. 25, sec. 17 (1765).

[13] 39 Geo. III, ch. 85 (1799).

[14] 20 and 21 Vict., ch. 54 (1857).

[15] See J. Hall, *supra* n. 8, p. 65, and the works cited therein.

[16] A gradual growth in awareness of the nature of problems—a slow sharpening of perception—is a crucial aspect of legal evolution. It is easy to criticize earlier generations for failing to see the full dimensions of a problem as we can now see it. We can be sure, however, that with poetic justice we shall also be dealt with similarly by future generations. For a full-dimensioned treatment of this and other problems of legal growth, see J. W. Hurst, *Law and Social Process in United States History* (1960).

[17] 20 and 21 Vict. ch. 54 (1857).

law each time a real, or sometimes a fancied, problem appears. They have never had the time, or at least have never taken the time, to try to comprehend the entire field of insurance, and to get it into perspective. Instead they have dealt merely on an *ad hoc* basis with specific and individual difficulties as they have arisen. In Wisconsin, for example, the legislature has dealt with insurance problems in over fifteen hundred separate statutes.[18]

Even after this extensive development, amounting now to perhaps 150,000 words, each session of the legislature sees some new, and many amending, statutes relating to various aspects of the subject. Many of the enactments are trivial but a large number have had important consequences. A similar pattern of development is to be found in other parts of the law. Very rarely does anyone take the trouble to prepare a systematic, unified, integrated treatment of any subject; this is especially true of insurance. It is not clear that any such attempt has ever before been made in the United States in the insurance field. The New York revision enacted in 1939 probably comes closest to meeting those specifications.[19] The Uniform Commercial Code is the characteristic member of the species—and perhaps the only member of such complexity.[20] In Europe, examples of systematic revisions are to be found, though they are not common even there. The best example for insurance is the German Insurance Regulation Law of 1901, which was decades in preparation.[21] It was followed closely by an equally systematic and "scientific" Insurance Contract Law in 1908.[22] The staff admires but does not plan to

---

[18] S. Kimball, *supra* n. 7, p. vi.

[19] Ch. 882 (1939), N.Y. Laws 2530.

[20] The literature on the Uniform Commercial Code is voluminous, and specific reference is therefore pointless. The code has now been adopted throughout the United States.

[21] Gesetz über die privaten Versicherungsunternhmungen vom 12. Mai 1901, in [1901] Reichsgesetzblatt 139. It is known as the Versicherungsaufsichtsgesetz, or VAG. Discussions leading to this statute were begun in 1869, were then delayed during the period of centralization of the German state and resumed in earnest about 1880. A draft was in existence in 1883; an amended one was published in 1896, and the legislature received the final proposal in 1900. For general historical background, see Büchner, *Die Entwicklung der deutschen Gesetzgebung uber die Versicherüngsaufsicht bis zum Bundesgesetz vom 31. Juli 1951,* in FÜNFZIG JAHRE MATERIELLE VERSICHERUNGSAUFSICHT NACH DEM GESETZ VOM. 12 MAI 1901 (Rohrbeck ed. 1952).

[22] Reichsgesetz über den Versicherungsvertrag, May 30, 1908, (1908) Reichsgesetzblatt 263. It is known as the Versicherungsvertragsgesetz, or VVG.

imitate such painstaking and prolonged analysis in the Wisconsin revision.

In Wisconsin, there have been one or two efforts to revise and consolidate the insurance laws[23] but there has never been any systematic and comprehensive attempt to reconsider and re-evaluate the underlying objectives of the law and to rationalize it. The most that such revisions could have achieved, even if they had been successfully enacted, would have been to smooth out the rough spots in the statutes and make them easier to understand and to use.

As a result, the Wisconsin insurance laws have developed into a complex and bewildering jungle of provisions which have never been carefully analyzed nor made internally consistent. The present code is an accumulation of specific *ad hoc* provisions, coming from different decades and responding to different problems, including many which are no longer problems or have an altogether different conformation than they had when first "solved." The insurance "code" of Wisconsin, like those of other states, is an antiquated legal instrument!

RECENT REVISIONS

Many states have developed new insurance "codes" in recent decades. It is far from our wish to denigrate the achievements of prior revisors of insurance laws. The contribution made by such revisions is important. The statutes have been tidied up, the most obvious contradictions eliminated, the terminology systematized and improved, and a semblance of rational structure given to replace the formless chaos that preceded them. Despite these gains, their achievements are seriously limited. No effort has been made, generally, to reexamine the presuppositions underlying existing statute law and determine whether long accepted premises and conclusions are valid.

The staff of the Wisconsin Insurance Laws Revision Committee, armed with the legislative mandate for a "comprehensive study," viewed with dissatisfaction the historical pattern of development of insurance law—not only the original enactments but also the limitations of the revisions—and set out to try to avoid the pitfalls that beset the path of previous draftsmen and revisors. A first step was

---

[23] See S. Kimball, *supra* n. 7, pp. 194–96.

for the staff to promulgate a set of guiding principles of insurance law revision; the second was to attempt to implement each by appropriate procedures. These principles and the method of implementing them may be of interest to those who are interested in insurance and the legislative process, not because they are the last word but because they may constitute a point of departure for subsequent discussion of insurance revision methodology.[24]

THE REVISION NOT TO BE IMPRISONED IN A STRAIGHT-JACKET OF RECEIVED DOGMA

It has been apparent from the outset, and is becoming increasingly apparent as thought is given to specific aspects of the revision, that received dogma is not necessarily sound. There is a paralyzing quality about long-accepted ideas that handcuffs the inquirer, straitjackets the mind, and discourages any attempt to blaze new pathways. The staff has agreed that no idea and no method of regulation shall be regarded as sacrosanct simply because it has the support of long tradition behind it. Indeed, the mere fact that a regulatory technique has not been questioned for a long time may itself be one of the best reasons for questioning it now. Members of the staff are no more free than other people from the debilitating effect of received doctrine, but a conscious awareness of the problem has led us to conceive of many new departures. None will be proposed to the legislature without extensive airing, but many will be suggested for serious consideration and discussion. None will be introduced merely because it is novel; but none will be rejected simply because it is not now to be found in any statute book.

Examples that have appeared up to this point include authorization of the use of federal receiverships by state insurance commissioners under special circumstances, an attempt to subordinate federal tax claims in liquidation, and the development of a technique of using forfeitures to apply compulsion to recalcitrant insurers and others, in a way borrowed from European practice. The federal receivership was first viewed with horror, but the logic of the supporting arguments prevailed and it has received general though not universal industry acceptance in the Delinquency Proceedings

---

[24] An abbreviated statement was contained in Wisconsin Legislative Council, Insurance Laws Revision Committee, Research and Drafting Procedures followed by Staff of Insurance Laws Revision Committee (February 10, 1967).

bill that became Wisconsin law in 1967.[25] The attempt at subordination of federal tax claims was also received skeptically at first but later accepted.

The ingenuity of the staff has by no means been exhausted, and many more novel suggestions will be made. Of course not all will nor should succeed. But some will succeed now and some will succeed later, after familiarity makes their merits clear. It has been especially encouraging that the commissioner and his staff, as well as most other interested persons, have recognized that this revision is expected to break new ground and have been very receptive to the free and uninhibited discussion of new ideas. A few persons have reacted vigorously, however, to any effort to break out of established patterns.

DRAFTSMANSHIP DEPENDENT UPON THOROUGH RESEARCH

From the beginning the staff has realized that much basic research needs to be done if a truly modern and systematic insurance code is to be produced rather than a mere paste-and-scissors compilation. Only with a meaningful research base can there be examination of the law in terms of fundamental issues such as: (1) What goals are to be sought? and (2) What are the most satisfactory means to achieve these goals without destruction of other values? On the other hand, limitations of time and resources prevent thorough research on every uncertain question. The result necessarily is a pragmatic compromise between the ideal and the practically possible.

The staff itself has launched some research projects and has also attempted to interest university groups and individuals in doing research in some areas in which uncertainties seem to exist, and where modest investments of time and resources may make large contributions. Up to the date of this publication, about a dozen substantial research projects have been launched, mostly in the form of projected doctoral dissertations. More are anticipated. Some will come to fruition in time to be of use in this project, and some will not. The University of Wisconsin, the Wisconsin Insurance Department and the University of Pennsylvania are all directly involved

---

[25] Ch. 89 (1967), Wis. Laws 220.

and have contributed substantial resources to the effort. More than $100,000 will be expended in these institutions in these various research activities, partly in fellowship support of the doctoral candidates and partly in other ways.

The University of Michigan Law School has been especially involved. A two-year program was begun July 1, 1967, utilizing the resources of the University of Michigan Law School and involving two faculty members, an experienced European insurance lawyer working as a senior research associate, and some graduate students. Over $50,000 in direct expenditures will be made by the University of Michigan, in addition to substantial commitments of faculty time. Hopefully, useful monographs will be produced that will lead to a better understanding of the legal and other aspects of some difficult regulatory problems, and will be available not only to improve the Wisconsin insurance laws, but also and more importantly, for use in future revision of other statutes.

Research initiated covers many topics. Examples are the regulation of loss reserves, the use of bonding as a regulatory tool, possible methods of early detection of insurer insolvency, the examination process, management contracts and other organizational questions, cancellation and non-renewal of automobile insurance policies, methods of assessment, mergers, and rate regulation including the use of investment income in rate making.

The rate regulation study is the most elaborate research project connected with the insurance laws revision. It is being undertaken with the full cooperation of the Wisconsin Insurance Department and the Rates and Rating Organizations Subcommittee of the National Association of Insurance Commissioners, of which the Insurance Commissioner of Wisconsin is currently chairman.[26] Formally it is a study of the latter committee, though much of the work, including a major share of the planning of the inquiry and interpretation of the results, is being done by the staff of the revision. The study is more elaborately conceived and carefully organized than past studies of the kind. In addition to actively assisting in the design and implementation of the Committee's study, the staff has obtained some non-Wisconsin support for this special study.

This catalogue of research topics is neither exhaustive nor closed.

---

[26] The activities of this committee may be followed in successive issues of the Proceedings of the National Association of Insurance Commissioners. The report leading to this study was adopted in Dallas, Texas, in December, 1966.

Most of these projects will be conducted at no cost to the state of Wisconsin, and none will be supported from the legislative appropriation for the project. It is not realistic, however much sense it would make, to expect a legislature to appropriate large sums of money for extensive basic research in connection with law revision —at least in the present environment. In an ideal society it would be more reasonable to expect it.

Some of the fruits of these studies have already been utilized in connection with the Delinquency Proceedings study,[27] and there will be further research findings to facilitate the future drafting activities of the staff, and to provide information for future revisions even more sophisticated than this one. Other steps are now being taken to generate further research on insurance regulation in business schools, law schools, regulatory bodies, trade associations, and insurers. This research will be on both legal and factual questions and will seek to determine sound public policy on difficult matters. All possible resources are being harnessed for the research tasks of this revision.

The research necessary for statute revision is not merely legal research. The insurance code regulates a legal contract, but insurance is far more than a contract. It is also a technique, a business, and an instrument of social planning, with ramifications extending throughout our social and economic life.[28] So complex a thing cannot be understood by legal analysis alone. There is room for, and in fact a necessity for, the work of the economist and the actuary in particular, supplemented by the whole team of social scientists. A modern code revision must take into account all the implications of the insurance concept for our society. It should utilize the ideas of "operations research," which relies on interdisciplinary teams as a fundamental practice in its work. The following statement, made to apply to operations research, is also true for code revision:

We should try as many approaches as possible so that we can select that one or combination of approaches that best fit the circumstances. This can be done by a team of researchers who come from different dis-

---

[27] That study is now law, Ch. 89 (1967), Wis. Laws 220.

[28] Kulp, "Social and Private Insurance—Contrasts and Similarities" in *Readings in Property and Casualty Insurance* (H. W. Snider, ed., 1959), pp. 28–32. For a development of these four viewpoints in the context of dental insurance, see Denenberg, "The Four Faces of Dental Insurance," *Journal American Society C.L.U.*, Vol. 18 (1964), p. 58.

ciplines or who are familiar with, respect, and know how to use the approaches of disciplines other than their own.

No team can feasibly contain every point of view. It is important, therefore, to use researchers who will subject their work to as wide a critical review by representatives of other disciplines as possible.[29]

DEMOCRATIC PARTICIPATION IN THE REVISION PROCESS

In addition to attempting to stimulate basic research, the staff also made immediate attempts to establish a continuing dialogue with informed and thoughtful persons interested in the revision. At all stages in the preparation of various drafts, the staff has attempted to consult interested individuals and groups, not only in Wisconsin but throughout the country. It was hoped that consultation would not only harness the expertise of interested persons, and lead to a better appreciation of their particular problems and viewpoints, but would ensure that legitimate interests were not violated. Of course, not all viewpoints can be given effect in the final product, which should protect the public interest, not special interests. However, all interests should be reckoned with in any planning for a new code, and all legitimate claims protected. Existing claims should be honored wherever appropriate.

The democratic dialogue deliberately designed as part of the revision process serves several useful purposes, in addition to the obvious one of giving everyone a day in court. The dialogue sparks research and highlights the strengths and weaknesses of statutory drafts. It also serves to require timely objections to any draft proposal, for those who lie back and fail to exercise their right of early objection, run the risk of having stale objections severely discounted. More positively, the democratic dialogue helps to produce a draft with a wide base of support. It produces a draft which many have helped to create and which many can, therefore, support as their own.

The main emphasis has been placed on the views of Wisconsin residents and interest groups. But the staff also recognized that insurance is less and less a local or an intrastate business and more and more an interstate if not an international business. Hence, there

---

[29] Russell A. Ackoff and Patrick Rivett. *A Manager's Guide to Operations Research* (New York: John Wiley & Sons, Inc., 1963), p. 23.

has been a systematic attempt to seek the views of interested persons throughout the United States. In trying to give due weight to non-Wisconsin interests, the Director served as a member of a committee appointed by the New York Superintendent of Insurance to consider the "holding company" question.[30] The NAIC rating study is an additional illustration.

The persons consulted have included not only prominent people in the insurance industry and its trade associations, but also regulators, insurance consumers, attorneys and academicians. This array of knowledgeable and expert consultants ensures that the ideas basic to the various drafts are not the product of armchair speculation but of the practical world, informed also by the more general thinking of those who have given these matters systematic attention. Curiously some of the provisions most widely attacked as visionary were suggestions of practicing insurance executives, not of academicians.

Attempts to sound out groups of interested people on both formal and informal bases took the following forms:

(A) Formal Activities of the Advisory Committee

This committee was appointed by the Insurance Laws Revision Committee, pursuant to Section 3 of Chapter 406, laws of 1965, authorizing the study of the insurance laws. It brings together in a formal way various interest groups.

Members of the advisory committee were consulted regularly on an informal basis, and significant results were achieved in formal day-long working sessions on each draft when it reached an appropriate stage of development. The meetings consisted of section by section discussions of drafts.

(B) Circulation of Draft Documents and Requests for Comment

Everyone on the mailing list of the committee has received copies of each generally circulated draft, and has been invited to comment on it. The first and third drafts of each chapter are generally circulated, while the second draft goes to all persons who indicated a desire to help in drafting that chapter by contributing suggestions to the staff on the improvement of the first draft. In addition to the

---

[30] *See Report to the New York Superintendent of the Special Committee on Insurance Holding Companies* (1968).

regular mailing list, the third draft went also to all state insurance departments and other presumptively interested persons. Many recipients have commented extensively on the draft documents. Most parts of the revision will be subject to this same elaborate and formal attempt to marshall the views of all interested parties.

During various stages of the drafts, many persons have been individually invited, on the basis of special interest or expertise, to comment on specific statutory language or specific legal problems relating to the proposed statutes. A special attempt was also made to get all possible help from the Wisconsin and national trade associations. The staff welcomes all such dialogue, and wishes to facilitate further exchange in all reasonable ways. Any interested persons are invited to enter into the dialogue. There is no membership fee for the club and the only dues are the expenditure of time and a willingness to make constructive suggestions.

(C) Speaking Engagements and Publications

The staff has attempted to stimulate interest in and suggestions for the revision by appearing before interested industry and academic groups, and by writing. The director of the staff organized a panel discussion on problems of insurance code revision at an annual meeting of the American Risk and Insurance Association, the national association of insurance teachers in universities. As a result, some papers were published.[31] The introduction to the Delinquency Proceedings chapter received wide readership by publication in the *Insurance Law Journal*,[32] and an expanded version appears in this volume. The director and associate director, with the cooperation of and financing by the University of Pennsylvania, launched in the fall of 1966 a lecture series on regulatory problems which ran into 1968. The papers from the lecture series, supplemented by a number of others obtained elsewhere, form this volume.

---

[31] Belth, "Observations on Solvency in the Context of Life Regulation," *Journal of Risk and Insurance,* Vol. 34 (1967), p. 539; McHugh, "Towards a Rational Regulatory System," *Journal of Risk and Insurance,* Vol. 34 (1967), p. 575; Mayerson, "How to Rewrite an Insurance Code," *Journal of Risk and Insurance,* Vol. 34 (1967), p. 95; Denenberg, "How to Rewrite an Insurance Code—Comment," *Journal of Risk and Insurance,* Vol. 34 (1967), p. 561.

[32] Kimball, Denenberg, and Bertrand, "Rehabilitation and Liquidation of Insurance Companies: Delinquency Proceedings in Insurance," *Insurance Law Journal,* p. 79 (1967).

(D) Systematic Interviews

The staff sought information and reactions to drafts from many interested persons, some by interviews at length and in person. The interviews included visits with personnel of the Wisconsin Insurance Department on many occasions, as well as, somewhat less systematically, the insurance departments of other states. Many knowledgeable insurance executives have been consulted at great length. So also were attorneys with appropriate special experience.

PRESERVATION OF THE UNDERLYING BASIS OF THE PROPOSED DRAFTS FOR LEGISLATIVE HISTORY

Virtually all of the work that has been done in connection with insurance law revision in the last 50 years has been lost, apart from the final drafts. Legislative bodies and staff technicians working on revisions elsewhere have been content to preserve only the final draft product, almost entirely without explanation of the way the draft reached final form and of the reasoning that went into it. Even those are difficult of access. To all intents and purposes, all background material on which those drafts were based has been lost to those who followed. This is not only a serious waste of resources, but it makes the draft product more difficult fully to understand, for the legislature which must enact it, the courts which must interpret it, the regulators who must administer it, and the public and industry which must be guided by it. To prevent this needless waste, the staff is preserving as much as possible of the research and thinking on which the draft in this revision is based, and is including extensive summaries and annotations in the draft documents themselves, in the hope of providing useful literature for the future. Later revisions will have this one as a foundation to build on.

One of the perennial difficulties of dealing with most state legislation, in or out of the insurance field, is that legislative history is either not generated at all or is difficult to locate and to verify. The statute must be construed without the aid of all those declarations of purpose and illuminating comments inherent in a complete legislative history. The states in effect throw the biography of the statute away before the statute is understood, construed, and given body. This contrasts sharply with federal legislation where there is an abundant and readily available legislative history, so much indeed that the courts are sometimes accused of psychoanalyzing Congress rather than reading the "plain words" of the statute.[33]

It is not enough merely to preserve the work product of a new insurance law for easy access by subsequent scholars, draftsmen, legislators, and revisors able and willing to undertake exhaustive inquiry. It must also be available for ready access and easy reference by the bar and the public. In order to ensure such availability, it is the present intention of the appropriate authorities to print the essential parts of the commentary on the drafts of this revision in the *Session Laws* of Wisconsin as the drafts become law. This was done with Laws of 1967, ch. 89.

The preservation of the work product has one other advantage. It facilitates borrowing and adaptation of the Wisconsin statutory proposals by other states. With respect to statutory language, Wisconsin should rather give than receive, and the Wisconsin revision should redound to the advantage of state regulation in general.

CONSTRUCTION OF A SOUND FRAMEWORK FOR THE DRAFT

One of the most serious defects of most American legislation is its unsystematic nature. This defect can only be avoided if constant attention is given to the building of a systematic structure rather than a patchwork.

This principle has several important corollaries. First, organization must be more than a series of convenient chapter headings. It should reflect the function, role, and purpose of the underlying law. It should provide a philosophy of regulation and suggest answers to the fundamental questions. Consequently, it is not sufficient simply to work out at the beginning a system of chapter headings and then pour existing statutory provisions into the mold thus created. *A*

---

[33] See, e.g., *United States* v. *Pub. Util. Comm.* 345 U.S. 295, 319 (1953), where Justice Jackson stated: "I should concur in this result more readily if the Court could reach it by analysis of the statute instead of by psychoanalysis of Congress. When we decide from legislative history, including statements of witnesses at hearings, what Congress probably had in mind, we must put ourselves in the place of a majority of Congressmen and act according to the impression we think this history should have made on them. Never having been a Congressman, I am handicapped in that weird endeavor. The process seems to me not interpretation of a statute but creation of a statute."

fortiori, no existing system can be accepted without question. In the early stages it is important to remain completely flexible in thinking about the ways the various parts of the statutes should be related to one another. Organization is as much a tool of communication as detailed statutory language, and should not be allowed to become an inflexible mold governing thought and stamping out legislative innovation. This principle is intimately related to the first—of resisting imprisonment of the revision in a straight-jacket of received dogma.

Second, the staff has recommended that it be left out of involvement in the hotly contested but isolated issues of insurance law and practice, as they now arise from time to time to puzzle and excite, if not to plague, the legislators. If the staff were continually diverted to give advice on every current legislative problem, systematic revision would be impossible. A staff put to work on each issue, however important, that came across the horizon, would have little time left for the systematic planning and building that is needed to avoid continuation of the present, or creation of another, legislative hodge-podge. The staff successfully avoided such involvement at first, though at the very beginning of its work there seemed some possibility that it might of necessity become embroiled in the automobile cancellation-non-renewal-rate increase problem that has excited legislators and the public everywhere. That degree of isolation has not remained possible, and inevitably the staff has been brought into some pressing but separate issues. In such cases, it has tried to integrate them into the whole.

Third, another corollary might be described, perhaps unduly pretentiously, as the adoption of "systems orientation." This is another notion borrowed from the emerging science of operations research:

The basic idea involved here is one that is generally accepted in principle by most managers and research men, but it is seldom followed in practice. The idea is that the activity of any part of an organization has some effect on the activity of every other part. It is a principle, which like Newton's law of gravity, connects each part of a system to every other part. Therefore, in order to evaluate any decision or action in an organization, it is necessary to identify all the significant interactions and to evaluate their *combined* impact on the performance of the organization as a whole, not merely on the part originally involved.[34]

---

[34] Ackoff and Rivett, *op. cit. supra* n. 30, p. 10.

This systems orientation is easier to illustrate than to describe in the abstract. It involves the full recognition of the organic unity of insurance regulation. It involves comprehension of the basic design of the whole system and understanding of the interrelatedness of its parts before a single component is built, or at least before it is accepted as final and complete.

One illustration will explain more than volumes of abstract analysis. When provisions relating to delinquency proceedings are drafted, consideration must be given to the question how soon after trouble appears, on what kind of proof and under what procedural controls the commissioner can act to seize a company. This in turn depends on many factors, including the efficiency of the examination system the commissioner is using and the skill and perceptiveness of his personnel. But the speed and efficiency with which he needs to act also depends on the cushion of capital and surplus that each company must maintain. The extent to which this cushion provides a safety factor depends in turn on other variables, such as how the cushion is related to changing premium writings and whether it is meaningfully protected by rate and investment regulation. It should be obvious that decisions on revision must be made in terms of a total system, however complex that task in fact becomes. There is no theoretical stopping point, of course, because decisions in insurance regulation depend inevitably on how the attorney general does his job, on the quality of judicial personnel, on the corporation law of the state, on the procedural rules under which courts must work, and on the political "climate" of the state. There is no logical stopping place, but naturally the limitations on human capacity, and especially on ours, makes it necessary for us to bound our "system" with some regard to what can practically be done. Fortunately a compulsory limit binds us in Wisconsin—the terms of reference of our assignment as given us by the legislature. That is a useful practical limit, if not a completely satisfying one.

MOVEMENT FROM AREAS OF AGREEMENT TO AREAS OF DISAGREEMENT

The purpose of an insurance revision project is to put sound legislation on the books, not to win debating points or create and get embroiled in controversy. This purpose can best be achieved by working from areas of substantial agreement toward areas of disagreement. By so doing, consensus can be exploited to the fullest, channels of communication can be established, conflicting viewpoints can be better understood and more easily resolved, and a base of agreement structured on which more controversial matters can be hammered out to mutual satisfaction.

By selecting a relatively uncontroversial subject like delinquency proceedings for the initial draft, the staff implemented this principle. A more controversial subject might have led to far less satisfactory results in getting the revision off the ground. Controversy could not be avoided, even here, and there was opposition to some provisions in the legislative bill, but it is noteworthy that concessions were made by many people, that most interested persons were reasonably happy with the final draft and were willing to terminate their opposition and acquiesce in some provisions with which they did not agree. Despite this compromise the draft managed to survive through all stages and get passed by the legislature while still retaining its organic unity.[35]

FUTURE ACTIVITY: OTHER DRAFTS NOW IN PROCESS

The chapter of the code dealing with the duties, powers and procedures of the commissioner and department also presented relatively little controversy and was before the legislature (with slight modification) without opposition when the session ended in 1967. It is again before the legislature in 1969.

The material on delinquency proceedings demonstrated that the revision process may sometimes require the expansion of several sections into a substantial chapter. The draft on the commissioner demonstrated the converse process. The draft consolidated numerous sections, now widely scattered throughout the code, into single sections. Two or three hundred sections became about thirty. Moreover, the sections were simpler. But the main economy of the draft chapter is not brevity so much as unification and organization of material now illogically and carelessly dispersed throughout the

---

[35] A joint legislative hearing was held on S.B. 303 on May 18, 1967. Many insurer representatives appeared to oppose one new provision in the bill, to eliminate setoff for reinsurers in liquidation proceedings. Without exception, all opponents of the clause took pains to praise the rest of the bill and to urge its passage, without the controverted clause, of course.

entire insurance law. If the chapter really succeeds, it will make of the material on the insurance department a simple and organically related unity.

The chapter on the commissioner was a logical choice for early revision. It lays the foundation on which the succeeding regulatory superstructure must be built. It announces the basic purposes and general powers of the commissioner and organizes the department charged with operating the regulatory process. With relatively few exceptions, its provisions did not produce acute controversy.

The next chapter drafted, relating to the corporation law of insurance companies, was also a logical early choice. The corporation law of insurance can be conceived of as a kind of generalized supervision. In fact, control of this body of law was one of the earliest methods of insurance regulation.[36] It is reasonable to design this generalized regulatory mechanism before building the more specific provisions of an insurance code. More controversy was generated in this area, however.

The work of revision is still continuing at this writing. In the meantime, the staff is determined to keep the principles here announced as effective working principles and not mere theoretical pronouncements. Perhaps for many readers the most attractive of those principles would be that of "democratic participation in the revision." Readers are a part of the public to which the revision is addressed, and suggestions of all kinds on the substance or procedure of the Wisconsin insurance code revision are welcomed.

---

[36] See Kimball, *op. cit. supra* n. 7, pp. 37 ff.

PART III

Financial Structure, Reserves, and Other Methods of Ensuring the Solidity of the Insurance Enterprise

chapter 6

Capital and Surplus Requirements

CAPITAL AND SURPLUS requirements provide one of the most important ways of providing solidity for the insurance enterprise. They provide the cushion of safety to absorb fluctuations in the value of assets and liabilities, as well as unexpected losses and expenses—contingencies that are inherent in the insurance process.

There has been widespread criticism of existing capital and surplus requirements. As a result, many states have increased their requirements, and the end of this trend is not yet in sight. Most of the changes, both proposed and enacted, have, however, been based on the roughest rules of thumb, with an assertion that existing levels are inadequate but with virtually no scientific work to determine what level would be appropriate.

Up to this point, moreover, formal statutory requirements of capital and surplus have been directed only to the initial phase of a company's existence. Yet requirements that are realistic for the formative stage are entirely unrealistic when the quite different question is put: what amount of capital and surplus is necessary to support safely an insurance operation with given characteristics? Up to this point in time, little scientific research has been done to solve this problem. Insurance departments have with more or less sophistication and with little uniformity imposed operating ratio limits on going insurance operations.

Only with the explosive development of insurance holding companies in the middle 1960's did the problem become acute, however. At that point, it became necessary to ask the question under circumstances when a holding company was formed for the express purpose (as some of them were) of diverting from the insurance operation as much surplus as possible in order to employ it in other enterprises deemed by management to be more profitable. At that point the regulator is forced to ask very seriously the question "How much surplus must the holding company leave behind in the insurance operation in order for it to be solid?" This question was asked in the *Report of the Special Committee on Insurance Holding Companies* made to the New York Insurance Superintendent on February 15, 1968. The following excerpt is Appendix One of that report.

THE CONCEPT OF SURPLUS SURPLUS

The Special Committee on Insurance Holding Companies*

The central objective of insurance regulation is to ensure the "solidity" of every insurance company. What is sought is more than "solvency" in the traditional senses, of (a) excess of assets over liabilities, or (b) ability to pay debts as they mature. What is sought is a more stringent test of soundness that will provide assurance of solvency lasting long enough into the future for any dangerous development to be detected and the surplus drain resulting from it stopped.

The "required surplus" is one that will be adequate to cover for a reasonable period of time any losses and expenses larger than those predicted and any declines in asset values, including all chance variations in the crucial factors of the operation. Any surplus beyond this cover is "surplus surplus" which, by definition, is unneeded; it may be treated quite differently in the process of regulation.

The notion of the "surplus surplus," or conversely, of the "required surplus" for a sound insurance operation, has a direct bearing on the "holding company problem," as it has been interpreted in this study. For example, if a holding company is formed to own the shares of existing insurers, and substantial portions of the assets of the existing insurers are expected to be transferred to the holding company for use in other enterprises, appropriate regulation of such insurers, whether domestic or foreign, demands that enough surplus be left in each operating insurer to support its insurance operation. Hence, only "surplus surplus" may be transferred.

Similarly, if an operating insurer is the "holding company," it

---

* Oscar M. Ruebhausen, Chairman; Newell G. Alford, Jr.; Samuel C. Cantor; Spencer L. Kimball; Stacy May; Oren Root. The committee's report was made to the New York Insurance Superintendent on February 15, 1968. This excerpt comes from pp. 43–47. See the next excerpt for work on which this appendix was based.

may wish to engage by investment or through subsidiaries in riskier, or at least different, enterprises than insurance. The investment or commitment of assets to subsidiaries that can safely be allowed out of the "required surplus" needed to support the insurance operation may not suffice to do what management wishes to do. However, it would be quite permissible from the viewpoint of policyholders' protection to subject any "surplus surplus" to the larger risks. Hence, it would be proper to invest or commit "surplus surplus" freely without any limit derived from insurance considerations alone. Other public policy objectives than the solidity of insurers are relevant, however, and may limit investment of "surplus surplus" in subsidiaries.[1] Thus, such investment must yield to considerations such as the undue concentration of economic power, or anticompetitive effects, or the enhanced opportunity for improper manipulation of assets or other possible abuses of power.

Further, when "surplus surplus" is ascertained, it could be freed for dividends or could be segregated as specific assets and used as pledges to secure the insurer's borrowing.

Thus it would appear to be sound and sensible for the Superintendent of Insurance to be authorized to prescribe standards and procedures by regulation which should be followed by insurers in calculating the amount of surplus that is excess to their insurance requirements and which could be free from those restrictions and controls that are dictated by the needs of the insurance business and the interests of the policyholders. In ascertaining the "surplus surplus," and in differentiating it from "required surplus," the Superintendent should use the scientific techniques and statistical data that now exist or may be further developed whether by advances in computer technology or through increasingly sophisticated mathematical analysis.

Because of the limits upon, and the relatively small size of, surpluses in New York life insurers, this concept of "surplus surplus" has less immediate importance for that branch of insurance operations. Accordingly, we do not recommend its application to life companies at this time.[2]

---

[1] See particularly Part II of this report.

[2] The concept has, in fact, already received some application to life insurers, even though not defined nor fully explored. N.Y. Ins. Law, sec. 90(1) (McKinney 1966) provides, in part, as follows: "For the purposes of this subsection, the investments of a foreign insurer shall be deemed to comply in substance with the investment requirements and limitations imposed by this chapter upon like domestic insurers . . . if, after disallowing as admitted assets

The "required surplus," which should be assured by regulation, is easy to state in the abstract, but difficult to implement in practice. It calls for analysis of the variables that the surplus to policyholders is expected to cover. Essentially they are three. First, the surplus must absorb any basic insurance costs (losses and expenses) which are in excess of the premiums charged. Second, the surplus must absorb any undervaluation of loss or claim reserves. Third, the surplus must absorb any declines in asset values. To this should be added any surplus required to finance necessary growth.

Though the principle, stated abstractly, is the same for both life and non-life insurance, its application is quite different for the two types of operation. If the concept is applied to life insurers, it will be found that they have insignificant undervaluation of loss or claim reserves, and little probability that any excess of insurance costs (above those reflected in the company's own calculations) will ever be incurred.

Thus, the problem for life insurers is, for practical purposes, reduced to making sure that there is enough surplus to absorb any decline in asset values, and to support necessary growth. Historically this need has been minimized partly by limitation of the investments in the life insurer's portfolio to those that are very stable in value and partly by creating artificial methods of valuation, like the amortization technique for bonds, that prevent fluctuations by defining them away. As more volatile investments were permitted, a mandatory securities valuation reserve was conceived as a way to dampen fluctuations in their value. The small margin of surplus allowed mutual life insurers under New York law necessitates such artificial limiting of asset value fluctuation, since surplus alone will not cover very much.

If investment laws were significantly relaxed to permit large amounts of investment in assets whose current market values are relatively volatile, the problem would take on new dimensions. Such investments would have to be restricted to an appropriate relationship to the policyholders' surplus. Put conversely, the "required surplus" would depend to a large extent on the amount of equity investments and thus the size of possible value fluctuations.

---

in whole or in part any of its investments which do not comply with such investment requirements and limitations, the superintendent finds that the resulting surplus to policyholders . . . would not be reduced below an amount which is reasonable in relation to the insurer's outstanding liabilities and adequate to its financial needs. . . ."

This problem has particular relevance to common stocks, but the same principles would apply for any investments where values fluctuate unpredictably, unless artificial means such as amortization are used to curtail the fluctuation.

The problem for non-life insurers is more difficult, and also more important. The loading factor built into the calculation of premiums and unearned premium reserves for non-life insurance is not comparable to that in life insurance. Premiums often prove inadequate and the combined loss and expense ratio frequently exceeds one hundred percent (100%) of premiums. Moreover, in some lines of insurance, notably liability, loss or claim reserves mount to enormous proportions, and inaccuracies in estimating them could prove disastrous. Finally, especially under current law, asset value fluctuations are even more important than for life insurers, because of the much greater freedom to invest in equities and the greater degree of unpredictability as to when investment values must be realized in cash to meet insurance claims.

The ascertainment of the required amount of policyholders' surplus for a given amount of current premium writings, loss reserves, and equity investments, is the key to rational insurance regulation for non-life insurers. It is an aspect of insurance regulation much neglected in the literature, largely because of its technical difficulty, though it is central to the whole regulatory enterprise. Indeed, the very possibility of doing it scientifically is sometimes doubted by practical insurance men.

Such doubts would clearly be soundly based, were reference made only to past and existing skills. However, while the necessary calculations are very difficult, the mathematical techniques for doing the job scientifically are now rapidly developing as a consequence of the increased use of computers. These techniques will certainly be operational for regulatory and management purposes in the foreseeable future, and the commissioners in the better-staffed insurance departments can look forward to dealing with the problem with real sophistication.

Whether the problem is difficult or not, however, it is a problem that has to be faced in the holding company context, for the reasons given earlier. Indeed, it has long been perceived as a problem, although solutions have been sought on the basis of experience and judgment. Nothing new needs to be contemplated immediately for there can only be a gradual substitution of hard facts and computation for experience and judgment. However, a clearer and more widespread appreciation of the nature of the problem would be helpful in contemplating the holding company development.

Well-known rules-of-thumb for making approximations have been developed. The so-called "two-to-one" rule constitutes an approximation to the specification of required surplus, and can be applied in the absence of anything better. Under most circumstances it is surely too stringent when used as a test of solidity. The rule is based on a theory developed by a former New York Insurance Department Chief Examiner and was utilized in the first draft of the 1939 Recodification of the Insurance Law as a yardstick for payment of dividends.

A similarly rough, but probably much too liberal, approximation is found in the English statutes. A non-life insurer must have a surplus of at least £50,000 if the general premium income of the company in the previous year did not exceed £250,000, a fifth of that income if it exceeded £250,000 but not £2,500,000, or the aggregate of £500,000 and a tenth of the amount by which that income exceeded £2,500,000.[3]

The insurance regulatory personnel of some states have concluded that premium writings of three times policyholders' surplus is safe but that four times is risky. Sometimes this is made a little more sophisticated by adding common stock investments to premium writings, in recognition of the fact that surplus must cover not only bad operational experience but also a stock market decline. In actual administration in a department as competent as New York's, actual application can be still more refined and discriminating, though New York, like the others, relies more on judgment than on precise quantitative standards.

In Finland, each company is required to have as a part of its claims reserve an "equalization reserve," which is to be "calculated according to risk theory, to provide for years with unusually heavy losses." [4] Under this provision, which was originally inserted in the Finnish law to provide a legal basis for tax-free accumulation of larger reserves, or more appropriately of more "surplus," in order to decrease the drain of foreign exchange through reinsurance, increasingly refined work in the calculation of the amount needed for the equalization reserve has been done by the regulatory agency.

Work on many related problems along the lines of the Finnish

---

[3] Companies Act 1967, s. 62(2), The Law Reports, Statutes 1967, ch. 81.

[4] Insurance Companies Act of 30 December, 1952, sec. 46, para. 3. Translated in *Insurance in Finland*, No. 2 (1964), p. 14.

approach is now being done elsewhere by a few people.[5] The prevalence of the high-speed computer makes computations practically possible that could only have been described in general and theoretical terms a few years ago. Consequently, it is possible now to anticipate, and to encourage the adoption of, increasingly sophisticated measurement as the new mathematical and electronic techniques are refined and perfected.

*   *   *

The appendix in the New York committee's report was an attempt to put into relatively simple terms an important evolving concept that must inevitably be based on more extensive scientific investigation of the problem. The following selection points toward (though it does not pretend finally to establish) a scientific basis for the determination of appropriate capital and surplus requirements in the day of the holding company that operates both insurance and noninsurance enterprises and that attempts to utilize its capital resources to maximize its profit. A satisfactory measure of the capital and surplus required to support a given insurance operation is the key to rational insurance regulation.

MINIMUM CAPITAL AND SURPLUS REQUIREMENTS FOR MULTIPLE LINE INSURANCE COMPANIES: A NEW APPROACH

Alfred E. Hofflander

Associate Professor of Finance and Insurance
University of California at Los Angeles

The insurance-oriented literature contains several levels of abstraction regarding the financial solvency of insurance companies.

---

[5] The mathematical problem is closely analogous to several others—for example, it is not unlike that involved in maximizing the return from a portfolio of investments. A recent paper containing some references to other literature is Borch, "The Theory of Control Processes Applied to Insurance Companies," *Journal of Risk and Insurance*, Vol. 34 (1967), p. 581.

The first level comes from those advances in actuarial science which are destined eventually to solve the double problem of capacity and capitalization (hereinafter referred to as the Ruin Problem).[1] Most of those works, however, are concerned with developing the tools necessary to determine the theoretical loss distribution in insurance. The emphasis is upon the mean and variance of the total loss distribution as they can be derived from the distribution of frequency and severity.[2]

At the other end of the spectrum lie the rules commonly called the Kenney Rules, which are simple and easy to apply in practice. As Kenney argues the matter, the equity of the insurer (known as policyholders' surplus) should be equal to the pure premium.[3] Houston argues[4] that intuitively one would expect a much smaller policyholders' surplus to be sufficient for the protection of insurers since its only purpose is to cover losses in excess of those envisioned in the rate, and that therefore the Kenney rule may provide an excessive margin.[5] Houston also examines a logical technique whereby a hypothetical insurer writing only one type of insurance could determine the appropriate amount of policyholders' surplus

---

[1] Capacity and capitalization problems in insurance are analogous to the debt/equity question in corporate finance. Thus, they are concerned with how much the total liability of an insurer can safely be with a given amount of equity so that the probability of ruin is smaller than some selected number e. Capacity corresponds to liabilities and capitalization corresponds to equity.

[2] For a description of the technique see Dickerson, Katti, and Hofflander, "Loss Distribution in Non-Life Insurance," *Journal of Risk and Insurance,* Vol. 28 (September 1961), pp. 45–54.

[3] *See* Kenney, *Fundamentals of Fire and Casualty Strength* (4th ed.; Dedham, Mass., 1967). Kenney was primarily concerned with conserving policyholders' surplus and did not attempt to define the precise limits of tolerance for his various ratios. Also, he was basing his ratios on pre–World War II experience. Probably a more meaningful set of ratios would be those established by the English companies and used by the surplus lines associations, specifically the *cover* ratio which is the ratio of total assets to premiums written. This ratio recognizes the possibility that loss reserves may not be accurate but that, whether they be excessive or inadequate, the impact of these errors will be in policyholders' surplus. Taking total assets, therefore, removes the problem of pinpointing the adequacy of reserves. The English feel that a cover ratio above 1.25 is increasingly desirable and a cover ratio below 1.25 is increasingly undesirable. There is no firm rule on this.

[4] Houston, "Risk, Insurance, and Sampling," *Journal of Risk and Insurance,* Vol. 31 (1964), pp. 511, 532.

[5] *Ibid.* Apparently Houston ignores the use of policyholders' surplus as a cover for loss reserves and fluctuating values of assets.

by making use of its frequency distribution of losses.[6] The extension of this approach to companies writing many different kinds of insurance is hindered by the varying face amounts (as well as units of exposure) and by the covariation between lines.[7] It should also be noted that a given insurer may not have sufficient exposure in one or more lines of insurance to allow it to make valid projections of its experience.[8]

Presented with these complexities, the insurance regulator must still answer the question of how much policyholders' surplus is sufficient for *each* insurer operating in his state. If the central objective of insurance regulation is to ensure the "solidity" of the enterprise, insurer by insurer, then what is desired is more than, or at least different from, "solvency" in the traditional sense. What is desired is an artificial measure of solvency that is considerably more stringent and provides assurance that assuming a continuation of present practices, with a margin allowed for chance variations in the crucial factors of the operation, a company is in a financial position to remain operative and technically solvent for a period long enough for any dangerous developments to be detected and corrected. The addition of "corrected" is important, of course—until deleterious developments are effectively changed, the danger of insolvency increases as the company loses surplus. Detection is not enough— for example, ascertainment that interest assumptions in life insurance policies of a certain vintage were higher than could be earned would continue to do damage to the finances of a life insurance company until all of the offending business was off the books.

The term "probability of ruin" should be defined at this point to represent the probability that an insurer will within a given period become technically "insolvent" in the sense that its assets will not

---

[6] Houston, *supra* n. 4, pp. 531–32.

[7] The variation and covariation between lines is briefly examined in Lambert and Hofflander, "Impact of New Multiple-Line Underwriting on Investment Portfolios of Property-Liability Insurers," *Journal of Risk and Insurance,* Vol. 33, No. 2 (1966), pp. 209–23.

[8] The problem here may well revolve around the definition of a line of business. For example, many would argue that auto property damage insurance written in New York is a different line than auto property damage insurance written in Wyoming. Obviously, this could be carried to extremes, since every subclass with either the average loss or standard deviation of losses significantly different from the average loss or standard deviation of losses of another subclass is in theory a separate line. Lack of usable data and time rather than theoretical considerations limit the number of classes used by a company for its analysis.

exceed its liabilities or that it cannot pay its debts as they mature, assuming a continuation of all existing facts except where it is known that they will be different in the future.

The acceptable "probability of ruin" in this paper is arbitrarily set at 0.001 and the time period for assurance of solvency at one year.

The key to the assurance of solidity is the policyholders' surplus, which is here defined as the difference between assets and liabilities (including reserves). The basic question, which is not yet definitely answered, is "how much policyholders' surplus is enough for the protection of insureds?"

Part I of this paper will focus on the basic problem of the need for capital and surplus. Emphasis will be on the theoretical problems of variation in the enterprise and how these movements affect the equity position of the insurer. Part II of the paper will deal with an analysis of some relevant data which is not intended to be definitive but rather illustrative. Part III is a brief summary with tentative recommendations.

I. THE NEED FOR SURPLUS

Shown in Table 1 is a streamlined balance sheet for a property-liability insurer. It is presented as an aid in viewing the manner in which policyholders' surplus protects insureds.

TABLE 1

Streamlined Balance Sheet for Property-Liability Insurers

Assets	Reserves
Cash	Unearned premium reserve
Bonds	Loss or claim reserves
Common stocks	Other required reserves
Preferred stocks	*Other Liabilities*
Mortgages	
Real estate	*Policyholders' Surplus*
Premium balances	Voluntary reserves
Other miscellaneous assets	Capital
	Surplus
Total Assets	Total Liabilities and Capital/Surplus

The first important potential source of drain on the surplus is the company's underwriting losses—a combined loss and expense ratio in excess of 100.[9] Thus, if an insurer has a combined loss and expense ratio of 110 on an earned premium of $1 million, the policyholders' surplus is drained to pay the excess loss of $100,000 above premiums. This would mean that the amount of losses anticipated by the unearned premium reserve in the above balance sheet is inadequate and that true liabilities are $100,000 greater than anticipated. The unearned premium reserve is the expected value of future losses and expenses,[10] a figure that may be either too high or too low. Thus, the first purpose of the policyholders' surplus is to absorb fluctuations leading to excesses in the operating characteristics of the insurer. The factors which may determine these movements are discussed briefly later.

Second, policyholders' surplus is needed to absorb declines in asset values. In most instances, this will be a decline in the value of the common stock portfolio because the bond portfolio is carried at an amortized value and declines only if there are defaults.[11] Common stocks, however, are carried at market value. A decline in the value of assets will directly result in a decline of equal amount in the policyholders' surplus (assuming, of course, no securities fluctuation reserves offset the decline). The question to be answered with respect to asset values is what might they be worth if they are valued at some point within the ensuing year. Again, some discussion of the anticipated fluctuations in value of these assets and the

---

[9] The use of the combined loss and expense ratio is theoretically indefensible but widespread. Its use in this paper is only as a surrogate for a more realistic measure. Such a measure would use accrued expenses and losses to earned premiums as a combined cost ratio. Unfortunately, the mixed "cash-accrual" accounting system developed for regulatory purposes has also been widely adopted by insurance management for general use. This makes it difficult for an individual not associated with a given insurance company to develop meaningful management information of the type generally available in other firms.

[10] Because of peculiarities of insurance accounting, a part (perhaps as much as 30–40 percent) of the unearned premium reserve, realistically speaking, is surplus, since prepaid expenses attributable to the whole life of the policy are written off as expenses at the outset. This constitutes an initial and artifical drain on surplus which is replaced as the policies run off. While the statement in the text is sufficiently accurate for present purposes, it would be appropriate to recognize that a portion of the unearned premium reserve is part of policyholders' surplus rather than a liability.

[11] There are sound arguments for valuing bonds at market, too, but nothing would be changed in principle if that were done—there would only be additional fluctuations to cover by surplus.

impact on (and hence the need for) policyholders' surplus will be discussed below.[12]

Third, the final major potential burden on policyholders' surplus arises out of the loss or claims reserves. The loss reserves are meant to aggregate that sum which when discounted for interest is equal to the known and unknown obligations that may arise from incidents which have already occurred. In the absence of fraud, the reserves set up are what the company expects these claims to cost. Any errors in the expected values will ultimately be reflected in the policyholders' surplus. This may not be entirely settled, however, until after the lapse of five years or more.

Some Theoretical Questions of Variations and Variance

This section will discuss in a nontechnical way some statistical questions respecting each of the above three items. In addition, some hypothetical data will be presented to give a better notion of the problems involved.

Unearned Premium Reserve

One wishes to know whether the margin of solvency—the degree of solidity—of the insurer is sufficient to protect against insolvency within a reasonable period in the future. The unearned premium reserve is an understated liability *if* the combined loss and expense ratio will exceed 100, for then as the premiums are earned, more will be paid out than came in as premiums. The deficiency must come from surplus. The more stable the ratio, the less need there is for policyholders' surplus to absorb fluctuations.

It is well to remember that insurance companies are poolers of risk. They utilize the law of large numbers to spread losses. However, the law of large numbers does not mean that there is no possibility of fluctuations which could cause large losses beyond those predicted from experience or judgment. As the number of risks increase, the relative size of the variations from the predicted will decrease, though there will always be fluctuations. The chance of failure from unanticipated variations is reduced, but it does not

---

[12] See pp. 77–78.

disappear altogether as the number of independent insured risks becomes large. By pooling risks in sufficient numbers an insurer can reduce its chance of failure but can never completely eliminate it.

For an initial illustration, assume the following:

1. Hypothetical line A has an industry combined loss and expense ratio of 100.0 with a standard deviation of 10.0.
2. The combined loss and expense ratios of the industry are normally distributed.
3. The test of solidity is to be 99.9 percent sure that an insurer will not become insolvent within a year because of bad underwriting experience.

If an insurer decides to write line A, the expected result will be 100.0, and that in 99.9 percent of the cases, the actual result will be less than 131.0.[13] If the above assumptions are valid, how much premium volume can this insurer write relative to its policyholders' surplus and still be 99.9 percent sure it will not become insolvent? Since there is 0.001 probability that it will have a combined ratio of 131 percent or larger, it should write no more than 100/31 of its policyholders' surplus. If it wrote that much and suffered the maximum loss contemplated, it would have just enough surplus to pay all claims without becoming insolvent. If the average result and standard deviation were 100.0 and 3.3 respectively, the range would be from 90 to 110 and the insurer could write 10 times policyholders' surplus with a probability of ruin of 0.001. Several practical problems complicate this simple analysis, however.

The analysis assumes that how well a company does is a completely random matter. That is, for any company we assume that a ratio of 131 percent or larger is as likely as one of 69 percent or smaller. But if a company has been operating with an extremely stable ratio over long periods of time, it may be reasonable to assume that the company has more stability than the industry as a whole. Should it be allowed to write more business in relation to its surplus than the amounts indicated by the industry variance? Simi-

---

[13] The value of 131 is arrived at through standard statistical techniques. It is noted from a table of normal curve areas that 99.9 percent of the area under the normal curve is found below the point determined by adding 3.1 standard deviations to the mean. Since the mean and standard deviation posited were 100 and 10, respectively, the equation is $100 + (3.1)(10) = 131$.

larly, should the reverse treatment be accorded firms with poorer experience?[14]

Secondly, is the "range of safety" a function of the size of the insurer or more correctly the amount of business it writes in a line?

Third, these tests show that the operating results of stock companies are different from those of mutuals. Should they be treated separately?

Fourth, the range of expected results will probably fluctuate over time. How is this to be handled in the final analysis?

Finally, since most operations are multiple line in nature, the above monoline analysis must be adapted to meet the complications of multiple line operation. The crux of the multiple line problem is to determine whether the various lines written by the insurer are "related," i.e., tend to follow each other and be unprofitable simultaneously and profitable simultaneously. This may be tested empiricially. Some studies have been done, with results one might have anticipated. The auto lines tend to move together, and most other lines are related only slightly. Some are even negatively related, which means that they tend to offset each other, with one line being up when another line is down. Unless two lines are perfectly related ($r = 1.0$), then writing two or more lines is safer than the writing of the most unstable line alone. As an example of this, assume:[15]

$$\text{For line A: } \bar{x}_A = 100.0 \qquad \sigma_{x_A} = 10$$
$$\text{For line B: } \bar{x}_B = 100.0 \qquad \sigma_{x_B} = 3.3$$

Further, assume A and B are highly related lines of business ($r = 0.75$). If a company writes only line A, it can expect with 99.9 percent confidence a combined loss and expense ratio of less than 131.0. If it writes only line B, it can similarly expect a ratio of less than 110.0. But when it writes 50 percent in A and 50 percent in B, it can expect results of less than 119.5. If lines A and B were completely unrelated ($r = 0.0$), then one could expect results to be less than 116.1. If they are perfectly but negatively related ($r = -1$), one would expect results less than 113.6. Summarizing the above:

---

[14] The analogy to the deviated rate problem and credibility of experience is almost perfect.

[15] $\bar{x}$ is the mean or expected result. σ_x is the standard deviation.

Line A alone, 99.9 percent sure of less than 131.
Line B alone, 99.9 percent sure of less than 110.
50 percent of each where:[16]

$$r = +1.00 \qquad 120.5$$
$$r = +0.75 \qquad 119.5$$
$$r = 0.0 \qquad 116.2$$
$$r = -1.00 \qquad 110.3$$

Finally, it is important to note that even where one can calculate the degree of relatedness (r) for a given time period, it is not clear that the value would be a stable one over time.

Investment Portfolio

The problem of the investment portfolio is not an easy one. The concern is that the value of the portfolio will fall to a level which

---

[16] Note that the result of writing 50 percent each where $r = -1$ is almost as stable as writing line B alone, even though the variance of line A is 10 times as great as that on line B. All of the above results are based upon the fact that if one has two random variables which are linearly combined the resultant mean is:

$$\bar{x} = P_1\bar{x}_1 + P_2\bar{x}_2 ,$$

where

$$P_1 + P_2 = 1$$

and the variance of the resultant distribution is given by:

$$\sigma_x{}^2 = P_1{}^2\sigma_1{}^2 + P_2{}^2\sigma_2{}^2 + 2P_1P_2\sigma_1\sigma_2r_{12} ,$$

where r_{12} is the coefficient of correlation between the two variables.
The results are perfectly general to n "lines":

$$\bar{x} = \sum_{i=1}^{n} P_i\bar{x}_i ,$$

where:

$$\sum_{i=1}^{n} P_i = 1$$

and

$$\sigma_x{}^2 = \sum_{i=1}^{n} \sum_{j=1}^{n} P_iP_j\sigma_i\sigma_jr_{ij} .$$

will impair the ability of the insurer to continue in operation. It should be pointed out at the onset that the concern here is not with liquidity but rather with the valuation of the assets.

The insurance commissioner is concerned with the continual (i.e., daily) solvency of each insurance enterprise in his domain. This problem may be expressed as "what is the probability (or how does one minimize the probability) that at some point during the year the value of the portfolio will fall to some dangerous or disastrous level?"

The problem is further complicated by the fact that one cannot solve it by requiring high-grade securities. There is a finite probability that a well-managed insurance company may select that particular portfolio of *good substantial equities* which can cause it ruin in any given year. To the management, and indirectly to the insurance commissioner, falls the job of making advance decisions regarding investments to minimize the probability of such an occurrence. On what basis are such decisions to be made. Even if one can assume that the recent past is a reasonable guide to the immediate future, the problem of establishing sufficient policyholders' surplus is not fully solved until the degree of "relatedness" (r) between variation in equity values and the combined loss and expense ratios is established. On the basis of common experience, one might suggest that the degree of relatedness is small, but it cannot be dismissed out of hand.

Loss Reserves

The last source of surplus drain is one which has been less adequately investigated. In addition, it is one which presents special problems since it is open to venal manipulation quite apart from the chance fluctuations to which it may be subject. The loss reserves are crucial in three lines of business: automobile bodily injury liability, general bodily injury liability, and workmen's compensation. The question is how accurately these reserves can be estimated. If they can be estimated with enough accuracy, then little policyholders' surplus is needed for this purpose. If the reserves cannot be estimated accurately, then a larger surplus will be required. In those lines where loss reserves are important, the actual results may not be known for five or more years. Hence, the problem of the adequacy of loss reserves arises.

The ratio of actual losses ultimately paid to the originally established loss reserves may be treated in a manner similar to the combined loss and expense ratio. As an example of this, assume a hypothetical line of insurance in which loss reserves of $100 million were established as of December 31, 1960. If after a passage of time it is found that only an average of $0.95 out of each dollar of reserves established is needed, then the ratio (in percentage terms) of actual to expected would be:

$$R = 95 .$$

If, through analysis of past experience, it is found that the standard deviation of R $(\sigma_{\bar{R}}) = 10$, then a company establishing a reserve in that year could have been 99.9 percent safe in assuming that their actual R would not have been greater than $1.26 (if they had had the results of the analysis in advance). Unfortunately, all of the problems which arose in the treatment of underwriting variance are again applicable:

a) Thus, this analysis assumes that a company's success in calculating reserves is completely random. That is, for any one company it assumes that a ratio of 1.26 or larger is as likely as one of 0.64 or smaller. But if a company has had success in estimating its loss reserves over long periods of time, is it reasonable to assume that the company has more stability or better analysis than the industry as a whole? Should it be allowed to have less policyholders' surplus than the amounts indicated by the industry variance? Again, should the reverse treatment be accorded firms with poorer experience in anticipating losses?

b) The stability of the ratio is almost certainly a function of size for at least the smaller firms.

c) Tests would probably show that the operating results of stock companies are different from those of mutuals. Different treatment may be justified, therefore.

d) The range of expected results will probably fluctuate over time, and this will have to be examined.

e) Finally, the variance in loss reserve estimates may be related to variance of returns in the portfolios and in underwriting. If so, it must be taken into account when these factors are combined with it.

II. ANALYSIS OF DATA

In order to give the reader some feeling for the orders of magnitude involved in the real world problems faced by regulators, the author has gathered data on some of the relevant items discussed in the earlier portions of this paper. The results presented below, however, are only to be used as rough measures of the problem, not as fine tools of calibration.

Variation in Underwriting

The problem of variation in underwriting may be put simply: if the industry combined loss and expense ration is 100, what is the probability that a specific company writing a given volume of business will deviate from this average by more than some number e.

In order to answer this question one must have the answer to several questions:

1. What is the shape of the curve representing distribution of results?
2. What is the standard deviation of the distribution of results?
3. To what extent is the variance of a company's results determined by its volume in the line?
4. What other nonrandom factors (e.g., territory, management ability, definition of a line) enter into and affect the variance of results? I can cast some light on the first three questions, but I am unable to do more than suggest the problems raised by the fourth question.

Source of Data

I gathered data on premiums earned and the combined loss and expense ratios of stock insurers on a company by company basis for 26 lines of insurance for 5 consecutive years (1959–63). For each year, every company listed in that year's "By-Line Underwriting" section of *Best's Aggregates and Averages* comprised the sample. These are the medium and large companies which write approximately 95 percent of the volume of stock insurers.

Results of Analysis

For each year, for each line the data were treated in the following manner:

1. The mean, variance, and standard deviation of the combined loss and expense ratio were calculated.
2. For each company, the deviation from the mean $(\bar{x} - x_i)$, the absolute deviation $|\bar{x} - x_i|$, the deviation squared $(\bar{x} - x_i)^2$, and the natural log of the absolute deviation $(ln|\bar{x} - x_i|)$ were calculated.
3. For each line, regressions were performed between the above measures of deviation and both premium volume and the reciprocal of the premium volume. This is done to test the assumption that there is some relation between size and variance results.[17]

The result of these calculations for 1959–63 are shown in Table 2.[18] One can note from Table 2 that there are substantial differences between the operating characteristics of the various lines. This is true of both the means and the standard deviations. The data on coefficients of correlation between the diverse measures of deviation and "size" present an interesting picture. First, let us hypothesize what one would obtain under various conditions and compare this with the actual results. Assume that underwriting profitability can be tied to size in one of three ways:

a) Size is a positive factor in underwriting profitability;
b) Size is unrelated to profitability; and
c) Size is a negative factor in profitability.

If size were a positive factor in profitability, one would expect a significant negative correlation between premiums earned and deviations from the mean combined loss and expense ratio. The results demonstrate that this is not generally the case. It must be pointed out, however, that the test for significance of *r* has certain

---

[17] See Hofflander and Duvall, "The Ruin Problem in Multiple-Line Insurance," *Journal of Financial and Quantitative Analysis,* Vol. 2 (June, 1967), pp. 150–65.

[18] Table 2 appears on pp. 82–86.

TABLE 2

Summary of Analysis of Combined Loss and Expense Ratios for
Twenty-six Lines* of Insurance—Stock Companies 1959–63

**Coding for lines of insurance:*

1 Fire	14 Workmen's compensation
2 Extended coverage	15 Miscellaneous bodily injury liability
3 Homeowners multiple peril	16 Miscellaneous property damage liability
4 Commercial multiple peril	17 Auto bodily injury liability
5 Allied fire	18 Auto property damage liability
6 Ocean	19 Auto collision
7 Inland marine	20 Auto, fire, theft and comprehensive
8 Accident	21 Fidelity
9 Health	22 Surety
10 Noncancelable accident and health	23 Glass
11 Unsegregated accident and health	24 Boiler and machinery
12 Group accident and health	25 Credit
13 Hospital and medical	26 Burglary and theft

Explanation of column headings:

Yr.	= Year
No. of Co's	= Number of Companies
W'ted Ave.	= Weighted Average of Combined Loss and Expense Ratio (weighted by premium volume)
Std. Dev.	= Standard Deviation of the Combined Ratio about Weighted Average
Net Prem. E.	= Net Premiums Earned
Dev. fm. Ave.	= Deviation from Average
Abs. Dev.	= Absolute Deviation from Average
Sq. Dev.	= Squared Deviation from Average

					Correlation Coefficients, R,					
					Net Prem. E			1/Net Prem. E		
Line Nos., Yr.	No. of Co's	W'ted Ave.	Std. Dev.		Dev. fm. Ave.	Abs. Dev.	Sq. of Dev.	Dev. fm. Ave.	Abs. Dev.	Sq. of Dev.
1 59	82	98.65	6.01		−0.09	−0.28	−0.22	0.21	0.34	0.28
60	78	99.81	5.49		−0.06	−0.24	−0.20	0.08	0.39	0.35
61	79	101.39	8.65		0.15	−0.09	−0.02	−0.17	0.30	0.24
62	75	103.20	6.95		0.11	−0.28	−0.23	−0.34	0.60	0.68
63	72	108.89	8.57		0.09	−0.20	−0.10	−0.08	0.25	0.15
2 59	89	95.91	7.54		0.00	−0.23	−0.19	−0.14	0.30	0.17
60	82	106.81	8.89		−0.07	−0.17	−0.17	0.00	0.15	0.14
61	76	115.18	11.43		−0.06	−0.21	−0.19	0.18	0.34	0.31
62	73	106.66	11.00		0.08	−0.11	−0.13	−0.25	0.32	0.34
63	70	98.28	8.88		0.19	−0.21	−0.13	−0.52	0.52	0.44

Source: Computed from *Best's Aggregates and Averages*, 1960–64, By-line Underwriting Section, *passim*.

TABLE 2—*Continued*

| | | | | | | Correlation Coefficients, R, | | | | |
| | | | | | *Net Prem. E* | | | *1/Net Prem. E* | | |
Line Nos.,	*Yr.*	*No. of Co's*	*W'ted Ave.*	*Std. Dev.*	*Dev. fm. Ave.*	*Abs. Dev.*	*Sq. of Dev.*	*Dev. fm. Ave.*	*Abs. Dev.*	*Sq. of Dev.*
3	59	68	91.03	7.27	−0.12	−0.06	−0.04	0.09	0.07	0.02
	60	76	97.99	7.97	−0.24	−0.20	−0.18	0.18	0.48	0.47
	61	80	104.26	10.26	−0.10	−0.11	−0.06	0.13	0.41	0.41
	62	83	104.88	8.54	−0.14	−0.19	−0.17	−0.16	0.53	0.47
	63	88	108.17	9.21	−0.08	−0.16	−0.11	−0.74	0.84	0.93
4	59	30	103.97	15.73	−0.02	−0.15	−0.23	0.25	0.09	0.17
	60	36	100.51	21.49	−0.07	−0.32	−0.18	−0.01	0.29	0.12
	61	54	93.23	17.66	0.03	−0.14	−0.07	−0.00	−0.03	−0.02
	62	68	91.10	12.04	0.04	−0.22	−0.15	−0.26	0.31	0.20
	63	73	93.50	11.65	0.01	−0.20	−0.16	−0.20	0.33	0.29
5	59	55	84.00	9.80	−0.34	−0.30	−0.27	0.31	0.22	0.26
	60	63	81.19	11.93	0.12	−0.39	−0.25	−0.43	0.62	0.60
	61	65	91.23	12.83	0.12	−0.25	−0.22	−0.18	0.34	0.26
	62	74	92.78	20.40	0.03	−0.32	−0.26	0.02	0.36	0.28
	63	73	95.13	18.16	0.09	−0.26	−0.22	−0.14	0.25	0.20
6	59	57	95.96	6.62	0.09	−0.26	−0.21	−0.06	0.33	0.30
	60	57	93.98	8.63	−0.01	−0.02	−0.07	−0.06	−0.05	−0.01
	61	58	98.57	7.12	0.10	−0.19	−0.16	−0.25	0.13	0.05
	62	55	93.44	7.85	−0.12	−0.14	−0.08	0.03	0.25	0.16
	63	51	97.85	7.52	0.16	−0.17	−0.14	−0.10	0.33	0.27
7	59	80	97.62	6.54	0.02	−0.23	−0.12	0.01	−0.00	−0.00
	60	80	97.95	6.83	−0.03	−0.29	−0.17	0.13	0.36	0.22
	61	79	98.74	8.23	0.13	−0.19	−0.12	−0.21	0.29	0.18
	62	75	95.14	6.51	0.07	−0.34	−0.20	−0.24	0.38	0.22
	63	74	100.11	7.34	0.16	−0.26	−0.13	−0.22	0.46	0.41
8	59	31	95.10	9.69	0.02	−0.32	−0.20	−0.12	0.36	0.33
	60	27	98.11	9.00	−0.08	−0.29	−0.23	−0.01	0.30	0.31
	61	27	97.43	12.27	−0.16	−0.09	−0.08	0.10	0.05	0.00
	62	27	99.35	9.49	−0.03	−0.18	−0.17	0.10	0.24	0.30
	63	29	93.86	11.48	−0.15	−0.12	−0.12	−0.14	0.19	0.21
9	59	7	87.30	5.09	0.01	−0.64	−0.59	0.24	0.90	0.92
	60	7	86.07	6.29	0.56	−0.32	−0.34	−0.68	0.61	0.63
	61	5	92.98	10.34	0.71	−0.36	−0.39	−0.62	0.50	0.50
	62	4	90.17	9.40	0.11	−0.90	−0.81	−0.03	0.68	0.61
	63	5	81.10	6.22	0.41	−0.49	−0.48	−0.62	0.41	0.51

TABLE 2—*Continued*

						Correlation Coefficients, R,			
					Net Prem. E			1/Net Prem. E	
Line Nos.,	Yr.	No. of Co's	W'ted Ave.	Std. Dev.	Dev. fm. Ave.	Abs. Dev.	Sq. of Dev.	Dev. fm. Ave.	Abs. Dev.	Sq. of Dev.
---	---	---	---	---	---	---	---	---	---	---
10	59	10	79.92	7.10	−0.46	−0.52	−0.42	0.51	0.53	0.46
	60	11	79.87	5.80	−0.15	−0.38	−0.31	−0.05	0.23	0.24
	61	13	80.33	6.24	−0.28	−0.25	−0.22	0.62	0.61	0.60
	62	14	78.95	7.62	−0.32	−0.29	−0.24	0.49	0.43	0.28
	63	12	81.49	4.23	−0.04	−0.55	−0.42	0.16	0.60	0.51
11	59	23	95.04	10.40	−0.07	−0.13	−0.09	0.06	0.25	0.20
	60	25	95.89	9.99	−0.14	−0.18	−0.15	0.08	0.37	0.31
	61	27	94.62	8.77	−0.03	−0.17	−0.13	−0.55	0.81	0.87
	62	29	95.03	9.99	0.03	−0.17	−0.13	−0.63	0.57	0.63
	63	28	98.74	8.13	−0.01	−0.18	−0.11	−0.68	0.77	0.88
12	59	42	97.90	4.50	−0.01	−0.14	−0.08	−0.04	0.24	0.15
	60	42	98.26	4.58	0.05	−0.13	−0.10	−0.38	0.72	0.71
	61	49	99.04	3.68	0.09	−0.16	−0.07	−0.73	0.80	0.96
	62	47	98.70	4.18	−0.01	−0.19	−0.11	0.14	0.45	0.38
	63	50	99.81	5.18	0.06	−0.19	−0.12	−0.55	0.63	0.75
13	59	28	95.89	7.73	−0.21	−0.09	−0.10	−0.12	0.11	0.08
	60	29	96.55	7.14	−0.09	−0.13	−0.15	0.01	0.09	0.15
	61	34	97.36	9.45	−0.20	−0.01	−0.03	−0.09	0.05	−0.02
	62	34	97.12	6.65	−0.15	−0.16	−0.11	0.10	0.28	0.27
	63	34	99.65	7.31	−0.03	−0.16	−0.12	−0.26	0.23	0.32
14	59	91	99.43	8.55	0.01	−0.19	−0.15	−0.03	0.20	0.16
	60	92	98.83	8.27	−0.06	−0.25	−0.16	0.08	0.19	0.18
	61	95	99.87	8.21	−0.03	−0.16	−0.12	−0.02	0.10	0.03
	62	93	97.27	7.27	0.04	−0.26	−0.18	−0.13	0.21	0.16
	63	95	97.33	7.62	−0.00	−0.23	−0.19	−0.02	0.30	0.26
15	59	102	96.57	8.49	0.07	−0.23	−0.19	−0.06	0.32	0.27
	60	114	94.65	8.95	0.06	−0.26	−0.14	−0.18	0.25	0.11
	61	113	93.14	9.83	0.04	−0.25	−0.20	−0.03	0.29	0.21
	62	114	89.33	7.41	0.03	−0.30	−0.20	−0.06	0.16	0.14
	63	108	92.13	11.29	0.08	−0.17	−0.13	−0.07	0.32	0.36
16	59	43	93.62	9.49	0.10	−0.33	−0.30	−0.03	0.35	0.37
	60	48	91.37	8.29	0.03	−0.24	−0.21	−0.11	0.43	0.42
	61	51	91.96	10.13	0.07	−0.31	−0.23	−0.08	0.36	0.31
	62	55	94.47	9.10	0.05	−0.36	−0.26	−0.08	0.35	0.28
	63	55	94.46	15.24	−0.01	−0.11	−0.12	0.10	0.34	0.27

TABLE 2—Continued

| | | | | | Correlation Coefficients, R, | | | | | |
| | | | | | Net Prem. E | | | 1/Net Prem. E | | |
Line Nos.,	Yr.	No. of Co's	W'ted Ave.	Std. Dev.	Dev. fm. Ave.	Abs. Dev.	Sq. of Dev.	Dev. fm. Ave.	Abs. Dev.	Sq. of Dev.
17	59	156	105.38	7.99	−0.03	−0.17	−0.14	−0.01	0.30	0.27
	60	156	102.61	8.65	−0.09	−0.16	−0.13	0.04	0.16	0.13
	61	159	103.44	7.55	−0.08	−0.16	−0.12	0.10	0.26	0.25
	62	169	102.37	8.16	−0.09	−0.15	−0.10	−0.11	0.31	0.28
	63	171	102.79	8.20	−0.06	−0.12	−0.08	−0.36	0.38	0.37
18	59	109	97.55	7.70	−0.12	−0.21	−0.20	0.03	0.33	0.35
	60	114	97.10	7.03	−0.10	−0.21	−0.17	0.13	0.17	0.14
	61	107	98.28	8.01	−0.05	−0.15	−0.14	−0.05	0.04	0.05
	62	108	101.86	7.53	−0.04	−0.22	−0.18	0.07	0.36	0.29
	63	105	104.62	7.61	−0.00	−0.18	−0.09	−0.62	0.76	0.92
19	59	138	92.66	10.17	−0.10	0.02	−0.01	0.08	0.01	0.03
	60	135	92.46	8.29	−0.13	−0.08	−0.08	0.19	0.07	0.04
	61	130	92.93	9.12	−0.16	−0.07	−0.09	0.05	0.00	−0.00
	62	129	96.88	8.80	−0.07	−0.07	−0.06	0.08	0.11	0.16
	63	132	100.48	8.22	−0.01	−0.07	−0.05	−0.30	0.46	0.52
20	59	88	92.80	10.01	0.10	0.03	0.02	−0.18	0.10	0.08
	60	89	94.12	9.20	0.06	0.03	−0.03	−0.20	0.13	0.13
	61	92	94.32	8.75	0.01	0.01	−0.04	−0.02	0.13	0.17
	62	98	95.77	8.62	0.04	−0.11	−0.10	−0.07	0.24	0.18
	63	97	93.06	8.40	0.03	−0.13	−0.10	−0.24	0.26	0.36
21	59	35	91.61	11.04	0.01	−0.34	−0.25	−0.09	0.23	0.18
	60	39	93.29	11.42	−0.04	−0.18	−0.20	0.07	0.12	0.15
	61	38	97.67	11.72	0.10	−0.29	−0.28	−0.09	−0.05	0.01
	62	37	85.19	9.76	−0.04	−0.48	−0.40	−0.30	0.54	0.54
	63	38	94.15	20.43	−0.07	−0.26	−0.14	−0.18	0.16	0.04
22	59	56	84.46	19.71	−0.21	−0.39	−0.32	0.16	0.42	0.34
	60	61	103.61	33.46	−0.10	−0.30	−0.21	−0.11	0.26	0.19
	61	64	90.70	20.45	−0.14	−0.21	−0.17	0.18	0.26	0.23
	62	65	86.39	17.88	−0.06	−0.27	−0.18	0.02	0.30	0.20
	63	64	93.66	25.48	0.11	−0.16	−0.16	−0.17	0.21	0.17
23	59	37	102.48	5.08	0.08	−0.13	−0.10	−0.00	0.29	0.27
	60	37	100.97	5.53	−0.20	−0.23	−0.22	0.17	0.37	0.37
	61	38	106.95	7.77	0.41	−0.04	−0.03	−0.31	0.16	0.22
	62	38	104.44	6.82	0.46	−0.25	−0.19	−0.45	0.56	0.53
	63	39	105.26	6.70	0.02	−0.26	−0.28	−0.12	0.28	0.30

TABLE 2—*Concluded*

| | | | | Correlation Coefficients, R, | | | | | |
| | | | | Net Prem. E | | | 1/Net Prem. E | | |
Line Nos.,	Yr.	No. of Co's	W'ted Ave.	Std. Dev.	Dev. fm. Ave.	Abs. Dev.	Sq. of Dev.	Dev. fm. Ave.	Abs. Dev.	Sq. of Dev.
24	59	17	93.17	5.48	0.14	−0.27	−0.18	−0.03	0.19	0.20
	60	17	91.05	7.01	0.07	−0.43	−0.30	0.37	0.49	0.53
	61	19	93.78	11.61	0.15	−0.33	−0.22	−0.09	−0.02	−0.07
	62	18	109.51	11.45	0.16	−0.33	−0.25	−0.17	0.33	0.25
	63	23	100.88	11.60	0.05	−0.28	−0.22	−0.14	0.24	0.16
25	59	3	71.06	8.46	0.66	−0.47	−0.56	−0.87	0.74	0.80
	60	4	78.56	6.16	−0.03	−0.78	−0.64	0.49	0.68	0.68
	61	3	108.21	7.38	−0.97	−0.89	−0.80	0.91	0.98	1.00
	62	3	100.22	5.12	0.92	−0.82	−0.74	−0.95	0.99	1.00
	63	4	98.89	7.82	−0.48	−0.52	−0.50	0.95	0.98	0.97
26	59	37	98.20	6.80	−0.26	−0.07	−0.09	0.06	0.26	0.28
	60	36	103.51	5.94	−0.33	−0.08	−0.12	0.17	0.18	0.21
	61	38	102.35	8.21	0.10	−0.01	0.05	−0.27	0.11	0.08
	62	40	99.50	6.92	0.09	−0.16	−0.19	−0.50	0.60	0.74
	63	40	102.86	7.33	−0.13	−0.29	−0.26	0.07	0.36	0.39

assumptions which have not been met. Hence, these results are only speculative. I continue in this analysis only because alternatives are not feasible.

If size were a deterrent or negative factor in underwriting profitability, one would expect a significant positive correlation between premiums earned and deviations from the mean value of the combined loss and expense ratio. The results similarly demonstrate that this is not generally the case. Hence, one can assume that within the range and extreme limitations of the data, size and underwriting profitability do not appear to be related. Since the relationship between size and profits is essentially neutral, one can proceed to the question of size and variance without fear of complications arising from the profit picture.

Again, one can hypothesize what might be expected and then compare this with actual results. The relationship between size and variance can also be broken into three alternatives:

a) Size is a positive factor in stability of results;
b) Size is an unrelated factor in stability of results; and
c) Size is a negative factor in stability.

If size were a positive factor, then one would expect that both the squared deviations and the absolute deviations from the average would *fall* as size increased. Thus, one would expect a significant negative correlation between size and both square and absolute deviations. *All* such correlations are negative. Only a few are statistically significant. (If the test of significance were applicable, then only three of the 26 lines would have had an *r* significantly different from zero in 1959). Few are of practical significance! In only isolated cases (where five or six insurers are the industry) can one say that this is important. For the linear measurement used, substantially less than 10 percent of the variation in underwriting results is accompanied by variation in premiums earned. This is in spite of the fact that the mean is a weighted average which would bias the results in favor of size.

Analysis also presented in Table 2 is used to test the hypothesis that variance is linearly related to the reciprocal of the premiums earned. In 11 of the 26 lines (1959) the degree of correlation fell when $1/P$ was substituted for P. In the remainder it rose. In only 4 of the 23 lines having more than 10 carriers did the degree of comovement (r^2) exceed 10 percent. Even though one does obtain very small values for r, they are almost all in the right direction.

In summary, one can say that for the firms in the sample, and with all of the reservations already raised, neither profitability nor stability appear to be *highly* related to size of premiums earned but that some such relationship does exist. Thus, the results a firm might be expected to achieve do not appear to be completely random with respect to size. I believe that these results would likely apply to other segments of the industry as well.

Other measurable characteristics may be available to insurance commissioners which they could use to further classify the companies in the sample. However, even if they exist, the following results will be presented under the assumption that such evidence is not appropriate and that underwriting results are completely random and are normally distributed (i.e., the relationship between size and variance is ignored). The question is what multiple of

TABLE 3

Permissible Ratio of Premium Writings to Policyholders' Surplus
for Monoline Operation under Simplified Assumptions

	1959	1960	1961	1962	1963
Fire..............................	5.8	5.9	3.5	4.1	2.8
Extended coverage...................	5.2	2.9	1.9	2.5	3.9
Homeowners multiple peril...........	7.3	4.4	2.8	3.2	2.7
Commercial multiple peril............	1.9	1.5	2.1	3.5	3.4
Allied fire..........................	6.9	5.5	3.2	1.8	1.9
Ocean marine.......................	6.1	4.9	4.9	5.7	4.8
Inland marine......................	5.6	5.3	4.1	6.6	4.4
Accident...........................	3.9	3.8	2.8	3.5	3.4
Health.............................32.1		17.8	4.0	5.1	312.5
Noncancellable accident and health....52.4		*	*	40.7	*
Unsegregated accident and health.....	3.7	3.8	4.6	3.8	4.2
Group accident and health............	8.4	7.9	9.6	8.5	6.3
Hospital and medical.................	5.1	5.4	3.8	5.7	4.5
Workmen's compensation.............	3.9	4.1	3.9	5.0	4.8
Miscellaneous bodily injury...........	4.4	4.5	4.3	8.2	3.7
Miscellaneous property damage.......	4.3	5.8	4.3	4.4	2.4
Auto bodily injury..................	3.3	3.4	3.8	3.6	3.5
Auto property damage..............	4.7	5.3	4.3	3.9	3.6
Auto collision......................	4.1	5.5	4.7	4.1	3.9
Auto, fire, theft and comprehensive....	4.2	4.4	4.8	4.5	5.2
Fidelity...........................	3.9	3.5	2.9	6.4	1.7
Surety.............................	2.2	.9	1.9	2.4	1.4
Glass..............................	5.5	5.6	3.2	3.9	3.8
Boiler and machinery...............	9.9	7.9	3.4	2.2	2.7
Credit.............................	*	*	3.2	6.2	4.3
Burglary and theft..................	5.2	4.6	3.6	4.8	3.9

* An almost unlimited amount could have been written with safety.
Source: Computed from data in Table 2.

policyholders' surplus could an insurer have written safely of *only*
one line of insurance in each of the five years examined? Table 3
presents these multiples. One must remember that this table also
assumes that there is no other possible source of drain on the
policyholders' surplus.

Investment Portfolio

Essentially, one would like to know what loss might be expected
on the portfolio of stocks owned. While it is impossible to forecast
the future, one can measure experience historically and then extrap-

olate these results to obtain some vague notion of what might occur in the future.

Sources of Data

Data were gathered for a population of 150 common stocks for the period of 1951 through 1965. The population (selected on the basis of 1962 data) included (1) the Dow Jones Industrials, (2) the 50 largest U.S. corporations on the basis of sales, (3) Clarkson's "B List" of 81 securities commonly considered by investment managers, (4) the 20 most actively traded common stocks on the New York Stock Exchange during 1962, and (5) a set of 33 randomly selected issues not included in any of the above. All of the 150 common stocks studied had been traded on the New York Stock Exchange since 1952 to insure data availability. All are of well-known established firms representing a wide spectrum of different industries. Clearly, they are good stocks for insurance-type portfolios. For each year, 50 portfolios of 35 stocks each were generated. Both the stocks *and* the levels of participation in each stock were selected randomly. Throughout the analysis, the period of consideration was one year. Stock prices, which reflect all stock splits and stock dividends, are mid-December closing prices for each year from 1951 to 1965. The dividends are the cash dividends paid during the respective years.

The central concern is that the portfolio's value will fall at some point during the year. Yet, this analysis only looks at the value at one point during the year, a point which approximates the annual valuation date. At least several states require quarterly evaluation, and so an analysis of quarterly results would be more appropriate. Clearly, this technique is artificial and can only be viewed as a rough approximation to reality. It should be noted, however, that since the mid-December prices are seldom the lowest of the year, it errs on the "wrong" side. That is, it would probably tend to overstate the average return, if not understate the variance. Despite these limitations, the results may be of some use. They are presented in Table 4.

The results are not surprising. Note, for example, that both the returns and variance of returns show a good deal of instability. One important fact, however, is that in only 2 of the 14 years was the average return negative, and that in only 4 of the 14 years would

TABLE 4

Yields on Randomly Generated Portfolios of
Quality Issues, 1952–1965

Year	Low Boundary $\bar{x} - 3\sigma$	Average Return $\bar{x}$	High Boundary $\bar{x} + 3\sigma$
1952	4.0%	11.3%	18.6%
1953	−7.3	2.0	11.1
1954	35.9	54.3	72.9
1955	12.0	22.8	33.6
1956	0.76	12.4	24.1
1957	−19.9	−6.1	7.7
1958	28.6	51.8	75.0
1959	3.9	16.6	29.3
1960	−12.0	0.64	13.2
1961	15.9	25.9	35.9
1962	−20.8	−11.8	−2.8
1963	8.5	23.5	38.4
1964	7.9	17.6	27.3
1965	5.4	18.2	31.1

Source: Computed from stock exchange quotations and
published earnings data.

one have obtained a negative return, even if they had selected that
portfolio representing the low boundary.

Loss Reserves

As in the case of variation in underwriting, the problem in loss
reserves is simply put. How accurate are loss reserve estimates?
That is, if an insurer establishes a certain amount as a loss reserve,
what is the range of confidence with respect to that figure? Again,
one must fall back on historical data to attempt to answer this
question.

Source of Data

The results presented here are based upon data taken from five
consecutive volumes of *Best's Reproduction of Principal Statements
from Fire and Casualty Companies*. They are exhaustive in the sense
that for each year *every* company listed was used. This means that
there is a mixture of both stock and mutual companies in the

sample. A separate analysis of stocks or mutuals alone, or other smaller classifications of companies, might be more revealing.

Results of Analysis

For each of the three categories of loss reserves, a ratio of actual losses (measured after a lapse of five years) to expected losses was calculated. Then, for each year a mean ratio with its attendant standard deviation was developed. These are shown in Table 5. The results are remarkably consistent over time. This picture is signifi-

TABLE 5

Mean and Standard Deviation of the Ratio of Actual to
Expected Loss Reviews, 1957–61

	1957		1958		1959		1960		1961	
	Mean	Sd. Dev.	Mean	Sd. Dev.	Mean	Sd. Dev.	Mean	Sd. Dev.	Mean	Sd. Dev.
Auto BI liability...	100.3	10.6	95.1	9.4	94.5	11.3	94.5	10.4	97.2	10.9
Miscellaneous liability........	91.7	18.8	89.3	18.4	89.7	15.9	90.1	19.9	90.7	21.4
Workmen's compensation.......	95.6	11.7	94.1	10.5	96.8	9.3	98.6	9.3	100.5	10.7

Source: Computed from data in *Best's Reproduction of Principal Financial Statements from Fire and Casualty Companies*, 1958–1962, *passim*.

cantly different from the one presented by the combined loss and expense ratios.

One odd item appeared in the result for 1960. An examination of the input disclosed that one insurer had a ratio of actual to expected losses in excess of 7000/1. Removing this insurer as being completely atypical yielded the results presented in the table.

The questions raised with respect to the relationship of size and variance in underwriting were again tested in the case of loss reserves. Here the deviations from average appear to be negatively correlated with size. This implies that larger firms tend to overreserve more frequently than smaller firms.[19] That they are also more

---

[19] That this may be of statistical significance but not of practical significance is apparent by the fact that the r^2 in each instance is less than 5 percent.

variable was illustrated by the fact that the correlation between size of reserves and both absolute and square deviations are negative.

Another interesting aspect of the results shows that the errors in forecasting loss reserves is *highly* correlated to the size of the reserves established. This is a much clearer relationship than in the case of the combined ratios.

It is also illuminating to observe that if the loss reserves are defined as the present value (discounting for interest) of claims incurred but not yet paid, then one would expect the average value of R to be greater than 100. In most instances, the value of R is less than 100.

Covariance in Underwriting

In each of the previous sections one central point has been ignored. That point relates to the degree of covariance between results. Because of the statistical limitations of this paper, no attempt is made to fuse the results into a "definitive" answer. Yet, some feeling for the relationship between underwriting lines should be presented, if possible.

Source of Data

The data used here are the stock company industry results for a period of nine consecutive years. This period was selected because of the short time that certain multiple line policies have been in effect. The data are from the Cumulative By-Line Underwriting Experience Section of *Best's Aggregates and Averages*.

Analysis of Results

Because most lines of insurance show noticeable trends, the first thing done was to eliminate the trends in the data. This was done because of the well-known problems involved in correlating time series containing strong trends. After eliminating the trend, the various lines were correlated with each other. The results for straight fire insurance are presented in Table 6. Because only nine years of data are available, one cannot place too much credence in the value of the r's which have been computed. If a test of the significance of the r's could be made (it cannot because of the violation of certain assumptions), the test would indicate that only two of the results are any better than an *r* value of zero (no correlation). Thus, few of the *r*'s would be accepted even if the test were valid. Add to this the understating of variance due to the auto correlation which exists in any data of this nature and it becomes apparent that the covariation may well be illusory. For this reason the resulting matrix of *r*'s computed by the author is omitted from this work.

TABLE 6

Time Series Correlation between the Annual Results for
Fire Insurance and Other Lines of Insurance
Stock Companies, 1956–64

Extended coverage	−0.40
Allied fire	0.17
Ocean marine	−0.83
Inland marine	−0.10
A & H insurance	−0.16
Group A & H	0.41
Workmens compensation	0.03
Miscellaneous bodily injury liability	0.05
Miscellaneous property damage liability	0.23
Automobile bodily injury liability	−0.06
Automobile property damage liability	−0.90
Automobile collision	0.15
Automobile fire, theft and comprehensive	−0.60
Fidelity	−0.18
Surety	0.02
Glass	0.26
Burglarly and theft	−0.07
Boiler and machinery	−0.40
Credit	−0.11
Homeowners	−0.09
Commercial multiple peril	−0.09

Source: Computed from data in *Best's Aggregates and Averages*, 1957–65. By-line Underwriting Section, *passim.*

III. SUMMARY

The problem of variations, or instability of results, in an insurance operation and the chance that these fluctuations may cause insolvency is a classical portfolio problem. In a sense, an insurance company has a portfolio of assets and liabilities. Random changes in the value of these items can cause even the best managed firm to become insolvent. The problem is further complicated by the fact that all the pertinent variables may well interact or be in some way related to each other.

From both the regulatory and management viewpoints, placing major emphasis upon simplistic ratios like premiums written to policyholders' surplus, as in the well-known Kenney rules, is an oversimplification of a complex problem. Yet, as a practical matter the problem of determining how far an insurer can go in building up premiums, loss reserves, and variable value investments on a supporting base of policyholders' surplus must be solved somehow. Theoretically, the amount of policyholders' surplus is a straightforward function of the amount and variance of the three aforementioned items. But as a practical matter, it is difficult if not impossible to measure the interrelationships involved. What then, is the solution? The following measures are offered as a first approximation:

a) Minimum capital and surplus requirements now in effect or to be worked out should remain in effect. They would ensure that an insurer would be safe until it was large enough to allow the requisite economies of scale and law of large numbers to become reasonably effective.

b) The variance characteristics of underwriting results for each major line of business should be determined. The same thing should then be done for various classes of investments and for loss reserves in different lines or with portfolios having other identifiable characteristics.

Then the variance of these characteristics would be combined in accordance with the mix of business and investments a given company has to determine the amount of policyholders' surplus necessary for that particular insurer. As a first step, it can be assumed that the degree of relatedness among the parameters is perfect unity ($r = 1$) or very high ($r = 0.7$). Then, as sufficient data is gathered and understanding acquired, less conservatism would be necessary in evaluating the parameters. Obviously, as in rate matters, it is necessary to assume that past results plus a judgment factor will yield reasonably valid estimates for the future.

Eventually, whenever the operating characteristics of an insurer are shown to deviate significantly and credibly from the results of other insurers, its own characteristics will be the sole determinant of the necessary amount of policyholders' surplus.

chapter 7

Life Insurance Reserves

ONE OF THE fixed stars in the life insurance regulatory constellation has been the net premium method of valuation of reserves, with its numerous modifications.

The following paper calls for a reevaluation of this traditional approach to setting reserves in the light of changes in accounting techniques, changes in the purposes served by financial statements, changes in technology, and changes in business practices generally.

A new method of valuation of reserves might revolutionize present conceptions of pricing life insurance and capitalizing life insurers. Hence, the analysis that follows and the further lines of research suggested should be followed with care.

LIFE INSURANCE RESERVES AND THE REGULATORY PROCESS*

Joseph M. Belth
Professor of Insurance
Graduate School of Business
Indiana University

The purpose of a life insurance company's "aggregate reserves for life policies" account is to measure in a conservative manner the amount by which the future premiums on the company's insurance in force are insufficient to meet the company's future obligations on

---

* The author wishes to acknowledge the assistance of Cheyeh Lin and S. Travis Pritchett who assisted in the tabulation of data. He also wishes to acknowledge the assistance of several actuaries who commented on a preliminary draft of the paper. The author alone, however, assumes full responsibility for the views expressed in the paper and for any errors that may remain. The computations were performed on the CDC 3600 in Indiana University's Research Computing Center.

that insurance. The policy reserves of a life insurance company appear on the liability side of its balance sheet and serve as a yardstick by which to measure the adequacy of the company's assets; if the value of the company's assets on the statement date exceeds the company's capital, policy reserves, and other liabilities on that date, the company is considered solvent for regulatory purposes.

Although this fundamental purpose of policy reserves seems simple and straightforward, the complexity that reserves introduce into the analysis of the financial condition of a life insurance company is enormous. This complexity is attributable to at least two factors. First, the measurement of policy reserves involves the computation of certain present values which in themselves are often difficult to comprehend. Second, reserves are calculated by the use of conservative methods and conservative assumptions which make realistic interpretation of the financial statements of life insurance companies extremely difficult.

The objective of this paper is to compare in a general way the two basic systems of reserve measurement now used for regulatory purposes in the United States to an alternative method of presenting the financial condition of a life insurance company. The alternative method is not presented as a recommendation but to stimulate discussion of a subject of great importance to the life insurance business.[1]

One other observation is necessary at the outset. Reference is often made to the need for different kinds of financial statements for different purposes. In life insurance, the various audiences for financial statements are present and prospective policyholders, regulatory authorities, taxing authorities, the management of the company, and in the case of stock companies, present and prospective shareholders. It is sometimes argued that the form of the statements needed by the regulatory authorities, whose primary concern is said to be the protection of policyholders, is quite different from the form of the statements that would be of maximum utility to present and prospective shareholders.

This argument is difficult to accept. On the one hand, if statements prepared for regulatory authorities fail to provide present and

---

[1] The paper deals solely with life insurance reserves; therefore, no attention is given to the important subject of asset valuation. For an extensive treatment of the latter, see Harold G. Fraine, *Valuation of Securities Holdings of Life Insurance Companies* (Homewood, Ill.: Richard D. Irwin, Inc., 1962).

prospective shareholders with useful information concerning the financial condition and earning power of the company, such statements can hardly be of maximum usefulness to the regulators. On the other hand, statements prepared to provide useful information to shareholders concerning the financial condition and earning power of the company should be equally useful to regulators. In any case, this paper will deal primarily with the relationship between life insurance reserves and the regulatory process, and only secondarily with some of the other possible applications of the concepts discussed.

NET-LEVEL-PREMIUM VALUATION

The reserve valuation system used in the United States is generally referred to as a system of net-premium valuation. However, as will be seen, the distinction between net-premium valuation and gross-premium valuation is not a clear one.

As one possible definition of net-premium valuation, a method of reserve valuation may be described as a net-premium method if only interest and mortality are reflected in the computation of the valuation premium. The technique that most nearly meets the definition is the so-called net-level-premium method, which in its usual form involves the selection of a level valuation premium (or net premium) such that the present value of the valuation premiums at issue date is equal to the present value at issue date of the death benefits (and endowment benefits, if any) under a block of policies.

In the computation of these present values, only interest and mortality are considered; expenses and lapses do not enter into the calculations. The interest rate selected is usually conservative—one that is low relative to the net rate the company expects to earn on its assets—in order to produce larger reserves than would be produced by a realistic interest rate. Although the mortality table selected is also usually conservative in the sense that the death rates are generally higher than those the company expects to experience, such a table does not necessarily produce larger reserves than would be produced by a more realistic mortality table.[2]

---

[2] The size of the reserves is determined more by the slope of the mortality rate curve from age to age than by the absolute value of the mortality rate at any age. For a discussion of this point, see Dan M. McGill, *Life Insurance* (rev. ed.; Homewood, Ill.: Richard D. Irwin, Inc., 1967), pp. 235–39.

The reserve at a valuation date is the excess of the present value of the future death benefits (and future endowment benefits, if any) over the present value of the future valuation premiums. In the computation of these present values, use is made of the same interest and mortality assumptions that are used in the computation of the valuation premium.

In view of the conservative interest and mortality assumptions invariably used in conjunction with the net-level-premium method, it can be argued that this method is not actually a net-premium method. The conservative assumptions provide a margin that can be used for expenses, contingencies, profit, and/or other items.[3] It can be argued that the only true net-premium valuation would be one in which the interest and mortality assumptions represent the actuary's best estimates rather than conservative estimates regarding these factors.

The use of net-level-premium valuation in the United States is generally attributed to the zeal of Elizur Wright. His fight for a stringent solvency standard apparently was influenced by numerous characteristics of the life insurance business in the middle of the 19th century. First, gross-premium valuation methods apparently were being abused. Second, most of the insurance being sold was on a participating basis with fairly high gross premiums, and as will be seen, this may present problems under certain gross-premium valuation techniques. Third, expenses were more nearly level in their incidence than later, as evidenced by first-year commissions of 10 percent of the gross premium and renewal commissions of 5 percent. These and other historical reasons for the adoption of net-premium valuation have been discussed extensively elsewhere and need not be repeated here.[4]

The first section of Table 1 illustrates the conventional manner of presenting net-level-premium reserves on a life insurance company's balance sheet. The figures represent the balance sheet at the end of the first 60 years of a hypothetical company's existence,

---

[3] One author has described net-level-premium valuation as a special form of gross-premium valuation in which expenses are assumed to be level in their incidence and exactly equal in each year to the difference between the gross premium and the valuation premium. See C. O. Shepherd, "The Legal Reserve System in the United States," *Record of the American Institute of Actuaries,* Vol. 28 (1939), p. 298.

[4] See, e.g., *ibid.,* pp. 269–315. This subject is also discussed in the *Study Notes* for the Part 6 examination of the Society of Actuaries.

TABLE 1

Balance Sheet at End of Sixtieth Year Based on Net-Level-Premium
Reserves, Policy A, and Sales Pattern A

(000 omitted)

I. CONVENTIONAL PRESENTATION:

ASSETS	LIABILITIES AND NET WORTH	
$1,036,215	Policy reserves.........	$ 967,912
	Net worth:	
	Capital.............$ 2,500	
	Paid-in surplus...... 10,000	
	Retained earnings 55,803	
	Total net worth.....	68,303
	Total Liabilities and	
	Net Worth........	$1,036,215

II. REVISED PRESENTATION SHOWING BREAKDOWN OF POLICY RESERVES:

ASSETS AND PRESENT VALUE OF FUTURE VALUATION PREMIUMS	LIABILITIES AND NET WORTH	
Assets................$1,036,215	Present value of future	
Present value of future	death benefits.....	$2,557,900
valuation premi-	Net worth:	
ums...............1,589,988	Capital.............$ 2,500	
	Paid-in surplus...... 10,000	
	Retained earnings.... 55,803	
Total assets and pres-	Total net worth.....	68,303
ent value of future	Total Liabilities and	
valuation premi-	Net Worth........	$2,626,203
ums..............$2,626,203		

Assumptions: Policy reserves are based on the net-level-premium method using the 1958 C.S.O. mortality table and 2½ percent interest (continuous functions). The other assumptions are described in the appendixes.

assuming that the company's initial capitalization is $12.5 million ($2.5 million capital and $10 million paid-in surplus); that sales pattern A, which is described in the appendixes, is followed; that gross premiums, cash surrender values, and dividends correspond to those of policy A, which is described in the appendixes; and that mortality, lapsation, and expenses correspond to the assumptions used in the computation of the gross premium for policy A. The reserves shown are based on terminal reserves under the net-level-premium method, using the 1958 C.S.O. mortality table and 2½ percent interest (continuous functions). The terminology used in the balance sheet presentation is intended to follow standard accounting terminology rather than the expressions currently found in life insurance company statements.

The policy reserves account in Table 1 may be broken down into its two components in the following manner (000 omitted):

Present value of future death benefits.................$2,557,900
Less: Present value of future valuation premiums........ 1,589,988
Net-level-premium reserve.....................$ 967,912

The balance sheet presentation may be revised in various ways to show the above breakdown. One possibility is to show the breakdown entirely on the right-hand side of the balance sheet. Another possibility is to show the present value of future death benefits on the right-hand side and the present value of future valuation premiums on the left-hand side. The latter approach is illustrated in the second section of Table 1. Note that this type of presentation eliminates the policy reserves account from the balance sheet. Although this type of presentation enlarges the totals on both sides of the balance sheet, it has no effect on the net worth section and might make life insurance statements more intelligible to the average reader.

MODIFIED NET-PREMIUM VALUATION

In the context of level-premium policies, a modified net-premium method of reserve valuation is one in which the valuation premium is not level. As in net-level-premium valuation, the present value of the valuation premiums at issue date is equal to the present value at issue date of the death benefits (and endowment benefits, if any), and conservative interest and mortality assumptions are used. However, in a modified net-premium method, the valuation premium in the first policy year is substantially below what it would be under net-level-premium valuation, and the difference is offset by valuation premiums that are larger in subsequent policy years than they would be under net-level-premium valuation.[5] The result of a modified net-premium method is a first-year

---

[5] A modified net-premium reserve is sometimes referred to as a "zillmerized" reserve after a German actuary named Zillmer, who suggested the idea in a paper published in 1863. See Thomas B. Sprague, "On the Proper Method of Estimating the Liability of a Life Insurance Company under its Policies," *Journal of the Institute of Actuaries*, Vol. 15 (1869–70), pp. 420–21. See also Spencer L. Kimball, "Sketches from a Comparative Study of American and European Insurance Regulation," *Journal of Risk and Insurance*, Vol. 32, No. 2 (June, 1965), p. 200.

reserve substantially smaller than the first-year reserve under net-level-premium valuation. Indeed, under some modified net-premium methods, first-year reserves are often zero for many policy types.

Many modified net-premium valuation techniques exist. Among them are the full-preliminary-term method, the Illinois Standard, the Ohio Standard, the New Jersey Standard, and the Commissioners' Reserve Valuation Method.[6] The latter, sometimes with minor variations, is today the most widely used of the modified net-premium methods. All of these techniques have a common purpose—to lighten the burden for a company whose surplus is not large and whose new business is substantial relative to its insurance in force.

Demands for modifications of the net-level-premium method were made as first-year expenses—particularly commissions—became larger. In other words, modified net-premium methods of reserve valuation were developed primarily because of the incidence of expenses. Under such circumstances, it is difficult to view the modified net-premium methods as net-premium valuation techniques. Although expenses are not directly reflected in the computation of valuation premiums under the modified net-premium methods, the development and nature of such methods reflect expense considerations. Thus, it can be argued that modified net-premium methods are, realistically considered, gross-premium valuation techniques, or at least that they fall somewhere between the net- and gross-premium categories.

The first section of Table 2 illustrates the conventional manner in which modified net-premium reserves are presented on the balance sheet of a life insurance company. The figures represent the balance sheet at the end of the first 60 years of a hypothetical company's operation, assuming that the company's initial capitalization is $2.5 million ($500,000 capital and $2 million paid-in surplus); that sales pattern A is followed; that gross premiums and cash surrender values correspond to those of policy B, which is described in the appendices; and that mortality, lapsation, and expenses correspond to the assumptions used in the computation of the gross premium for policy B. The reserves shown are based on terminal reserves under the Commissioners' Reserve Valuation Method, using the 1958 C.S.O. mortality table and $3\frac{1}{2}$ percent interest (curtate functions).

---

[6] For a discussion of modified reserves, see McGill, *op. cit.*, pp. 276–90.

TABLE 2

Balance Sheet at End of Sixtieth Year Based on Modified Net-Premium
Reserves, Policy B, and Sales Pattern A

(000 omitted)

I. CONVENTIONAL PRESENTATION:

ASSETS	LIABILITIES AND NET WORTH		
$591,974	Policy reserves.........		$ 397,668
	Net worth:		
	Capital.............$	500	
	Paid-in surplus......	2,000	
	Retained earnings....	191,806	
	Total net worth......		194,306
	Total Liabilities and		
	Net Worth........		$ 591,974

II. REVISED PRESENTATION SHOWING BREAKDOWN OF POLICY RESERVES:

ASSETS AND PRESENT VALUE OF FUTURE VALUATION PREMIUMS		LIABILITIES AND NET WORTH		
Assets................$	591,974	Present value of future		
Present value of future		death benefits......		$1,112,575
valuation premi-		Net worth:		
ums..............	714,907	Capital.............$	500	
		Paid-in surplus.......	2,000	
Total assets and pres-		Retained earnings....	191,806	
ent value of future		Total net worth.....		194,306
valuation premi-		Total Liabilities and		
ums..............$1,306,881		Net Worth........		$1,306,881

Assumptions: Policy reserves are based on the Commissioners' Reserve Valuation Method using the 1958 C.S.O. mortality table and 3½ percent interest (curtate functions). The other assumptions are described in the appendixes.

The second section of Table 2 shows the breakdown of the policy reserves account into its two component parts. Note that the figures in Table 2 are not comparable to those in Table 1 for three reasons: a different policy is used, different lapsation and expense assumptions are used, and a different initial capitalization assumption is used.

GROSS-PREMIUM VALUATION

In accordance with the earlier definition of net-premium valuation, a method of reserve valuation may be described as a gross-premium method if more factors than interest and mortality are reflected in the computation of the valuation premium. Admittedly, this is a broad definition that comprehends a considerable variety of possible valuation techniques, two of which are discussed below.

Gross Premium as Valuation Premium

One technique that meets the definition of a gross-premium method is the same as a net-premium valuation except that it uses the gross premium as a valuation premium in the computation of the reserve. Although gross-premium methods usually connote a much more refined technique, the crude method referred to in the preceding sentence is important in at least two respects.

First, some of the writings of Elizur Wright suggest the possibility that one of his main reasons for strongly advocating net-level-premium valuation was the abuses he had witnessed in the name of gross-premium valuation. Most of the life insurance written at that time was on a participating basis, and written at high gross premiums with generous margins. Use of these high premiums, together with omission of any provision for future expenses and future dividends, had a tendency to produce very small policy reserves. Wright may have felt that it would be easier to regulate on the basis of net-level-premium valuation than on the basis of a refined and more complex gross-premium valuation.[7]

Second, a crude gross-premium method under which the gross premium serves as the valuation premium is really what is now used in the name of net-premium valuation under the questionable title of "deficiency reserves." A deficiency reserve is required in addition to the usual net-premium reserve when the present value of the company's future valuation premiums on a policy exceeds the present value of the company's future gross premiums on that policy, both being computed on the interest and mortality assumptions used in the computation of the company's net-premium reserve. The value of the deficiency reserve for the policy is simply the difference between these two present value figures. In other words, the sum of the net-premium reserve and the deficiency reserve for such a policy is precisely equal to the reserve under the crude gross-premium method.[8] In summary, the American system might be described as

---

[7] See, e.g., "1859 Report of the Massachusetts Commissioners," reprinted in *The Bible of Life Insurance* (Chicago: American Conservation Co., 1932), pp. 44–49.

[8] For a discussion of deficiency reserves, see McGill, *op. cit.*, pp. 243–45. The system is actually more complex than this simplified statement, since it is also required that reserves be equal to or greater than cash values. Additional reserves must be established for any policies on which the cash value is greater than the reserve. See line G(3) of Exhibit 8 in the life insurance annual statement blank promulgated by the National Association of Insurance Commissioners.

one under which (1) net-premium valuation is used when the gross premium is larger than the valuation premium, and (2) gross-premium valuation is used when the gross premium is smaller than the valuation premium.[9]

Refined Gross-Premium Methods

When the expression "gross-premium valuation" is used today, however, the reference is generally to a refined technique that takes into account numerous factors that are omitted from net-premium valuations and from the crude gross-premium method mentioned above. Moreover, the expression generally connotes the use of assumptions that reflect the actuary's best estimates concerning future developments rather than the conservative interest and mortality assumptions discussed earlier.

Gross-premium valuations are frequently employed. Such a technique is usually considered an essential part of the determination of the value of a company when it is to be purchased. Although not generally employed for regulatory purposes, an argument can be made for the use of gross-premium valuation in the regulatory process. This point is discussed later.

One particular gross-premium valuation method is used in this paper for illustrative purposes. Under this method, the gross-premium reserve may be defined as the present value of future face-amount payments, plus the present value of future cash-surrender-value payments, plus the present value of future dividends, plus the present value of future expenses, minus the present value of future gross premiums. In the computation of the various present values, the assumptions are intended to represent the actuary's best estimates regarding future experience, and lapsation is reflected in the computations as well as interest and mortality.

The first section of Table 3 shows the manner in which gross-premium reserves would appear on the balance sheet if the conventional method of presentation were used. The figures correspond to those in Table 1, except that gross-premium reserves are used instead of net-level-premium reserves. The assumptions used in the

_g.p.r._

---

[9] To draw an analogy to a famous question relating to the subject of slavery, one might ask whether the United States system of valuation can survive half-net and half-gross.

TABLE 3

Balance Sheet at End of Sixtieth Year Based on Gross-Premium
Reserves, Policy A, and Sales Pattern A

(000 omitted)

I. CONVENTIONAL PRESENTATION:

ASSETS	LIABILITIES AND NET WORTH		
$1,036,215	Policy reserves.....		$ 859,871
	Net worth:		
	Capital.........$	2,500	
	Paid-in surplus...	10,000	
	Retained earn-		
	ings..........	163,844	
	Total net worth..		176,344
	Total Liabilities		
	and Net Worth.		$1,036,215

II. REVISED PRESENTATION SHOWING BREAKDOWN OF POLICY RESERVES:

ASSETS AND PRESENT VALUE OF FUTURE GROSS PREMIUMS	LIABILITIES AND NET WORTH		
Assets.................$1,036,215	Liabilities:		
Present value of future	Present value of		
gross premiums....... 1,226,238	future face-		
Total assets and present	amount pay-		
value of future gross	ments.........$770,549		
premiums............$2,262,453	Present value of		
	future cash-		
	surrender-value		
	payments...... 697,580		
	Present value of		
	future divi-		
	dends......... 518,342		
	Present value of		
	future expenses. 99,638		
	Total liabilities..		$2,086,109
	Net worth:		
	Capital.........$	2,500	
	Paid-in surplus...	10,000	
	Retained earn-		
	ings..........	163,844	
	Total net worth....		176,344
	Total Liabilities		
	and Net Worth.		$2,262,453

Assumptions: See explanation in text.

computation of the gross-premium reserves are the same as those
used in the computation of the gross premium for policy A.

Note that the gross-premium reserves are approximately $860
million in contrast to the net-level-premium reserves of approxi-

mately $968 million. Similarly, the company's retained earnings under the gross-premium method are approximately $164 million in contrast to retained earnings of approximately $56 million under the net-level-premium method.

It is important to note that the only meaningful manner in which to express the relationship between the retained earnings figures on the two valuation bases is in terms of the absolute difference of approximately $108 million. The ratio of $164 million to $56 million is meaningless in this type of analysis because the ratio depends on the company's initial capitalization. To illustrate, one of the assumptions underlying Tables 1 and 3 is that the company began operations with $12.5 million. If the company had started with $10 million, retained earnings in the current balance sheet would have been about $23 million under net-level-premium valuation and about $131 million under gross-premium valuation. Although the absolute difference is still $108 million, the ratio of $131 million to $23 million is approximately twice the ratio of $164 million to $56 million.

Note also that the net worth in Table 3 should be equal to the initial capital and paid-in surplus accumulated for 60 years at the assumed interest rate, because the same assumptions were used in computing the gross premium and the gross-premium reserves, and because no profit factor is included in the gross premium for policy A. Since the initial funds are $12.5 million and since the amount of 1 at the end of 60 years at $4\frac{1}{2}$ percent interest is about 14.027408, the net worth in Table 3 should be approximately $175,343,000. The discrepancy between this figure and the $176,344,000 shown in Table 3 is attributable to rounding. For example, in the computation of the assets at the end of 60 years, the gross premium to the nearest cent per $1,000 of face amount ($23.13) was used. If a gross premium of $23.12 had been used, the discrepancy would have been in the opposite direction, since the net worth would have been approximately $174,644,000.

The gross-premium reserve of approximately $860 million may be broken down in the following manner (000 omitted):

Present value of future face-amount payments	$ 770,549
Present value of future cash-surrender-value payments	697,580
Present value of future dividends	518,342
Present value of future expenses	99,638
Total of outgo items	$2,086,109
Less: Present value of future gross premiums	1,226,238
Gross-premium reserve	$ 859,871

A revised presentation of the balance sheet showing the above breakdown of the gross-premium reserve is contained in the second section of Table 3. Note again that this particular type of revised presentation eliminates the policy reserves account from the balance sheet.

The impact of the company's growth rate may be illustrated by reference to the reserve figures at the end of the 60th year of operations under the assumption that sales pattern B, which is described in the appendices, is followed. Under such circumstances, the gross-premium reserves are approximately $1,123 million, in contrast to net-level-premium reserves of approximately $1,344 million. The difference of $221 million is substantially larger than the difference of $108 million under sales pattern A. Under sales pattern B and the assumption that the company begins operations with initial funds of $12.5 million, the net worth at the end of 60 years with gross-premium valuation is approximately $177 million, in contrast to a net worth of *minus* $45 million under net-level-premium valuation. Indeed, the 10 percent compound annual rate of sales growth under sales pattern B, in conjunction with net-level-premium valuation, produces a situation in which the company goes steadily deeper into deficit after the initial funds are exhausted. In other words, net-level-premium valuation tends to impose a ceiling on a company's rate of growth.[10]

The figures in Table 4 correspond to those in Table 2, except that gross-premium reserves are used instead of reserves under the Commissioners' Reserve Valuation Method. The assumptions used in the computation of the gross-premium reserves are the same as those used in the computation of the gross premium for policy B. Note that the gross-premium reserves are approximately $229 million in contrast to the reserves of approximately $398 million under the Commissioners' Reserve Valuation Method. The absolute difference in reserves on the two bases is approximately $169 million. Similarly, the company's retained earnings under the gross-premium method are approximately $361 million in contrast to retained earnings of approximately $192 million under the Commissioners' Reserve Valuation Method.

---

[10] This characteristic of net-level-premium valuation is mentioned in Owen C. Lincoln, "Should the Commissioners Reserve Valuation Method Be Adopted by a Participating Company Which Has Traditionally Used the Net Level Premium Method?" *Transactions of the Actuarial Society of America,* Vol. 47 (1946), p. 22.

TABLE 4

Balance Sheet at End of Sixtieth Year Based on Gross-Premium
Reserves, Policy B, and Sales Pattern A

(000 omitted)

I. CONVENTIONAL PRESENTATION:

ASSETS	LIABILITIES AND NET WORTH		
$591,974	Policy reserves.....		$ 228,867
	Net worth:		
	Capital.........$	500	
	Paid-in surplus...	2,000	
	Retained earn-		
	ings..........	360,607	
	Total net worth..		363,107
	Total Liabilities		
	and Net Worth.		$ 591,974

II. REVISED PRESENTATION SHOWING BREAKDOWN OF POLICY RESERVES:

ASSETS AND PRESENT VALUE OF FUTURE GROSS PREMIUMS		LIABILITIES AND NET WORTH		
Assets...................$	591,974	Liabilities:		
Present value of future		Present value of		
gross premiums......	529,231	future face-		
Total assets and present		amount pay-		
value of future gross		ments.........$286,135		
premiums............$1,121,205		Present value of		
		future cash-		
		surrender-value		
		payments......	411,432	
		Present value of		
		future expenses.	60,531	
		Total liabilities..		$ 758,098
		Net worth:		
		Capital.........$	500	
		Paid-in surplus...	2,000	
		Retained earn-		
		ings..........	360,607	
		Total net worth..		363,107
		Total Liabilities		
		and Net Worth.		$1,121,205

Assumptions: See explanation in text.

Once again, the impact of the company's growth rate may be
illustrated by reference to the reserve figures for the 60th year of
operations under the assumption that sales pattern B is followed.
Under such circumstances, the gross-premium reserves are approximately $215 million in contrast to modified net-premium reserves
of approximately $581 million. The difference of $366 million is

TABLE 5

Net-Premium Reserves and Gross-Premium Reserves for Policies A and B,
with Aggregate Reserves Based on Sales Pattern A

Policy A

Policy or Company Year	Per-Policy Figures ($)		Aggregate Figures ($000)	
	Net-Level-Premium Reserve	Gross-Premium Reserve	Net-Level-Premium Reserve	Gross-Premium Reserve
1..........	15.98	6.80	72	−31
2..........	32.27	9.80	222	5
5..........	82.81	61.22	1,256	588
10..........	171.53	147.33	5,822	3,877
20..........	360.17	336.76	35,997	28,228
40..........	707.15	682.79	297,236	255,113
60..........			967,912	859,871

Policy B

Policy or Company Year	Per-Policy Figures ($)		Aggregate Figures ($000)	
	Modified Net-Premium Reserve	Gross-Premium Reserve	Modified Net-Premium Reserve	Gross-Premium Reserve
1..........	0.00	−43.14	0	−172
2..........	13.63	−32.65	48	−322
5..........	56.56	3.25	499	−651
10..........	134.16	69.21	2,619	−739
20..........	307.75	240.38	16,424	3,179
40..........	654.21	613.49	128,828	59,990
60..........			397,668	228,867

Assumptions: See explanation in text.

much larger than the difference of $169 million under sales pattern
A. Under sales pattern B and the assumption that the company
begins operations with initial funds of $2.5 million, the net worth
at the end of 60 years with gross-premium valuation is approximately $444 million in contrast to a net worth of approximately
$78 million under modified net-premium valuation.

The contrast between net-premium valuation and gross-premium
valuation may also be illustrated by reference to the data in Table 5.
Shown there are per-policy reserves in selected policy years on both
bases for policies A and B. Also shown are aggregate reserves, under
sales pattern A, for policies A and B on both reserve bases for
selected years of company operations.

Natural Reserves and Asset Shares

The expressions "gross-premium reserve," "natural reserve," and "asset share" are closely related. As suggested earlier, a refined gross-premium reserve calculation includes assumptions relating to interest, mortality, and lapsation, and reflects face-amount payments, cash-surrender-value payments, dividends, and expenses. Moreover, such a calculation usually involves the actuary's best estimates rather than conservative estimates regarding future developments.

A natural reserve is a specific type of gross-premium reserve in which the assumptions used in the calculation of the reserve are exactly the same as those used in the calculation of the natural premium, and the natural premium is calculated to be sufficient to pay expenses as well as death claims. Although lapsation and cash surrender values are not included in the computation of either the natural premium or the natural reserve, the definition of these terms usually includes the assumption that lapses will produce neither gains nor losses.[11]

The natural premium and the natural reserve make no provision for dividends. Although the gross-premium reserves in Table 3 make specific provision for dividends, their effect is neutralized. This is perhaps best illustrated in the second section of Table 3, which shows that provision for dividends is made on the left-hand side of the balance sheet through the present value of future gross premiums and on the right-hand side through a specific liability item.

The natural premium and the natural reserve also make no provision for a profit element. Such an item is not included in the gross premium for policy A; however, a specific profit element is included in the gross premium for policy B. Therefore, the gross-premium reserves shown in Table 3 are also natural reserves, and the gross-premium reserves shown in Table 4 differ from natural reserves to the extent of the profit element.[12] The latter discrepancy

---

[11] See Bruce E. Shepherd, "Natural Reserves," *Transactions of the Actuarial Society of America,* Vol. 41 (1940), p. 463.

[12] If a company's outstanding business is revalued periodically on the basis of new assumptions made in the light of developing experience, the identity or near-identity of gross-premium reserves and natural reserves would disappear. This point is discussed later in the paper.

could be remedied by the establishment of a liability item equal to the present value of future profits on the business in force on the valuation date.

An asset share calculation shows the assets generated by a block of business under a given set of interest, mortality, lapsation, and expense assumptions. Gross premium, face-amount payments, cash-surrender-value payments, dividends (if any), and expenses are taken into account in the calculation. If the assumptions used in the calculation of the gross premium are also used in the asset share calculation, if no profit element is included in the gross premium, and if lapses and cash surrender values neutralize themselves so as to produce neither gains nor losses, the assets generated by a block of business as of the end of any given policy year are equal to the natural reserves on that business.

Since no profit element is included in the gross premium for policy A, the gross-premium reserves shown in Table 3 are equal to the assets generated by the business. The gross-premium reserves in Table 4, however, are smaller than the assets generated by the business. The difference is equal to the present value at issue date of the profit element, accumulated at $4\frac{1}{2}$ percent interest to the point of valuation. Similarly, the gross-premium reserve per policy in Table 4 is smaller than the asset share per policy. The difference is equal to the present value at issue date of the profit element per policy, accumulated at $4\frac{1}{2}$ percent interest and with benefit of survivorship and persistency to the valuation point.[13]

GROSS-PREMIUM VALUATION FOR REGULATORY PURPOSES

In contrast to net-level-premium and modified net-premium valuation, the main distinguishing characteristics of a refined gross-premium valuation of the type described earlier are (1) a relatively high degree of complexity, (2) the use of the actuary's best estimates with regard to future developments rather than highly conservative assumptions, and (3) the creation of significant changes in net worth and in the incidence of earnings. Some of the ramifications of these three characteristics, if gross-premium valuation were

---

[13] For a discussion of asset share calculations, see McGill, *op. cit.*, pp. 265–73.

to be used for regulatory purposes, are discussed in this section of the paper.

Complexity

A refined gross-premium valuation is more complicated than a net-level-premium or a modified net-premium valuation for at least two reasons. First, a gross-premium valuation takes into account many factors in addition to interest and mortality. For example, future expenses are considered, since it is inappropriate to take future gross premiums into account and disregard future expenses that will have to be paid out of future gross premiums. If the company sells participating insurance, future dividends are considered even though such dividends are not guaranteed; in the event of future changes in the dividend scale, the present value of future dividends may be adjusted accordingly. Lapse rates should be taken into account, and if they are, cash surrender values must also be considered. Lapse rates are usually much larger, much more susceptible to wide fluctuations, and much more variable as among companies than mortality rates. But as two British actuaries said many years ago, ". . . we consider that this fact does not supply a justification for the exclusion of the one element [lapse rates], and the inclusion of the other [mortality rates], in the calculation of valuation reserves."[14] This is especially true because the greater variability exists in the element most often ignored.

Second, gross-premium valuation, by its very nature, implies that the assumptions used in the valuation will be changed frequently —presumably once each year when the annual statement is prepared. Under the present system used in the United States, a reserve basis (method and assumptions) is decided upon at the time a block of business is issued, and such basis is normally maintained throughout the life of that block of business. Occasionally the reserve basis is changed through what is termed "reserve strengthening" (or, in the opposite direction, "reserve weakening"), but such a change is the exception rather than the rule. In the case of net-premium valuation, changes in basis presumably are considered unnecessary because of the conservatism inherent in the original

---

[14] Thomas G. Ackland and James Bacon, "On the Valuation of Whole-Life Industrial Assurances, with Allowance for Lapses," *Journal of the Institute of Actuaries,* Vol. 38 (1904), p. 541.

basis. But in a gross-premium valuation, when the actuary's best estimates are used instead of conservative estimates, revaluation is imperative. Although the computations involved in an annual revaluation of a company's entire portfolio of business are seemingly awesome, they are well within the capabilities of today's powerful electronic computers.

The idea of annual revaluation also raises interesting questions relating to cash surrender values. Although the computation of cash surrender values by the adjusted-premium method is technically separate from the computation of net-premium reserves, the two computations are essentially linked together by a strong similarity of method and by the use of common interest and mortality assumptions in many instances. Moreover, the idea of a guaranteed cash surrender value is consistent with the idea of a fixed reserve basis that is not subject to change in the normal course of events. If cash surrender values are deemed to be merely a form of guaranteed benefit payable to those who discontinue their policies, such values can be incorporated into a gross-premium valuation in the manner described earlier in this paper. However, if cash surrender values are deemed to represent an attempt to provide an equitable distribution of funds to withdrawing policyholders,[15] it can be argued that, consistent with the idea of annual revaluation of the company's liabilities, the cash surrender values should be nonguaranteed and should reflect the actuary's best estimates with regard to the future experience of the company. A thorough development of this point is beyond the scope of this paper.

Actuary's Best Estimates

The use of the actuary's best estimates with regard to future developments, rather than the use of conservative estimates, leaves much more to actuarial judgment in the preparation of the annual statement. One actuary recently characterized "generally accepted accounting principles" as requiring reporting on a "most likely" basis in contrast to "insurance accounting principles" as being on a "most unlikely" basis in the direction of conservatism.[16]

[15] See McGill, *op. cit.,* pp. 291–96.

[16] Dale R. Gustafson, "Life Actuary Cautions that 'Force Fit' of Accounting Method May Be Detrimental," *Best's Insurance News* (Fire and Casualty Ed.), December, 1966, pp. 21–22.

On the one hand, it might appear that the use of the actuary's best estimates of future developments would impose new responsibilities on the company's actuary. On the other hand, however, it can be argued that the actuary is already involved constantly in the making of such estimates because of his responsibilities in the development of gross premiums, of cash surrender values, and in the case of participating insurance, of dividends.

The actuarial judgment inherent in gross-premium valuation has one other treacherous aspect. The use of a great deal of judgment in the presentation of a company's solvency position may make manipulation of the financial statements more likely than under the present system. Indeed, it appears that the susceptibility of gross-premium valuation to venal manipulation was one of the reasons for Wright's advocacy of net-level-premium valuation.[17] Although it may now be assumed that the majority of actuaries would operate in a professional manner and would have no part in a "rigged" statement, the fact remains that there may always be a few who would abuse the privilege of being allowed to exercise judgment in preparing the financial statements. This in turn would impose a heavy responsibility and burden of competence on the regulatory authorities, because it would be they to whom the actuary would have to justify the assumptions used in the preparation of the financial statement. An important question concerning gross-premium valuation, therefore, is whether the states are now equipped or could be equipped in the foreseeable future to exercise sound judgment as well as cope with the general complexity of gross-premium valuation.

Change in Net Worth and in Incidence of Earnings

It is often said that the total earnings of a corporation cannot be determined accurately until the corporation is finally liquidated, and that the purpose of periodic financial statements is mainly to attempt to allocate such earnings to the various time periods prior to liquidation. To the extent that net-premium methods of valuation are conservative, the result is an understatement of the annual earnings of a growing company and an understatement of net worth

---

[17] See, e.g., C. O. Shepherd, *op. cit.*, p. 273.

relative to corresponding figures based on the actuary's best estimates regarding future developments.

When a refined gross-premium valuation is made, the changes in
net worth and in the incidence of earnings are attributable not only
to the use of more realistic assumptions but also to the difference in
the treatment of acquisition expenses. When net-level-premium
valuation is used, the effect is a total write-off of acquisition expenses in the year in which such expenses are incurred. When one
of the modified net-premium methods is used, the effect is the same
as though part of the acquisition expenses is written off in the year
in which the expenses are incurred and the remainder of the
expenses is capitalized. When a refined gross-premium valuation is
used, the effect is the same as though all of the acquisition expenses
are capitalized. For example, in the case of policy A, the present
value of the gross premiums at the instant before the payment of
the first premium is exactly equal to the sum of the present values
of the four outgo items (face-amount payments, cash-surrender-
value payments, dividends, and expenses), so the gross-premium
reserve at that point is zero. At the end of the first year, however,
the gross-premium reserve per policy is −$6.80. The main reason
for the negative figure is the fact that by the end of the first year, the
present value of future expenses is sharply reduced because the
company has paid the acquisition expenses associated with the
policy. Since the acquisition expenses exceed the first year's gross
premium, the present value (at the end of the first year) of the
future gross premiums exceeds the present value of the outgo items.
In short, gross-premium valuation amounts to a capitalization of the
acquisition expenses and their gradual write-off over the entire
lifetime of the particular block of policies.

No attempt is made in this paper to study the extent to which
gross-premium valuation would affect the incidence of earnings.
However, the simple models developed for this paper can be used to
illustrate the extent to which gross-premium valuation would affect
net worth. Moreover, the figures can be compared to certain rules of
thumb that are sometimes used to adjust the net worth shown in the
financial statements of life insurance companies.

The rule of thumb used in adjusting reserves under the Life
Insurance Company Income Tax Act of 1959 is that reserves are
decreased by 10 percent for each percentage point by which the

company's actual earnings rate on investments exceeds the interest rate used in the computation of its reserves.[18] In the case of policy A, the interest rate assumed in the computation of the net-level-premium reserves is 2½ percent, while the earnings rate used in the illustrative computations is 4½ percent. If the above rule were applied to this situation, the "adjusted reserves" would be 20 percent lower than the net-level-premium reserves.

TABLE 6

Comparison of Reserves and Net Worth in Selected Years
on Two Bases Using Policy A, Sales Pattern A,
and Initial Funds of $12.5 Million
(in thousands of dollars)

Year	Net-Level-Premium Reserve Basis		Gross-Premium Reserve Basis		Percentage by Which Gross-Premium Reserves Are Smaller Than Net-Level-Premium Reserves
	Reserves	Net Worth	Reserves	Net Worth	
1................	72	12,960	−31	13,063	143.1%
2................	222	13,433	5	13,651	97.7
5................	1,256	14,912	588	15,579	53.2
10................	5,822	17,473	3,877	19,418	33.4
20................	35,997	22,408	28,228	30,177	21.6
40................	297,236	30,824	255,113	72,947	14.2
60................	967,912	68,303	859,871	176,344	11.2

Assumptions: See explanation in text.

The net-level-premium reserves and the gross-premium reserves for policy A for selected years, assuming sales pattern A, are shown in Table 6. Note that the gross-premium reserves are below the net-level-premium reserves by percentages that differ widely among the different years of analysis. The above rule of thumb used for

[18] For a discussion of this adjustment, see McGill, op. cit., pp. 914–20. The rule of thumb is based on such model company studies as those found in Horace Holmes, "The Standards of Policy Reserves in America and Their Effect on the Life Assurance Business," Transactions of the Actuarial Society of America, Vol. 39 (1938), p. 284, and Vol. 40 (1939), p. 180. See also Taxation of Income of Life Insurance Companies (Hearings before the Subcommittee on Internal Revenue Taxation of the Committee on Ways and Means, U.S. House of Representatives, 85th Cong., 2d sess.) (Washington, D.C.: U.S. Government Printing Office, 1958), pp. 255–59.

federal income tax purposes is intended to adjust only for the difference between the interest rate actually earned by the company on its assets and the interest rate assumed by the company in computing its reserve liabilities. Nevertheless, it is interesting to compare the above-mentioned figure of 20 percent with the percentage figures in the last column of Table 6. Perhaps by coincidence, the figure of 20 percent is very close to the figure of 21.6 percent shown in Table 6 for the 20th year of the company's operations.

In the case of policy B, the interest rate assumed in the computation of the modified net-premium reserves is 3½ percent, while the

TABLE 7

Comparison of Reserves and Net Worth in Selected Years
on Two Bases Using Policy B, Sales Pattern A,
and Initial Funds of $2.5 Million
(in thousands of dollars)

Year	Modified Net-Premium Reserve Basis		Gross-Premium Reserve Basis		Percentage by Which Gross-Premium Reserves Are Smaller Than Modified Net-Premium Reserves
	Reserves	Net Worth	Reserves	Net Worth	
1...............	0	2,517	−172	2,690	...
2...............	48	2,534	−322	2,904	770.8%
5...............	499	2,573	−651	3,723	230.5
10...............	2,619	2,559	−739	5,917	128.2
20...............	16,424	2,744	3,179	15,989	80.6
40...............128,828		24,744	59,990	93,582	53.4
60...............397,668		194,306	228,867	363,107	42.4

Assumptions: See explanation in text.

earnings rate used in the illustrative computations is 4½ percent. Thus, the above rule would involve a reduction of 10 percent in the modified net-premium reserves. The modified net-premium reserves and the gross-premium reserves for policy B for selected years, assuming sales pattern A, are shown in Table 7. Note again that the percentages differ widely among the different years of analysis and that the figure of 10 percent is not close to any of the percentage figures in the last column of Table 7.

Note that the gross-premium reserves are negative in the first year of operations in Table 6 and in a number of early years in

Table 7. Such negative results occur when the present value (at the valuation date) of the gross premiums exceeds the present value of the outgo items. Perhaps because negative reserves are the same as assets in their effect on net worth, some authors have expressed great concern not only about showing aggregate negative reserves but even about permitting negative reserves on some blocks of business to be offset against positive reserves on other blocks of business.[19] Indeed, the fact that negative reserves are possible under gross-premium valuation and virtually impossible under net-premium valuation may be an important reason for the avoidance of gross-premium valuation for regulatory purposes in the United States. Yet, the arguments against the use of negative reserves appear to be merely indirect suggestions that the present value of future profits be established as an additional outgo item in the computation of gross-premium reserves.

A rule of thumb sometimes used to adjust the net worth of a life insurance company from the stockholder's point of view is to increase the statement net worth by $20 to $25 per $1,000 of level-premium life insurance in force when the business is valued on a net-level-premium basis and by $15 to $20 per $1,000 of level-premium life insurance in force when the business is valued on a modified net-premium basis.[20] In the case of policy A and sales pattern A, the net worth on the gross-premium reserve basis exceeds the net worth on the net-level-premium reserve basis by between $22 and $23 per $1,000 of insurance in force throughout the 60 years of analysis. Although this result is consistent with the above-mentioned rule of thumb, great care must be exercised in any attempt to use such a rule, as emphasized in the paper cited in footnote 20.

In the case of policy B and sales pattern A, the net worth on the gross-premium reserve basis exceeds the net worth on the modified net-premium basis by amounts ranging from about $43 to about $57 per $1,000 of insurance in force, depending on the year of analysis selected. Although the range itself is fairly small, the figures are not consistent with the above-mentioned rule of thumb.

---

[19] See, e.g., Sprague, *op. cit.*, p. 422.

[20] These figures are presented as part of a "typical schedule" in Melvin L. Gold, "Valuing a Life Insurance Company," *Transactions of the Society of Actuaries,* Vol. 14 (1962), pp. 139–57.

CONCLUSION

Net-level-premium valuation became well established in the United States primarily through the efforts of Elizur Wright to provide a stringent solvency standard for life insurance companies. Modifications of the net-level-premium system were made subsequently in response to increased acquisition expenses and the pressure that they imposed on certain types of companies, particularly the company desiring to grow at a fairly rapid rate relative to its surplus position.

In relation to a refined system of gross-premium valuation, net-premium valuations generally, including net-level-premium valuation and the various modified systems, are characterized by conservative methods and conservative assumptions. Thus, the financial statements prepared for regulatory purposes generally overstate liabilities and understate net worth and earnings relative to the results that would be achieved by more realistic methods and the use of actuaries' best estimates of future experience.

Because of the conservatism inherent in the financial statements of life insurance companies, various methods of adjusting the statements have been developed in attempts to obtain more realistic figures. Such adjustment techniques, however, are open to question and in some cases have been the cause of considerable concern.[21]

Moreover, there is no assurance that net-premium valuations always produce conservative results. Because such valuations employ hypothetical premiums instead of gross premiums and disregard expenses, dividends, and lapse rates, it is possible for a company to show a larger net worth under the present system than would be shown under a system utilizing realistic methods and realistic assumptions.[22] Similarly, it is possible for a company to appear solvent under the present system when a realistic gross-premium valuation would show the company to be insolvent. An example of such a company would be one that should realistically

---

[21] See, e.g., Jon S. Hanson and Duncan R. Farney, "New Life Insurance Companies: Their Promotion and Regulation," *Marquette Law Review,* Vol. 49, No. 2 (Fall, 1965), pp. 230–44.

[22] In commenting on a preliminary draft of this paper, the chief actuary of a large mutual company indicated that his company's gross-premium reserves are larger than its statement (net-level-premium) reserves.

anticipate high renewal expenses relative to its more efficient competitors but uses gross premium rates comparable to (or even lower than) those competitors. In the case of nonparticipating insurance, this problem is mitigated (but not completely solved) through the use of deficiency reserves. In the case of participating insurance, net-premium valuations ignore illustrated dividends, which would be included in a realistic gross-premium valuation. The fact that dividends are not guaranteed would not excuse a company from the questionable practice of illustrating a dividend scale so large that the company would be insolvent if such a scale were shown as a part of its reserve liabilities.

The present systems of valuation were developed at periods when the emphasis in accounting was on conservatism and when attention focused primarily on the balance sheet. There has been a gradual shift, however, so that today more emphasis is placed on realism and greater attention is given to the income statement.[23] These changes have been attributable at least in part to a rapid rise in the number of persons owning shares of stock in widely held corporations and to the emergence of net income as a primary element of the federal tax base.[24]

Moreover, the present systems were developed at periods when the computational difficulties made refined gross-premium valuations virtually impossible to achieve. Today, with the increasingly widespread availability of powerful electronic computers, such valuations are entirely feasible.

If the amount of assets held today by life insurance companies is larger than necessary when viewed in the light of realistic methods of valuation and realistic assumptions, such a situation may have important implications for the private life insurance business as

[23] See, e.g., C. Aubrey Smith and Jim G. Ashburne, *Financial and Administrative Accounting* (2d ed.; New York: McGraw-Hill Book Co., Inc., 1960), pp. 8–9, 50–51, 53–54, 75.

[24] Financial statements generally, and not just those of life insurance companies, have been criticized in recent years. For an interesting discussion of this subject, see "What *Are* Earnings? The Growing Credibility Gap," *Forbes*, May 15, 1967, p. 28. However, the criticism of life insurance company statements has been particularly severe. See Corporate Information Committee of National Federation of Financial Analysts Societies, "Twelfth Annual Report" (1960); and "Subcommittee Report on Life Insurance Company Annual Reports for Shareholders" (December, 1963).

well as the public at large.[25] However, the question of whether the industry-wide net worth of life insurance companies (including the net worth built into conservatively valued reserves) is larger than necessary is beyond the scope of this paper, which is intended solely to discuss one possible alternative to the present methods of reserve valuation.

In short, changes in accounting techniques, changes in the purposes served by financial statements, changes in technology, and changes in business practices generally may suggest that the time has come for basic changes in the methods by which the financial condition of a life insurance company is presented to the regulatory agencies. In the author's opinion, the subject of reserve valuation is overdue for careful reappraisal in the light of today's circumstances.

APPENDIX A: HYPOTHETICAL POLICIES AND SALES PATTERNS

All of the data used to illustrate the various reserve valuation techniques discussed in this paper are derived from two policies, which for convenience are referred to as policy A and policy B, and two sales patterns, which are referred to as sales pattern A and sales pattern B.

Policy A

Policy A is a $10,000 participating straight life policy issued to standard males aged 35. The cash surrender values and annual dividends for the first 50 policy years are shown in columns 3 and 5 in Appendix B. These figures pertain to the policies issued by a major life insurance company, which furnished the figures to the author. The cash surrender values beginning in the 10th policy year are equal to the terminal reserves under the net-level-premium method using the 1958 C.S.O. mortality table and 2½ percent interest (continuous functions). The dividends are illustrations based on the company's 1967 dividend scale.

---

[25] Some of these implications are discussed in Joseph M. Belth, "Observations on Solvency in the Context of Life Insurance Regulation," *Journal of Risk and Insurance,* Vol. 34, No. 4 (December, 1967), pp. 539–60.

The gross annual premium for policy A is $231.30. This premium is computed on the basis of a number of assumptions made by the author and is not the one actually charged by the above-mentioned company.[26] In the computation of the gross premium, the assumed interest rate is 4½ percent.[27] The assumed mortality rates, which are shown in column 6 in Appendix B, are those in the X_{18} table, with Buck's select modification at issue age 35.[28] The assumed lapse rates, which are shown in column 7 in Appendix B, are those in Linton's A table,[29] with an arbitrary extension to the 50th policy year. The assumption is made that all policyholders will have either died or lapsed their policies by the end of the 50th policy year.

In the computation of the gross premium for policy A, it is assumed that the expenses that vary with the gross premium are 67 percent of the gross premium in the first policy year, 10 percent in the second through tenth policy years, and 5 percent thereafter. These figures are based on the assumptions that the agent's commissions are 55 percent of the gross premium in the first policy year, 5 percent in each of the next nine years, and 2 percent thereafter; that the corresponding general agent's commissions are 10 percent, 3 percent, and 1 percent; and that the state premium tax is 2 percent each year. Per-policy expenses are assumed to be $100 per policy in the first policy year and $5 per year per continuing policy thereafter.

The assumption is made that gross premiums and expenses are paid at the beginning of the respective policy years and that face-amount payments, cash-surrender-value payments, and dividend pay-

---

[26] The method used in the computation of the gross premium is described in Joseph M. Belth, "Calculation of Life Insurance Gross Premiums: A Suggested Modification of the Traditional Textbook Approach," *Journal of Risk and Insurance,* Vol. 34, No. 3 (September, 1967), pp. 385–96. Assumptions are made concerning interest, mortality, lapsation, cash surrender values, dividends, expenses, and profit, and the gross annual premium is computed by solving a linear equation.

[27] The net rate of interest earned by United States life insurance companies on their invested funds in 1967 was 4.83 percent. See *1968 Life Insurance Fact Book* (annual; New York: Institute of Life Insurance), p. 58.

[28] See Norman F. Buck, "Discussion of Charles M. Sternhell's Paper on the New Standard Ordinary Mortality Table," *Transactions of the Society of Actuaries,* Vol. 9 (1957), pp. 38–39.

[29] See M. A. Linton, "Returns under Agency Contracts," *Record of the American Institute of Actuaries,* Vol. 13 (1924), p. 287.

ments are made at the end of the respective policy years. It is also assumed that dividends are not contingent upon the payment of subsequent premiums.

Policy B

Policy B is a $10,000 nonparticipating straight life policy issued to standard males aged 35. The cash surrender values for the first 50 policy years are shown in column 4 in Appendix B. These figures are equal to the minimum cash surrender values under the Standard Nonforfeiture Law, using the 1958 C.S.O. mortality table and 3½ percent interest (curtate functions).

The gross annual premium for policy B is $196. In the computation of the gross premium, the assumed interest rate and mortality rates are the same as those mentioned above for policy A. The assumed lapse rates, which are shown in column 8 in Appendix B, are those in Linton's B table, with an arbitrary extension to the 50th policy year. Once again the assumption is made that all policyholders will have either died or lapsed their policies by the end of the 50th policy year.

In the computation of the gross premium for policy B, it is assumed that the expenses that vary with the gross premium are 87 percent of the gross premium in the first policy year, 10 percent in the second through tenth policy years, and 5 percent thereafter. These figures are based on the same assumptions mentioned above for policy A, except it is assumed that the agent's commissions are 75 percent of the gross premium in the first policy year. Per-policy expenses are assumed to be $200 per policy in the first policy year and $10 per year per continuing policy thereafter. Once again it is assumed that gross premiums and expenses are paid at the beginning of the respective policy years and that face-amount payments and cash-surrender-value payments are made at the end of the respective policy years.

In the computation of the gross premium for policy B, an additional element is included for each policy sold. It is assumed that this additional factor has a present value per policy at issue date of $50 plus 50 percent of one gross annual premium. This may be considered a profit factor, or a margin for contingencies, or a combination of the two. When this item is mentioned in the paper, it is referred to as the profit element of the policy.

Sales Patterns

In any discussion of reserve valuation techniques, the company's rate of growth is extremely important. To illustrate, two different growth patterns, designated as sales pattern A and sales pattern B, are used in this paper.

Sales pattern A is shown in column 9 in Appendix B. In the company's first year, it is assumed that $5 million of life insurance (500 policies of $10,000 each) is placed in force. It is assumed that sales in the second year exceed the sales in the first year by 20 percent. Thereafter, it is assumed that the rate of increase in sales declines by one percentage point in years 3 through 7, by one half of a percentage point in years 8 through 17, by one fourth of a percentage point in years 18 through 37, and by one eighth of a percentage point in years 38 through 60.

Sales pattern B is shown in column 10 in Appendix B. Once again it is assumed that first-year sales are $5 million, but it is assumed that sales increase thereafter at an annual compound rate of 10 percent throughout the 60-year period of analysis.

APPENDIX B

Cash Surrender Values, Dividends, Mortality Rates, Lapse Rates, and Sales Patterns
Assumed in Illustrative Calculations

(1) Policy or Company Year	(2) Attained Age	(3) Cash Surrender Values* Policy A	(4) Cash Surrender Values* Policy B	(5) Dividends* Policy A	(6) Mortality Rates	(7) Lapse Rates A	(8) Lapse Rates B	(9) Sales Pattern† A	(10) Sales Pattern† B
1	35	7.00	0.00	2.12	0.00077	0.100	0.200	500	500
2	36	24.00	0.00	2.48	0.00100	0.060	0.120	600	550
3	37	41.00	10.83	2.88	0.00116	0.050	0.100	714	605
4	38	59.00	25.39	3.28	0.00141	0.044	0.088	843	666
5	39	77.00	40.27	3.72	0.00164	0.040	0.080	986	733
6	40	96.00	55.46	4.16	0.00236	0.036	0.072	1,144	806
7	41	115.00	70.95	4.60	0.00264	0.032	0.064	1,316	887
8	42	133.00	86.75	5.06	0.00295	0.029	0.058	1,507	976
9	43	153.00	102.83	5.50	0.00328	0.027	0.054	1,718	1,074
10	44	172.00	119.21	5.98	0.00363	0.025	0.050	1,950	1,181
11	45	190.00	135.88	6.46	0.00402	0.024	0.048	2,204	1,299
12	46	209.00	152.81	6.96	0.00445	0.023	0.046	2,480	1,429
13	47	228.00	170.00	7.46	0.00492	0.022	0.044	2,778	1,572
14	48	246.00	187.42	7.96	0.00546	0.021	0.042	3,097	1,729
15	49	265.00	205.05	8.48	0.00606	0.020	0.040	3,438	1,902
16	50	284.00	222.88	8.88	0.00672	0.020	0.040	3,799	2,092
17	51	303.00	240.88	9.29	0.00745	0.020	0.040	4,179	2,301
18	52	322.00	259.04	9.70	0.00821	0.020	0.040	4,586	2,531
19	53	342.00	277.36	10.12	0.00902	0.020	0.040	5,022	2,784
20	54	361.00	295.80	10.53	0.00992	0.020	0.040	5,487	3,062
21	55	380.00	314.36	10.93	0.01091	0.020	0.040	5,981	3,368
22	56	399.00	333.00	11.32	0.01201	0.020	0.040	6,504	3,705
23	57	418.00	351.69	11.73	0.01322	0.020	0.040	7,057	4,076
24	58	437.00	370.41	12.13	0.01455	0.020	0.040	7,639	4,484
25	59	456.00	389.14	12.53	0.01599	0.020	0.040	8,250	4,932
26	60	475.00	407.83	12.93	0.01757	0.024	0.048	8,889	5,425
27	61	493.00	426.46	13.31	0.01928	0.028	0.056	9,556	5,968
28	62	512.00	445.01	13.69	0.02112	0.032	0.064	10,249	6,565
29	63	530.00	463.45	14.07	0.02310	0.036	0.072	10,966	7,222
30	64	548.00	481.74	14.46	0.02525	0.040	0.080	11,706	7,944
31	65	566.00	499.83	14.80	0.02761	0.044	0.088	12,467	8,738
32	66	583.00	517.69	15.08	0.03021	0.048	0.096	13,246	9,612
33	67	600.00	535.24	15.37	0.03308	0.052	0.104	14,041	10,573
34	68	617.00	552.44	15.66	0.03624	0.056	0.112	14,848	11,630
35	69	633.00	569.24	15.92	0.03966	0.060	0.120	15,664	12,793
36	70	648.00	585.65	16.16	0.04330	0.064	0.128	16,486	14,072
37	71	664.00	601.69	16.40	0.04709	0.068	0.136	17,310	15,479
38	72	679.00	617.43	16.61	0.05100	0.072	0.144	18,154	17,027
39	73	693.00	632.94	16.78	0.05501	0.076	0.152	19,016	18,730
40	74	708.00	648.25	16.96	0.05923	0.080	0.160	19,895	20,603
41	75	722.00	663.35	17.12	0.06380	0.088	0.176	20,790	22,663
42	76	736.00	678.20	17.28	0.06885	0.096	0.192	21,700	24,929
43	77	749.00	692.72	17.43	0.07452	0.104	0.208	22,622	27,422
44	78	762.00	706.80	17.57	0.08092	0.112	0.224	23,555	30,164
45	79	775.00	720.35	17.70	0.08799	0.120	0.240	24,497	33,180
46	80	787.00	733.36	17.86	0.09564	0.136	0.272	25,446	36,498
47	81	798.00	745.80	17.98	0.10378	0.152	0.304	26,400	40,148
48	82	809.00	757.73	18.09	0.11232	0.168	0.336	27,357	44,163
49	83	819.00	769.19	18.19	0.12120	0.184	0.368	28,314	48,579
50	84	829.00	780.27	18.26	0.13045	0.86955	0.86955	29,270	53,437
51								30,221	58,781
52								31,165	64,659
53								32,100	71,125
54								33,023	78,238
55								33,931	86,062
56								34,822	94,668
57								35,693	104,135
58								36,541	114,549
59								37,363	126,004
60								38,157	138,604

* Per $1,000 of face amount.
† Number of $10,000 policies.
Source of data: See explanation in Appendix A.

chapter 8

Regulation of Investment

THE REGULATION of insurance company investment practices has sweeping implications not only for the solidity of the enterprise but also for the operation of our capital markets in particular, the economy in general, and for the achievement of overriding social purposes such as the rebuilding of our cities. The following selection discusses the problems of investment regulation and newly proposed solutions.

THE REGULATION OF INVESTMENTS: A WISCONSIN VIEWPOINT*

Spencer L. Kimball
Dean and Professor of Law
University of Wisconsin

Herbert S. Denenberg
Harry J. Loman Professor of Insurance
Wharton School of Finance and Commerce
University of Pennsylvania

Regulation of the investment of assets is inevitably an important part of the total regulation of the insurance enterprise.

The assets constitute the security of the insured that his claims will be paid and his interests protected. Unless they are safeguarded against dissipation and are available if needed, the insurance policy does not really insure. The law has adequate justification for intervention, therefore, to the extent that sound judgment decrees that dangers to the insured and the public from dissipated assets should be anticipated and precluded.

---

* This essay is adapted from Wisconsin Legislative Council, Insurance Laws Revision Committee, *Regulation of Investments,* Second Draft, August 23, 1968. The draft was prepared by the authors, with the aid of Werner Pfennigstorf and Barbara Heaney.

In both major branches of insurance, but especially in life insurance, investment income is an important part of the economics of the enterprise. In life insurance, the long-range character of the obligations and the level-premium mode of operation puts large sums into the insurer's hands to be held for the policyholders, and compound interest has an opportunity to work its wonders. Investment income therefore becomes a major factor in determining the necessary level of premiums to be charged. In computing premiums, a rate of return on invested assets is assumed and guaranteed. The long-run solidity of the life insurer depends on its actually earning a rate at least as large as that assumed; if it earns more, dividends can be paid from the excess either to participating policyholders or to shareholders or kept as retained earnings.

On the property-liability side of the business, investment income has kept many an insurer safely afloat during recent years when some insurers have had substantial underwriting losses in some lines of business. Though the different nature of the insurance operations means that less sizable reserves are accumulated and investment income is consequently smaller in comparison with premium income and therefore not so large a factor in the level of premium rates as it is in life insurance, it is still important in the earnings picture. It is a source of policyholder or shareholder dividends. It is the major source of internally generated capital for expansion. Moreover, and perhaps most important of all, it is a fruitful source of misunderstanding, disagreement, and controversy in the area of regulation of rates. In a few states it has even been expressly treated as a factor in the regulation of rates.

Bad investments can drain surplus and render an insurer unsound as easily as good investments can add to surplus and make the insurer profitable; it is for this reason that some regulation of investments is necessary. Although insurers are in general very sophisticated investors, not all of them are equally wise or skilled.

GENERAL OBJECTIVES

The laws regulating the investments of insurers have a number of objectives. In the first place, on those occasions when the management of an insurer is incompetent, they seek to prevent management from making speculative or otherwise unsuitable investments that endanger policyholder interests. To achieve this purpose, the laws historically prescribe minimum standards of quality and diversification of the portfolio, both among broad classes of investment and among individual investments.

Second, they seek to stabilize the financial position of insurers, to prevent them from being unduly vulnerable to shifts in economic circumstances.

Third, laws concerning investments may have objectives concerned with concentration of economic power and not directly related to ordinary insurance regulatory purposes. The laws may, for example, prohibit an insurer from purchasing a bloc of stock in another corporation large enough to permit the insurer to establish control.

Fourth, the investment laws may have other specific "social" objectives. For example, in authorizing investments in housing, §84 of the New York Insurance Law states: "To promote and supplement public and private efforts to provide an adequate supply of decent, safe and sanitary dwelling accommodations for persons of low and moderate income and to assist in relieving the housing situation any domestic life insurance company may, wherever it is actively doing the business of life insurance, acquire or construct housing projects. . . ." Social objectives like this are more numerous than they were—it is no longer possible, if it ever was, for the insurance industry to regard the great needs of our society as irrelevant to the insurance business, nor does responsible leadership in the insurance community wish to do so. The recent billion dollar investment program of the life insurance industry in the urban core indicates that social purpose is very much a real objective in practice as well as in theory.

Sometimes in its pursuit of legitimate objectives, the law has erred and has unduly restricted or channeled management initiative and judgment. It may, in the process, have interfered with management's attempt to achieve maximum return consistent with safety, thus raising the price of insurance and sometimes restricting its supply.

Sometimes the objectives of investment regulation may collide with one another. For example, social purposes such as that of investment in the urban core could conceivably be in conflict with objectives relating to solidity. In that event, the special social purpose would have to give way since the paramount and overriding social purpose of insurance is to provide security, which is only possible if insurers have assets soundly invested. Insolvent insurers solve no social problems. On the other hand, it should never be forgotten that our total security in the most fundamental sense also depends on realizing social objectives designed to assure a society just enough to be viable and orderly.

PRESENT WISCONSIN LAW

Uniformity

Wisconsin has in general followed a pattern of investment regulation that is not uncommon in the United States, especially where there is a fairly detailed regulation of investments. It is rather like New York's law, for example. There are, of course, many specific differences between the laws of Wisconsin and of other such states, but interstate variations in investment law and practice have been minimized in several ways. First, the National Association of Insurance Commissioners has exerted some influence in the direction of uniformity of law and, even more, of regulatory practice. Second, some key regulatory and insurance states, among which New York is the most prominent, have exerted pressures for uniformity of insurer practice far beyond their borders by requiring substantial compliance with their own investment laws from all insurers seeking authorization to do business within them. Third, and conversely, there has sometimes been competitive pressure on the more restrictive states, such as New York, to authorize domestic insurers to capitalize on legitimate investment opportunities available to their out-of-state competitors.[1]

History of Wisconsin Investment Regulation

The last century has witnessed a continuous liberalization of the investment laws of Wisconsin.[2] Two highly restrictive laws of 1870, controlling separately life and nonlife insurers, established strict standards of control over insurer investments. Thereafter, a steady process of amendment expanded the list of permitted investments and liberalized their terms.

[1] See, e.g., Report to the New York Superintendent of the Special Committee on Insurance Holding Companies (1968), pp. 21–26.

[2] For a detailed history of the Wisconsin statutes, see S. Kimball, *Insurance and Public Policy* (1960), pp. 129–43.

This process of widening the investment discretion of management was not even interrupted by the investigations of the insurance industry after the turn into the 20th century. Widespread abuses uncovered in large eastern companies resulted in restrictive legislation in New York as well as other states, especially for life insurance. But no serious abuses were discovered in Wisconsin, and in addition the existing laws were already stricter. Hence there was no resulting legislative reaction in this state.

While the amendment process liberalized the Wisconsin investment law, it failed to systematize it or restructure it, since the detailed enactments were each in response to a separate need or problem. The law is too complex, too detailed, too unsystematic, and still too restrictive for the rapidly unfolding investment environment of the last half of the 20th century.

Investment of Capital

Among the basic similarities between Wisconsin's investment control and that found elsewhere is the requirement that any domestic insurer invest an amount equal to the capital required of a stock company in limited classes of high-quality fixed-dollar investments.[3] Unlike New York and some other states, Wisconsin has no specific restrictions on the investment of assets equivalent to reserves. The special requirement for capital seems to lack clear purpose and justification and is omitted from the proposed Wisconsin revision.

Authorized List of Investments

Like New York and many other states, Wisconsin limits the investments of both life and nonlife insurers to an authorized list of investments,[4] which grows in length as new types of investments are invented or become popular and are added by the legislature. As each new class has been added, special qualifications and limits applicable only to the new class have been added with it. They are not always the same, thus complicating the structure of investment

---

[3] Wis. Stat. sec. 201.25(2) (1967). Unless otherwise indicated, section references are to the Wisconsin Statutes, 1967.

[4] Secs. 201.25(1) and 206.34(1).

regulation and removing the details farther and farther from basic principles.

Life Insurers' Investments in Common Stocks

Wisconsin, like other states, has specific limitations on a life insurer's investments in variable value investments, and in particular in common stocks, including an aggregate limitation (when combined with preferred stocks) of 15 percent of admitted assets, measured at cost.[5] New York is even more restrictive. It limits a life insurer's investment in common stocks, when measured at cost, to 5 percent of admitted assets or one half of surplus, whichever is smaller.[6] The *Report to the New York Superintendent of the Special Committee on Insurance Holding Companies* conservatively recommends a 10 percent limit.[7] Most other states are more liberal. There are noteworthy cases where there is virtually no limit on common stock investments. Thus, a number of states permit virtually unlimited investments in common stocks except for the requirement of fixed-dollar investments for capital, and sometimes minimum surplus.[8]

Some states, including Wisconsin, place a single limitation on common and preferred stocks taken together. Wisconsin places a limit of 15 percent of admitted assets on the combination.[9] Florida, Indiana, and North Dakota have a 10 percent limitation applicable to all stock, common and preferred.[10]

---

[5] Sec. 206.34(1)(es).

[6] N.Y. Ins. Law, sec. 81(13)(c) (McKinney 1966).

[7] *Report to the New York Superintendent of the Special Committee on Insurance Holding Companies* (1968), p. 23. The report was submitted in early 1968.

[8] See, e.g., Deering's Cal. Ins. Code Ann. secs. 1190, 1191 (West Supp. 1967); Conn. Gen. Stat. Rev. secs. 38–37 (1958) (only limitation is that purchase does not substantially lessen competition); secs. 38–144 (life companies limited to stock which has paid at least $3\frac{3}{4}$ percent interest during previous five years); Va. Code Ann. secs. 38.1–182 (Supp. 1966) (excess capital and surplus). See also *Report to the New York Superintendent of the Special Committee on Insurance Holding Companies* (1968), p. 22, n. 1.

[9] Sec. 206.34(1)(eg).

[10] Fla. Stat. sec. 625.0104(2)(a) (1967); Ind. Ann. Stat. sec. 39–4202(22) (Supp. 1968); N.D. Cent. Code sec. 26–08–11(11)(d) (1960). New York has no limit on qualified preferred stocks. N.Y. Ins. Law sec. 81(3) (McKinney 1966).

Real Property Investments

In dealing with real property the Wisconsin statutes still seem to reflect, in 1968, an archaic prejudice, that may go as far back as the English mortmain statutes of the 13th century, against the holding of real estate by persons with perpetual life. The stringent limitations traditionally placed on real estate ownership by insurance corporations transcend sound investment considerations.

There is in Wisconsin a common kind of limitation on home office property to 20 percent of admitted assets.[11] This limitation has a diversification objective, and also helps to restrain conspicuous consumption beyond the insurer's means. The present limitation prevents investment of nonadmitted as well as admitted assets in home office real property beyond the specified percentage.

Moreover, income producing real property is ordinarily subject to unduly conservative limitations. An insurer may invest only 5 percent of its admitted assets in income producing real property.[12] For life insurers, the rule is liberalized by permitting extra investment in certain specialized types of real property.[13] Of course, real property poses special liquidity problems, but they are not insurmountable and can be solved within the overall framework of a proper investment portfolio. In life insurance, liquidity is not generally even important.

Finally, real property acquired in the bona fide enforcement of creditors' rights, at least unless they are investments otherwise permissible under the provisions mentioned in the previous paragraph, must now be sold within five years of acquisition unless the commissioner authorizes an extension of time to prevent loss on a forced sale.[14]

Qualitative Requirements

Wisconsin follows the general control pattern by prescribing a variety of qualitative requirements for investments. For both life

---

[11] Sec. 201.24(2).
[12] Sec. 201.25(1) (hh) and sec. 206.34(1) (k).
[13] Sec. 206.34(1)(n) and (s).
[14] Sec. 201.24(3).

and nonlife insurers, for example, common stocks must be those of corporations that meet certain minimum earnings tests.[15] Roughly similar earnings tests are applied to equipment securities or certificates,[16] to bonds of private companies organized under the laws of the United States or Canada,[17] to preferred stocks,[18] and to public utility indebtedness.[19]

Portfolio Distribution

Wisconsin, like other jurisdictions, also employs many limitations relating to portfolio distribution. Those applied to nonlife insurers are few. They are as follows: (1) stocks, bonds, and other evidences of indebtedness, which do not meet minimum earnings requirements, 5 percent of admitted assets;[20] and (2) income-producing real property, 5 percent of admitted assets.[21]

Portfolio distribution limitations are much more detailed for life companies. They comprise: (1) bonds of the International Bank for Reconstruction and Development and the Inter-American Development Bank, 2 percent of admitted assets;[22] (2) common and preferred stock, 15 percent of admitted assets (determined at cost);[23] (3) vessels, machinery, and equipment subject to contracts of sale or use, 3 percent of admitted assets;[24] (4) certain foreign investments, 2 percent of admitted assets;[25] (5) income-producing real property, 5 percent of admitted assets;[26] and (6) dormitories, 5 percent of admitted assets.[27]

The limitation of 20 percent of admitted assets for a home office, already discussed above, applies both to life and nonlife insurers.[28]

---

[15] Secs. 201.25(1) (ff), (fg), (fh) and 206.34(1) (es).
[16] Secs. 201.25(1) (hk) and 206.34(1) (fc).
[17] Secs. 201.25(1) (ff) and 206.34(1) (ef).
[18] Secs. 201.25(1) (ff) and 206.34(1) (eg).
[19] Sec. 206.34(1) (ec).
[20] Sec. 201.25(1) (fh).
[21] Sec. 201.25(1) (hh).
[22] Sec. 206.34(1) (bl).
[23] Sec. 206.34(1) (eg) and (es).
[24] Sec. 206.34(1) (fp).
[25] Sec. 206.34(1) (fs).
[26] Sec. 206.34(1) (k).
[27] Sec. 206.34(1) (s).
[28] Sec. 201.24(2).

For town mutuals organized under ch. 202, the value of the home office may not exceed one mill on the dollar on the amount of insurance in force.[29] The different nature of the town mutual's operations requires this different treatment. As an assessment mutual its assets are greatly limited.

Individual Investment Limitations

Wisconsin also utilizes many limitations relating to individual investments. These limitations have diversification as one objective. They may have others, too, such as a concern for undue concentration of economic power.

For nonlife insurers the only limitation on individual investments is that no such insurer may invest more than 10 percent of its admitted assets in the stock, securities, or evidence of indebtedness of any one private or municipal corporation.[30] Similar limitations applicable only to life insurers are as follows: no such insurer shall invest (1) more than 2 percent of its admitted assets in a single issue of the secured bonds or other evidence of indebtedness of a corporation;[31] (2) more than 1 percent of its admitted assets in a single issue of the unsecured bonds or other evidence of indebtedness of a corporation,[32] (3) more than 2 percent of its admitted assets in the preferred stock of a single issuer;[33] (4) more than 1 percent of its admitted assets in the common stock of a single issuer;[34] (5) more than 2 percent of its admitted assets in a single issue of equipment securities or certificates;[35] or (6) more than 10 percent of its assets in the securities of one corporation.[36] There is no obvious reason for having more restrictive attitudes toward life insurers than for others, at least in these respects. No difference of principle or policy is apparent.

Modern thinking about investment policy may challenge the validity of these percentages, on the ground that portfolio diversifi-

---

[29] Sec. 201.24(2).
[30] Sec. 201.25(4).
[31] Sec. 206.34(1)(ee).
[32] Sec. 206.34(1)(ef).
[33] Sec. 206.34(1)(eg).
[34] Sec. 206.34(1)(es).
[35] Sec. 206.34(1)(fc).
[36] Sec. 206.34(2)(a).

cation should be balanced with sufficiently careful and continuous study of securities held, which requires limiting the number of different investments to manageable proportions.

Other Quantitative Limitations

Insurance codes generally relate the amount that may be loaned on the security of real or other property to some percentage of the market value of the collateral. For nonlife insurers Wisconsin now requires that a loan on real property be no more than ⅔ of market value.[37] The figure is 75 percent for life companies,[38] having been raised from ⅔ by recent amendment.[39] In contrast, loans on security of certain securities may not exceed 90 percent of market value for life insurers[40] but 100 percent for nonlife insurers.[41]

Leeway Provisions

Wisconsin, like other states, has recently adopted so-called "leeway" or "basket" provisions which permit an insurer to invest a limited fraction of its assets in otherwise unauthorized investments. Such provisions serve as a safety valve, permitting the insurer an additional measure of flexibility to allow for a difference of interpretation, or for shifting circumstances that change the status of an asset, and permitting the insurer to take advantage of investment opportunities that may not yet be or may never be specifically authorized. A nonlife company may invest up to 10 percent of its admitted assets in this category,[42] a life company 5 percent.[43]

Foreign and Alien Companies

Wisconsin statutes, unlike those of some other jurisdictions, do not expressly provide for the regulation of investments of foreign or

---

[37] Sec. 201.25(1)(c).
[38] Sec. 206.34(1)(c).
[39] Ch. 392, sec. 1 (1965) Wis. Laws 638.
[40] Sec. 206.34(1)(g).
[41] Sec. 201.25(1)(g).
[42] Sec. 201.25(1)(n).
[43] Sec. 206.34(1)(m).

alien insurers, though they do regulate the investments of deposits of such insurers.[44]

CHANGES PROPOSED IN THE WISCONSIN REVISION PROJECT

Recent staff work of the Wisconsin Insurance Laws Revision Committee proposes fundamental changes in the pattern of investment regulation. For the most part, they are liberalizing changes, based on the assumption that most insurance managements are both able and willing to pursue a sound investment policy and that present investment laws do more to hinder than to help in achieving that goal. Only for new or marginal insurers is there need to provide the detailed rules that now characterize investment regulation. In a few respects the changes are toward more stringent control, but the overall effect of what is proposed will be to give sound insurers much more freedom.

Changes in Method of Control

The main change proposed is not substantive but procedural. The proposed revision seeks to enlarge greatly the rule-making responsibility of the commissioner and to reduce the amount of detail contained in the statute. This change is closely related to and makes possible a classification of insurers, freeing most of them from detailed control over investments, but intensifying control where such intensification seems necessary.

The statutes relating to investments have required a continuous stream of statutory amendments to keep pace with economic developments, legal changes, and evolving investment philosophies. To ensure that investment laws permit application of sound but recent trends and that new investment insights can be promptly utilized, the proposed revision is content to outline investment principles and objectives, leaving it to rules of the commissioner to spell out the details and to implement needed changes more expeditiously. In particular, the authorized list is retained in form, but the list is stated with great generality and the commissioner has wide discretion to add to it. While change in investment regulation should not

---

[44] Sec. 201.32(6).

be lightly undertaken, sound investment opportunities should not have to be foregone simply because the legislative process is inherently and properly slow in adapting to change. The authority to make such needed changes expeditiously can be safely entrusted to the commissioner if he is properly guided by general statutory standards. The changes required from time to time are only in detail and not in principles. Moreover, the legislature can always deal explicitly with any matter that it considers important enough to deserve embedding in a statute. The temptation is constantly present to deal explicitly with details that do not deserve legislative attention.

In order to avoid any possibility of a regulatory vacuum, the proposed revision includes proposed rules to implement the statute. These rules, which should be promulgated by the commissioner with the same effective date as the statutes they interpret, basically codify but also simplify those details of existing statutes that need not rise to the level of statutory enactment.

Liberalization of Controls of the Majority of Insurers and Imposition of Special Restrictions on Certain Insurers

Investment regulation has long presented the horns of a dilemma to the insurance commissioner and to the legislature. Either legislation and regulation must be so detailed and strict as to put handcuffs on the competent investment managers of strong and well-run insurers, or so general and lacking in detail as to make it possible for inexperienced investment personnel to endanger seriously the interests of insureds and the public. The Wisconsin revision attempts to go in between the horns by imposing special restrictions on certain insurance corporations, leaving others relatively free. All new insurers for their first five years and older insurers on specific order of the commissioner are subject to more restrictive investment regulation than is applicable to other insurers—to most insurers. The commissioner may reclassify an insurer in either direction by an order, which would be subject to judicial review. For most insurers, therefore, only the statutory provisions and a few simple implementing rules will apply; they provide much greater freedom and flexibility than the current law. For insurers subject to special restrictions, something comparable to the present law will ordinarily be applicable through more explicit and detailed rules, but there will also exist the possibility of more direct supervision by the insurance commissioner, as well as the greater flexibility that results from the more extensive use of rules.

This approach assumes that the commissioner and his staff should not replace nor interfere with experienced and skilled investment management of strong and mature insurers; as to most insurers it contemplates virtually no interference nor surveillance. It does assume, however, that when management is demonstrably lacking in competence or reliability or the financial condition of an insurer demands close watchfulness, the commissioner should be empowered to protect insureds and the public. In such cases, stringent rules and close control are needed. This is the underlying principle that the present law already expresses; the revision merely tries to make it more workable and to focus the commissioner's attention where it belongs, almost exclusively on the weak insurers, simultaneously freeing the sound ones from the undue strictness and detail of the present control. When the commissioner does undertake close surveillance of an insurer's investments, he should and will be empowered under ch. 601 to create an advisory committee or group of investment men from sound insurers to help him.

It goes without saying that special restrictions on investment should not be taken to indicate that an insurer is second class. An insurer thus restricted, whether new or old, may be potentially excellent; its temporary financial condition or other conditions, however, may make closer control over investments important for the time being. An insurer should be rehabilitated or liquidated, not merely restricted in its investments, if its situation is such as to endanger the interests of insureds or the public. The formulation of the proposed statute is intended to ensure this.

As experience develops, the commissioner may develop a series of classifications applicable to restricted insurers and develop differentiated controls for the various classes. The proposed law gives him flexible power to do so under broad rule-making authority. In giving the commissioner this power carefully to modulate the law to match regulatory needs, the proposal seeks to implement a fundamental principle of the entire investment law in particular and of the Wisconsin revision in general—the notion that a sharp separation should be made between the statement of general principles and the formulation of detailed applications.

It is the legislature's role to concern itself with statements of principle and the establishment of general direction, not with detail. The circumstances of the securities markets of this country change so much over time that it would be unfortunate if even closely restricted insurers were locked into a detailed investment framework without the possibility of quick changes in the details to meet new circumstances. The history of investment statutes is one of constant legislative amendment to keep pace with changing legal forms and investment opportunities. But the legislative process is often too slow to keep up with the swift tides of legal and economic change, and legislatures lack the facilities for the continuity of study and decision-making essential to the regulatory process. *A fortiori* this is true in dealing with the troubles of restricted insurers.

Exercise by the commissioner of his rule-making power under the proposed revision, within an overall legislative framework and subject to the controls of the Administrative Procedure Act, is a much sounder way to deal with changing circumstances than is constant legislative concern with the changing details of the securities markets. The latter is a mere facade, anyway—the reality is that interested parties ask for what they want, and in the absence of strenuous opposition from the commissioner, the legislature complies with the request.

The commissioner may make use of his system of classification by making various classes of restricted insurers subject to prior approval, to subsequent disapproval, to reporting requirements, or to other procedural devices.

The commissioner may go even further in tailor-making his regulatory control of investments by the use of specific orders directed to a single insurer. Under certain circumstances, the investment policy of an insurer may present special dangers, special opportunities or special needs, that make the statutes and the promulgated rules undesirable to apply. Under such circumstances, the commissioner should be able to intervene in an individual insurer's investment policy by order. Thus, the revision recognizes that investments not otherwise authorized may occasionally be satisfactory for a given company and gives the commissioner power to authorize an otherwise unapproved investment.[45] However, the danger of abuse is great, and a wise commissioner will exercise such powers

---

[45] This provision is adapted from Wash. Rev. Code Ann. sec. 48.13.250 (1961).

sparingly to avoid the charge of unjustified discrimination and arbitrariness. In all but truly exceptional cases, the rules should apply evenly to all. Moreover, the new freedom accorded to unrestricted insurers should obviate the necessity for more than occasional approval of such consent investments.

Unification of Life and Nonlife Requirements

There are some significant differences between the investment needs of nonlife and life insurers. The nonlife insurer must place greater emphasis on liquidity, faces a much more substantial risk of catastrophic loss, and deals in short-term commitments. The life insurer, basically dealing in long-term fixed-dollar commitments and operating on the basis of premiums that guarantee a specified rate of interest to be earned, must select its investments accordingly.

Despite these operational differences, however, the types of eligible investments for both life and nonlife insurers are basically the same, even under existing law. The differences are mainly in portfolio distribution rather than in eligibility of assets.

In drafting both the proposed statutes and the accompanying rules, an attempt was made, wherever possible, to unify life and nonlife prescriptions. Differences should exist only for good reasons related to the operational differences between the classes.

Liberalization of Common Stock Investments for Life Insurers

The existing Wisconsin law limits the common and preferred stock investments of a life insurer to 15 percent of its admitted assets. This figure was recently raised from 5 percent for each.[46] It is more permissive than New York's comparable requirement which limits investment in common stocks to 5 percent of admitted assets or one half of surplus, whichever is less.

However, it is worth noting that a recent authoritative study of the life insurance investment process concluded that "the capacity of life companies for risk taking is appreciably greater than the degree of risk taking reflected in their investment portfolios."[47] Further liberalization of common stock investments for life insurers would

---

[46] Ch. 392, sec. 1 (1965), Wis. Laws 638, amending sec. 206.34(1)(eg) and (es) (1963).

[47] J. Walter, *The Investment Process* (Boston: Harvard University Graduate School of Business Administration, 1962), p. 62.

help in achieving several goals. It would help make life insurance a more attractive savings medium by providing greater opportunities for growth and yield. It would provide greater protection against the effects of inflation for policyholders as well as insurers. It would provide more satisfactory alternative investment outlets for insurers when the yield on fixed-dollar investments dips very low, as it did in the late 1940's. It would help increase the supply of equity capital, thus contributing to the growth of the economy and enlarging the options of small and medium-sized as well as larger insurers.

The proposed revision would permit a life insurer to invest up to 20 percent of its admitted assets in common stocks, an apparent increase of 5 percent over the present authorization. This is qualified, however, by a change, for purposes of this limitation, to valuation at market. This may in fact be more stringent than the present law, depending on the circumstances. Such an extensive commitment as 20 percent would not be appropriate for every life insurer; each would decide for itself whether to commit so much of its assets to common stocks. This, as well as any generalized investment control, should not prevent variation to reflect the peculiar financial position and individual history of individual insurers. But conversely, strong insurers should not be needlessly straitjacketed by unnecessary restraints devised for weak insurers. The best way to provide some specific statutory control over individual insurers whose financial position is weaker than the normal is to establish an independent limit on common stock (and other equity) investments that relates these more volatile categories of assets to policyholders' surplus. This recognizes that a main function of policyholders' surplus is to cover short-term fluctuations of value of the portfolio of invested assets. That limit is patterned after (but is more liberal than) the New York limitation on common stock investment and is even more liberal than that recommended by the *Report to the New York Superintendent of the Special Committee on Insurance Holding Companies* (1968). Its function is to ensure that the most extreme fluctuation of the stock market that one can reasonably anticipate will not wipe out policyholders' surplus as a result of a decline in the market value of shares held.

Investments in Real Property

The authorization to invest in real property is liberalized by the proposal in four ways. First, the limitation on home office real property to 20 percent of admitted assets is made inapplicable to the extent that the insurer is able to treat any excess over 20 percent as assets it does not need to meet tests of solidity or solvency. Second, real property (like any other asset) acquired in the bona fide enforcement of creditors' rights may be held indefinitely if not needed for those purposes and may be held for a reasonable period of time even if so required. Third, an insurer may commit a larger portion of its portfolio to income-producing real property. The present limit of 5 percent applicable to life and nonlife insurers is raised to 20 percent of admitted assets or twice policyholders' surplus for a life insurer and to 10 percent of admitted assets for a nonlife insurer.[48] Finally, the sharp lines dividing real from personal property are partially erased.

Foreign and Alien Insurers

The present Wisconsin law does no more than regulate the investment of deposits of alien insurers.[49] The proposed revision, however, requires substantial compliance with the investment laws of this state by all admitted insurers. There is both precedent and justification for this new requirement. New York regulates the investments of foreign and alien insurers, requiring them to "comply in substance with the investment requirements and limitations" imposed on domestic insurers.[50] Other states have similar provisions.[51] Nothing relates so clearly to the solidity of an insurer as the character of its investments, and while it is unjustified both for a state to apply an unduly stringent regime of control to any insurer, domestic or foreign, or for one state to extend its regime of general regulatory control in detail to all insurers doing business within its borders, one of the basic presuppositions of a system of state control of insurance is that each state may decide what insurers are safe enough for its domestic market. Even literal compliance probably could be constitutionally imposed, but that would lead to absurd results when, as would surely be inevitable, state requirements were

---

[48] Wisconsin Legislative Council, Insurance Laws Revision Committee, Regulation of Investments, sec. 5(2)(d) (2d Draft, August 23, 1968). (The limit is now higher for life insurers if certain narrow categories of real property investment are added. See *supra,* p. 132).

[49] Sec. 201.32(6).

[50] N.Y. Ins. Law sec. 90 (McKinney 1966).

[51] See, e.g., Fla. Stat. sec. 625.0139 (1967).

found to be inconsistent, instead of merely to differ in the degree of severity of the restrictions imposed. "Substantial" compliance should be enough for even the most important restrictions. In the investment field, the liberalizing of the investment laws applicable to unrestricted domestic insurers makes a requirement of merely "substantial" compliance very reasonable, indeed, for nondomestic insurers of the same caliber. Moreover, as with New York's law,[52] substantial compliance would require satisfaction of this state's laws only to the extent that the assets are needed to establish soundness of operation.

Liberalization of Investment of Excess Surplus

Both for domestic and foreign insurers, the liberalization described above is not the end. The proposed revision also calls for virtually complete investment freedom for surplus in excess of optimum surplus.

"Optimum surplus" is a newly coined term used to describe the amount of surplus that ideally should be available as a minimum to support the insurer's operation. The term is new, but the concept is not. It is not *required* for solvency, and failure to maintain it is not alone ground for drastic action like rehabilitation. Nor is it a maximum—it is the least amount of surplus the insurer should have to be regarded as solid, but no sound public policy prohibits management from having even more. Failure to maintain the optimum surplus, appropriately subjects the insurer to administrative surveillance—with respect to dividends and other distributions, for example. In a variety of ways, the existing regulatory patterns in the United States already recognize a point beyond which an insurer has funds not essential for the insurance operation. Thus in applying a "substantial compliance" concept to a foreign insurer, the commissioner may ignore improper investments if the insurer does not need them to satisfy him as to solidity.[53] Likewise, when a holding company is formed for the purpose of freeing unnecessary surplus for other activity, as in some recent cases, the commissioner must decide how much surplus needs to remain to support the insurance operation. Again, the commissioner might begin to put pressure on a property-liability insurer to do various things when its policyhold-

---

[52] N.Y. Ins. Law sec. 90(1) (McKinney 1966).

[53] For explicit statutory enactment of this application, see N.Y. Ins. Law sec. 90(1) (McKinney 1966).

ers' surplus drops below a certain ratio to its premium writings, perhaps plus investments in equities. The Kenney rules are well known,[54] and are sometimes used, with or without modification.[55] If policyholders' surplus declines below the appropriate amount, the insurer does not have the optimum surplus, but it may still be far from insolvent. But if an insurer has surplus in excess of the optimum it should be almost completely free to deal with that excess as it likes.[56]

For life insurers, the concept would have only limited application. The valuation of life insurance reserves is generally done on such a conservative basis that to be sound a mature insurer does not really need surplus beyond its reserves. In the present state of the art of insurance regulation, thus, optimum surplus for life insurers should probably be the same as compulsory surplus. However, this statute is being drafted, so far as possible, to provide room for future developments in the art of regulation. Completely free surplus is that in excess of the optimum, however the latter is eventually defined or ascertained.

An important corollary of this new view of surplus is a new approach to sanctions against violations of the limitations on investments. Traditionally, divestment is required by the insurance law. The new revision permits instead the treatment of investment in excess of statutory or administrative provision first as leeway and thereafter simply declines to count it toward satisfaction of either compulsory or optimum surplus requirements. As long as remaining surplus is adequate—in excess of optimum surplus—the insurer can continue to hold assets irrespective of any limitation. Of course, this liberalization is not applicable to investments that are prohibited on public policy grounds—there divestment is required in the event of violation.

Investment Fluctuation Reserves

The proposed revision empowers the commissioner to establish, by rule, reserves for investment fluctuations in order to lessen the

---

[54] R. Kenney, *Fundamentals of Fire and Casualty Insurance Strength* (4th ed.), pp. 19–20, 97.

[55] Far more liberal ratios are in fact more commonly applied in practice.

[56] For more extensive discussion, see *Report to the New York Superintendent by the Special Committee on Insurance Holding Companies* (1968), pp. 43–47.

impact of variation in values of specific classes of assets held by insurers. Establishment of such reserves would reduce the amount of optimum surplus—they are alternative devices for dealing with fluctuation of asset values. Such a provision would not only authorize securities valuation reserves in life insurance but could extend it to all types of companies.

There is no thought that the Wisconsin commissioner would go off on a tangent of his own in providing for such reserves beyond the life field. Whatever he does should be done in parallel with other important insurance states and only after close consultation with and probably (though not inevitably) agreement of the affected industry.

CONCLUSION

The proposed investment law is designed to give new freedom to the regulated, the regulator, and the legislator.

To sound insurance companies, it gives freedom to their technically skilled, well-staffed, and responsible management to perform a task in which their normal management objectives are largely the same as those demanded by their policyholders and the public interest.

To the regulator, it gives freedom to concentrate on those insurers and on those aspects of regulation most in need of attention. The commissioner is free to concentrate his efforts on new insurers, marginal insurers, and those apparently badly managed. He need not squander his limited resources in giving detailed guidance and control to those whose capital, surplus, and management are such as to require only the broadest regulatory guidelines.

By virtue of the rule-making power granted him, the commissioner can tailor his regulatory controls to fully protect the public and the policyholder without unnecessarily and uneconomically interfering with the prerogatives of management.

Finally, to the legislator it gives freedom from the necessity of dealing repeatedly with technical, detailed minutiae of the investment statutes, leaving him free to concentrate his attention where it should be concentrated, on the setting of broad policy guidelines.

chapter 9

Regulating the Solidity of Property and Liability Insurers

THE THREE PREVIOUS selections focus on specific methods of ensuring the solidity of the insurance enterprise—capital and surplus requirements, reserves, and investment control.

The selection that follows is an attempt to state more comprehensively the regulator's responsibilities and available techniques for ensuring solidity of property and liability insurers. The author proposes changes in insurance laws and in the practices of insurance departments to enable the regulator to see that insurance companies keep their promises.

ENSURING THE SOLVENCY OF PROPERTY AND LIABILITY INSURANCE COMPANIES

Allen L. Mayerson
Professor of Insurance and Actuarial Mathematics
University of Michigan

The major purpose of insurance is to turn uncertainty into certainty and thus provide a sense of security for the policyholder. Insurance companies assume risks and by pooling them turn a large, potentially disastrous loss into a small, certain loss. But the insurance mechanism cannot provide certainty to others unless it is itself secure. Thus it is proper that from time to time, we examine the security of the insurance mechanism, the solvency of insurance carriers, and consider the function of insurance supervision in assuring and maintaining solvency. Certainly an institution that attempts to provide a sense of security for the public must itself be secure; the solvency of insurance companies is an important goal of society and one of the principal reasons for the existence of insurance regulation.

What Is Solvency?

Solvency in the technical sense in which I propose to use it means that an insurer is in a position to meet all its obligations, not only those which fall due in the near future but also those obligations that will not mature for many years. Colloquially but not technically, we might say that solvency means the capacity for permanent performance.

Professor Kimball[1] distinguishes between technical solvency and another concept which he calls "solidity," which describes the broad purpose of assuring the ability of insurers to keep their promises. Certainly insurance regulation has as a general goal the assurance of more than mere technical solvency. This general purpose must, however, be made explicit by setting minimum legal standards which an insurer must meet in order to continue in business. We will be primarily dealing with these legal standards, hence with "solvency" rather than the more vaguely defined "solidity."

Solvency is more than a purely accounting concept. From an actuarial point of view, solvency requires (*a*) that premiums are sufficient to meet expected claims and expenses and (*b*) that assets are adequate to meet known liabilities, with an appropriate safety margin. Temporarily, large assets may balance out inadequate premiums, but long-run solvency requires both adequate premiums and a contingency reserve or surplus to meet unexpected fluctuations.

We cannot define solvency in a way that gives any certainty that an insurer can meet its obligations. Catastrophes are conceivable that could exhaust the assets of even the soundest insurer; even in the absence of a catastrophe, an insurer can sustain a long run of bad experience that can eventually cause insolvency. All we can ask is that solvency imply an ability to meet those obligations that can now be predicted, using the best judgment of which we are capable, with a safety margin to guard against those adverse fluctuations which good judgment and past experience indicate may occur.

---

[1] Spencer L. Kimball, *The Purpose of Insurance Regulation*, Minn. L. Rev., Vol. 45 (1961), p. 471.

Since insurance involves an aleatory process, solvency can be viewed in probabilistic terms. We can pose the question: "What is the probability that an insurer with a given capital and surplus, with assets invested in a certain way, and with a given portfolio of insurance risks will become insolvent (be ruined) during a given time period?" If we ignore the probability that insolvency can occur because of poor investments, economic or social trends that cannot be foreseen, or dishonest management, the ruin problem can be formulated mathematically. It would, of course, be helpful to be able to incorporate economic and financial risks in the model as well as claim fluctuations, but the mathematical methods needed to handle such a complex problem have not yet been developed.

The ruin problem has been studied in considerable detail by the collective theory of risk, which treats insurance as a stochastic process wherein during a given time interval, an insurer collects premiums at a given rate and sustains random losses according to a specified mathematical function.[2] By using this theory, we can define a solvent insurer as an insurer whose probability of ruin during a specified time interval is less than a predetermined amount. We might, for example consider an insurer solvent if its probability of ruin, during a 5-year period, is less than 1 in 1,000.

Something of this sort is done in Finland where insurers are required by the statutes to establish an equalization reserve whose size is determined by collective risk theory. "The reserve, when accounts of a certain year are closed, is the amount the company would need in addition to future premiums in order to be capable, with a probability of $1 - e$, of meeting its present and future liabilities if the company ceased to make new contracts after one year."[3] By taking e sufficiently small,[4] any desired degree of solvency can be prescribed.

Unfortunately, the insurance business embraces business risks as well as mathematical risks. Even as to the latter, the mathematical function applicable in each individual case and its parameters are

---

[2] Paul Kahn, "An Introduction to Collective Risk Theory and Its Application to Stop-Loss Reinsurance," *Transactions, Society of Actuaries,* Vol. 14 (1962), p. 400.

[3] Address by E. Pesonen, "Solvency Measurement," Proceedings, 17th International Congress of Actuaries, Special Meeting, Edinburgh, June 1, 1964.

[4] The term *"e"* is the "probability of ruin." For further discussion see Hofflander's essay in Chapter 6.

not fully known. The forces which threaten solvency are varied and complex. What formula for solvency devised even two years ago would have allowed for the large riot losses of July, 1967, and April, 1968? What is the probability of a 25 percent decline in the market value of the common stocks included in an insurer's investment portfolio? How can the competence and integrity of a company's management be measured and included in the formula? The kind of claim fluctuation which can be considered as a chance variation and measured by the calculus of probability may be the least important facet of the solvency problem.

The Role of the Insurance Department

Solvency is one of the principal concerns of insurance company management, and it is the insurance commissioner's primary responsibility. The management of any enterprise has two major objectives: to manage the company so that it will be profitable and grow, and to ensure that the company will continue to exist. Thus prudent management does not normally risk the future of a company on a gamble which may prove highly profitable but which entails a substantial risk of bankruptcy. The task of insurance company management is in essence similar to the management of any other type of company. Insurers differ from most other companies, however, in that the solvency of an insurance company is of great importance not only to its stockholders but to its policyholders as well.

Prudent management dictates that solvency should rank very high on the list of an insurer's goals. In its quest for solvency, management has the advantage of certain "inside" information about the company: its operations, the ability of its personnel, and its future plans. And, of course, management has considerable control over the processes that determine the company's future, and an alert management can stop a dangerous situation before it gets out of hand. Management can change a company's retention, enter into reinsurance agreements, enter or withdraw from territories, cease writing a type of insurance which is producing underwriting losses, or change its premium rates or policy provisions. These decisions are often made on the basis of knowledge that is not available to persons outside the company.

However, solvency is only one of the aims of insurance company management. The desire to show a current operating profit may be an equally strong motivation for some managers, as may the desire to expand rapidly into other territories or branches of insurance, or to capture a larger share of a given market. Some company managements may be most interested in doing things which will convince the financial community that the company is growing more rapidly than its competitors and hence will lead to a higher price for the company's stock. A study of how management attempts to maintain company solvency, though interesting, would be a complex and difficult undertaking.

Our concern will be with the insurance commissioner's problem: how to be sure that every company doing business in his jurisdiction is solvent and has a high probability of remaining solvent. And since the problems of life insurance companies and property and liability insurers are quite different, we will limit our consideration to the latter.

The insurance commissioner has limited authority—he may exercise only those powers which the law grants to him, either specifically or by reasonable implication. Despite inadequate laws which often give him less power than he needs to deal directly and realistically with the ruin problem, the public expects the insurance commissioner to see to it that only solvent insurers are permitted to solicit insurance. The policyholder expects that his insurer will remain solvent until after his claim, if any, is paid in full, or his policy expires. Lacking the requisite technical knowledge, he relies on his state insurance commissioner to see that each insurer is and remains solvent.

It is his job not to permit the incorporation of a new insurer which may soon become insolvent, nor to permit a shaky insurer incorporated elsewhere to sell insurance in his state. Once an insurer, whether newly incorporated or with years of experience in other states, has been given a certificate of authority to commence writing insurance in his state, its continued solvency is an important concern of the insurance commissioner.

The commissioner endeavors to ascertain and preserve solvency (*a*) by scrutinizing the company's annual statement and, where needed, interim financial reports; and (*b*) by conducting periodic examinations to verify the correctness of the company's annual statement and to ensure its compliance with statutes and with prudent management practices. To understand how an insurance department attempts to test the solvency of companies subject to its supervision requires a careful and critical study of the property insurance annual statement blank, of insurance accounting procedures, and of the periodic examination as a tool for determining and maintaining solvency.

Standard of Solvency—New Companies

When an insurer begins operation in a state, either by becoming incorporated as a new company or by being licensed by a state other than its state of incorporation, it must meet certain minimum capital and surplus requirements. These requirements vary greatly by state, by line of business, and often by form of corporate organization. An insurer can become incorporated in Arizona with only $25,000 capital and $12,500 surplus[5] while Michigan requires $1,000,000 capital and $500,000 surplus.[6]

The initial capital and surplus requirements of most states are much too low under present conditions, but they are gradually being increased. For example, the Pennsylvania governor's 1967 legislative program included an increase in the minimum capital and surplus for a new insurer writing automobile liability insurance from $150,000 to $750,000.[7] Many states have increased the minimum capital for a multiple line property insurance company to $1,000,000 or more.

The purpose of requiring a substantial initial capital is, presumably, to provide a cushion to absorb any unforseen losses and the expenses of starting in the insurance business, thus preventing the invasion of policyholder reserves. Since capital is a sort of "last ditch" fund which cannot be drawn upon without forcing a company into insolvency, hence receivership, its primary purpose is, perhaps, to permit an orderly receivership and liquidation of an insurer that does not succeed, with minimal or no loss to policyholders and other claimants.

If an insurer is permitted to continue operation as long as it has even one dollar of surplus, as appears to be true under most state insurance laws, the capital must be sufficient to cover (1) losses

---

[5] Ariz. Rev. Stat. secs. 20–210 and 211 (Supp. 1967).

[6] Mich. Comp. Laws Ann. sec. 410.410 (1967).

[7] Special Message on Insurance to the General Assembly by Governor Raymond P. Shafer, June 13, 1967 (mimeographed press release).

sustained prior to the date as of which an insolvent financial statement is filed but concealed from the insurance department and, perhaps, even from management; (2) losses and expenses of operation during the two or three months during which the financial data are assembled and filed and the insurance department investigates, confirms the insolvency, and takes action to place the company in receivership; (3) losses due to forced liquidation of assets; and (4) the expenses of a receivership. Since many insolvencies, perhaps most, involve inefficient or dishonest management, capital should also be sufficient to allow for a substantial margin to cover the disappearance of some of the assets claimed in a company's balance sheet between the time difficulties begin to be apparent and the time the insurance commissioner, armed with an appropriate court order, takes possession of the assets.

Since the initial capital required by law applies to all insurers licensed to do business in the state, regardless of the length of time since incorporation, the volume of business written, and the competence and integrity of management, some compromise is necessary. It is obviously impractical to set the minimum initial capital required of a new insurer at a level which would be adequate for a giant company with hundreds of thousands of policyholders; it must be assumed that capital and surplus will grow as a company grows and that the contingency reserve needed to protect against claim fluctuations and asset depreciation will be accumulated gradually, out of earnings. The legal minimum capital should rather be set at a level which will provide for the new company which has not yet "turned the corner" and started to earn a profit from its insurance operations. The minimum capital should provide for the unsuccessful company, one which never "got off the ground" or which early in its history suffered reverses which made it impossible for it to build a sound, substantial operation and led, in time, to insolvency.

One measure of the amount needed as minimum initial capital can be obtained by comparing the assets and liabilities of insurers which have become insolvent, preferably by studying only companies becoming insolvent within 10 years of incorporation. An adequate initial capital would be an amount which would cover the excess of liabilities over assets of such companies, hence would prevent loss to policyholders.

Unfortunately, adequate data are not readily available. The Senate Antitrust and Monopoly Subcommittee gathered a great deal of information,[8] but for most of the 58 defunct companies studied, the data are incomplete and the relevant information is not available. A few examples may, however, provide some guidelines.

When the Career Insurance Company of Texas went into receivership in July, 1964, after having written substandard automobile insurance for less than one year, it had 27,200 policyholders, liabilities of $922,000, and assets of $300,000. Its required minimum capital under Texas law was $200,000.

Equity General Insurance Company of Florida, placed in receivership in June, 1961, operated in 49 states. It had liabilities of $1,116,605 and assets of $800,000.

The Banner Mutual Insurance Company of Illinois, placed in receivership June, 1965, had claims of more than $2,000,000 and assets of $500,321.

The International Automobile Insurance Exchange of Indiana, placed in receivership in March, 1964, had 8,300 claims totaling $6,265,731 and assets of $1,700,000.

The Exchange Casualty and Surety Company of Michigan, placed in receivership in March, 1962, had 12,400 claims approved by the court totaling $3,022,131 and assets of $398,633.

The Commonwealth Mutual and the Empire Mutual, both of Pennsylvania, both placed in receivership in 1964, had $1,500,000 and $2,520,000 of liabilities respectively, and assets of $1,107 and $4,070. The Delaware Mutual of Pennsylvania was not in much better shape, with assets of $40,238 to cover claims of $1,140,000.

The Security General Insurance Company of South Dakota was found by the South Dakota insurance department to have a capital impairment of $137,000 as of December 31, 1961. By November 30, 1963, when the insurance department commenced conservatorship proceedings, the impairment had grown to $1,158,267. The cost of the receivership undoubtedly increased the loss to policyholders considerably. South Dakota requires initial capital of $200,000.

Lake States Casualty, an Illinois reciprocal insurer, was organized on September 30, 1960, and placed in receivership in September,

---

[8] *The Insurance Industry, Hearings before the Subcommittee on Antitrust* and *Monopoly of the Senate Committee on the Judiciary* (U.S. Senate, 89th Cong., 1st Sess., 1965), pt. 12, p. 6850, exhibits 1–3. The following information on insolvencies was gleaned from this source, as well as pp. 7172–75, 7190, 7354, and *passim*.

1965, with assets of $361,329 and liabilities of $1,061,418. The minimum paid-in surplus required of reciprocals by Illinois law was $133,333.

It should be apparent from these examples that a minimum capital of less than $1,000,000 may prove to be inadequate as a cushion to protect policyholders and claimants. An insurance company writing a high-volume and easily entered branch of insurance, such as automobile insurance, can readily acquire 20,000 policyholders and a premium volume of $4,000,000 in a year or two. If the premium turns out to be 15 percent inadequate, a not unheard of circumstance, a capital of $600,000 would be needed to absorb the loss. Excessive expenses, unwise investments, and the cost of a receivership can easily bring the total deficiency to $1,000,000 or more.

Companies writing branches of insurance other than automobile also need paid-in capital. A tornado which swept through southwestern Michigan in April, 1965, caused more than $2½ million in losses in 15 minutes and so severely reduced the financial capacity of a small mutual fire insurance company, despite prudent underwriting, a surplus equal to 70 percent of premiums, and what had appeared to be adequate reinsurance, as to force it to merge. Had the tornado lasted a few minutes longer, the company might have sustained irreparable financial damage and been unable to meet its claims.

Most states vary the required amount of initial capital and surplus according to the line or lines of business an insurer plans to write. In some states this variation, though of doubtful validity, is at least simple. Illinois, for example, enumerates three classes of insurance: class 1, life, accident and health; class 2, casualty, fidelity and surety; and class 3, fire and marine.[9] Class 1 has two subdivisions, class 2 has eleven, and class 3 eight. To write any one of the 11 kinds of insurance included in class 2, an insurer needs a minimum capital (initial surplus for a mutual or reciprocal insurer) of $400,000 and to write more than one type of casualty insurance, $600,000. To write one or more of the eight kinds of fire and marine insurance encompassed by class 3 requires a minimum capital of $400,000, while a multiple line operation, writing any or

---

[9] Ill. Ann. Stat. ch. 73, sec. 616 (Smith-Hurd, 1965).

all of both class 2 and class 3, casualty and fire insurance, requires $1,000,000 initial capital and surplus.[10]

By contrast with the simple Illinois statute, New York has requirements that are not only ineffectual but confusing as well. New York enumerates 22 different kinds of insurance[11] and specifies various minimum capital requirements depending upon the kind or kinds of insurance a company wishes to write. A stock company may write glass insurance, or boiler and machinery, or elevator, or animal or property damage liability insurance, with a paid-in capital of $100,000. It needs $200,000 to write theft insurance, $300,000 for bodily injury liability insurance, $300,000 for workmens' compensation, and $500,000 to write fidelity or surety bonds. An insurer wishing to write more than one kind of casualty insurance (e.g., N of the above types) must have a minimum capital equal to the sum of the required capital for each of the N branches of insurance, less $50,000 times N — 1. A company wishing to write only fire (including water damage and other miscellaneous property insurance) or only marine insurance must have $250,000 capital, but a company wishing to write both fire and marine insurance needs $500,000. A company wanting to write multiple line insurance (comprising both fire and casualty coverages) must have "a minimum capital of $500,000 and a surplus to policyholders equal in the aggregate to the minimum capital and minimum surplus required on organization by this section and by section 341 and as otherwise required by this section for all the kinds of insurance business which it is to be licensed to do and shall maintain a surplus to policyholders equal in amount to such minimum capital prescribed by such sections."[12] The actuarial foundation for this complex series of requirements is, presumably, lost in antiquity.

A statute such as New York's, a state with a well-deserved reputation for strict insurance laws and conscientious and rigorous insurance supervision, raises some fundamental questions. Is an insurer writing only boiler and machinery insurance, a type of coverage which includes insurance against loss of or damage to any

---

[10] *Ibid.*, secs. 625, 655, and 678.
[11] N.Y. Ins. Law sec. 46 (McKinney 1966).
[12] *Ibid.*, sec. 311.

property of the insured resulting from the explosion of a boiler, engine, turbine or generator, in need of less initial capital and surplus than a company writing only inland marine insurance, which might be insuring packages sent by parcel post, golf clubs, musical instruments and stamp collections, and other personal property, under an all-risk form of coverage? Is a company writing glass and elevator and boiler and property damage liability insurance in need of more capital than an insurer writing only one of these types of insurance, perhaps in greater volume than the first company's total for all branches? Is it not more likely that an insurer writing a variety of coverages, with its exposures widely diversfied both geographically and by type, is inherently safer than one which writes only fire and windstorm insurance on property clustered in one county or one city? It is less likely that a company writing many types of insurance will suffer unfavorable experience in all of them at once than that a company specializing in one branch will because of conditions peculiar to that branch have to call upon its capital and surplus to make up its underwriting losses.

Paid-In Surplus

In addition to the required initial capital, most states also require a stock insurer to have an initial paid-in surplus, often expressed as "50% of the amount of its paid-in capital"[13] or "50% of its required minimum capital."[14] The contrast between the statutes of New York and Illinois is interesting. Though it will permit an insurer with a paid-in capital of $500,000 and a paid-in surplus of $250,000 to write fire and marine insurance, New York insists that an insurer with $1,000,000 capital have an initial surplus of $500,000. Illinois, by contrast, appears to permit higher-than-minimum capitalization without requiring an increase in paid-in surplus.

Some states tend to confuse the function of capital and paid-in surplus. Capital is intended to constitute a cushion of protection for policyholders, not to be drawn upon except in case of insolvency. An insurer whose capital is impaired may not continue to operate; either more capital must be contributed or the company is placed in

---

[13] *Ibid.*, sec. 311(1).
[14] Ill. Ann. Stat. ch. 73, sec. 625(2) (Smith-Hurd Supp. 1967).

receivership. Paid-in surplus, however, is intended as an initial working fund to pay expenses until the company obtains a sufficient volume of business to meet its overhead and to cover losses due to fluctuations in claim experience. Surplus may in the normal course of business drop well below its initial level without causing any real concern to the insurance commissioner.

Though many state statutes recognize this, some do not. Maryland, for example says: "For authority to continue in the insurance business, in addition to the minimum capital stock required by section 48, every insurer commencing business in this state on or after July 1, 1966 must maintain surplus assets or funds in an amount of not less than one hundred percent of such minimum capital stock."[15] Such a statute presumably requires the insurance commissioner to place in receivership any insurer whose surplus drops below its statutory minimum capital. New York requires for life insurers that "every such corporation organized prior to April 4, 1962 shall at all times maintain a minimum capital of at least $300,000 and a surplus at least equal to 50% of such capital."[16] Colorado insists that "no insurance company . . . shall be permitted to do any business in this state . . . unless . . . it is possessed of an actual paid-up cash capital or guaranty fund and an accumulated surplus not less than the following."[17] It would seem more sensible to establish an adequate required capital and an initial paid-in surplus of sufficient size to cover expenses and provide a contingency reserve during the "growing up" phase of an insurer's life span, but to permit an insurer to continue to operate so long as its capital is intact and it has enough surplus to see it through the next calendar year.

Some states permit the formation of mutual insurers or reciprocal exchanges with lower initial capital requirements than stock companies. Illinois, for example, requires a multiple line stock property insurance company to have $1,000,000 initial capital and a paid-in surplus of $500,000.[18] However a multiple line mutual property insurance carrier needs only a paid-in surplus of $1,000,000. Furthermore, while the stock insurer must keep its initial capital intact

---

[15] Md. Ann. Code art. 48A, sec. 49 (1968).

[16] N.Y. Ins. Law sec. 191 (McKinney 1966).

[17] Col. Rev. Stat. Ann. sec. 72–1–36 (1963).

[18] Ill. Ann. Stat. ch. 73, sec. 625 (Smith-Hurd Supp. 1967).

(though it may, of course, use its surplus in the conduct of its business), a mutual insurer must only maintain a minimum surplus equal to two thirds of the original paid-in surplus required.[19] Reciprocal exchanges, too, are often permitted to operate with less surplus than a stock or mutual insurer writing the same type of insurance.[20]

Although there seems to be no logical reason why a mutual or reciprocal insurer should be permitted to issue nonassessable property insurance policies unless it is financially as strong as a stock company writing the same kind of insurance, practical considerations have often dictated this result. Requiring equivalent financial strength for stock and mutual insurers makes it almost impossible to start a mutual company. Few individuals are willing to contribute paid-in surplus to start a mutual insurer, thereby assuming the risk of loss if the insurance operation goes badly, with no corresponding hope of profit if it succeeds.

To compensate for the weaker financial requirements for mutual and reciprocal insurers, statutes often stipulate that such companies have a certain minimum number of initial subscribers. For example, the *Michigan Insurance Code* requires[21] that a domestic mutual property or casualty insurer have at least 20 members and insure not less than 200 separate risks (20 employers with at least 5,000 employees for workmen's compensation insurance) before it can obtain a certificate of authority to commence an insurance business. It is difficult to see how this requirement contributes very much to the insurer's solvency.

A mutual or reciprocal insurer which does not have a surplus equivalent to that required of stock companies writing the same types of insurance may, in most states, issue only assessable policies. Thus the *Illinois Insurance Code* requires[22] a reciprocal exchange to issue contracts providing for a "cash deposit and a contingent several liability of the subscriber in an amount not less than one nor more than ten times the amount of the cash deposit stated in the contract." It states however that "if a reciprocal shall have a surplus equal to the minimum capital and surplus required in Section 13 for

---

[19] *Ibid.*, sec. 655(2).

[20] Dennis F. Reinmuth, *The Regulation of Reciprocal Insurance Exchanges* (Homewood, Ill.: Richard D. Irwin, Inc., 1967), pp. 102–16.

[21] Mich. Comp. Laws Ann. sec. 500.5810 (1967).

[22] Ill. Ann. Stat. ch. 73, sec. 687 (Smith-Hurd Supp. 1967).

a stock company transacting the same kind or kinds of business, such reciprocal may issue policies without contingent liability."[23]

Although the notion that a group of individuals should have the right to get together and organize a mutual or reciprocal insurer to protect each other against fires, automobile accidents, or other insurable perils appeals to our sense of fairness and our predilection for cooperative, self-help enterprises, it seems doubtful whether this has really been the motivation behind the formation of most assessable mutuals or reciprocals. In recent years, at least, it seems more likely that this type of organization has been used as a device to avoid the stiffer legal requirements for the organization of stock insurers and nonassessable mutuals. By starting a mutual or reciprocal, hence taking advantage of a sort of statutory loophole, an entrepeneur interested in starting an insurance company can avoid investing his own capital in the enterprise.

The question may well be asked: "How many policyholders of assessable companies really understand what their obligation is, in case of insolvency, and have carefully assessed the probability that they will be called upon for an additional premium?" Despite the statutory requirement that assessable insurance contracts state that fact in prominent print, most policyholders do not read their policies. Many holders of assessable policies are probably not even aware of their contingent liability. In any case, the difficulty of collecting assessments, particularly in case of insolvency, makes them of questionable value as protection against the inability of an insurer to meet its obligations.

It is impossible, without considerable research, to establish the amount of minimum capital that ought to be required of new insurers. Ideally, we would like to specify an amount that will be adequate to perform the function capital is intended to accomplish, yet is not so large as to severely inhibit the formation of new insurers. It is clear, however, that the amount of minimum capital specified by the insurance laws of most states is grossly inadequate as a safeguard for policyholders. It is also apparent that a differentiation of the required amount of initial capital by line of business contributes little or nothing to solvency. Mutual insurers and reciprocal exchanges should not, unless they write assessable policies and

---

[23] A similar provision applicable to mutual insurers, though not providing for several liability, is found in *Ibid.*, sec. 667.

their policyholders fully understand the risk of assessment, be permitted to operate with less surplus than the capital and paid-in surplus required of stock companies. The distinction between paid-in surplus, intended as a working fund during the period before an insurer begins to earn a profit, and capital, intended as a guaranty fund to protect policyholders against loss due to insolvency, should be made clearer than it is in some state statutes.

Standards of Solvency—the Annual Statement

One of the state insurance commissioner's most useful tools for testing company solvency is the annual statement filed by each insurer. The statement, on a form common to all the states and adopted in 1950, shows an insurer's assets and liabilities, underwriting and investment income, and changes in capital and surplus; it also includes many detailed exhibits and schedules which support the final accounting figures. The statement showing an insurer's financial condition for a given calendar year must be filed by March 1 of the following year; an addendum, the Insurance Expense Exhibit, showing premiums, claims, and various types of expenses for each line of insurance, must be filed by April 1.

Besides the annual statement, many states require quarterly or semiannual statements from new companies and companies in which financial problems are believed to exist. These statements are considerably more abbreviated than the annual statement but provide the basic asset, liability, income, and expense data needed to determine whether an insurer is solvent. In some isolated instances, companies are required to furnish monthly financial statements to the insurance commissioner. Thus an alert insurance commissioner can keep close track of the financial status of his insurers if he deems it necessary.

If an insurance company doing business in several states had to furnish accounting data in a different form to each state, the work would be considerable. Conducting an interstate insurance business without uniformity of accounting practices and uniform financial statements would be well-nigh impossible. That a considerable degree of uniformity does exist is due to the National Association of Insurance Commissioners and its Committee on Blanks, which is charged with the duty of establishing rules and forms for reporting accounting data and financial information.

Although the National Association of Insurance Commissioners is a voluntary body with no statutory authority or coercive power and each insurance commissioner is free to ignore the Association's recommendations if he wishes, a considerable degree of uniformity exists in many areas. The work of the Blanks Committee, which has produced a standard form of annual statement acceptable to every state, is a notable example of uniformity achieved by voluntary agreement.

Some states stipulate by law that the annual statement filed with the insurance commissioner shall be the form promulgated by the NAIC Blanks Committee.[24] Others leave complete discretion in the hands of the insurance commissioner.[25] However the statute is worded, state insurance commissioners have universally adopted the NAIC form of annual statement blank, though certain states require certain supplementary information in addition to the voluminous data contained in the standard blank.[26] The advantage of uniformity in insurance accounting procedures is obvious.

The Periodic Examination

Perhaps the most potent weapon of a state insurance department in preserving the solvency of the companies under its jurisdiction is the periodic examination. Most states examine companies every three years, but the insurance commissioner generally has the right to examine companies whenever he deems necessary; some commissioners have recently inaugurated an annual examination of new companies and those with recent financial difficulties or major management changes.[27] Michigan and certain other insurance departments have followed a similar policy by administrative ruling.

---

[24] E.g., Ill. Ann. Stat. ch. 73, sec. 747(1) (Smith-Hurd 1965): ". . . such statements, which shall conform substantially to the form of statement adopted by the National Association of Insurance Commissioners. . . ."

[25] E.g., N.Y. Ins. Law sec. 26(1) (McKinney 1966): "[the] statement shall be in such form and shall contain such matters as the superintendent shall prescribe."

[26] Thomas F. Tarbell, "The Combined Fire and Casualty Annual Statement Blank," *Proceedings of Casualty Actuarial Society,* Vol. 37, No. 67 (1950), pp. 74–81; Vol. 38, No. 69 (1951), pp. 113–40.

[27] The 1967 legislative program of the Pennsylvania insurance commissioner calls for annual examination of a new insurance company during the first five years of its life.

While it is true that many insurers need to be examined more frequently than once every three years, it is also true that some companies need to be examined less frequently. Recognizing this, the New York insurance law was amended in 1966 to provide that only domestic casualty, surety, fraternal, and cooperative insurers must be examined every three years; domestic life insurance companies and other domestic insurers need be examined only once every five years.[28] The superintendent of insurance is, of course, at liberty to examine any insurer more frequently. "The superintendent may make any examination into the affairs of any insurance corporation or other insurer doing any insurance business in this state . . . as often as he deems it expedient for the protection of the interests of the people of this state."[29]

The 1967 Pennsylvania legislative program, too, proposes "changing the mandatory examination of all companies from once every three years to once every five years" so that "the strength of the Department can be focused on auditing as often as the Commissioner feels necessary those companies clearly in danger of failing."[30]

The primary purpose of an examination is to verify the financial condition of an insurance company as shown in its annual statement. In the course of a periodic examination, every item shown in the company's financial statement for the latest calendar year is checked in detail, and the financial statements for the two previous years are spot-checked. The actual documents evidencing the ownership of stocks, bonds, mortgages, and other assets are inspected and counted. Accounting checks are made from the original vouchers, through the journal and ledger, to the financial statement. The legality and propriety of the company's disbursements are verified, and any violations of law or sound insurance practice are called to the attention of company officers and the insurance commissioner. A careful periodic examination ensures that the surplus shown in the company's annual statement (or a modified surplus, as changed by the examiners) really exists.

In the course of the examination, the insurer's claim reserves and

---

[28] N.Y. Ins. Law sec. 28 (McKinney 1966).

[29] *Ibid.*

[30] Special Message on Insurance to the General Assembly by Governor Raymond P. Shafer of Pennsylvania, June 13, 1967 (mimeographed press release).

unearned premium reserve are carefully checked, and a search is made to find any unrecognized liabilities that may have been omitted from the balance sheet. Reinsurance treaties are reviewed, and a determination is made whether the company's own insurance program, to protect its own property against fire, theft, liability claims, etc., is adequate.

The examiner force is the backbone of a state insurance department. Most of the better insurance departments have a carefully selected and well-trained staff of examiners, protected in their jobs by civil service status and given the opportunity to advance in responsibility and salary as they learn and qualify by experience and, sometimes, by passing promotion examinations. Some of the larger insurance departments also permit examiners to specialize either in examining life insurance companies or property insurance companies, and sometimes in specific phases of an examination. Some states require an examiner trainee to have a college degree in accounting, economics, or business administration, and almost all insurance departments with a well-qualified civil service examiner crew look to the examiners to fill many of the higher administrative posts in the department.

Despite the importance to a state insurance department of a capable and well-trained staff of examiners, only 24 states have 10 or more examiners and 9 states have no examiners at all.[31] A comparison of the number of examiners with the number of companies doing business in a state[32] leads one to question how the examiners can manage to examine every insurance company every three years (or five years in some states). The answer is to be found in the Zone system of examination.

If each insurance department were to conduct a separate examination of a company which operates in 50 states, this would obviously be uneconomic duplication, as well as disrupting to the operations of the insurer. To avoid this, the National Association of Insurance Commissioners has devised the Zone system of examinations. The United States is divided into six zones, each containing eight or nine states. When an insurance company is due to be examined, the home state commissioner calls the examination and

---

[31] Preliminary Report, State Insurance Department Statistical Data, year ending December 31, 1964, compiled by the Insurance Industry Committee of Ohio.

[32] 385 in Alaska; 1,772 in Texas.

invites participation from the other zones in which the company does business. Thus a company domiciled in zone 4 comprising eight midwestern states and operating countrywide would be examined by the insurance department of its state of incorporation plus one representative from each of the other five zones in which it does business.

The Zone system has many advantages but also some defects. It makes it possible for all states to participate, some indirectly, in the examination of an insurer which operates countrywide, while avoiding duplication of effort and multiple scrutiny of the same figures. The Zone examiner represents not only his own state but also all other states in his Zone and is charged with the responsibility of reporting to his Zone chairman and to all states in the zone as to the financial condition of the company he is examining.

The Zone system, however, is only as good as the caliber of the examiners who actually do the work. Some states send capable examiners on out-of-state zone examinations, but others do not. Many states prefer to keep their best examiners at home to examine their domestic companies; New York, whose 400 examiners constitute one third of the total pool of trained insurance examiners in the United States, refused until recently to participate in Zone examinations at all. Some states, lacking their own civil service examiner staffs, use outside accounting firms which supply men of varying abilities. Some states have, on occasion, used an examining assignment in New York, which may last a year or more, as a sinecure for an examiner whose training and ability were dubious.

A state which does not participate in a Zone examination or which sends its weaker men on out-of-state assignments is, in effect, depending on evaluation by the state of incorporation of the financial soundness of an insurer and the accuracy of its financial statement. The logical end result of this process is to make each state responsible for its own domestic companies, resulting, perhaps, in a different standard of solvency depending on the state in which an insurer is incorporated.

The cost of an insurance examination is paid by the company being examined. A few states permit their examiners to bill the company directly for their per diem salary and expense allowance, but most states pay their examiners directly and bill the companies for the time the examiners spend there. The National Association of Insurance Commissioners Committee on Examinations adopted in

1964 a recommendation "that an Examination Revolving Fund be established by each Insurance Department from which to pay the expenses and salaries of Insurance Company Examiners, whose examiners are not on the state payroll, and that examiners not be authorized to draw expenses and salary, or per diem, direct from the company being examined."[33]

Despite some defects, it can fairly be said that the power of examination is on the whole being properly used as a device to ascertain the true financial condition of insurance companies and to detect financial problems before they result in insolvency. Few incipient insolvencies have gone undetected because an examination failed to discover information that should have been found. Some insolvencies have gone undiscovered because an examination was not made in time. In general, however, the examination system cannot be blamed for very many of the insolvencies that have occurred, and it is probable that some insolvencies that would otherwise have happened have been prevented by timely examinations which uncovered some fundamental problems while there was still time to correct them.

Insurance Accounting

Insurance accounting methods differ in many respects from commercial accounting procedures. In part this is due to inherent differences between insurance and other businesses and in part to historical development.

Since an insurance policy is a long-term, aleatory contract, the eventual disbursements of an insurer are not known with any degree of certainty at the end of a calendar year. Thus an insurer collects premiums during the year for policies whose effective protection extends beyond the end of the year. Certain claims incurred during the year are not reported at year-end, and the insurer will not even find out about them until the following year. Even claims which occurred during the year are often pending at year-end, and their true value can only be estimated.

Because of the need to estimate rather than record exactly so many of the liabilities of an insurer, it is difficult to make book

---

[33] *Proceedings of National Association of Insurance Commissioners,* Vol. 1 (1965), p. 91.

entries for them, and the practice has grown up of not putting most liabilities "on the books." Thus the major reserve liabilities of a property insurer are not found on its ledger, do not arise from a journal entry and a subsequent posting procedure, but instead are calculated by an inventory method at year-end.

As a consequence, the ledger has lost its importance; and many accrual items, such as accounts receivable and payable, interest due and accrued, premiums due but not yet collected, etc., are not posted to the ledger. The result is that insurance accounting, instead of following the accrual accounting methods which are standard in most other businesses, is done by a modified or incomplete double-entry bookkeeping system, and the traditional books of account, the journal and ledger, do not truly reflect the position of the company.

To determine an insurer's financial status requires a careful scrutiny of its annual statement, since the ledger trial balance omits many important items and understates many others. The annual statement, not the general ledger, is the principal book of account and the vehicle for maintaining continuity from year to year. This is apparent from the insurance company practice of starting a new ledger each year in contrast to the commercial accounting procedure (at least before the advent of electronic computers) of carrying forward the general ledger, suitably ruled and balanced, from year to year.

Asset Valuation

From an accounting point of view, the surplus of a property insurance company is equal to the total of its assets minus the total of its liabilities; thus the method of determining the value of various kinds of assets is extremely important. Asset valuation is as crucial to solvency as, though considerably less complicated than, the valuation of liabilities.

The assets of a property insurer comprise bonds, stocks, agents' balances, and to a lesser extent, mortgages and real estate. In 1965, the 805 stock fire and casualty companies included in Best's Fire and Casualty Aggregates and Averages held 43.1 percent of their assets in bonds, 39.4 percent in common stocks, 2.5 percent in preferred stocks, 6.9 percent in agents' balances (uncollected premiums), and 1.4 percent in mortgages and real estate, largely in home office and branch office buildings. The 344 mutual companies included in Best's held 64.9 percent of their assets in bonds, 18.4 percent in common stock, 3.1 percent in preferred stock, 4.5 percent in agents' balances, and 3.2 percent in real estate and mortgages.

In a property insurance company, unlike a life insurance company, fluctuations in asset values are carried directly to surplus. If the stock market rises, thus increasing the market value of a property insurer's common stock portfolio, these paper profits go directly into the balance sheet and increase the stockholder's equity. The Underwriting and Investment Exhibit of the property insurance annual statement includes in net income only "realized" capital gains and losses. Realized capital gains are usually defined as the excess of profits over losses on the sale or maturity of assets. Unrealized gains and losses, so-called "paper profits," are charged or credited directly to surplus. Thus it is possible for a property insurer to consistently lose money on its insurance operations yet build up its surplus by a judicious investment policy. If the stock market continues to rise, the solvency of most property insurers is assured, despite inadequate rate levels and even, in some cases, mediocre management. However, the stock market can go down as well as up, and one function of adequate capital and surplus is to ensure solvency even in the event of a drop in the stock market.

The practice of permitting unrealized capital gains to flow directly to surplus is suspect from another standpoint. Although realized capital gains are subject to a 25 percent federal income tax, no tax liability is required by NAIC accounting rules to cover the potential tax on unrealized gains. This represents a surprising departure from the conservatism underlying most NAIC accounting rules.

As stated above, the average stock property insurance company holds nearly 40 percent of its assets in common stocks. Its surplus constitutes 44 percent of assets.[34] Thus a 40 percent decline in stock prices—a decline of this magnitude has occurred eight times in the 20th century—[35] could wipe out 16 percent of an insurer's assets (if it held the average portfolio) and one third of its surplus. Some insurers have more than 40 percent of their assets in common stock and less than a 44 percent surplus to assets ratio; they could be hurt

---

[34] *Best's Aggregates and Averages* (1966).

[35] Harold G. Fraine, *Valuation of Securities Holdings of Life Insurance Companies* (Homewood, Ill.: Richard D. Irwin, Inc., 1962), p. 101.

much worse; the 1962 stock market recession reduced some insurers' invested assets by 20 percent. As we will see later, this could have a considerable effect on an insurer's underwriting capacity. McDiarmid states: "I suggest that an institutional owner of common stocks should probably feel rather uneasy unless it is able to absorb a decline in the market value of its holding, measured from year end to year end, of 20 per cent. It should proceed, therefore, to build up a reserve of this size not only from realized capital gains and market appreciation but also by some contribution from earnings. I also suggest that a company with an established reserve equal to 30 per cent or more of the market value of its stock holdings would probably feel able to weather any likely storm without any substantial drain on its surplus."[36]

Bonds and stocks held by insurance companies must be valued in a company's annual statement according to rules established by the Committee on Valuation of Securities of the National Association of Insurance Commissioners. High-quality bonds are carried at amortized values; bonds of lower quality and preferred and common stocks are carried at market values. The determination of which bonds are eligible for amortization is governed by rules promulgated by the NAIC Valuation of Securities Committee; each year a listing is published of all securities held by insurance companies stating which bonds are amortizable and giving the value, usually the December 31 market value, at which nonamortizable bonds and all preferred and common stocks must be shown in the annual statement.

For life insurance companies, the NAIC Committee on Valuation of Securities performs one additional task—it classifies stocks and bonds into various categories for establishing the Mandatory Securities Valuation Reserve. This reserve, carried as a liability in the balance sheet of life insurers and fraternal societies, is intended to smooth out fluctuations in asset values and to provide an additional solvency margin against capital losses on securities. It is not required for property insurance companies.

The Mandatory Securities Valuation Reserve is built up by allocating to the reserve each year a percentage of the statement value of each category of assets: 0.1 percent of high-quality bonds; 0.5

---

[36] Fergus J. McDiarmid, "Valuation of Life Insurance Company Investments," *Transactions of Society of Actuaries,* Vol. 16, No. 390 (1964), p. 405.

percent of medium-quality bonds; 0.25 percent of most preferred stocks; 1 percent of common stocks, low-quality bonds and low-quality preferred stocks. Realized and unrealized capital gains are also credited to the Mandatory Securities Valuation Reserve, and capital losses are charged against it. The reserve thus acts as a buffer for changes in asset values, avoiding fluctuations in surplus which would otherwise occur because of capital gains and losses. The reserve does not grow indefinitely, however; a maximum reserve buildup is stipulated. The maximum reserve is 20 times the annual allocation for bonds and preferred stocks and 33⅓ times the annual reserve allocation for common stocks. Thus the maximum reserve is 2 percent for high-quality bonds, 5 percent for high-quality preferred stocks, 10 percent for medium-quality bonds, 20 percent for lower quality bonds and preferred stocks, and 33⅓ percent of the statement value for common stocks.

Is a Mandatory Security Valuation Reserve Needed for Property Insurers?

In his excellent study of asset valuation for life insurance companies, Fraine states: "To promote real solvency, a system should provide for the retention in all years of a portion of the revenues in order to build up real rather than 'paper' assets sufficiently, so that when the value of some of the assets shrinks, there will still remain an adequate coverage of liabilities by the total value of all assets."[37] The Mandatory Securities Valuation Reserve is intended to achieve this for life insurance companies. We may well ask the question: Why isn't such a requirement equally appropriate for property insurers?

This question was, of course, asked by the National Association of Insurance Commissioners and was, in April, 1964, answered in the negative. The Laws and Legislation Committee of the NAIC resolved that "the Subcommittee on Valuation of Securities, NAIC, having heretofore affirmed the principle of extending the mandatory securities valuation reserve to property and casualty insurance companies, has concluded that this requirement be not effectuated at this time, and recommends that a study be made by the Laws and

---

[37] Harold G. Fraine, *Valuation of Securities Holdings of Life Insurance Companies* (Homewood, Ill.: Richard D. Irwin, Inc., 1962), p. 125.

Legislation Committee of the NAIC with the objective of drafting model legislation to relate holdings of equity investment to the surplus of the insurance company."[38]

The Subcommittee to Draft Model Legislation to Relate Holdings of Equity Investments to the Surplus of the Insurance Company was appointed and began its deliberations in 1964. The subcommittee considered various methods of asset valuation which would eliminate or dampen surplus fluctuations arising from changes in stock market levels, and also considered whether it was possible to establish a maximum amount of common stock, perhaps in relation to a company's capital and surplus, which might be held by a property insurer. The committee was unable to agree on a limitation on the proportion of an insurer's assets which may be invested in common stocks, hence it broadened its sphere of inquiry to encompass not only asset fluctuation but also the relationship between premium writings and surplus. In December, 1966, the subcommittee proposed a rule to govern these matters.[39] The subcommittee stated that it is desirable for nonlife insurers to maintain the sum of investments in common stock and net written premiums (net of reinsurance) at an amount less than three times the insurer's capital and surplus. The subcommittee also proposed that if the sum of common stock investments and net written premiums exceeds four times capital and surplus, "the continued operation of the insurer under such conditions shall be deemed hazardous to the public and to the policyholders." The "three times" and "four times" standards were derived empirically, based on a study of the amount of surplus held by well managed companies.

At the June, 1967, meeting of the National Association of Insurance Commissioners, considerable opposition was expressed by insurance company trade associations to the subcommittee's proposal. The subcommittee, now comprising different members from those appointed in 1964, voted that "the regulatory standard not be promulgated and that this Subcommittee be discharged."[40] As a result, no action has been taken on this important regulatory prob-

---

[38] *Proceedings of National Association of Insurance Commissioners,* Vol. 2 (1964), p. 514.

[39] *Proceedings of National Association of Insurance Commissioners,* Vol. 1 (1967), p. 111.

[40] *Proceedings of National Association of Insurance Commissioners,* Vol. 2 (1967), p. 373.

lem, and the NAIC continues to ignore the need for adequate solvency standards.

The Unearned Premium Reserve

The two principal liabilities of a property insurer are the unearned premium reserve and the claims reserve. The former, comprising some 25 percent of the average insurer's total assets, represents the unearned premium on unexpired policies, while the latter comprises the reserve for claims which have occurred but have not yet been paid, as well as the claim expenses which must be incurred to settle these claims.

The unearned premium reserve on an individual policy may be viewed in two ways, retrospectively and prospectively. Retrospectively, the unearned premium reserve is the balance of the premium paid by the insured after deducting his share of claims and expenses incurred since the policy was written. Prospectively, the unearned premium reserve may be viewed as the amount needed to discharge all future liabilities on the policy, expenses as well as claims, until the policy expires. The prospective reserve may also be viewed as the amount which would have to be returned to the insured if the policy is cancelled, or the amount which would have to be paid to another insurer if the business were to be reinsured and the new insurer assumed all future liabilities under the policy. These various ways of viewing the unearned premium reserve lead to different calculated results.

Since an insurance premium actually comprises two parts, a claim portion and an expense portion, a case could be made for recognizing the incidence of both claims and expenses over the policy term when calculating the unearned premium reserve. If the expense loading in the rate is 35 percent, for example, perhaps 65 percent of the premium, the part available to pay claims should be considered earned uniformly over the policy term, while recognizing that most of the 35 percent expense loading, the portion used to pay the agent's commission, premium tax, and underwriting and issue expenses, is spent at the time the policy is written. Commercial accounting practice, for businesses other than insurance, does this by establishing prepaid expenses as an asset on the balance sheet.

In line with the principle of conservatism that governs insurance accounting, however, the practice universally used in the United

States is to establish the unearned premium reserve on a gross basis. It is assumed that the full gross premium paid by the insured is earned uniformly over the policy term. This method has the advantage that the unearned premium reserve is sufficient, at any point of time, to cancel all policies and to return the unearned premium for the balance of the policy term to the insured. Unless the quality of the business is exceptionally poor or the rate level is inadequate, the unearned premium reserve would also be ample to reinsure the company's entire portfolio of insurance. Thus the gross unearned premium reserve is sufficient for solvency on a liquidating basis.

On a "going concern" basis, the unearned premium reserve is excessive, since it does not recognize that the expense portion of the premium has already been spent and has been reflected in the insurer's accounts. Most investment analysts and insurance company managements, therefore, consider that a property-liability insurer has an "equity" in the unearned premium reserve of some 25 percent to 30 percent, reflecting prepaid expenses. When calculating the net worth shown in their annual reports to stockholders, some companies add this equity in the unearned premium reserve to the capital and surplus shown in their annual statements. From a regulatory point of view, the equity in the unearned premium reserve provides an additional solvency margin and a check on unwise or excessive growth. I would not advocate a change in insurance accounting procedures to release the equity in the unearned premium reserve to surplus until proper solvency standards have been established, by law or regulation, governing the amount of surplus an insurer must possess relative to its common stock holdings, its rate level, and the size and nature of its insurance portfolio.

Claim Reserves

The largest liability of a company which writes mostly casualty insurance and the second largest of a company which writes mostly fire insurance is the claim reserve. This reserve is also the most difficult of a company's liabilities to evaluate and the one most likely to be understated if an insurer is in financial difficulties. The claim reserve consists of three parts: a reserve for claims which have been reported but are still pending, a reserve for claims incurred before the statement date but not yet reported to the company, and a claim expense reserve.

Various methods are used by property insurers to determine the amount of their claims reserves. The reserve for reported claims and the reserve for claims incurred but not reported (the latter is often called the IBNR or ICNR reserve) may be established on a case estimate, statistical, or formula basis. The case estimate approach, formerly the most common, and still used for many types of insurance, sets a reserve on each reported claim individually, based on the judgment of the claim department as to the amount for which the claim will eventually be settled. The statistical method, favored by most insurers for lines like property damage liability, automobile collision, and other types of insurance in which the average claim payment is modest in amount, consists of determining the average claim cost for each line or subline of insurance, projecting it for inflation or trends, and multiplying by the number of outstanding claims. The formula basis assumes that a certain percentage of the premium will be used for claims and establishes the claim reserve for a given policy year as the stipulated percentage of earned premiums, less claim payments already made. Companies generally use a case estimate or a statistical basis, or a combination of the two, in establishing their claim reserves. The formula method is usually used only in schedule P of the annual statement.

The reserve for incurred but not reported claims is usually determined pragmatically, based on past experience as to claims which, though incurred before December 31, are not reported to the insurer until after that date. Obviously, the volume of such claims will vary greatly by line of business. An automobile liability claim is much more likely to be reported late, for example, than is a fire insurance claim. It is necessary to use some type of statistical approach to calculating the ICNR reserve since an individual case estimate cannot be made for a claim which has not yet been reported. Of course the time lag between the statement date, December 31, and the date the statement must be filed, usually March 1, gives the insurer some opportunity to obtain a partial count of delayed claims, but there will often be a substantial number of claims incurred during the previous year which have not yet been reported by March 1. An analysis of previous years' late claim reports will usually afford a basis for estimating this reserve.

The claim expense reserve is usually determined as a function of the claim reserve. Since its purpose is to establish as a liability the claim expenses that will have to be paid on outstanding claims, which is properly a charge against the accounting period when those claims were incurred, a percentage of the claim reserve, based on the company's previous experience as to the ratio between claim expense and claim payments, usually gives a reasonably accurate result.

The claim reserve, including the ICNR, and the claim expense reserve are shown on the first two lines of the "Liabilities, Surplus and Other Funds" page (page 3) of the property insurance annual statement. These reserve totals are supported by part 3A (page 9) of the statement, which shows the various components of the claim reserve by line of business. Part 3A shows the gross claim reserve, the amount of reinsurance recoverable, the ICNR, and, separately, the claim expense reserve. The claim reserve (including ICNR), net of reinsurance, is also used in part 3 (page 8) of the statement where the increase in the claim reserve is added to losses paid to obtain the incurred losses and the loss ratio for each line of business.

In addition to the reporting of claim reserves by line, in part 3A these claim reserves are tested in schedules O and P. These schedules test the insurer's claim reserve, as reported at the end of the previous year, to attempt to determine whether it was redundant, inadequate, or accurate. The theory behind such a test is that if the insurer has not changed its method of determining its claim reserves, any redundancy or inadequacy in last year's reserve may indicate a similar redundancy or inadequacy in this year's claim reserve. Schedule O provides a one-year claim reserve runoff for 25 of the 28 lines of business shown in part 3A. Schedule P provides a more detailed runoff, covering eight policy years, for three branches of insurance: automobile bodily injury liability, bodily injury liability other than automobile, and workmen's compensation. Schedule P also performs another function: it establishes by formula a minimum reserve for each of the three lines of business. This minimum formula reserve, which applies to each of the three latest policy years, is 65 percent of earned premiums for workmen's compensation and 60 percent for the two liability coverages, less claims paid.

Schedule O, for each of its 25 lines of insurance, splits the losses paid during the current calendar year into losses incurred during the same calendar year and losses incurred in prior years. The claim reserve on December 31, as shown in part 3A of the statement, is split into the reserve for losses incurred in the current calendar year and the reserve for losses that were unpaid at the previous year-end and have still not been settled. For each line of business, a comparison of the losses paid on prior years' claims, plus the December 31 reserve on prior years' claims, with the claim reserve at the end of the previous year, indicates the degree of redundancy or inadequacy in last year's claim reserve. If this test indicates a substantial degree of inadequacy in last year's claim reserve, it would presumably impel the insurance department to check this year's claim reserve in detail, unless given assurance by the company that steps have been taken to avoid a similar inadequacy in the current year's claim reserve.

The usefulness of schedule O as a test of claim reserves depends upon the fact that most claims incurred prior to the current year have been liquidated by the current December 31. Although some old claims are, of course, still outstanding, they constitute only a small portion of the total claims in reserve at the prior year-end. For the three lines of business included in schedule P, automobile liability, general liability, and workmen's compensation, some claims may be outstanding for many years; as a result, a one-year claim reserve runoff is not sufficient, and more sophisticated methods must be used.

Schedule P

Schedule P attacks the problem of determining the adequacy of claim reserves for its three lines of insurance by subdividing the claim reserve (including the claim expense reserve) by policy year. Thus all claims outstanding on policies written in 1966 (whether the claim occurred during 1966 or 1967) are assigned to policy year 1966. To the claim reserve and claim expense reserve for each policy year is added the claim and claim expense payments made in all prior years. Earned premiums are then determined for each policy year, and the loss ratio, the ratio of losses incurred (payments plus reserve) to earned premiums, is calculated.

For the older policy years, most claims have been paid and the current claim reserve forms only a small portion of the claims incurred. For the last three policy years, however, a substantial portion of the claims incurred may still be unpaid, and the loss ratio may not be reliable. Schedule P requires, therefore, that an additional reserve be established, on a formula basis, whenever the loss ratio for any one of the three latest policy years is less than 65 percent for workmen's compensation insurance or 60 percent for automobile or general liability insurance. "The theory implicit in Schedule P is that of setting an arbitrary minimum value on third-party loss valuations until sufficient time has elapsed to remove most of the uncertainty surrounding these valuations."[41] The excess of the schedule P formula reserve over the company's own case estimate (or statistical) reserve must be carried to the liability page of the annual statement where it constitutes an additional liability of the insurer.

In addition to the incurred loss ratio for each policy year and the comparison of the formula reserve with the case estimate reserve for each of the three latest policy years, schedule P contains, in part 5, a claim reserve runoff for each of the six latest policy years, each subdivided into two accident years. Thus policy year 1965, comprising all policies written during 1965, is divided into accident year 1965, claims that occurred in 1965 on policies written in 1965, and accident year 1966, claims that occurred in 1966 on policies written during 1965. The latest policy year, since it coincides with the calendar year for which the annual statement is filed, can have a reserve only for claims which occurred in the first of its two accident years—the second accident year has not yet begun.

For each of these 11 policy-year and accident-year combinations, the incurred claims (payments plus claim reserve) are traced from year-end to year-end. Each year, of course, more and more claims have been paid, and their ultimate value definitely determined, while the reserve, representing an estimate of the value of claims still outstanding, is correspondingly decreased. Thus the successive totals of incurred claims for a given policy year and accident year, at consecutive year-ends, indicate whether prior years' claim reserves were redundant, accurate, or inadequate. If the successive incurred claim totals decrease, it indicates a conservative reserving policy, with claims overvalued when the reserve is established, and gradually finding their true level as more and more of the policy year's claims find their way from the claim reserve to the paid column. If the successive incurred claim totals increase, it indicates that the reserve was initially set at too low a figure, which might indicate to an alert insurance department the possibility that current claim reserves, too, are understated.

---

[41] "Report on the Annual Statement," *Proceedings of Casualty Actuarial Society,* Vol. 52, No. 244 (1965), p. 255.

Criticisms of Schedule P

Schedule P has been subject to incessant criticism over a great many years—primarily by actuaries. A committee of the Casualty Actuarial Society said in 1948: "Undoubtedly the chief purpose of minimum reserves is to guarantee adequate reserves. After careful study, the Committee has concluded that this purpose cannot be met by the present Schedule P method or any other formula method for establishing minimum reserves. In actual practice, it is believed that the present Schedule P method has not succeeded in preventing or reducing losses to policyholders when carriers have become insolvent."[42]

In his 1962 presidential address, the president of the Casualty Actuarial Society said: "Another cause of difficulty is the famous, or should I say infamous, Schedule P which, except for its fifth part has, I believe, long outlived its usefulness. The Schedule is most expensive to prepare and little understood even by those who have been associated with casualty insurance for years."[43] In 1965, another committee of the Casualty Actuarial Society stated: "The entire Schedule P adds measurably to recording and preparation expense without contributing material of equivalent value, and without achieving the purpose for which it was intended."[44]

The major specific criticisms of schedule P can, perhaps, be summarized as follows:

a) The formula approach to setting minimum loss reserves employed in schedule P is invalid; in any case, the 60 percent and 65 percent expected loss ratios on which the formula is based are out-of-date. The 60 percent and 65 percent figures for expected loss and claim-expense ratios were adopted many years ago when most insurers were members of rating bureaus and charged the same rates. Since then, premium rates, particularly for automobile insurance, have increased severalfold and the portion of the premium needed for expenses has decreased. Also, companies using bureau

[42] "Report of Committee on Compensation and Liability Loss and Loss Expense Reserves," *Proceedings of Casualty Actuarial Society,* Vol. 35, No. 58 (1948), p. 58.

[43] Laurence H. Longley-Cook, "Actuarial Aspects of Industry Problems, *Proceedings of Casualty Actuarial Society,* Vol. 49, No. 91 (1962), p. 107.

[44] "Report of the Annual Statement," *Proceedings of Casualty Actuarial Society,* Vol. 52, No. 244 (1965), p. 245.

rates now write only a small proportion of automobile insurance, and rate deviations and independent ratemaking have become the rule rather than the exception. The percentage of the earned premium available for automobile liability losses and claim expense for companies using rates calculated by the National Bureau of Casualty Underwriters is 65.5 percent as compared with the 60 percent stipulated by schedule P.[45]

Independent and deviating companies generally use a still higher expected loss ratio. It is clear that a loss reserve formula which requires a company to set aside 60 percent of premiums for losses and claim expense, when the company's premium scale contemplates that 65 percent or more of the premium will be used for this purpose, contributes nothing to insurer solvency.

b) Separating automobile bodily injury from automobile property damage and putting the former in schedule P and the latter in schedule O causes unnecessary complications, particularly as single limit policies become more common. The Special Automobile Policy, which combines bodily injury and property damage for an indivisible premium is becoming more and more popular. In general liability insurance too, more and more liability insurance is being included in homeowners and commercial property package policies, often combined with other coverages for an indivisible premium. It would be simpler and more accurate to combine bodily injury and property damage insurance claim reserves and test them together. Since schedule O and schedule P use different methods of testing the claim reserve runoff, it might be wise to put the combined bodily injury and property damage reserve in both schedules. Unnecessary restrictions on the reporting of claim reserves in the annual statement should not stand in the way of simplification of automobile and general liability rating and underwriting practices; companies which prefer to offer a single limit liability insurance policy to the public should not be deterred by schedule O and schedule P requirements.

c) Schedule P should be on a calendar-accident year basis instead of a policy year basis. All the accounting data in the annual statement, except schedule P, pertain to a calendar year. Automobile and general liability insurance loss statistics are compiled on an

---

[45] Philipp K. Stern, "Ratemaking Procedures for Automobile Liability Insurance," *Proceedings of Casualty Actuarial Society,* Vol. 52, No. 97 (1965), pp. 139, 165.

accident year basis, which can be related to calendar year earned premiums. The policy year method, which assigns the entire premium for a policy to the calendar year in which the policy was written, even though coverage extends over several calendar years, was a practical expedient adopted in the precomputer age to avoid the work necessary to split each premium into the portion allocable to each calendar year. Now that insurers have electonic computers to expedite their calculations, there is no longer any reason why schedule P should be compiled on a basis which differs from the rest of the annual statement. "With calendar-accident year data in Schedule P, the recording of policy year will no longer be necessary for annual statement purposes. This saving can be made without any loss in the real value of Schedule P, because loss and loss expense reserves can be tested equally well on an accident year basis."[46]

d) A test of loss reserves requires a reporting not only of dollar figures but also of the number of claims outstanding. It would be much easier for an insurance department to detect inconsistencies in claim reserves if the number of claims and the average claim cost were reported separately. This poses a difficult problem, however, in the definitions of what is meant by a claim. Different companies use different definitions; some consider every claim notice as a claim and set up a file. Other companies exclude from their accounting system claims on which there is obviously no liability, as well as claims closed without payment soon after receipt of the claim notice. Since the purpose of schedule P is to verify the current claim reserve by testing whether previous claim reserves were correct, differences in claim definitions should not be an insuperable obstacle to the reporting of the number of claims outstanding. All that is required is that an insurer be consistent in its definition of a claim and that it not change its practice from year to year, without indicating the nature of the change as a footnote to schedule P. The trend in average claim cost would be particularly useful, given a sufficient volume of business, in verifying that adequate allowance for inflation and upward trends in claim payments has been made in setting the current claim resurves.

e) Schedule P should, perhaps, be on a "direct" instead of a "net" basis. Reinsurance can distort the schedule P results and make

---

[46] Ruth Salzmann, "Schedule P on a Calendar/Accident Year Basis," *Proceedings of Casualty Actuarial Society,* Vol. 54, No. 101 (1967).

them of doubtful value as a check on claim reserves. For example, reinsurance which covers the excess of loss ratio, involving a variable reinsurance commission depending on the ceding company's loss ratio, transfers fluctuations in loss experience from the claim reserve to the commission account. Thus schedule P may show considerable stability while, in fact, underwriting experience may be deteriorating badly; claim reserves may be too low, but schedule P would not flash a warning signal to the insurance department.

Unlike most parts of the annual statement blank, whose form is governed by the Blanks Committee of the National Association of Insurance Commissioners and ratified by its acceptance by each state insurance commissioner, schedule P is specifically required by statute in 20 states. Nineteen other states, though having no statutes requiring completion of schedule P, give the commissioner authority to adopt NAIC accounting rules; the remaining states have no specific statutes.[47] The existence of specific schedule P statutes in 20 states makes it more difficult to change this part of the annual statement than other portions. However, responding to various criticisms of schedule P, the NAIC Laws and Legislation Committee appointed in December, 1963, a subcommittee "to prepare model legislation to modify schedule P." The subcommittee reported to the 1964 meeting of the NAIC that "it was the consensus of the Subcommittee members that new legislation should be attempted as a replacement for and improvement over present Schedule P statutes, taking into account the changing needs of the insurance business. This was confirmed in executive session, and it was unanimously agreed that legislation be drafted to include adequate procedures as guidelines for specifically achieving the objective of providing reasonable and conservative reserves for losses and loss expense."[48] Studies and meetings have continued, and at the June, 1967, meeting of the NAIC, the actuarial subcommittee of the Property, Casualty and Surety Committee, which has taken over the task of attempting to find a satisfactory method of testing loss reserves, requested that an industry advisory committee be appointed to work with the Actuarial Subcommittee "to prepare and test various proposals to test the accuracy of loss reserves for the

---

[47] *Proceedings of National Association of Insurance Commissioners,* Vol. 2 (1963), p. 464.

[48] *Proceedings of National Association of Insurance Commissioners,* Vol. 2 (1964), p. 524.

Schedule P lines of business and to prepare a report in time for the December, 1967 meeting of the NAIC."[49]

The adequacy of claim reserves is perhaps the most important imponderable in attempting to determine an insurer's solvency from its financial statement. Without being sure that claim reserves are adequate, no insurance department can be confident that the surplus shown in an insurer's annual statement is correct and that the insurer is, in fact, as solvent as it appears to be. It is, therefore, unfortunate, that schedule P, intended as a test of claim reserves, has so many shortcomings and that it appears to be so difficult to reach agreement on necessary corrective measures. A new schedule P, with an actuarially sound test of claim reserves, should be a priority item for the NAIC and its Blanks Committee.

Relationship of Premium Volume to Surplus

The minimum capital and surplus required by present state insurance laws is not often adequate for a new insurer and is even less so for a company which has been in business for several years and has written a substantial volume of insurance. A company's capital and surplus is its ultimate guarantor of solvency; it provides the cushion to absorb fluctuations in experience, asset losses, excessive expenses, needed increases in claim reserves, or any of the other perils which may beset an insurance company. Since an insurer's potential of sustaining these types of losses is not independent of its size, a statutory standard which simply sets a fixed amount of capital and/or surplus for an insurer writing a certain type of insurance is not adequate. The amount of capital and surplus an insurer needs is a function of its size.

Since the amount of capital and surplus in relation to size is clearly the most important measure of solvency, many people have thought that a formula which relates the volume of business an insurer may do to its surplus, might serve as an automatic regulator. If, for example, an insurer were limited to writing a premium volume equal to twice its capital and surplus, an insurer which sustained operating losses, either due to inefficiency or bad luck, would find that it was required to curtail its operations and write

---

[49] *Proceedings of National Association of Insurance Commissioners,* Vol. 2 (1967), p. 497.

less business the next year. If operating losses continued over a period of years, the insurer would have to keep reducing its premium volume until when insolvency finally became its fate, it had very little business in force and few, if any, policyholders would suffer by its demise.

The New York insurance department has for many years applied an administrative rule to relate the premium volume written by an insurer to its capital and surplus. New York uses as a measure a ratio of 2:1 between premiums written (net of reinsurance) and surplus for a company writing casualty insurance and a ratio of 1:1 for a company writing fire or surety coverage. A rationale for this formula was set out by Roger Kenney.[50] For fire insurance companies, Mr. Kenney postulates that "the unearned premium reserve . . . is a measure of the outstanding potential liability of the company in the form of risks accepted. It therefore follows that the larger the cushion of safety (the policyholders' surplus) looms against the unearned premium reserve, the greater the strength of the organization."[51] Since, however, the relationship between written premiums and the unearned premium reserve depends upon the term of the policies in force (a three-year policy generates a much larger unearned premium reserve than a one-year policy) and their distribution by month of issue (the unearned premium reserve on December 31 is 1/24 of the annual premium for a one-year policy written in January and 23/24 for one written in December), the translation of a 1:1 ratio between surplus and unearned premiums to a 1:1 ratio between surplus and written premiums is approximate at best. A mathematically forbidding rationalization of the 2:1 rule relating premiums written and surplus for casualty insurers can be found in a memo by Harwayne.[52]

For casualty companies, the 2:1 rule was nearly embodied in law. In the late 1930's it was proposed that the New York insurance law contain a provision that "no such company (meaning stock casualty company) shall at any time pay any cash dividend on its capital stock unless, after providing for such dividend, its surplus to policyholders is at least equal to fifty per cent of the net prem-

[50] Roger Kenney, *Fundamentals of Fire and Casualty Insurance Strength* (Dedham, Massachusetts, 1949).

[51] *Ibid.,* p. 20.

[52] Frank Harwayne, "Insurance, Risk, Investment and Profit," *Proceedings of National Association of Insurance Commissioners,* Vol. 2 (1966), p. 451.

iums written during the next preceding calendar year. . . ."[53] This proposal met considerable opposition, however, and the statute finally adopted states: "No such company shall declare any cash dividend to stockholders which together with all such dividends declared by it during the next preceding twelve months exceeds ten per cent of its then outstanding capital stock unless either it has surplus to policyholders at least equal to twenty-five per cent of its unearned premium liability, as shown by its last statement on file with the superintendent, or it has surplus at least equal to fifty per cent of the minimum capital required for the kinds of business it is authorized to transact, whichever shall be greater."[54] This, of course, is a much weaker statute which does not impose any realistic solvency standard. Despite its lack of statutory sanction, however, the 2:1 rule applied with discretion is still the standard used by the New York Insurance Department as a rule of thumb to determine whether an insurer's financial condition requires further scrutiny.

As mentioned above, the NAIC Committee to Draft Model Legislation to Relate Holdings of Equity Investments to Surplus made a proposal to use a 3:1 ratio between written premiums (and investment in common stocks) and surplus as a red flag and a 4:1 ratio as an absolute limit, in the absence of demonstration by the insurer that it is safe to write a larger volume of insurance. The recommendation was, however, rejected by its parent committee after it encountered the opposition of the insurance business.

The NAIC subcommittee embarked on a new and possibly fruitful approach to solvency standards when it saw fit to combine the question of equity investments with the relationship of premium writings to surplus. So long as the stock market continues to advance, an insurer with a substantial investment in equities can absorb even a quite adverse loss experience without a threat to its solvency. On the other hand, an insurer can withstand a substantial drop in its asset values if it is earning underwriting profits. If underwriting losses and asset depreciation strike together, however, an insurer's capacity to meet its obligations may be compromised.

The position of the insurance business has been consistent, and successful in opposition to legislation imposing any rule, whether 1:1, 2:1 or 3:1. It is contended that any such rule of thumb does not

---

[53] Kenney, *supra* No. 50.

[54] N.Y. Ins. Law sec. 313 (McKinney 1966).

really consider all the factors that make for solvency and that should be examined to evaluate the soundness of an insurance company's operation. It is claimed that any standard which ignores the caliber of management, the quality and liquidity of assets, the adequacy of claim reserves and unearned premium reserves, the type of reinsurance arrangements, operating results over a period of years, and the distribution of business by type of insurance and geographical area cannot distinguish between a sound and an unsound insurer. Insurers and their trade associations cloak themselves with the mantle of free enterprise and managerial freedom and state that no formula will replace good judgment, management ability, integrity, and financial capability.

While an insurer may well believe that its management is better able than the insurance department to judge the amount of surplus it needs, this does not really solve the problem. A state insurance department has a responsibility to the public not to allow an insurer in danger of insolvency to continue to write business. Furthermore, its powers are limited by statute; neither lack of confidence in management nor a vague, general belief that an insurer is not financially sound is sufficient ground for license revocation or receivership. An insurance department must use objective standards to decide which insurers should be permitted to continue and which should be asked to withdraw from business or curtail their operations. In the absence of some enforceable rule relating required surplus to volume of business written, or exposure to loss, an insurance department may have no ground for moving against an insurer until its capital drops below the statutory minimum. By this time, the insurer is likely to be hopelessly insolvent, and loss to policyholders becomes inevitable.

It is no answer to say that an insurance department has the power, by auditing the annual statement and by examination, to scrutinize the adequacy of claim reserves and unearned premium reserves and to ascertain the quality of a company's investment portfolio. After all reserves have been checked out and found adequate, after assets of doubtful value have been excluded from the balance sheet or reduced in value, there will still, it is hoped, remain a surplus of a certain amount. At this point, the insurance department must make a decision that this surplus is or is not adequate for the kind and volume of business the company writes. In the absence of some formula, it is difficult to see how such a decision can be arrived at and, without appropriate statutory support, enforced if it is adverse to the company.

Reinsurance and Solvency

The size of a company's retention on an individual risk and the degree of protection it enjoys against catastrophes are vital in any study of solvency; hence we must discuss reinsurance, the functions it serves, and the way it operates.

There are five purposes of reinsurance:

a) Protecting company assets against adverse fluctuations in frequency or severity of losses that might threaten an insurer's financial stability. This might be called insuring the solvency of the insurance company.

b) Avoiding violent swings in underwriting experience which, though well within the insurer's financial capacity, might shake the confidence of investors and the public, hence stabilizing operating results and avoiding surplus fluctuations.

c) Preserving surplus by the early recovery of prepaid expenses. An insurer can write a larger volume of business than its surplus would normally permit by sharing with the reinsurer the burden of the unearned premium reserve, hence minimizing surplus depletion.

d) Sharing the risk when a company enters a new or unfamiliar line of business. An inexperienced company can draw on the knowledge, as well as the surplus, of a reinsurer.

e) Providing capacity for individual risks larger than a primary company is willing or able to assume. An insurer need not decline to write a risk too big for it to handle; reinsurance permits it to service its agents, even on large policies.

Reinsurance treaties (as agreements between reinsurers and ceding companies are called) generally fall into two main categories, each of which has several subtypes. All reinsurance treaties may be classed as pro rata or excess of loss. Pro rata treaties, in turn, are either quota share or surplus share. Excess of loss (sometimes called nonproportional reinsurance) in turn comprises three types of reinsurance treaties.

Quota-share reinsurance is an agreement by the primary insurer to cede to the reinsurer a fixed percentage of every risk it writes. Quota share treaties are common between members of a group which operate under common management and are sometimes used for other purposes as well. A surplus share treaty provides for ceding to the reinsurer any amount written by the primary insurer over its retention, i.e., the maximum amount it is willing to keep for its own account. Thus there will be some risks, those that fall within the retention, on which there will be no reinsurance, while larger policies are shared in varying proportions between the ceding company and the reinsurer. Surplus share reinsurance is the traditional way of handling fire insurance, fidelity and surety, and many other types of coverage. In both quota share and surplus share reinsurance the reinsurer reimburses the ceding insurer, by means of a reinsurance commission, for its share of taxes and underwriting expenses incurred by the ceding insurer.

Excess of loss or nonproportional reinsurance may be written (*a*) on an "each risk, each occurrence," basis; (*b*) on an "each occurrence" basis; or (*c*) an annual aggregate excess of loss (stop-loss) reinsurance. In each of these types, the ceding insurer pays a premium to the reinsurer in return for a promise by the reinsurer to pay a portion of each loss which exceeds a specific amount. The reinsurer's liability may fluctuate between very wide limits, and its proportion of a ceding company's risk is not determined until a loss occurs; in pro rata reinsurance, by contrast, the reinsurer assumes a percentage of each risk (or a percentage of each risk larger than the ceding company's retention) and pays its share of any loss that ensues on a partially reinsured policy, no matter how small.

Basis (*a*), "each risk, each occurrence," is usually used for casualty reinsurance. Thus a reinsurer might agree, for a premium, to pay an automobile bodily injury claim in excess of $25,000 per accident. The ceding company would pay the first $25,000 of claims arising out of any accident and could be sure that no matter how large the claim or how many claims were filed because of one automobile accident, the reinsurance treaty would protect it against having to pay more than its retention.

Basis (*b*), "each occurrence," is often called catastrophe reinsurance, since its purpose is to protect a direct insurer not only against large individual claims but also against many claims arising from one windstorm or other catastrophe. Of course the retention limit under this type of reinsurance would normally be substantially greater than under type (*a*).

Basis (*c*), stop-loss reinsurance, guarantees the primary insurer that it will not have to pay out losses totaling more than a given

amount during a calendar year. Thus stop-loss insurance protects
not only against loss severity but also against loss frequency, from
whatever cause. It is generally used for hail insurance on growing
crops; its use in other areas is sporadic and a stop-loss reinsurance
treaty would normally be rather expensive.

When properly used, reinsurance can be very helpful in preserving an insurer's surplus, hence protecting its solvency; it can also be
misused to conceal an insolvency which would otherwise be evident.
Reinsurance is a particularly attractive device for the unscrupulous
because reinsurance contracts are so complex and the average property insurer has so many of them that it is quite difficult for an
insurance department to discover an improper reinsurance contract
among the maze of legitimate reinsurance treaties usually found on
examination of a property insurer.

Reinsurance treaties intended to conceal rather than to prevent
insolvency may be made between companies operating under common management, or, less often, between unrelated companies.
Generally, though not always, they take the form of surplus aid
treaties. A surplus aid treaty may best be described as a loan
masquerading as reinsurance. If one insurer lent money to another,
the borrower would be able to show the amount borrowed as an
asset but would have to set up a liability of the same amount, and
its surplus position would not change at all. If the loan is accomplished in the guise of a reinsurance treaty, however, the "ceding"
company can reduce its unearned premium reserve by the amount
ceded to the "reinsurer," thus increasing its surplus. Any transfer of
premium from ceding to reinsuring company can be kept at a
minimum by a generous reinsurance commission allowance made
by the reinsuring to the ceding company. After the end of the year,
when the ceding company has filed its solvent-looking financial
statement, the loan can be repaid by cancelling the reinsurance
treaty retroactively or by the ceding company reassuming the business ceded.[55]

Surplus aid reinsurance may have some legitimate uses, for example when with the knowledge and consent of the insurance department, an insurer uses surplus aid reinsurance to conceal a temporary
surplus problem which will have been corrected soon after the date

---

[55] A classic case of surplus aid reinsurance intended to conceal insolvency is
described in *Insurance Industry Hearings, supra* n. 8, pp. 7168–72, 7230–50.

of the financial statement. If used to cover up a surplus deficiency which cannot be corrected, especially if the treaty is made without the insurance department's knowledge, surplus aid reinsurance merely postpones the inevitable insolvency and ensures that policy-holders will suffer a greater loss.

Because of the vital importance of reinsurance to insurer solvency and the many possibilities of abuse inherent in this important tool, it is essential that insurance departments be thoroughly cognizant of the reinsurance contracts used by companies under their supervision. Unfortunately, few insurance departments are equipped to study this aspect of insurance as intensively as necessary.

Rate Regulation and Solvency

The rate regulatory statutes in force in almost every state assign to the insurance commissioner the task of approving fire and casualty insurance premium rates to ensure that they are not "excessive, inadequate or unfairly discriminatory." It is often argued that by preventing inadequate rates, rate regulation is an important aid to solvency.[56]

It is clear that adequate premium rates are essential to the solvency of an insurance company. Even if funds are carefully invested and assets conservatively valued, even if loss reserves are established with scrupulous care, even if management is honest and capable, insolvency is inevitable if premium receipts over a long period of time are less than claims plus expenses minus investment income. What is less clear is that the insurance commissioner, through his rate approval powers, can have much positive influence on rate adequacy. He can, of course, have an important negative influence by vetoing needed rate increases.

A rate filing submitted by a property-liability insurance company or a rating bureau representing a number of property insurers usually consists of a statistical demonstration, using data for a previous calendar year or policy year, indicating the "pure premium" that would have had to be charged to pay the claims and claim expenses for each classification or group of classifications in the rating system. When a loading for expenses and profit is added,

---

[56] Allen L. Mayerson, "How to Rewrite an Insurance Code," *Journal of Risk and Insurance*, Vol. 34, No. 95 (March, 1967), p. 116.

we obtain the gross premium which would have been reasonable and adequate for the period whose statistics are under review. This figure, perhaps projected for cost-of-living changes or trends in average claim frequency and claim cost, may be taken as the premium rate which the insurance commissioner is asked to approve to become effective at some future date specified in the filing. Or, the filing may simply compare the "expected" and actual loss ratios for each classification or group of classifications and indicate the percentage change in the premium rate which is needed to bring the actual loss ratio in line with the expected ratio.

For a large, well-established insurer having access to competent actuarial advice, this method of ratemaking, using previous years' statistics and assuming, in effect, that next year will, except perhaps for inflationary increases, be very much like last year, has worked satisfactorily. At least this has been true in those branches of insurance where actuarial procedures have been carefully designed and properly used like workmen's compensation insurance; considerable doubt has been cast on the actuarial soundness of rating procedures used in fire insurance and some other types of coverage.

Fortunately for policyholders but unfortunately for the theory that rate regulation helps ensure solvency, the stable, well-managed companies are not generally the ones which become insolvent. Most of the 65 insurers which failed since 1960[57] were engaged in insuring substandard drivers, a heterogeneous class in which the "product mix" underwritten by the insurance company may sharply influence the loss ratio and the adequacy or inadequacy of the premium scale. Furthermore, the companies engaging in this rather hazardous branch of insurance often lacked competent actuarial advice and experienced management. No insurance commissioner when approving a schedule of premium rates for a new insurer, a company entering a new line of business, or one engaged in insuring a heterogeneous group such as substandard drivers can have any assurance that future loss experience will bear any very close relationship to the statistics on which the rates are based. Loss ratios depend on underwriting standards and claim practices as well as rate level, and these are not under the control of the insurance commissioner.

---

[57] Dean Sharp, "It's Too Late to Defend the Status Quo," *Insurance,* October 8, 1966, p. 25.

The history of rate regulation indicates clearly that insurance commissioners are quite zealous when rate reductions are indicated but are much less inclined to approve rate increases. Legislators and the public like lower automobile and fire insurance rates; the commissioner who crusades for lower rates, regardless of the effect on solvency, wins plaudits in the newspapers. The insurance commissioner who urges an insurer to increase its premium rates because its solvency might be in question is rare indeed.

Conclusion

The principal reason for the existence of state insurance departments is to see that insurance companies keep their promises, a condition that requires as a prerequisite unquestioned solvency. From 1960 to 1966, 65 property-liability insurers failed causing substantial losses to policyholders and third-party accident victims.[58] Where solvency is concerned, state insurance departments have not done a completely satisfactory job. Changes in state insurance laws and in the practices of state insurance departments are badly needed, and ambitious programs of improvement are being undertaken in many states. It is hoped that the analysis in this paper will contribute a few ideas that may help state insurance regulation to fulfill its responsibilities.

---

[58] *Ibid.*

PART IV
Rate Regulation in Property and Liability Insurance

PART IV

chapter 10

More Federal Regulation and/or More Competition

DOES RATE REGULATION by the states serve the public well? What alternatives are available to present rate regulatory patterns? The Stewart proposal in Chapter 3 deals in part with those questions. Others have also spoken on the subject.

After seeking to answer those questions, the following selection makes a specific proposal to amend the McCarran Act to create an entirely new method of regulating rates for automobile insurance.

THE REAL ISSUE: STATE VERSUS FEDERAL OR REGULATION VERSUS COMPETITION?

Donald P. McHugh
Vice President and General Counsel
State Farm Mutual Automobile Insurance Company

The stage is now being set for a new congressional drama which might appropriately be styled "McCarran Act Revisited." The focus will certainly be on automobile insurance, but before the final curtain is rung down, it is highly likely that other lines of insurance will play a role.

It is probably no exaggeration to state that the future of the automobile insurance business may be at stake, certainly in its present form. Congressmen and senators refer to the mounting press of complaint letters they are receiving from policyholders around the country concerning a variety of practices in the automobile insurance business. Knowledgeable congressional informants describe the public pressures as exceeding anything experienced in all other areas of consumer interest. How widespread the discontent, how genuine the public clamoring, or how deeply disturbed the congressional mood will only be known as the story unfolds.

A mood of change seems to permeate all gatherings of automobile insurance officials, regulators, and academicians. There is great uncertainty as to the nature and extent of the changes which are imminent. But despite dire predictions by some alarmists and unsupported charges by hostile critics, the industry is not running scared. Indeed, most industry leaders have welcomed the probe and have offered full cooperation to both congressional and executive department inquiries. Thoughtful leaders in the industry recognize that legitimate concern on the part of the insurance buying public cannot be ignored or swept under the rug. Better that wellsprings of public discontent reach the surface so that fears can be aired, and, hopefully, doubts and distrust dispelled. For too long, the public has harbored suspicions that the industry deliberately enshrouds its operations in some occult mystique to ward off its critics. Insurance accounting, ratemaking techniques, measures of profitability, reserving practices, and underwriting evaluations are issues bewildering to insurance buyers and public officials alike. While the enormous complexities of the business will not all yield to simplified explanation which will satisfy everyone, much can be done to overcome past failures in communicating with the public about the business.

There is considerable apprehension in many quarters that insurance is a natural whipping boy for the public and its elected officials and that a fair and impartial hearing of the case is virtually impossible. Insurance officials frequently find themselves between pressure for lower rates and broadened benefits on the one hand and on the other shrill demands that insurance be sold to all persons with no right to select customers, and very little to vary their rates. But such contradictory pressures should not dampen our faith in the inherent fairness of the American public to judge the ultimate questions. And while the industry might not march joyously into the congressional arena to face its interrogators, the overwhelming precedents would indicate that fair, competent, and considerate treatment will be accorded.

For these reasons, most companies do not fear the prospect of having to make a public accounting of their conduct. Indeed, while some imperfections may be bared and some derelictions revealed, the prevailing mood is that, on balance, more good than harm can come from these searching federal inquiries.

CONGRESSIONAL MOOD AFTER McCARRAN ACT

The congressional setting is considerably different today than the frantic atmosphere in which Public Law 15 was enacted following the Supreme Court's South-Eastern Underwriters Association decision. Prevailing patterns of business behavior were then squarely in conflict with federal law; some type of legislative relief was urgent, and the imprecise draftsmanship of the McCarran Act of 1945 reflected the need to achieve hasty compromises, with implications not clearly understood. The deliberations over the All-Industry Rate Bills during the moratorium suffered from the same disabilities.

But, in the main, the challenge was to the system of regulation. The congressional debate centered around the issue of federal versus state power and the merits of differing forms of regulatory supervision. The issues today involving automobile insurance may be more deep-seated. It is true that the initial focus of the Dodd Committee study was upon alleged failure of state regulation to forestall failures of a number of high-risk auto insurers. The introduction by Senator Dodd, cosponsored by other influential members of the Senate, of the Motor Vehicle Insurance Guaranty Bill, immediately sparked public interest in numerous other aspects of auto insurance. Heading the list was the problem of market capacity, i.e., cancellation, nonrenewals, and availability of product. The dimensions of the problem expanded as legislators raised related questions: blackout of whole regions and areas; mass cancellations; termination of agencies with injury to innocent policyholders; discrimination based on race, color, and age; restrictive underwriting rules and classification plans; ratemaking in concert; ratemaking techniques and their regulation; inclusion of investment income in ratemaking; claims handling; and anticompetitive issues such as blacklisting and tie-in practices. These are largely areas where insurance companies come into direct conflict with the public, and the conflict causes irritation and tension.

But congressional and executive department thinking soon moved into a third round. As any informed critic might predict, the attention of staff probers was quickly drawn to the more fundamental questions which dealt not with symptoms but with the real malignancy eating at the business. The cost of automobile insurance —now a virtual necessity under state law—may be reaching beyond what the public will pay, and for reasons not within the power of industry effectively to control—the slaughter on our highways and the malfunctioning of the tort liability system. Undoubtedly, these matters are overdue for examination in depth. To the extent that the subject is examined in its totality, the industry looks forward hopefully to sympathetic understanding of management's problems with the distinct likelihood that national focus on these problems may point the way to workable solutions not hitherto found.

On August 29, 1961, the Senate Judiciary Committee issued a report on the insurance industry and reasserted its belief "that the regulation of insurance by the States is in the public interest."[1] Significantly, the report noted, "Furthermore, the subcommittee found absolutely no support for Federal regulation from any groups representing any of the important segments of the industry. From certain academic sources and from representatives of the insurance-buying public come the only support for a limited kind of Federal supervision."[2] Patently, the members of the Senate were not then disposed to upset state regulation or even tamper with the McCarran Act.

CONGRESSIONAL MOOD TODAY

The mood of the Congress may be considerably different today. It is evident that many prominent House and Senate members see a need for a new role by the federal government in insurance regulation, although no clear outlines of this role are yet discernible. In announcing the staff study, Congressman Celler referred to his vigorous opposition in 1945 to the McCarran-Ferguson Act as contrary to the nation's basic antitrust policy.[3] Presumably, his disenchantment continues.

A 183-page report[4] by the staff proposing alternative means for further study concluded by recommending that the Federal Trade

---

[1] *The Insurance Industry, Insurance: Rates, Rating Organizations and State Regulation* (S. Rep. No. 831, 87 Cong., 1st sess., 1961), hereinafter cited as 1961 Report.

[2] *Ibid.*, p. 18.

[3] Statement of Emanuel Celler, chairman of Committee on Judiciary and its Antitrust Subcommittee of House of Representatives, July 25, 1967 (press release).

[4] House of Representatives, Committee on the Judiciary, *Automobile Insurance Study*, Report by the Staff of the Antitrust Subcommittee (Subcommittee No. 5) (90th Cong., 1st sess., 1967).

Commission be authorized to conduct a comprehensive investigation into the automobile insurance business. This recommendation was later endorsed by a special subcommittee of the Judiciary Committee.[5] However, a joint resolution[6] authorizing a two-year study by the Department of Transportation became law on signature by the President on May 22, 1968. Endorsement, repeal, or modification of the McCarran Act are possible as a result, and inevitable demands will be heard for a completely new federal law calling for an exclusive system of insurance regulation by the federal government.

Some political analysts predict that the Congress may be entering into a period of "political turbulence." The implications are that the relatively inactive-to-moderate pace of the Eisenhower-Kennedy-Johnson era may be replaced by bolder and more activist legislative programs on the domestic front. Surprisingly enough, leading liberal intellectuals are warning their confreres about the perils of further concentration of power in the federal bureaucracy. Even Daniel P. Moynihan, whose several recent pronouncements sharply attacked the insurance business—automobile liability insurance in particular—admonishes industry leaders to effect whosesale internal reforms or suffer the specter of a frightening federal colossus regulating every aspect of the business.

It was the abusive practices of price-fixing combinations in fire insurance which brought down the wrath of the Department of Justice upon the insurance business and led ultimately to the enactment of Public Law 15. For some time thereafter, property and casualty insurers, in conjunction with state insurance commissioners, wrestled over the form of rating laws which would meet the regulatory test of Section 2(b), and thus insulate industry pricing activities, including rating bureaus, from federal antitrust prosecution. It could hardly have been anticipated that the resulting All-Industry Fire and Casualty Rate Laws and their subsequent administration would create deep antagonism within the industry against state regulation and would alienate many of its staunchest supporters.

---

[5] See *Washington Insurance Newsletter,* No. 932, November 3, 1967 and House of Representatives, Committee on the Judiciary, *Automobile Insurance Study,* Report by the Staff of the Antitrust Subcommittee (Subcommittee No. 5) (90th Cong., 1st sess., 1967).

[6] S.J. Res. 129 and H.J. Res. 958 (90th Cong., 1st sess., 1967).

It was not surprising that the Senate Judiciary Committee would later find that state laws making bureau membership compulsory and prohibiting deviations contravened cherished federal policy. The Senate Judiciary Committee Report of 1961 declared: "The requirement of several state statutes for mandatory bureau membership substantially lessens competition and appears to be in conflict with the McCarran Act. . . . The McCarran Act can certainly not be viewed as justifying the acts of States in compelling all insurers to be members of rating bureaus or requiring that all rates be uniform by legislative fiat."[7] The committee recommended a judicial test of such laws, concluding that if the Supreme Court upheld their validity, "The Congress then has no alternative but to bring about a drastic revision of the McCarran Act."[8] The last effort to upset the North Carolina compulsory uniform auto rate law died in 1966 when the Supreme Court declined to review the Fourth Circuit ruling upholding this law.[9] With both the House and Senate Antitrust Subcommittees expressing interest in current automobile insurance inquiries, the imperfections in the McCarran Act which suffer such distortions of national policy to persist will receive thorough reappraisal. The Office of the Attorney General, which urged legislative correction of a restrictive fire rate law in the District of Columbia,[10] is not likely to be silent as Congress reopens this issue.

Nevertheless, state regulation of rates will not be judged by such abnormalities but rather by the success or failure of the prevailing pattern of state prior approval laws. The National Association of Insurance Commissioners is for the second time since 1959 taking a comprehensive look at the rating laws. The preliminary results to date indicate much dissatisfaction with the states' performance in discharging regulatory responsibility over property and casualty rates.[11]

---

[7] 1961 Report, p. 77.

[8] *Ibid.*, p. 78.

[9] *Allstate Ins. Com.* v. *Lanier*, 361 F.2d 870 (4th Cir. 1966), certiorari denied 385 U.S. 930 (1966).

[10] Statement of Lee Loevinger, Assistant Attorney General, Antitrust Division, Department of Justice, before the Subcommittee on Business and Commerce, Senate Committee on the District of Columbia, June 21, 1962.

[11] "First Report on Analysis of Insurer Questionnaire, N.A.I.C. Rates and Rating Organizations (F1) Subcommittee," *Proceedings of the National Association of Insurance Commissioners,* 1967.

The principal public pressures which generated support for federal reexamination of insurance stemmed from cancellation, nonrenewals, and inability to obtain auto insurance. It can be fairly well documented that these market capacity problems are directly traceable to inadequate rate levels.[12]

PRICE OF INSURANCE AS CRITICAL ISSUE

Lack of capacity is not uniform throughout the country but intensifies in those states where politically minded insurance commissioners utilize prior approval procedures to prevent rates from reaching their proper levels.[13] The public concern which first developed several years ago was, naturally enough, over symptoms experienced and not over underlying causes which could not be known. Insurers, like other businessmen, solicit the patronage of their customers. It is not natural to turn customers away or refuse to make services available. Only hard economic realities dictate such business judgment. The demand was urgent; there were no physical limitations to availability of supply; and yet the market was not being fully served. The principal answer must be price. The delicate mechanisms that operate in a free economy to match supply and demand were out of kilter. The finger points inexorably at rate regulatory laws and their administration by the states.

This answer will not meet all the criticisms against the conduct of the business during these trying periods of adverse underwriting experience. Whatever the self-interest justification, precipitate response on a blanket basis which fails to distinguish between customers does vast harm to many innocent buyers. The loud outcries of the innocent victim left without automobile insurance for no fault of his own was bound to be heard in regulatory agencies and

---

[12] *Commonwealth of Virginia ex rel. State Corporation Commission* v. *Aetna Casualty & Surety Co., et. al.,* Case No. 17680 (1966), transcript, testimony of Morton White, p. 746. Statement of J. Victor Herd before Subcommittee on Antitrust and Monopoly of the Committee of the Judiciary of the United States Senate, June 28, 1968.

[13] "Only a year ago there were some 350–400 companies writing auto liability in South Carolina. Today there are only 150–160 and ONLY 80 of them are writing any substantial volume. Many companies, even some of the largest have long since stopped accepting any new business at all." South Carolina Association of Insurance Agents, *Special Bulletin to Members No. 66–46,* November 16, 1966. See also *The Miami Herald,* December 13, 1965, sec. B, p. 1; *Orlando Sentinal,* December 14, 1965, p. 1–C; and *Today,* August 26, 1966.

legislative halls. The problem called for more statesmanship than was exhibited by all members of the industry. But final judgment must be based on the overall performance of the business, not the isolated acts of a few, and the industry is confident that, on balance, it has served the public well in the face of serious obstacles.

The question the Congress will ask is whether rate regulation by the states has served the public well. As a result of the 1959–60 hearings, a devastating case was carefully documented in the records and report of the Senate Antitrust Subcommittee to demonstrate how state rating laws were used in the fire insurance field to suppress competition, block and delay innovation, and deny the public the benefits of lower rates, through competition.[14] While this was occurring, state regulators either failed to take corrective action or actually abetted the process. The Senate Committee noted: "Apart from the possibility of Federal antitrust abuse, it would appear that State insurance departments have not been diligent in overcoming attitudes hostile to the felt needs of the buying public."[15]

In the face of the rising automobile insurance rates in recent years, resulting from mounting highway losses and spiraling inflation, the subsequent record of state regulation is hardly an inspiring one. The All-Industry Rate Laws have in numerous instances become the vehicle for devious political manipulations. Politics—not business judgment—and public pressures—not market forces—became the touchstone for measuring rate levels. In this atmosphere, many companies have felt impelled to withdraw from states or curtail their writings.[16]

The requirement of prior approval of automobile insurance rates is not explicit in the All-Industry Laws, but by accepted usage, advance approval has become the order of the day in most insurance departments. The "deemer" provision,[17] designed originally to pro-

---

[14] 1961 Report, pp. 21–66.

[15] *Ibid.*, p. 59.

[16] Statement of Ralph E. Moulton, President of Auto-Owners Insurance Company of Lansing in *Journal of Commerce*, May 13, 1966.

[17] A typical deemer provision is contained in N.Y. Ins. Law sec. 184 (McKinney 1966). "[E]ach filing shall be subject to a waiting period of fifteen days, which period may be extended by the superintendent for an additional period not to exceed fifteen days if he gives notice within such waiting period to the insurer or rating organization which made the filing that he needs additional time for the consideration of such filing. . . . A filing shall be deemed to meet the requirements of this article unless disapproved by the superintendent within the waiting period or any extension thereof. . . ."

tect insurers against needless departmental delay, has become the villain in the piece. It provides that after 30 days (15 days and generally one 15-day extension) the filing is deemed to be approved, even if the commissioner has not acted. It would be a brave if not foolhardy filer who relied upon the passage of time to make rates effective without receiving affirmative approval by the commissioner.

The attempt to justify All Industry Laws on the basis of solvency and equity considerations is a hollow exercise. It is doubtful if any filings in recent times were disapproved because they were too low, and even more unlikely that commissioners directed that rates be increased. Yet if the "inadequacy test" was really used as a device to regulate for solvency, such action could be expected to be routine. On the contrary, most rate regulatory efforts center around the "not excessive" standard where the political pressures are at work.

If rate regulation is a tool for achieving solvency, it is passing strange that most insolvencies occur in the closely regulated lines of automobile and fire insurance while the nonrate-regulated lines of life and health insurance have good solvency records. The Senate Committee in 1961 found no evidence that price competition caused insolvency;[18] and Senator Dodd's more recent inquiry into high-risk automobile insurance company failures,[19] while bitterly critical of the failure of state regulation to forestall such insolvencies, concluded there was no information indicating that any of the many insolvencies examined was brought about by inadequate rates as such.[20]

While rate regulation may achieve desired results in some lines, its utility is doubtful in the highly competitive lines such as automobile insurance where the influence of the ratemakers in concert has never been too pronounced. Independent automobile insurers write over half the total business with the two major independents being the largest by wide margins. There is certainly no dangerous concentration in the property-casualty business where almost 1,400 companies operate and where in automobile insurance alone over

---

[18] 1961 Report, p. 116.

[19] U.S. Senate, Subcommittee on Anti-trust and Monopoly of the Committee on the Judiciary, *Hearings on the Insurance Industry* (89th Cong., 1st sess., 1965).

[20] See address by Senator Thomas J. Dodd in *Proceedings, 20th Anniversary Meeting, National Association of Independent Insurers* (November 1–4, 1965), p. 85.

800 companies actively compete for the business. Significantly, those companies having the largest share make rates independently, outside the rating bureaus,[21] and generally at significantly lower levels.[22]

The debate continues within the industry over liberalizing the rating laws to make them more responsive to competition. While the Gerber Committee study of the 1959–61 era achieved few constructive results despite congressional prodding,[23] the current NAIC study has hopeful portents. Great strides forward were accomplished at the last session of the state legislatures when Florida[24] and Georgia[25] enacted California-type rating laws and Indiana[26] passed a file and use law with concessions to agents along the lines of the modified prior approval proposal.

But in the experience gained under 20 years of all-industry laws, the question remains: Is state regulation of rates in highly competitive lines an adequate substitute for competition? Professor Allen L. Mayerson of the University of Michigan, and former insurance superintendent of that state, noted: "In my view, a better solution may be found along the lines of the Idaho statute which requires rate filings for casualty insurance only if the Commissioner finds that reasonable competition does not exist in a particular line of commerce."[27] In other words, there will be no rate regulation if the commissioner makes a positive finding on the existence of reasonable competition. This may be begging the question, which is the perplexing affirmative burden of establishing the existence of competition. To many congressmen the simpler solution will be the time-honored federal device of the antitrust laws, which simply

---

[21] See generally, *Best's Fire and Casualty Aggregates and Averages* (28th ed.; Morristown, N.J.: Alfred M. Best Co., Inc., 1967).

[22] For example the liability rates at basic limits for a typical driver in Chicago are as follows:

Bureau	$58.50
Independent 1	47.50
Independent 2	45.50

[23] "To Review Fire and Casualty Rating Laws and Regulations (L1) Subcommittee Report," *1963 Proceedings of the National Association of Insurance Commissioners,* Vol. I, No. 262 (December 3–7, 1962).

[24] Fla. Stat. ch. 627 (1967).

[25] Ga. Code Ann. ch. 56–5 (Supp. 1967).

[26] Ind. Ann. Stat. sec. 39–5239 to sec. 39–5262 (Supp. 1968).

[27] Allen L. Mayerson, "Some Considerations in the Regulation of Rates," *Insurance,* Vol. 68, No. 50 (December 23, 1967), p. 19.

provide workable tools to attack whatever forces may unreasonably interfere with and restrain the normal working of free competition.

A NEW APPROACH TO RATE REGULATION

As Congress surveys the automobile insurance scene and the intricacies of its regulation, the prospect of a wholly new federal machinery to take over this job may seem appalling. But if it concludes that state rate regulation has not worked, it will certainly take a hard look at bringing automobile insurance rating back under the federal antitrust laws. The procedures for accomplishing this are manageable and can be accomplished in such a way as to retain the essential regulatory role of state insurance departments. Provision could be made for preserving all concerted rating bureau activities which can be publicly justified because of the peculiar nature of insurance pricing.

Amendment of McCarran Act

In its simplest terms, an amendment could be drafted to the McCarran Act which would exempt all automobile insurers engaged in interstate commerce from the provisions of any state law with respect to the regulation of motor vehicle insurance rates, rating plans, or rating systems, with the proviso that Section 1 of the Sherman Antitrust Act shall not apply to the making of rates by any such insurer through any rating bureaus or rating organizations unless such activity unreasonably restrains competition with other persons not members or subscribers to the rating bureaus. Thus, exempt from the "regulation" by the state required by the provisions of Section 2(b) of the McCarran Act, automobile insurance rating would become subject to the antitrust laws. This would accomplish a meaningful partnership between federal and state governments in which each sovereign would be assigned the role which it is most competent to discharge. The preservation of competition and sophisticated techniques for accomplishing it have been perfected through long years of experience by the federal government. The states, on the other hand, would retain their responsibility over licensing of companies and agents, entry into the market, capital and surplus requirements, control over the insurance contract, policy forms and endorsements, protection of the public against fraud and manipulation, examination of companies and organizations, complaint handling, investments, and finally, the opportunity to concentrate upon the single most important regulatory objective, the preservation of solvency.

Competition as Regulator

It seems unlikely that the federal government would itself attempt direct regulation of rates when another time-tested federal mechanism is available. As federal and state officials make common cause in seeking solutions to the nation's auto insurance problems, this venture into creative federalism seems worthy of exploration.

Past experience with price controls, both state and national, strongly indicates that only the most urgent considerations of national interest justify bureaucratic interference with the sensitive pricing machinery which makes our economy such a marvel of efficiency. Government inquiry or supervision cannot effectively be substituted for our traditional ideal of prices set in response to free market forces. Only the ebb and flow of buyers' pressures reflected through free markets should mold pricing decisions. As the Supreme Court announced in the *Socony-Vacuum* case, antitrust's prime goal is to assure the determination of prices by free competition alone. "The fact that, as here, they (prices) are fixed at the fair going market price is immaterial."[28] For, "the reasonableness of prices has no constancy due to the dynamic quality of business facts underlying price structures."[29] The "difference between legal and illegal conduct in the field of business relations" as enunciated by the Supreme Court in the *Trenton Potteries* case cannot "depend upon so uncertain a test as whether prices are reasonable—a determination which can be satisfactorily made only after a complete survey of our economic organization and a choice between rival philosophies."[30] Professor Spencer L. Kimball in examining state rate regulation expressed a similar view: "With respect to the former (the excessive test) it is possible to argue that free competition is not only a better guarantee that rates will not be excessive than is administrative regulation, but also is the only reliable way to decide the basic question of value. . . ."[31]

That the even hand of competition works to produce the level of

---

[28] *U.S.* v. *Socony-Vacuum Oil Co.,* 310 U.S. 150, 222 (1940).

[29] *Ibid.,* p. 221.

[30] *U.S.* v. *Trenton Potteries Co.,* 273 U.S. 392, 398 (1926).

[31] Spencer L. Kimball, "The Goals of Insurance Laws: Means vs. Ends," *The Journal of Insurance,* Vol. 29, No. 1 (March, 1962), p. 26.

rates which best serves all sectors of the economy was graphically demonstrated in a study made by the California Rating Department under its competitive nonfiling law.[32]

In the chronically unprofitable automobile lines, the California experience was consistently better for insurers than in the country as a whole where prior approval of rates prevail. But, conversely, in the lines of insurance traditionally profitable nationwide, California showed higher loss ratios with competition obviously working to depress prices and profits.[33]

The argument has never been supported that competition as a regulator will not work in insurance since it causes insolvencies in a business where insolvencies cannot be tolerated because of harm to innocent persons. If the danger exists, it is declining as more states require that uninsured motorist protection cover when tortfeasors' insurers become insolvent. The vast majority of states have now enacted mandatory uninsured motorist laws, with or without right of rejection, and an increasingly larger number of states are including insolvency protection. Thus, as the percentage of insured vehicles in America increases with uninsured motorist coverage including insolvency protection, the harmful consequences of insolvency to injured claimants become minimal. Against this background, the argument that excessive competition might lead to insurer insolvencies loses much of its weight.

Problems Created by Rating Bureaus

The need to preserve rating bureaus' concerted pricing functions is the reason generally advanced against application of the antitrust laws to property and casualty insurance. Conceivably, Congress might conclude that the only socially useful role of the bureaus is the collection and dissemination of loss experience. If bureaus operated to compile only pure loss experience with members and subscribers making their own rates, it is probable that no further antitrust exemption would be necessary. But assuming that Congress will want as little interference with existing industry practices as possible, it is suggested that an exemption from only Section 1 of the Sherman Act could achieve the objective of preserving price

---

[32] "Twenty Years Experience under California Rating Law," Address by Mark Kai-Kee, *Proceedings 21st Annual Meeting, National Association of Independent Insurers* (November 14–17, 1966), p. 53.

[33] *Ibid.*

fixing in concert. Rating bureaus would thus continue concerted ratemaking for members and subscribers on a voluntary basis. However, the amendment could be drawn narrowly so that rating practices or any other business conduct which restrained competition of any third person could still be prosecuted under Section 1. The proscriptions of Section 1 against conspiratorial conduct which allocates markets or customers, suppresses production, causes boycotting, or results in tie-in or unlawful exclusive dealing would apply to rating bureaus. Section 2 of the Sherman Act, the monopoly section, would apply to all automobile insurers. By making Section 2 applicable to all, the danger that rating bureaus either singly or in combination could monopolize the business is eliminated. All automobile insurers outside the bureaus would, of course, be fully covered under these laws.

The rating bureau issue poses some thorny questions, but they are not beyond solution. A proposal to keep rating bureaus only subject to state rating laws would ease the antitrust question, but probably creates an unworkable situation in which independent filers are free to move responsively to market conditions while competitors in rating bureaus are delayed and handcuffed by regulatory supervision. Historically, where Congress has granted exemptions from the antitrust laws, it has sought to safeguard the public by substituting some form of regulation, either state or federal. However, in 1963 Congress granted an exemption to member clubs of a professional team sport to pool their television rights for package sale by the league. Other sections of this law provide that other restrictive broadcast and telecast practices remain under the antitrust laws.[34] There is thus some legislative precedent for limited antitrust exemption without substitute controls. However, if the prospect of unregulated price fixing, however narrowly circumscribed, is disturbing to congressional sensibilities, consideration could be given to requiring rating bureaus to file reports and subject them to periodic rating examination by the states for corrective action, but excluding advance approval power.

Other Issues to be Resolved

In sketching this brief outline of a plan within the framework of the McCarran Act for bringing automobile insurers under the

---

[34] 15 U.S.C. sec. 1291 (1964).

antitrust laws by exempting them from state rating laws, no effort is being made to resolve all other questions of antitrust application to the automobile insurance business. Obviously, the question of price discrimination under the Robinson-Patman Act, along with other questions, requires very careful study. Joint underwriting and joint reinsurance are matters which will require special attention. This concept is advanced in order to focus upon an approach which is vastly different from the politically charged question of whether the federal government or the state government should maintain the exclusive bureaucratic machinery for the regulation of insurance. The federal antitrust laws are not regulatory statutes. They express America's abiding faith that, in general, free competition will keep the country's economic machinery in good working order. They have been described as charters of economic freedom.[35] Their function is to eliminate unreasonable restraints or restriction upon the healthy operation of our free enterprise institutions.

Benefits of New Approach

It is respectfully suggested that such a proposal could bring relief in areas now deeply troublesome and would have positive benefits for state governments, federal officials, the insurance business, and the purchasing public. How long will state governors and insurance commissioners suffer the unbearable political pressures in approving automobile insurance rates? How long will a few of the public be denied a necessity of modern American life because insurers must pull out or drastically restrict writings in the face of faulty rate regulation? Even liberal rating laws are no sure guarantee against such consequences, since experience has demonstrated that the difficulty often lies in the administration of the laws and the type of personnel administering them.

Today, insurers are facing public challenges on the issue of including investment income in ratemaking. A persuasive case can be made that there is no practical way to include returns from investment in the ratemaking formulas. But the industry is in an untenable position when it attempts to tell public officials they should not look into such income in measuring a company's performance. In point of fact, income from all sources must in some

---

[35] Report of the Attorney General's National Committee to Study the Antitrust Laws (1955), p. 1.

way be considered by insurers in establishing the rate levels needed to accomplish the company's long-term or short-term corporate goals and properly serve the market. Under antitrust policy, pricing is a function of the market; and the force of competition will require due consideration of all relevant factors in the making of rates. Margins of profit are not set in advance by administrative fiat. They result naturally from the free play of supply and demand. The current inclusion of a profit factor in automobile insurance rate filings is an arbitrary and unrealistic fiction which is seldom reflected in the facts, and which exposes the absurdities of administrative rate making procedures.

In another vein, insurers are now obliged to make rates upon the basis of the political boundaries of each state. Obviously, the artificial demarcations marking the boundaries of political subdivisions have little or no relation to the economic factors which determine natural marketing areas. Competition under the antitrust laws serves to relate prices to costs and other natural economic phenomena.

In reviewing the various alternatives for regulating the automobile insurance business, the goal should be the system which serves best the interest of all the people. Congress will surely seek to evaluate the merits of the antitrust approach before reaching a final judgment.

chapter 11

Price Discrimination in Property and Liability Insurance

THE FOLLOWING SELECTION examines the concept of price discrimination, its economic and ethical basis, and its regulatory and legal status.

The conclusions reached on the concept of price discrimination in property and liability insurance have important implications for rating methods, pricing in concert, dividends, group insurance, and regulation.

UNFAIR RATE DISCRIMINATION IN PROPERTY AND LIABILITY INSURANCE

C. Arthur Williams, Jr.
Professor of Economics and Insurance
University of Minnesota

All states require under their rate regulatory laws or other legislation that subject to a few exceptions, property and liability insurance rates be not unfairly discriminatory. Although this legislation usually makes no attempt to define unfair rate discrimination, few persons have questioned the desirability or the feasibility of requiring property and liability insurance rates to conform to the standard. This is surprising in view of the fact that (1) it is much more difficult to regulate insurance rates with respect to unfair discrimination than with respect to their reasonableness or their adequacy, (2) there are no strong economic arguments in favor of this standard, and (3) some of the recent proposals for converting model rating laws to less restrictive regulation have important implications for the regulation of unfair discrimination.

This paper will (1) define unfair rate discrimination in insurance and describe the three forms it may take, (2) present the economic and ethical arguments supporting and opposing the prohibition of unfair discrimination in insurance, and (3) explain and evaluate current regulation and proposals for change.[1]

DEFINITION AND TYPES OF UNFAIR INSURANCE RATE DISCRIMINATION

A widely accepted economic definition of price discrimination states that unfair price discrimination exists if, allowing for practical limitations, there are price differences that do not correspond to differences in costs or cost differences that are not reflected in price differences. The qualifying adjective "unfair" is generally omitted because, as will become apparent later, price discrimination is a neutral term in economics and to label this practice "unfair" prejudges the practice. On the other hand, because price discrimination does not include all types of price differentiation, the absence of some qualifying adjective is also misleading. Instead of attempting to solve this terminological issue here, this paper will refer to unfair price discrimination because this is the accepted terminology in insurance.

The definition stated above is not operational because it does not indicate (1) whether the costs are marginal costs or average costs or (2) what relationship should exist between prices and costs. A more precise definition preferred by many economic theorists states that a price structure is unfairly discriminatory if the prices are not *proportional* to *marginal* costs. They prefer this definition because they wish to avoid the problems associated with allocating overhead costs and because the principal economic argument advanced against unfair price discrimination depends upon this price-marginal cost relationship. On the other hand, despite the arbitrary nature of overhead cost allocations, most public officials and citizens generally would probably prefer a definition in terms of average costs. The theorists' requirement that prices be proportional to costs is more generally acceptable than their preference for marginal costs, but some observers have argued that the proper price-cost relationship is not equal ratios of prices to costs but equal returns on

---

[1] This paper, prepared in 1967, updates and restates material first presented in C. A. Williams, Jr., *Price Discrimination in Property and Liability Insurance* (Minneapolis: University of Minnesota Press, 1959).

the investment required in connection with each good or service. Determining the associated investments, however, is generally agreed to be impractical.[2]

Examples of unfair price discrimination have been classified in many ways. For example, unfair price discrimination may be open or secret, systematic or sporadic, purposive or incidental, and permanent or temporary.[3] A useful classification for this paper includes three categories: (1) unfair *personal* discrimination as illustrated by a surgeon's fees for the same type of operation that vary according to the patient's income; (2) unfair *group* discrimination as represented by special ladies' day prices, new customer magazine rates, and milk prices for cheese and ice cream processors; and (3) unfair *product* discrimination as represented by relatively higher prices for deluxe model automobiles, relatively lower prices on unbranded merchandise, and off-season rates at resort hotels.[4]

Although many persons believe that a monopoly or some collusion is necessary for a seller to discriminate unfairly among his buyers, this is not the case. All that is necessary is that the seller be able to divide his market into segments, each of which can be charged a separate price, and that resale among the buyers be held to a minimum.[5] This market segmentation can be accomplished by imperfect knowledge among the buyers or by product differentiation, as well as by collusion or monopoly.

UNFAIR INSURANCE RATE DISCRIMINATION DEFINED

An insurance rate structure will be considered to be unfairly discriminatory for the purposes of this paper, if allowing for practi-

---

[2] See Joel Dean, *Managerial Economics* (New York: Prentice-Hall, Inc., 1951), pp. 505–6.

[3] John Perry Miller, *Unfair Competition* (Cambridge: Harvard University Press, 1941), pp. 125–26.

[4] D. S. Watson, *Price Theory and Its Uses* (Boston: Houghton Mifflin Co., 1963), p. 312. Watson also discusses the famous classification of the English economist, A. C. Pigou, who distinguished between price discrimination of the first, second, and third degrees.

For another clear, comprehensive discussion of the personal-group-product dichotomy, see Ralph Cassady, Jr., "Techniques and Purposes of Price Discrimination," *Journal of Marketing,* Vol. 11, No. 2 (October, 1946), pp. 135–44. This is one of a series of four important articles by the same author on unfair price discrimination.

[5] Joe S. Bain, *Pricing, Distribution, and Employment* (rev. ed.; New York: Henry Holt & Co., 1953), pp. 401–2.

cal limitations, there are premium differences that do not correspond to expected losses and average expenses or if there are expected average cost differences that are not reflected in premium differences. This definition (1) recognizes the aleatory characteristic of insurance contracts; (2) embodies the concepts of (a) average cost, not marginal cost and (b) price-cost proportionality; (3) does not inquire into the "justness" of the costs incurred; and (4) implies that there is a family of "premium structures," not only one premium structure, that will satisfy the test of fair discrimination. The special problems posed by bureau pricing, reference filings, assessments, and dividends will be ignored for the present.

Some Dichotomies and Relationships

Expected Costs, Not Actual Costs. Insurance poses a more difficult pricing problem than most other products because the expected cost of insuring a particular policyholder almost always differs substantially from the actual costs incurred. Indeed insurance would not serve much purpose unless some insureds incurred actual losses that greatly exceeded their expected losses. On the other hand, it would not be feasible unless most insureds incurred actual losses that were less than their expected losses or unless all insureds incurred actual losses equal to their expected losses. For this reason it is necessary to define unfair insurance rate discrimination in terms of expected costs, not actual costs. Determining relative expected costs, however, is a highly complicated, technical task involving considerable judgment and many compromises. For example, in determining how many rating classes should exist, one must balance the desire for a refined classification against the desire for credible statistical information.

Even if a satisfactory compromise is reached with respect to the number of classes of insureds, there are many ways in which these classes can be defined. True causal factors that would serve as a basis for these definitions are extremely difficult to identify; the compromise with respect to the number of classes limits the number of causal factors that can be considered; and practical problems involved in applying the definitions cannot be ignored.[6]

---

[6] Professor Kimball, for example, has criticized the common practice of placing all young male drivers in the same rating class for automobile insurance and of using race as a rating factor in life insurance. Difficulties such as these

Average Costs, Not Marginal Costs. The preference of economic theorists for marginal costs has already been explained, but insurance rate discrimination has been defined above in terms of average costs. In insurance the distinction between marginal costs and average costs is much less important than in many other businesses because of the relative importance of variable costs. For example, at least 80 percent of the expected costs incurred in writing property or liability insurance for a particular insured are typically marginal costs. These include the expected losses and allocated loss adjustment expenses, the agent's commission, and the state premium tax. When an insurer elects to underwrite a new group of insureds or a new product (or stops underwriting an old group or product), a larger percentage of the costs incurred (or saved) will be marginal costs. Hence the effect of choosing average costs instead of marginal costs will be most significant when testing the existence of unfair personal discrimination. Tests of unfair group or unfair product discrimination will be much less affected.

As mentioned earlier, one reason many economic theorists prefer to define unfair discrimination in marginal costs terms is to avoid the arbitrary allocation of overhead costs. Determining marginal costs, however, may in itself be a rather arbitrary process. At this time most accounting records are not designed to produce this information. In addition there are some important conceptual problems with respect to the common costs incurred in servicing two or more customers or producing two or more products that are not resolved by turning to a marginal-cost concept.[7]

Finally, a definition of unfair rate discrimination in terms of marginal costs has never been considered seriously and is not likely to be acceptable as a guide for public policy in the future. If, as will be maintained later, the primary reason for prohibiting unfair rate discrimination is an ethical one, acceptability of the definition becomes an extremely important criterion.

---

lead Professor Kimball to conclude that no other objective of insurance regulation is so difficult to apply as fair rate discrimination. See Spencer L. Kimball, "The Purpose of Insurance Regulation: A Preliminary Inquiry in the Theory of Insurance Law," *Minnesota Law Review,* Vol. 45, p. 471 (1961), pp. 495–96.

[7] *Cost Behavior and Price Policy* (New York: National Bureau of Economic Research, 1943), pp. 170–88.

For a discussion of the problems involved in determining the marginal costs in insurance, see Lewis H. Roberts, "Actuarial Note: Fixed and Variable Expenses," *Proceedings of the Casualty Actuarial Society,* Vol. 50, Pt. I, No. 93 (May, 1963), pp. 1–2.

Premium-Cost Proportionality. The definition states that an insurance rate structure is unfairly discriminatory unless the premiums are proportional to the expected costs. In other words, each premium should contribute the same percentage of expected costs to the profit of the insurer.

This test, however, is usually properly modified to permit greater expected percentage profits in those lines where the risk or possible variation in the possible costs is large. Indeed it can be argued that the expected profit percentage should be greater with respect to those insureds whose actual losses as a group are the least predictable. Determining the appropriate variation in profit percentages, however, would be an almost impossible task. In addition to recognizing variations in risk, perhaps the portion of the insurer's investment income made possible by each insured should be considered. For many years state insurance commissioners have debated whether insurers' investment income should be considered in determining the allowable profit factor, and they have recognized that this allowance should vary among lines of insurance. A few states have recently required insurers to recognize their investment income in some rate filings. This issue, however, is too important and complicated to be resolved here. All that can be done is to note its implications with respect to unfair discrimination.

Reasonableness of Incurred Expenses. The definition of unfair discrimination under discussion does not question whether the expenses incurred in servicing a particular insured are reasonable in comparison with the expenses incurred in servicing some other insureds. It is concerned solely with the fair allocation of the expenses that are incurred. For example, assume that the commission rate is 20 percent of the premium. If the premium for one insured is $100 and for another $200, the second insured pays twice as high a commission as the first insured. Is this fair? If each of two insureds pays a $100 premium but the agent must spend much more time selling and servicing one insured, should both insureds pay the same dollar commission? Testing the reasonableness of the expenses themselves would seem to be a natural extension of the test of unfair discrimination, but it would make the regulatory process even more difficult.

Family of Acceptable Premium Structures. The definition of unfair price discrimination then that is probably in accord with prevailing value judgments is phrased in terms of *expected average* costs. Important but reasonable differences of opinion can exist with respect to the estimation of expected losses and allocated loss adjustment expenses, the estimation of variable expenses, and the estimation and allocation of overhead costs. Consequently it would clearly be unreasonable to insist on theoretical grounds that for each insurer there is only one premium structure that is not unfairly discriminatory. Instead there is a family of premium structures that would satisfy the test. A particular premium structure should be acceptable if it is a member of this family.

Some may argue that it is useless to test a premium structure with respect to unfair discrimination because some method of estimating the expected losses or allocating the overhead costs can always be devised to make the structure a member of the acceptable family. Such a liberal interpretation of the standard is not being advocated here. Many situations involving overt, unfair discrimination, particularly unfair personal or individual discrimination, should be readily apparent. For example, some allocations of overhead cost or classifications with respect to expected losses would be so strained as to receive almost universal condemnation. Nevertheless the test of unfair discrimination using this definition should be recognized for what it is—a rough yardstick and not a vernier caliper.

Types of Unfair Insurance Rate Discrimination

Unfair insurance rate discrimination can, like unfair price discrimination in general, be divided into three types. Unfair personal or individual rate discrimination is illustrated by rebates, arbitrary schedule credits, misclassifications, and competitively influenced judgment rates that favor one insured over another even though their expected costs of protection are the same. Most cases of unfair group rate discrimination are associated with class rating plans under which the rate variations among the classes are not related to cost differences. However, the concept includes any situation in which two or more insureds with different expected costs of protection are charged premiums that do not vary in accordance with these costs. Finally unfair product discrimination occurs when an insurer "overprices" or "underprices" one product relative to another. In this instance it has already been recognized that the ratio of premiums to costs may vary among lines in accordance with the risk or uncertainty involved and may in the future vary with respect to the contribution to investment income.

Opportunities for Unfair Rate Discrimination

In a perfectly competitive economy there would be no unfair rate discrimination because in the equilibrium state all prices would equal their respective marginal costs. The insurance business, however, operates under conditions closely approximating monopolistic competition or, in some instances, oligopoly. Through actual or alleged (through advertising) differences in contracts or in the performance of their obligations under those contracts, insurers have created differentiated products in the minds of the consumer. In addition, consumers have far less than perfect knowledge of insurers and their services.[8] Finally the purchaser of insurance protection cannot resell the product to another prospective buyer. Market segmentation and unfair premium discrimination, therefore, are clearly possible. On the other hand, because of the relatively great importance of marginal costs and the competition among insurers, who are continually looking for classes of insureds whose premiums are too high, the potential for unfair group and product discrimination is considerably more limited than in most other lines of business.

REASONS FOR PROHIBITING UNFAIR INSURANCE RATE DISCRIMINATION

The concept that insurance rates should be not unfairly discriminatory is almost universally accepted in insurance literature. For example, in his recent text on *Corporate Risk Control*, Professor MacDonald states that the "great goal of the insurer, in the United States at least, in determining the premium rate of an insured is achievement of equity."[9] In their recent report to the Virginia State Corporation Commission, Woodward and Fondiller, a New York

---

[8] Professor Crane has observed that price and product proliferation are more serious problems in insurance than in other businesses because price and quality comparisons are more difficult to make. Frederick C. Crane, *Automobile Insurance Rate Regulation*, Bureau of Business Research Monograph No. 105 (Columbus: Ohio State University, 1962), p. 82.

[9] Donald L. MacDonald, *Corporate Risk Control* (New York: Ronald Press Co., 1966), p. 82.

actuarial consulting firm recommends open competition as the simplest formula for rate regulation; but they would retain the enforcement, upon complaints, of prohibitions against unfair discrimination and unfair competition, thus demonstrating their acceptance of this standard.[10]

The reasons for prohibiting unfair insurance rate discrimination can be classified according to whether they are based upon economic or ethical considerations. Each of these two classes of arguments may in turn be classified according to whether they apply to business in general or to insurance in particular.

Arguments Based upon Economic Theory

The major economic argument against unfair price discrimination in any business states that in order to achieve an ideal allocation of resources among uses, *ceteris paribus,* all prices, including insurance premiums, should be proportional to the marginal costs of producing the purchased good or service. On the assumption that prices and costs are acceptable indications of satisfactions and sacrifices, respectively, no other price-cost relationship will yield as satisfactory a distribution of resources because otherwise the total satisfaction could be improved by moving resources from the underpriced use to the overpriced use.[11]

Most economists, however, regard price discrimination as a neutral term.[12] To quote Joel Dean, "no blanket condemnation of price discrimination is possible in the real world of widely disparate incomes. Some forms are good and some forms bad in terms of the sound criterion of the general welfare."[13] Dean rests his case primarily upon the fact that prices and costs are not accurate indications of the satisfactions and sacrifices associated with the goods or services. To illustrate, assume that an advertising executive must pay 35 cents for the same quality shoeshine that a clerk can obtain from the same shoeshine boy for 10 cents. The shoeshine boy can be

---

[10] "Significant Studies Advocate More Flexibility in Insurance Rating," *Best's Insurance News,* Vol. 67, No. 6 (October, 1966), p. 11.

[11] J. S. Bain, *Pricing, Distribution, and Employment* (rev. ed.; New York: Henry Holt & Co., 1953), pp. 413–14, 443.

[12] D. S. Watson, *Price Theory and Its Uses* (Boston: Houghton Mifflin Co., 1963), p. 311.

[13] Dean, *op. cit.,* pp. 508–9.

accused of favoring the clerk because of the lower price but because of differences in the marginal utility of money, the shoeshine actually costs the advertising executive less, psychically, than the clerk.[14] Dean argues, therefore, that to achieve an optimum allocation of resources, it would often be necessary to adopt a pricing system in which prices in dollars are not proportional to marginal costs in dollars.

Not all economists share this negative position. For example, A. R. Oxenfeldt recognizes that the relationships between money costs and sacrifice and between money demand and satisfaction are complex. However, he notes that economists who have investigated these problems "conclude that money costs are the best, perhaps the only, available indicator of sacrifices incurred in production and that money demand is the best available measure of satisfaction obtained from consumption."[15] Nevertheless most of these economists agree with Professor Dean that it would not be wise public policy to require that all prices be proportionate to their respective marginal costs because (1) the resulting allocation may have some undesirable welfare implications, (2) in an imperfect economy this is an almost impossible goal to achieve, and (3) there are instances in which total output may be increased and prices reduced for all customers because of unfair price discrimination.[16] For example, a monopolist with relatively large fixed costs and joint costs *may* find that by segmenting his market into two parts and charging those customers with the more elastic demand a lower price, he can benefit both himself and all his customers. He benefits himself because his profit is increased. His output, however, *may* be more than under a simple monopoly, and the customers in *both* submarkets *may* pay lower prices than if there were no unfair discrimination. Many similar situations can be developed.[17]

Unfair price discrimination is sometimes criticized because it is

---

[14] *Ibid.*, fn. 3, p. 509. The relationship *may* be the reverse of that stated because the personalities of the two individuals is a factor as well as their incomes.

[15] A. R. Oxenfeldt, *Industrial Pricing and Market Prices* (New York: Prentice-Hall, Inc., 1951), p. 96.

[16] See, e.g., Myron W. Watkins, "Price Discrimination," *Encyclopedia of the Social Sciences* (New York: The Macmillan Co., 1962), Vol. 11, pp. 350–55; and Sidney Weintraub, *Price Theory* (New York: Pitman Publishing Corp., 1956), pp. 435–38.

[17] Bain, *op. cit.*, p. 414.

associated with incipient or actual monopoly,[18] which generally is assumed to have undesirable economic effects. It is true that a large business may temporarily lower its prices to certain customers in order to drive out its competitors. This is undesirable, but as noted earlier a monopoly position is not required for unfair price discrimination. Imperfect knowledge on the part of buyers or product differentiation is a sufficient condition.

In summary, there is no clear economic justification for requiring prices to be proportional to *average* costs. An economic justification does exist for requiring prices to be proportional to *marginal* costs, but it is subject to many qualifications. Essentially the same conclusion applies to unfair insurance rate discrimination. However, the qualification that unfair price discrimination *may* reduce prices and increase output carries much less weight than in most other industries. It is doubtful that economic arguments alone would support or deny the extensive regulation of unfair rate discrimination that now exists.

Arguments Based upon Ethical Considerations

One ethical argument against unfair price discrimination, which also has an economic base, states that prices should be proportional to marginal costs because each person should be expected to pay a price that is proportional to the added social burden associated with that service. This argument assumes a value judgment that most persons are not prepared to accept as a universal rule. Although unfair personal discrimination is the least defensible type of discrimination because it suggests deliberate favoritism,[19] this and other types of unfair discrimination are commonly accepted and justified on such grounds as charity, friendship, patriotism, convenience, or personnel policy. The value judgments of a society at a given point in time are far more complex than this standard would suggest. Furthermore, not all members of a society accept the prevailing judgments, and these judgments themselves tend to change over time.

Economic-ethical arguments in favor of a certain pricing structure are not new. Indeed at one time they occupied a much more dominant position than at present. Aristotle, St. Augustine, and

---

[18] Watkins, *op. cit.*
[19] Watkins, *op. cit.*, p. 352.

Thomas Aquinas are among the famous philosophers and theologians who supported the concept of a "just price" at various stages in world history. Instead of explaining how prices are in fact determined, these writers were concerned primarily with the realization of justice. Aristotle's definition of a just price has been explained as follows:

> Justice applies not to the inanimate but to the animate, not to the commodity but to the laborer; it is revealed not in the magnitude of an isolated unit but in the correct relation of that unit to the organic whole. Hence the just price does not attach to house or flour or shoe alone. There is rather a just price relationship between house and flour and shoe—a relationship corresponding to that between builder and farmer and shoemaker.[20]

This doctrine was rediscovered by theologians in the Middle Ages. At first when the influence of the Church was great and a static natural economy existed with relatively simple products and services, the doctrine was readily accepted. How the just price was to be determined was not specified, but it was generally agreed that most prices at the time were just because they were related to costs. There was no credit nor constant infusion of new products to cloud the picture. As a money economy, credit, and more complicated goods and services developed, pricing structures became more complex; and it was no longer clear that they were just. Consequently, the "just price" supporters tried to modify their doctrine to fit the changing environment. They permitted new elements such as the creativity of an entrepreneur, scarcity, pleasurableness, and risk to influence price. This change permitted prices to vary among persons, places, and times. In other words, "justice was conceived as a sliding scale rather than an objective norm."[21] Demand considerations were recognized as well as cost considerations.

Since the 18th century and the development of classical economics, which viewed price as a purely market phenomena, the doctrine of the just price is of interest mainly to historians.[22]

Although the importance of ethical arguments as a guide for

---

[20] Edgar Salin, "Just Price," *Encyclopedia of the Social Sciences* (New York: The Macmillan Co., 1962), Vol. 8, p. 504. In other words, Aristotle's just price structure was not unfairly discriminatory in the ethical sense.

[21] *Ibid.*, p. 506.

[22] Professor Edgar Salin has observed, however, that the socialistic labor theory of value is a closely related concept and that a decline of capitalism could be accompanied by a reappearance of the "correct" price doctrine.

price policy in general must be discounted, it should be recognized that the public attaches far more importance to these arguments as the degree of competition declines or as the "public interest" of the business increases. As long as there is extensive competition, the public reasons that the resulting price structures cannot be too unfairly discriminatory, at least in the intermediate or long run. Also as the degree of "public interest" increases, the public has become more concerned with "fair" treatment.

The property and liability insurance business is considered to be a "business affected with a public interest."[23] Consequently it is not surprising to find a rather strong emphasis on ethical principles.

This importance attached to ethical pricing has been reinforced by the mutual character of all insurance.[24] Because all insurers are basically middlemen combining the resources of many persons to compensate the few who suffer losses, insurers, it is argued, should relate their premiums to expected costs. Professor MacDonald states the principle in these strong terms. "Insurers . . . strive endlessly to reduce inequities to insignificant degrees. Their zeal stems from recognition of the fact that the essence of inequity in rating is involuntary subsidization of one policyholder by another. Their abhorrence of subsidization within policyholder groups rests in part upon their belief that redistribution by an insurer of the resources of its policyholder without the consent of every other policyholder is immoral."[25]

Unfair rate (or underwriting) discrimination has also been considered undesirable because it may exclude certain groups from coverage. Both ethical and social implications are involved. If premiums are set unduly high for some groups, they may be unable to pay the premiums and thus indirectly be denied coverage that they could afford at a correct price. Insurers may also refuse to write individuals whose true expected costs would place them in an acceptable class.[26] Discrimination of this sort, however, is not necessarily purposive. It may result instead from the inability of the insurer to estimate expected costs accurately.

Finally this emphasis upon ethical principles was supported until

---

[23] *German Alliance Insurance Co.* v. *Lewis,* 233 U.S. 389 (1914).

[24] Robert Riegel, "Fire Insurance Rates: Problems of Cooperation, Classification, Regulation," *The Quarterly Journal of Economics* (August, 1916), pp. 704–37.

[25] MacDonald, *op. cit.,* p. 82.

[26] Kimball, "The Purpose of Insurance Regulation," *op. cit.,* pp. 496–97.

recently by the dominance of bureau insurers who, through a common pricing structure, reduced the degree of effective price competition.

These ethical arguments, however, have not gone unchallenged, and the challenges seem to be increasing in number.

In a recent report on Florida automobile liability insurance, a committee of businessmen appointed by the Florida Insurance Commissioner questioned the concept of insurance as a "public interest" business. In their words, the "states do not regulate price for the other major section of the automobile transportation system. Insurance is no more of a utility in this connection than the manufacturer. In fact, even less as they are in the 'risk' business."[27] Later in their study, however, they express great concern over the equity of automobile rate class differentials and rating territories.[28]

Even if the "public-interest" label does apply, however, this does not mean that insurers must avoid unfairly discriminatory premium structures. Indeed the public interest nature of the business may suggest unfair discrimination in favor of certain groups whom society in general would prefer to help. Professor Kimball has suggested that the socialization of risk is an objective of insurance regulation that competes with the objective of equity among policyholders.[29] For example, society may prefer some unfair rate discrimination to pricing out of the market certain automobile insurance drivers with high expected losses.

H. J. Lowry, president-elect of the American Mutual Alliance, has speculated that at some future date the government may pay subsidies to private insurers to allow them to write some insureds at rates based upon political rather than economic factors. He argues that one type of insurance buyer is already being subsidized at the expense of another through assigned risk plans, unsatisfied judgment funds, and the rejection in certain states of sorely needed rate increases.[30]

Professor Richard N. Farmer has advanced the interesting thesis that the life insurance business may be on the verge of decay

---

[27] Florida Action Committee for Traffic Studies, *Florida Automobile Liability Insurance Study and Conclusions,* June, 1966, p. 17.

[28] *Ibid.,* pp. 26–28.

[29] Kimball, "The Purpose of Insurance Regulation," *op. cit.,* pp. 512–14.

[30] *The Mutual Memorandum,* Vol. 50, No. 18 (November 15, 1966), item 74.

because of incorrect ethical attitudes on the part of its managers and state regulators.[31] In his opinion these persons reason incorrectly that the life insurance business is a morally superior industry and should act accordingly. Professor Farmer agrees that in 1930 this attitude may have been correct because there was no extensive social insurance program; individual life insurance and annuities provided the only means by which many members of the population could avoid orphanages and poorhouses, insurers were major mobilizers of savings, and only highly regarded businesses were regulated so closely by the state. Today he argues that social insurance, widening vocational horizons for widows, declining death rates, a lesser role for insurers in the mobilization of savings, and other recent developments have made life insurance much less of a virtuous industry. State regulation no longer creates the halo effect it once did because states now regulate closely some not so desirable enterprises such as dealers in alcoholic beverages, horse racing, and growers of opium poppies. In short, he argues, "insurance is a vocation like many others, without any particular claim to special status. If this is true in our private enterprise economy, it seems wise for insurance companies to behave much like other types of firms."[32] Price discrimination receives the following specific notice:

Certain types of price discrimination would enhance the profitability of the company, but such pricing is not applied, since it is improper to price in this manner, given the moral superiority of the industry. The long struggle over quantity discounts and the reluctance of many companies to apply this sort of pricing suggests that non-economic aspects of this pricing question were very important. But if the result is to be less profitable, grow less, or give business to other firms (and perhaps Federally sponsored programs) such an attitude may actually contribute to the decline of the industry.[33]

Professor Farmer may underestimate the degree to which life insurers now practice unfair price discrimination,[34] but purposive unfair discrimination has seldom been so forcefully advocated. If

---

[31] Richard N. Farmer, "The Long Term Crisis in Life Insurance," *The Journal of Risk and Insurance,* Vol. 33, No. 4 (December, 1966), pp. 621–29.

[32] *Ibid.,* p. 626.

[33] *Ibid.,* pp. 626–27.

[34] See H. D. Mohring, "The Life Insurance Industry: A Study of Price Policy and Its Determinants" (unpublished doctoral dissertation, Massachusetts Institute of Technology, August, 1958).

unfair price discrimination in life insurance is now acceptable, can it be any less appropriate in property and liability insurance? At present most persons are probably not prepared to accept Professor Farmer's thesis, but his article serves as a strong reminder that ethical attitudes do change.

Ethical considerations also seem to fade into the background when challenged by self-interest. For example, in 1950 the residents of Massachusetts were asked to vote on whether the rates charged throughout the Commonwealth should be uniform. The vote against the proposal was three times the vote in favor, but the measure passed in Suffolk county, the highest-rated area in the state.[35]

Ethical considerations vary among nations. For example, in Great Britain unfair discrimination is not prohibited, and British insurers engage in many practices that would be illegal in the United States.[36] This international variation can influence domestic regulations. For example, when United States insurers engage in international insurance activities, which pit them against insurers of other countries with different ethical standards, they are subject to much less regulation with respect to unfair discrimination.[37]

SPECIAL PROBLEMS IN DEFINING UNFAIR INSURANCE RATE DISCRIMINATION

Before turning to the present status and prospects for the regulation of unfair insurance rate discrimination, it is desirable to describe briefly some of the special problems that arise in determining a test for unfair rate discrimination. The section on the definition of unfair insurance rate discrimination sheds some light on the feasibility of regulations against unfair discrimination. This section supplements those earlier observations.

---

[35] George H. Kline and Carl O. Pearson, *The Problem of the Uninsured Motorist* (New York: New York State Insurance Department, 1951), pp. 58–59.

[36] A. J. Bohlinger and T. J. Morrill, *Insurance Supervision and Practices in England* (New York: New York State Insurance Department, 1948), pp. 25–43 and 75–79.

[37] For a similar observation with respect to control of insurance contract terms, see Spencer L. Kimball and Werner Pfennigstorf, "Administrative Control of the Terms of Insurance Contracts: A Comparative Study," *Indiana Law Journal*, Vol. 40, No. 2 (Winter, 1965), pp. 220–21.

Bureau Rates and Reference Filings

To this point the discussion has proceeded as if the test of unfair discrimination were being applied to the expected costs incurred by a single insurer in servicing its insureds. In practice the test is often applied to some cost structure other than that of the insurer involved. Two examples are the testing of (1) bureau rates and (2) reference filings.

Bureau rates are based on the average expected costs for the insurers submitting their loss and expense experience. The expense pattern in particular may vary among insurers. For example, the expenses involved in servicing a particular class of insureds may be higher for insurer A than for insurer B while the opposite may be true with respect to some other class of insureds. Hence the bureau rate structure is not equally suitable for all insurers using it. However, if the principle of bureau pricing is acceptable on other grounds, this should not be sufficient reason to discredit it because the family approach to acceptable structures would probably encompass all or most of these variations.

Reference filings pose a similar problem and suggest a similar conclusion. Here the insurer adopts the price structure of some other insurer or group of insurers as its own. The correspondence with its expected cost structure is probably not the same as for the other insurer or insurers but the difference is likely to be defensible on some reasonable grounds.

Assessments and Dividends

Assessments and dividends are usually not considered in discussions of unfair rate discrimination but as determinants of the final cost to the insured they probably should be.

Assessments are almost always expressed as a percentage of the original premium. Consequently they are related to the expected cost of protection as estimated at the beginning of the policy period. The actual costs do not affect the relative amount paid, and assessments can be tested with respect to unfair discrimination in the same way as the initial premiums.

Because dividends determine the final cost to the insured, the equity of the final cost structure depends upon the way in which dividends are distributed. The regulation of dividends, however, is a highly controversial issue. First, many observers who believe that initial rates should be subject to strict regulation with respect to unfair discrimination oppose regulation of dividends. The payment of dividends, they argue, is strictly a function of management and at most regulators should concern themselves with excessive dividends that would endanger the solvency of the insurer. Second, even if the desirability of prohibiting unfair discrimination is accepted, it is not clear what constitutes unfair dividend discrimination. Those accepting the definition already stated for rate discrimination favor a constant percentage dividend for all insureds because in this way the net prices are related to the expected costs. Others argue that it would be improper to ignore the additional information obtainable from the experience during the policy period because it is now possible through some credibility weighted average of the expected and the actual costs to obtain a better estimate of the "true" relative expected costs. Still others believe that dividends should be distributed primarily on the basis of relative actual loss ratios because the insureds with the lowest ratios contributed most of the money available for dividends and because the initial expected cost figure is at best an intelligent guess.

Clearly the regulation of dividends at this time with respect to unfair discrimination is, to put it optimistically, difficult. However, failure to regulate dividends in this respect may enable an insurer to accomplish through dividends what it could not accomplish through its initial premium structure. Consequently one cannot evaluate the feasibility and effectiveness of *rate* regulation without considering the status of *dividend* regulation.[38]

REGULATION OF UNFAIR RATE DISCRIMINATION

Although there may be many questions concerning the desirability and feasibility of prohibiting unfair discrimination in insurance

---

[38] In his comprehensive study of "The Regulation of Ex-Post Insurance Rates," Dr. A. R. Whitaker makes the same point forcibly as follows: "The law is, at best, not clearly in favor of a rate-reduction interpretation of insurance policy dividends but it cannot be denied that dividends could be used to effectively restructure any set of rates, or that they are frequently so used, or that they cannot be regarded as mere distributions of surplus when they are so used. Even if dividends were absolutely undifferentiated according to loss structure, they are regarded as potential reductions in the cost of insurance, and are so represented by agents." A. R. Whitaker, "The Regulation of Ex-Post Insurance Rates" (unpublished doctoral dissertation, University of Pennsylvania, 1965), p. 61.

rates, extensive regulation does in fact exist. Before turning to this insurance regulation, the nature of such regulation in other fields will be described briefly. Insurance regulation cannot be considered in a vacuum. If insurance is subject to different treatment than other goods and services, there should be some reason for the difference.

Businesses Not Affected with a Public Interest

Most businesses such as automobile and cigarette manufacturers and retail stores are not considered to be affected with a public interest. Common law does not prohibit these businesses from practicing unfair price discrimination except when it is part of an unreasonable agreement to fix prices. The principal federal legislation, namely the Robinson-Patman Act of 1936, prohibits price differences not justified by cost differences if they are symptomatic of monopoly or collusion or if they tend to hinder competition. Uniform prices are not prohibited even if there are cost differences; quantity discounts justified by cost differences may be forbidden if there are only a few buyers of the larger quantities; and price differences not justified by cost differences may be permitted if a lower price is made in good faith to meet an equally low price of a competitor. Thus this legislation is designed primarily to prohibit only those practices in which the unfair price discrimination (1) is overt and (2) tends to hinder competition. The ethical arguments and the economic argument concerning misallocation of resources apparently carry little weight.

Businesses Affected with a Public Interest

Businesses affected with a public interest are subject to much more extensive price regulation. At the present time these businesses include (1) transportation carriers, (2) public utilities, and (3) miscellaneous businesses such as public warehouses, hotels, stockyards, and insurers. The only characteristic these businesses have in common is that at some point in time a sufficient number of people became dissatisfied with private management in these businesses, the legislatures responded with statutes authorizing special price regulation, and the courts upheld the new regulation. Once a business is considered a "public interest" business it is almost impossible to remove it from this category but the degree of price regulation can be changed.

The regulation of the rates charged by common carriers has been relaxed recently, but the situation with respect to unfair discrimination has not changed much. Rates cannot be "unjustly" discriminatory. Unfair personal rate discrimination is always unjust, primarily because of ethical considerations. Unfair group and product discrimination, on the other hand, is fairly common, purposive, and legal. The relatively high fixed costs and the complex competitive nature of the industry have forced the regulators to recognize demand considerations.

Public utility rate regulation follows a similar pattern. State statutes prohibit unfair personal rate discrimination and "unreasonable" group and product discrimination. Because of their monopoly position one might expect these utilities to be subject to the most stringent regulations against unfair rate discrimination of all types, but because of their relatively high fixed costs, a considerable degree of unfair group and product rate discrimination has been permitted in order to increase output and lower the average unit cost. On the other hand, the unfair discrimination is probably of a lesser degree than it would be without any regulation. An ethical argument can be made against any unfair discrimination, but the economic arguments in the other direction are more persuasive.

Insurance

Unfair personal discrimination in fire insurance rates was first prohibited by an 1886 Louisiana statute forbidding rebates.[39] Although several other states soon adopted legislation prohibiting rebates and unfair personal discrimination in life insurance, there was little activity with respect to property and liability insurance. In 1910 there were only four antirebate laws applicable to fire insurance.[40] These statutes were considered by the courts to be a proper exercise of the police power of the state. They were enforced only after a violation had occurred and been discovered, usually by customer complaint.

In 1909 Kansas adopted the first comprehensive rate regulatory law affecting property and liability insurance. This law required

---

[39] *Cyclopedia of Insurance in the United States, 1913–1914* (Hartford: The Insurance Journal Co., 1914), p. 356.

[40] *Cyclopedia of Insurance in the United States, 1909–1910* (Hartford: The Insurance Journal Co., 1910), pp. 47–64.

insurers to file their rates and gave the superintendent of insurance certain approval and disapproval powers but, explicitly at least, it prohibited only unfair *personal* discrimination. The 1911 New York law, which is remembered mainly for its sanctioning of rating bureaus, also specifically prohibited only unfair personal discrimination. However, the legislative committee that proposed the legislation believed that regulation of unfair group discrimination was desirable and urged the superintendent to discuss a common plan of classifying loss experience with the National Association of Insurance Commissioners. Furthermore the superintendent acted as if he had the authority to regulate unfair rate discrimination of any type.

With the passage of time more states adopted rate regulatory laws. In many states the law no longer limited unfair discrimination to unfair personal discrimination. Antidiscrimination and antirebate laws also became more common. As late as the early forties, however, except with respect to workmen's compensation insurance, relatively few of these laws were effectively enforced.

The June 5, 1944, decision of the Supreme Court in the South-Eastern Underwriters Case and the passage in 1945 of Public Law 15 are too well-known to merit detailed comment here. The principal provision in Public Law 15, as far as rating practices and rate regulation were concerned, stated that after January 1, 1948 (later extended to July 1, 1948) the Sherman Act, the Clayton Act, and the Federal Trade Commission Act, all as amended, were to apply to insurance to the extent that such business was not regulated by state law and in all cases of boycott, coercion, or intimidation.

The principal question facing the states was whether to place primary reliance upon competition or strict regulation of insurance rates as the way to avoid application of these federal laws. Public Law 15 was conceived in an atmosphere that favored price competition in reaction to the practices that brought about the SEUA decision, but it was silent on the respective roles of competition, rating bureaus, and approval requirements.[41]

---

[41] That Congress itself probably preferred more extensive use of competition as a regulator than had previously existed is indicated by the following statement of the Committee on the Judiciary of the House of Representatives: "It is the opinion of Congress that competitive rates on a sound financial basis are in the public interest." Report No. 143, Committee on the Judiciary, to the 79th. Cong., 1st. sess., House of Representatives, Expressing the Intent of Congress with Reference to the Regulation of the Business of Insurance. Appears in *Proceedings of the National Association of Insurance Commissioners* (1946), pp. 130–31.

Model Rating Laws

After debating the relative merits of several proposals, which varied dramatically in the relative roles of competition and regulation and all of which in the eyes of their supporters would be adequate to prevent federal regulation, the National Association of Insurance Commissioners in 1947 adopted two model rate regulatory bills, one of which applied to fire insurance and the other to casualty insurance. These model laws, which were developed in cooperation with an All-Industry Committee, produced more restrictive regulation than had previously existed. Because most states passed laws modeled after these two bills and most still have such laws in effect, their major provisions affecting the regulation of unfair discrimination deserve special attention. Of particular interest are (1) the rating standards, (2) the filing requirements, (3) the "prior approval" and "deemer" provisions, and (4) the permissive sections with respect to rating bureaus and deviations from rating bureau rates.

The model laws require that rates be not unfairly discriminatory, but this term is not defined. Other provisions concerning the factors to be considered and the information to be offered in support of a rate filing strongly suggest that the concept includes unfair personal, class, and product discrimination and that it is cost-based. Unlike the Robinson-Patman Act, the model laws do not excuse unfair discrimination if it does not affect competition or if it is practiced in good faith to meet competition. However, in laws otherwise patterned quite closely after the model law, some states do provide more information concerning unfair discrimination. A few, like the Robinson-Patman Act, relate the standard to competition; some imply that only unfair personal discrimination is forbidden. On the other hand, a few specifically prohibit unfair group discrimination. The reluctance to define such a complex term as unfair discrimination is understandable, but the vagueness of the present approach creates many severe operational problems for the persons charged with the application of the law.

All rate manuals, rating schedules, rating rules, and rating plans must be filed and may not be used until the end of a waiting period or until approved, if earlier. The commissioner is expected to review each filing as soon as possible after it has been made. Rates may also be disapproved after they go into effect. Because of the "prior approval" requirement, the filing provision is a necessary part of the model rating laws, but the desirability of a filing provision can be considered independent of the prior approval requirement. The principal advantage of this provision is that the most important information required for the regulation of unfair discrimination is readily available to the regulators. It is possible to conduct a rather extensive investigation without requesting special information or even alerting the insurer involved to the fact that it is being investigated. It is not necessary to rely upon random examinations or consumer complaints to uncover violations of the law. On the other hand, filing can be a burden, particularly if the rates must be fully supported. All states with laws patterned after the model laws have a filing requirement except two, and the classification of these two laws as model laws is perhaps dubious. Montana does not require independent casualty insurers to file rates. Bureau insurers must file, but the standards are assumed to be satisfied as long as there is reasonable competition. The Idaho law suspends all of its model rating law including the standards unless a biennial review by the commissioner reveals a lack of reasonable competition with respect to a particular line of insurance.

The "prior approval" requirement has been the most debated feature of the model laws since the day it was introduced. Actually when it was adopted it was not considered to be a prior approval requirement. Filed rates were deemed to be approved at the expiration of a waiting period unless earlier approved or disapproved. The principal disadvantage of the requirement is that it may result in unnecessary delays and unreasonable denials which in turn may discourage product innovations and cause underwriting standards to be tightened. The "deemer" or waiting period clause is designed to encourage a prompt review, but it may also result in a perfunctory check on the proposed rates. Commissioners are understandably reluctant to allow rates to go into effect by default and may prefer any positive action to this alternative. Once a rate goes into effect under such a provision, there may be considerable reluctance to exercise the right of subsequent disapproval.[42] These possibilities coupled with the workload created by such reviews may lead to less

---

[42] For similar observations with respect to the approval of insurance contracts, see Spencer L. Kimball and Werner Pfennigstorf, "Administrative Control of the Terms of Insurance Contracts: A Comparative Study," *Indiana Law Journal*, Vol. 40, No. 2 (Winter, 1965), pp. 155–56.

effective control than laws providing only for subsequent disapproval. Another possibility is that an overburdened or overly rigid department may automatically and unduly question any departure from the prevailing rate relativities, which in many states is the bureau structure. On the other hand, the prior approval requirement has the advantage that it enables and encourages a review of a proposed rate structure before it goes into effect. The process is systematized and simplified and the responsibility is clearly fixed. Furthermore serious doubts are more likely to lead to rejections at that point than after a rate has gone into effect. In defense of this requirement it has also been argued that it prevents "flash filings" designed to favor particular customers that are withdrawn before they become applicable to others. It also avoids the problem of correcting premiums on existing business in the event of a subsequent disapproval. Final judgment, if any judgment is ever final, would seem to depend upon the importance assigned to unfair discrimination as a rating standard, both absolutely and relative to reasonableness and adequacy; the decisions made with respect to these other two standards; one's confidence in competition as a regulator; and the relative effectiveness and cost of the alternatives.

Several states generally considered to be in the model rating law camp have more restrictive requirements. Either the waiting period is longer or, as in the case of the District of Columbia (fire rates only), explicit approval by the commissioner is necessary. On the other hand, several states have "file-and-use" versions of the model laws under which the rates go into effect immediately and are subject only to subsequent disapproval.

Indiana and Louisiana have new modified file-and-use laws[43] under which a prior approval requirement goes into effect if there is any change in the anticipated expense ratio. One may well question why state insurance departments should possess different authority with respect to the regulation of the expected loss and expected expense portions of the premiums.

The other sections of the model laws that are most relevant to the regulation of unfair discrimination are those permitting the formation of rating bureaus and deviations from rating bureau rates. Rating bureaus can be formed and can require that members and subscribers adhere to their rates, but deviations are permitted under certain conditions. Bureaus are also permitted to make

---

[43] Louisiana, however, still requires all fire insurers to belong to the Louisiana Rating and Fire Prevention Bureau.

"agency filings" on behalf of insurers who wish to take more independent action but use the filing machinery of the bureau. If the regular bureau rates are based upon the pooling of the experience of many insurers, it is argued that because of the Law of Large Numbers the rate relativities produced in this way are more accurate than those based on the experience of any single member or subscriber. Even those who advocate that bureaus limit their function to the determination of advisory pure premiums recognize the validity of this argument. Regular bureau filings also reduce the burden of the filing requirement upon the member insurers and upon state regulators who can afford to devote more time to this one filing. On the other hand, unless many insurers choose to remain independent, the advantages of competition as a prodder and as an outlet for experimentation is weakened. The optimum balance is a delicate one.

The deviation route is one way to combine competition with bureau rating, but on this score the model laws are quite restrictive. Deviations do not go into effect until approved by the commissioner; the rating bureau is entitled to a hearing before the commissioner acts on the deviation, and the deviation is effective for only one year. Deviations with respect to rate relativities are more restricted with respect to casualty insurance than fire insurance because the independent route is much more accessible in casualty insurance. If a casualty insurer wishes to deviate from the bureau rates, the deviation must be the same percentage change for a kind or a class of insurance. In other words the rate relativities among classes must be preserved. The fire rating law permits a change in the rate relativities.

All states with model rating laws or close approximations thereto permit rating bureaus to exist but do not require insurers to join. The relative importance of rating bureaus varies greatly among these states. A few states impose more restrictive deviation provisions with respect to changes in rate relativities; some others are more liberal in this respect than the model laws. In a few states a deviation goes into effect at the expiration of a waiting period if no action has been taken by that time. The new Indiana statute applies the file-and-use privilege to deviation filings and permits the deviation to remain in effect until terminated or subsequently disapproved. In accordance with the prevailing trend, provisions of this sort will probably become more common.

On balance, the model rating laws represent a rather restrictive approach to the regulation of unfair discrimination. Although the range of possible and actual interpretations is great, the laws imply that (1) unfair discrimination is an important rating standard and (2) regulation supplemented by some competition is the best way to prevent unfair discrimination.

Other Rating Laws. The major departures from the model rating laws, in addition to the file-and-use legislation which is a departure in lesser degree, are those associated with (1) state-made rates, (2) mandatory rating bureau membership, and (3) the no-filing, no-bureau-rate-agreement approach.

State-made rates are best exemplified by Texas which through its State Board of Insurance promulgates rates in fire, automobile, workmen's compensation, and title insurance.[44] Massachusetts establishes automobile insurance rates in this way. The result is one set of rate relativities for all insurers.

Mandatory rating bureaus, coupled with a prior approval requirement, exist in one or more lines in the District of Columbia, Louisiana, Mississippi, North Carolina, and Virginia. Because deviations are usually permitted from the bureau rates, it is legally possible for an insurer to use a different set of rate relativities but not classes, and there are practical limits to this flexibility.

Those who favor these laws point to the arguments advanced earlier in favor of prior approval and rating bureaus. The opponents adopt the negative arguments with state-made rates being considered a particularly unwarranted interference with private enterprise. Some states such as South Carolina have considered recently a move toward a mandatory-bureau approach for automobile insurance.

California, Florida, Georgia, and, with respect to casualty insurance only, Missouri, represent the no-filing, no-bureau-rate-agreement approach. California does require that rates be not unfairly discriminatory, but an insurer may adopt a rate and use it immediately without notifying the California Insurance Department. The law is enforced primarily through periodic and spot examinations of insurers and advisory rating organizations, supplemented by customer complaints. Supporters of this approach point primarily to the flexibility it provides insurers, but they also note how it reduces the political pressures upon the department and lightens its workload. Competition becomes a more effective regu-

---

[44] R. W. Strain, "Insurance Pricing and Its Role in Relation to Economic Theory and Marketing Management," *Journal of Risk and Insurance,* Vol. 33, No. 3 (September, 1966), p. 453.

lator and the state insurance department can better perform its more circumscribed role. Opponents argue that the no-filing, no-bureau-rate-agreement approach leads to a proliferation of forms and rating procedures and to unfair discrimination. Mark Kai-Kee, the able Chief Rating Deputy of the California Insurance Department, agrees that "while the business should be allowed considerable freedom to exercise business judgment in the establishment of rate levels, a reasonably detailed policing of the rating practices of insurers is necessary to assure fair treatment of policyholders and to guard against unfair discrimination. . . . Competition itself does not prevent unfair discrimination." He admits that at times California may have had too many variations in forms or practices, but he believes that this disadvantage has been more than offset by growth and the capacity to meet change.[45] He believes that on the whole the efforts of the department to prevent unfair discrimination have been successful. Indeed he believes that the examination procedure used by his department permits a surveillance of the actual application of the rates that is not possible under the model laws. Customer complaints have not been excessive, and in his opinion they have been expeditiously handled. On the other hand, he acknowledges that the greatest difficulty in administering the California law has been deciding what constitutes unfair discrimination. It is also probable that insurers have greater permissiveness in this respect in California because the Commissioner must make a stronger case to terminate an existing rate than to prevent one from going into effect.[46] Finally although Mr. Kee does not consider this point, it is interesting to speculate to what extent the success of the California approach depends upon the influence upon insurer practices of more restrictive approaches in most jurisdictions.

Eighteen states have separate statutes applicable to workmen's compensation insurance rates. Under these statutes the supervisory authority has the power to establish rates or to require prior approval of rates. Many of these states require all insurers to belong to a single rating bureau and prohibit any rate deviations. The result is strict regulation of rates with respect to unfair discrimination and other standards. Included among these states are several such as

---

[45] "California Rating Law: How It Works and Is Implemented," *The National Underwriter,* November 21, 1966, pp. 22–24.

[46] *Proceedings of the National Association of Insurance Commissioners,* Vol. 2 (1966), p. 494.

Florida, California, and Missouri, which in other lines favor greater reliance upon competition as a regulator. The major reason ostensibly is the quasi-social insurance nature of workmen's compensation insurance and the resulting emphasis upon rate adequacy. It is interesting to speculate whether automobile insurance rate regulation would become more restrictive if the Basic Protection proposal or some similar automobile compensation plan were to be widely adopted. This special treatment of workmen's compensation insurance rates deserves much more thorough investigation.

Some jurisdictions such as Louisiana and the District of Columbia have radically different patterns of statutory regulation for fire insurance and for casualty insurance. These differences appear to be as outdated as the compartmentalization they perpetuate. The different treatment of life insurance and health insurance in most states should also be reexamined.

Other Statutes Regulating Unfair Discrimination. Rate regulatory laws are not the only statutes regulating unfair discrimination. Other relevant statutes include separate antirebate laws, antidiscrimination statutes, fair-trade practices acts that contain a general prohibition of unfair practices, and laws regulating the payment of dividends. These statutes are significant because (1) they regulate matters not always covered under the rating laws, such as rebating by producers or dividends that are unfairly discriminatory; and (2) they provide the only regulation with respect to lines not covered under rate regulatory laws. Because they raise the most interesting questions, only the regulation of rebates and dividends will be considered here.

Rebates are a clear example of unfair personal discrimination. They are prohibited in all states in most lines of insurance under rate regulatory laws or one of the special statutes noted above. Yet there is no universal agreement that rebates should be prohibited, especially if the rebate represents a sharing of the agent's commission with his customer. Spencer Kimball and Bartlett Jackson have questioned both the feasibility and desirability of antirebating legislation. Their arguments are so relevant to the present discussion that they deserve extended notice. They are convinced that rebating is common, but there are "few prosecutions, fewer convictions, and almost no application of sanctions."[47] They attribute this situation to

---

[47] Spencer L. Kimball and Bartlett A. Jackson, "The Regulation of Insurance Marketing," *Columbia Law Review,* Vol. 61, (February, 1961), p. 187.

the difficulty of detection and proof and the subtlety of the forms in which rebating can be cast. A cash payment, compensation under an advisory board contract, a loan that must be repaid, and a luncheon invitation motivated partly by friendship illustrate the variety of ways in which a person may be induced to purchase a contract. It is doubtful that the legislature meant to prohibit all of these practices. Some may argue that even if an antirebate law cannot be effectively enforced, it may designate "a moral standard to which members of a profession can make obeisance, toward which they should strive and against which their conduct can be judged. There seems little doubt that . . . the mere existence of the law reduces rebating to some extent."[48] On the other hand, those agents and policyholders who are the least deserving because they do not hesitate to violate the law gain an unfair advantage because they can violate the law without serious risk. Removing the penalties on the policyholder would remove one of the barriers to enforcement. Creating in competing agents a statutory cause of action against those who grant rebates would also help. A more basic question is whether rebating is undesirable. All insurance men contacted by Kimball and Jackson agreed that rebating was bad and should be prohibited.[49] They ascribed this finding in part to professional conditioning and in part to self-interest. The level of commissions is protected by antirebate statutes and this was in fact probably the most important motivating force when this legislation was passed. People not connected with the insurance business, however, did not see anything objectionable in rebates. Kimball and Jackson conclude with two observations that are relevant to the entire field of unfair discrimination. First, although they are not prepared to recommend abolition of the rule against rebating, they deny that such a rule is obviously desirable. Second, if such a rule is desirable, it should be made more operational than is presently the case.

This issue is currently being spotlighted by the proposal being advanced more and more frequently that producers be remunerated on the basis of a fee negotiated with the client instead of a specified commission rate. It is argued that under a fee system the producer's advice will be more objective because it will not depend upon the amount of insurance purchased. It will be independent of rate increases and can be made commensurate with the services per-

---

[48] *Ibid.,* 188.

[49] *Ibid.,* p. 190.

formed.[50] Although this point is usually avoided in discussion of the fee system, presumably the producer will be permitted to lower his fee when faced by competition from some other producer. If adjustments of this sort are to be permitted, the antirebating laws will have to be revised or abandoned. If not, it will be interesting to observe the effectiveness of the policing mechanism.

To test public attitudes toward the fee system in an unscientific fashion, I asked one of my classes composed mainly of graduate students not interested in insurance as a career whether they would prefer such a system. All 21 students favored a variable fee system for business insurance because they argued (perhaps naively) that a business purchase is or should be more carefully made by knowledgeable people. On the other hand, 13 of the 21 students opposed rebates or variable fees based upon competitive forces in connection with family insurance. When pressed to explain their reasons for this position, they explained that it would add one more element of uncertainty to a difficult decision. This uncertainty was particularly distasteful in a purchase that was motivated by the desire to eliminate uncertainty. They also noted the social or "public interest" flavor of private insurance. On the other hand, they had no objection and in fact preferred price competition among insurers and even among agents as long as it did not involve unfair *personal* discrimination.

The regulation of dividends with respect to unfair discrimination is diverse and generally ineffective. In most states the only restriction on dividends is that the total amount paid not endanger the solvency of the insurer. The NAIC has taken no position on the matter except that if liberally interpreted, the optional rebate section under the rating law and the unfair trade practices act might provide authority for such regulation. The antirebate section states specifically that no insurer shall give any advantage in dividends to any insured, which probably prohibits any unfair personal discrimination but is silent on unfair group or product discrimination.

Only 17 states have statutes that prohibit unfair discrimination in the payment of dividends. These statutes differ according to (1) how specifically they prohibit unfair group discrimination, (2) the insurers affected (for example, all participating insurers or only domestic mutuals), and (3) how specifically and in what manner

---

[50] Donald W. Berry, "Producer Remuneration," *Best's Insurance News, Fire & Casualty Edition,* Vol. 67, No. 4 (August, 1966), pp. 20–23.

they define unfair discrimination.[51] Most laws do not define the term. A few require that class dividend rates vary according to relative loss experience, but some require that for a given kind of insurance the dividend rate be the same for all insureds. This variation in definitions is not surprising in view of the comment on pages 225–26 with respect to unfair dividend discrimination.

New York and Texas have the most complete statutory apparatus for regulating dividends. The New York law, which varies in its application by type of insurer, requires as a minimum prior approval of the dividend classes as reasonable—and as a maximum prior approval of the dividends themselves as fair and equitable. In Texas the dividend structures in most casualty lines are required to be equitable and cannot take effect until approved by the state board. Fire and marine insurance dividend rates must be the same for all insureds. Such tight dividend regulation appears consistent with the tight rate regulation that is characteristic of these two states if unfair discrimination is an important pricing standard. This consistency can be contrasted with the situation in many states that require initial workmen's compensation insurance rate structures to be uniform but do not regulate dividends with respect to unfair discrimination.

The goals of dividend regulation with respect to unfair discrimination need to be more extensively and intensively discussed.[52] These goals must be defined before the current statutes can be evaluated and where necessary revised.

CONCLUSION

Although the prevailing view in insurance literature and among insurance personnel and state regulators is that property and liabil-

---

[51] Whitaker reports that as a matter of practice, "no state regulates dividends paid within its boundaries by foreign companies. In many cases the regulation consists solely of a requirement that dividends be equitable, without further specification or filing requirement." Whitaker, *op. cit.*, p. 253.

[52] One starting point for such a discussion would be Dr. Whitaker's suggestion that initial rate filings include a specific loading for dividends. The dividends paid could be less than this loading if the insurer's financial condition could not support the full dividend and the commissioner approved. All reductions would be a uniform percentage of the warranted dividend rates. In other words, the initial rate relativities would be preserved. Whitaker, *op. cit.*, p. 227. This position is consistent with Dr. Whitaker's opinion expressed on page 226 that fundamental changes in the underlying structure of loss expectations cannot ordinarily be detected in one year.

ity insurance rates should be not unfairly discriminatory, it is not obvious that these rates should be required to satisfy this standard. Unless an insurer practices unfair discrimination in order to lessen the degree of competition, there are no strong economic arguments against this practice. Instead the justifications for prohibiting unfair discrimination rest primarily upon ethical considerations. Because the insurance business is always essentially mutual in character, all policyholders should, it is argued, be treated fairly with respect to the other policyholders. Because insurance is a business affected with a public interest, the public is more concerned about fair treatment than would otherwise be the case.

Although the opposition to the prevailing view is a small and relatively ineffective group, they are vocal and their number seems to be increasing. They deny that mutuality implies fair treatment as long as the purchase of insurance from a particular insurer is not compulsory. They argue that insurance is no more a public-interest or virtuous business than many other businesses not subject to such a strict unfair-discrimination standard. Socialization of risk, they observe, often runs counter to private equity among policyholders, but it may be a more important goal of rate regulation. They also observe that although much lip service is paid to the prohibition of unfair discrimination, public feelings on this subject are more apparent than real. Finally, as insurance becomes more international in scope, the provincial nature of domestic attitudes will become more obvious and less controlling.

If insurance regulation does rest primarily upon ethical grounds, it should be in accord with prevailing ethics. At present most persons seem to accept the thesis that insurance rates should not be unfairly discriminatory. Consequently it seems appropriate to have rules prohibiting unfair discrimination. However, the evidence concerning current attitudes is meager and indirect. There is need for more dialogue on this point in order to determine how strongly the regulators, insurers, and the public feel about this goal of insurance regulation. Such information will be important in resolving an issue that involves competing goals of insurance regulation and in determining what resources should be devoted and restrictions imposed in order to prohibit unfair discrimination.

If unfair discrimination is to be prohibited, should restrictions apply equally to the three types of discrimination? Unfair personal discrimination is apparently the most distasteful and fortunately the easiest to detect.

Abandoning regulation and accepting competition as the sole regulator of unfair discrimination is apparently not a satisfactory solution. Although competition among insurers prevents much unfair discrimination, the pressures of competition encourage some insurers to engage in this practice. Insurers have some ability to discriminate unfairly among their customers because of product differentiation and imperfect knowledge; indeed although insurance pricing structures compare favorably in this respect with those used by other industries, the fairness of several practices developed under regulated conditions has been questioned.

If some regulation is desirable, how much? Although my views are far from fixed, my current preferences are as follows: At the minimum it would seem reasonable to require that rates be not unfairly discriminatory and to authorize the insurance department to disapprove any rate that failed to meet this standard. The standard, however, needs to be defined in terms of the desired price-cost relationship. It should be interpreted liberally to permit a family of premium structures because there are many acceptable ways to classify insureds, estimate relative expected losses, and allocate expenses. A filing requirement would also be desirable because of the information it provides the regulator. The presence or absence of a prior approval requirement is probably not nearly as important as a department staffed with a large number of highly qualified and highly motivated, but flexible, examiners. However, given my assessment that the public is less concerned about unfair discrimination than has been supposed and the fact that a vigorous policing of a subsequent disapproval provision will uncover overt cases, a prior approval provision is probably not necessary. Rating bureaus should be permitted to exist because of the stability they lend to rating practices, the credibility of their experience, and their contribution to more effective regulation. Deviations, however, should not be required to be uniform and should be effective until terminated by the deviator or disapproved. Independent insurers should be subject to the same standards and other requirements as bureau insurers.

Rate regulation without dividend regulation is incomplete because an insurer can accomplish through dividends what it would be prevented from doing through its initial rate structure. Although a strong argument can be made for requiring the payment of the same dividend rate to all insureds purchasing a given type of property and liability insurance, the subject needs to be much more intensively investigated and discussed before any firm recommendation can be made. The regulation of dividends presents the most unanswered questions with respect to unfair discrimination.

In conclusion, it can be said that the current regulation of unfair discrimination in insurance rates is supported by certain rebuttable presumptions with respect to both the objectives and the means of such regulation. More research and objective discussion are needed with respect to both the presumptions and the rebuttals.

chapter 12

Multiple Line Regulation

MULTIPLE LINE LEGISLATION represented a much needed but long delayed reform of the American insurance system. The monoline tradition, however, had tenacious roots in history, industry organization, and regulatory philosophy. As the next selection indicates, we may have multiple line laws but we are still far from a true multiple line insurance system.

MULTIPLE LINE INSURANCE REGULATION

William B. Pugh, Jr.
Assistant General Counsel
Insurance Company of North America

This sordid and depressing story opens in Phoenicia about the year 1000 B.C. It appears that at that time if a person had property and wished to protect himself against financial loss because of its loss, he went to see his friendly, independent agent who for a sum agreed to reimburse the owner of the property for the loss regardless of the particular perils involved. Unfortunately, for those who believe in the progress of man, the truth is that things have gone down hill ever since the days of the Phoenicians. Despite some progress in recent years, there are still too many instances where the only way you can obtain multi-peril or all risk insurance is to go to foreign insurance markets free from beneficent state regulation.

The subject of the discussion today is how we got into this mess and the basic forces behind its development, with a description of some possible rays of hope for the future.

EVOLUTION OF THE AMERICAN SYSTEM

By the 1750's in Philadelphia, stimulated by the brilliance of Benjamin Franklin, man's institutions had evolved to the point

243

where houses could be insured against fire and lightning but not under trees. By 1792 the citizens of Philadelphia had organized a company to write fire, marine, and life insurance which were, practically speaking, all of the known forms of insurance of the day. In subsequent years the operators of this concern, the Insurance Company of North America, in what must be considered one of the colossal blunders in the history of American industry, decided there was no future in life insurance. One wonders whether this story would have been different had INA decided otherwise.

However, there was progress throughout most of the 19th century with companies being organized to write various kinds of insurance, including after about 1860 the first glimmerings of casualty insurance. Progress continued until the day Mrs. O'Leary's cow kicked over the lantern. The insurance industry hasn't recovered yet. The New York Insurance Department, anticipating the conflagration, was the first state to require separate life companies (apparently about 1865); and the second meeting in 1871 of what was then known as the National Convention of Insurance Commissioners (NCIC),[1] influenced by company failures after the Chicago fire, recommended model legislation to accomplish the same purpose.[2]

This recommendation was adopted in most states and in the years which followed was refined into what was called the American System, which in many instances required separate casualty as well as surety and workmen's compensation insurance companies in contrast to the English System which has always permitted multiple line powers. By 1910 New York, unsatisfied with the regulatory efforts of most states, adopted the Appleton Rule, applying its restriction to all companies who wished to be licensed in New York, and extending it to their entire operations wherever they might be.[3] One ridiculous aspect of the matter is that the two largest present-day stock companies in effect were given grandfather rights, including life, which they have maintained throughout the period even in

---

[1] The NCIC is now entitled the National Association of Insurance Commissioners or NAIC.

[2] *Proceedings of Second Session of the National Association of Insurance Commissioners,* Appendix, p. 257.

[3] See address by A. Bohlinger, Deputy Superintendent of Insurance, "The Appleton Rule—A Barrier to Multiple Line Underwriting?" before Savings Bank Insurance Forum, June 12, 1947, in *Insurance Broker—Age,* June, 1947.

New York. Every new insurance code solemnly reenacts these provisions, and it is considered humorous at code hearings to suggest that either the restriction be removed or the grandfather rights be taken away.

There was some basis for the so-called American System in the early period. Companies were comparatively small, and catastrophes such as those of Chicago and San Francisco were comparatively large. Failures were common. Besides, most of the dominant fire companies weren't interested in writing other forms of insurance.

Shortly after 1900, forces began to develop outside the industry and its regulation which would eventually force change. These centered around accelerating growth and increasing complexity of the American economy, both on the commercial and industrial levels and among individuals as well.

EARLY TREND TOWARD MULTIPLE LINE INSURANCE

The first major effort towards change was made by Burton Manfield, the Connecticut commissioner, at the NCIC in 1914, where he presented a paper calling for the abandonment of the American System. He concluded: "Why hamper and restrict the immense insurance activity in this country by needless practices of laws? That activity should be enlarged to find its normal expansion into all reasonable fields and in all reasonable ways."[4]

World War I seems to have interrupted further study. In 1920 the NCIC reaffirmed its position favoring the American System, but the important states of Pennsylvania, Connecticut, and Massachusetts registered a position in favor of giving companies multiple line powers other than life.[5] Benjamin Rush, then president of INA, supported this position, and the company has been in the forefront of the proponents of multiple line powers since that time.[6]

In 1922 the NCIC actually went on record as favoring the abolition of the American System, except for life insurance. The

---

[4] "Should We Abandon the American Restrictions upon Classes of Insurance Written (a) by a Company Doing Direct Writing and (b) by a Company Doing Reinsurance?" *Proceedings of the National Convention of Insurance Commissioners* (1914), pp. 161–68.

[5] *Proceedings of the National Association of Insurance Commissioners, 1921* (December 7–8, 1920), pp. 17–30.

[6] *Ibid.*

report of that year pointed out that American business was unable to secure needed insurance. Strong emphasis was made of the point that change was required to permit broader policies and not merely to permit a single company to write various kinds of insurance in separate policies. The report stated: "The coverages for which there seemed to be a demand and which cannot be given in one policy as is done by London Lloyds, are Jewelers' Block Policy, Householders Comprehensive Policy, Automobile Comprehensive Policy and insurance against damage to valuable objects of art."[7] The report concluded that "there is no apparent reason why most of the coverages should not be permitted."[8] Perhaps there was not, but 25 years still had to elapse before even the basic changes were made in state laws opening the door to the development of these policies.

It is not completely clear why the delay resulted. It appears probable, however, that the major reason was the extremely refined and dominating industry power structure which emerged during the twenties and thirties. Its organization and controls were single line in nature. By 1932, with the organization of the Insurance Executives Association, the industry was regulated by a pyramid of advisory organizations, topped by the IEA, a fire rather than a multiple line organization, which was in turn controlled by its Committee of Fifteen, the chief executives of the largest fire insurance companies in the United States. Inland marine was sold through departments of these companies and the leading casualty companies were subsidiaries. The power structure dictated the price and form of insurance. Because of the nature of the power structure, it was not capable of dealing with a multiple line policy. As a result, multiple line insurance was suppressed until the day when the form of the power structure was changed and, in fact, its effectiveness failed. It must be remembered that it was not until 1944 that insurance was held to be interstate commerce subject to the federal antitrust laws.

INLAND MARINE DEVELOPMENTS

A classic example of how the system worked is demonstrated by the extension of controls over the emerging field of inland marine

---

[7] *Proceedings of the National Association of Insurance Commissioners* (1924), pp. 6–9.

[8] *Ibid.*

insurance as it developed after World War I. Because of the changing nature of the perils to which property is exposed in transportation, inland marine policies from the beginning were all risk or broad-named peril in nature. During the twenties these were applied to risks associated with transportation such as bridges and tunnels. When the advantages of the coverages were recognized, these policies were used for multiple location risks and efforts were made to extend them even further. In one case an underwriter insured a chain of movie theaters and pacified his conscience by inserting the words, "This policy covers the property while in transit or otherwise."[9]

These efforts challenged the power structure. For one thing, they were comparatively free of any regulation by the industry or by the states, and when done on an individual company basis were competitive, which seems to have been about the worst sin. The system reacted quite effectively. First, the Interstate Underwriters Bureau was organized in 1929 to fix the forms and rates for writing multiple location insurance. The major fire insurance companies all became members; and they effectively forced compliance by agreeing not to furnish reinsurance, essential for this type of business, to any company who did not agree to abide by the rules.[10] The Inland Marine Underwriters Association was organized as a trade association in 1931 for inland marine insurance, and it fixed the policies of the business under the watchful eyes of the fire company executives.

In 1933, with the assistance of the Superintendent of Insurance of New York, industry drew up and the NCIC approved the Nation-Wide Marine Definition, defining and limiting what could be written as inland marine.[11] In the following year the industry nominated and the NCIC approved an industry committee known as the Joint Committee of Interpretation to interpret the definition. This committee had the power to try companies and levy fines if they issued policies contrary to the definition. As indicated in *Interpretative Bulletin No. 90,* dated November 20, 1940, referred to again later in this paper, the committee took the position, which was enforced, that it had the power to determine what could be written under Marine or Inland Marine Powers whether or not the

---

[9] Review of period by Donald Bowersock, subsequently President of the Boston Insurance Company, in *Weekly Underwriter,* February 21, 1938.

[10] See articles of agreement of the Interstate Underwriters Bureau.

[11] See Hamlin, "Inland Marine Insurance," *Spectator* (May 19, 1938), p. 12.

coverage was written on a marine form.[12] In this regard, the committee always took the position that it could make uniform findings applying throughout the United States even though the definition of inland marine insurance in the state laws varied widely. In the approximately 20 years up to about 1950, the IUB, the IMUA, the definition, and the joint committees, served in effect as a keystone between fire and casualty insurance, preventing any form of uncontrolled multiple line type underwriting which would threaten the controls of the power structure.

In the 1930's there were some pressures, such as the development of the personal property floater, which tended to be upsetting, but the power structure assigned "jurisdiction" of this form to segments of the business making it single line in practice even though multiple line in nature. During this period also, the extended coverage endorsement was developed. While this created no multiple line problem as such, its success and experience with the personal property floater, plus early experiments with the forerunners of automobile comprehensive coverage, stimulated thinking toward package policies.

DIEMAND COMMITTEE

The final decisive step came in 1943 when Commissioner Harrington of Massachusetts appointed an eight-man committee with John A. Diemand, president of INA, as chairman, to review the problem of multiple line insurance and to make recommendations. The composition of the committee was noteworthy because of the absence from its membership of representatives from the major New York and Hartford fire companies.[13] Also, the previous year the IEA had sent a special committee to Philadelphia to attempt to chastise Mr. Diemand (not an easy task) for giving a speech calling for, among other controversial subjects, the repealing of laws preventing multiple line underwriting. His appointment obviously was not to their liking even though he continued to serve as a member of the IEA until he resigned early in 1945.

---

[12] The Joint Committee of Interpretation issued interpretative bulletins numbered consecutively from the time of its organization on January 22, 1934.

[13] The members of this committee included the following: Kenneth C. Bell, S. Bruce Black, William H. LaBoyteaux, Arthur F. Lafrentz, J. Arthur Nelson, William D. O'Gorman, William D. Winter, John A. Diemand (Chm.).

The committee was an able one, as a review of some 1,200 pages of stenographic notes of some 17 meetings from December 15, 1943, to May 17, 1944, will indicate. There were differences of opinion, but there was also a strong esprit de corps which encouraged compromise in a forward direction. It is impossible to read the transcript without appreciating the key contribution made by the chairman in producing an effective and unanimous report.

The recommendations appear today to have been somewhat limited. The first two were that companies with sufficient resources would be permitted by law full multiple line powers other than life (*a*) in the foreign market and (*b*) in reinsurance. The last three recommendations were that companies be given powers to write comprehensive automobile policies, comprehensive aviation policies, and the personal property floater. An addendum indicated most members favored a comprehensive householders policy, but it was not recommended because it would endanger acceptance of the report.[14] The committee felt that if they were able to gain acceptance of a limited report, the rest would follow. The opposition apparently felt the same way, and in fact, the broader result did follow almost immediately in most states, at least so far as fire and casualty insurance was concerned.

The great contribution of the committee was its high purpose, conditioned by a very practical approach, and a great deal of careful and painstaking work which made intelligent opposition difficult if not impossible. Opposition did erupt immediately, highlighted by a long statement made jointly on behalf of the IEA and the Association of Casualty and Surety Executives, which must rank as one of the most misguided statements of the organized insurance industry.[15] Despite this opposition, the report was accepted by the NAIC in 1944 and the laws of most states were modified to give multiple line powers for fire and casualty insurance by 1949. By 1947 more than a majority of states had adopted the changes. This was the same year that the All Industry Rating Laws were presented to the states for approval and indicates, contrary to some arguments, that

---

[14] *Proceedings of the National Convention of Insurance Commissioners* (1944), pp. 125–29.

[15] Presented to Laws and Legislation Committee of NAIC by E. L. Williams, president of the Insurance Executives Association, at meeting on June 15, 1944. *Proceedings of the National Association of Insurance Commissioners* (1944), p. 233.

the two laws were considered coextensively and in contemplation of each other.

It is hard for me to leave the Diemand Committee story without one further comment indicating the simplicity and directness of the chairman. During one discussion of the householder's policy, one insurance executive spoke strongly in favor of it but expressed the opinion that the policy would require premiums so large that only the rich could afford the policy. The chairman said: "I am not thinking of it from the standpoint of the rich man. In my own territory I am thinking of the 400,000 individually owned homes around Philadelphia. . . . I think this form can be made to appeal to that particular fellow."[16]

There was several years' delay in the developing of new forms. New York did not amend its law until 1949, thereby changing the effect of the Appleton Rule as it applied to fire and casualty companies (its restrictive, extraterritorial effect still applies to prevent combination of life and property and liability powers). Furthermore, the fire insurance industry attempted to continue the same controls regardless of the change in the law. The only shift was in effect to recognize the state regulators as more nearly equal partners in attempting to stifle independence and competition. Efforts shifted to the use of the new rate laws to prevent competition. The independent became faced with the concerted arguments of the "best minds in the industry" and rating bureaus and trade associations assumed the new role of "aggrieved parties" in harassing litigation efforts. In short, the power structure attempted to maintain its historic position that there should be no competition in rates and forms at the policyholder level. Change within the structure came only after majority agreement. However, it became possible for a large, independent company with substantial resources and the courage to gamble on its future, particularly in relation to its producers, to develop and introduce new forms with competitive rates, but the going was very difficult for at least 10 years.

Lest one be accused of overemphasis, it is relevant to note that one prominent exponent of the status quo in speaking to a national trade association stated the following:

---

[16] *Proceedings of the National Association of Insurance Commissioners Multiple Line Underwriting Committee of the Subcommittee on Laws and Legislation* (1944), pp. 13–14.

I would be remiss if I did not impress upon you that to my mind this is the day and time to strike back unrelentingly at every manifestation of whatever nature that would disturb the orderly process of insurance. So long as we realize our trusteeship in this business we will always be alert to maintain its integrity and keep all subversive wolves from our pastures.[17]

CONTINUED OPPOSITION TO MULTIPLE LINE LAWS

Time, of course, does not permit a detailed review of the incidents of the fifties which led to the breakdown of industry opposition and restraints, but the more important problems illustrate many of the essential issues involved which continue in somewhat different form to the present day.

First, the industry opposition to the Manufacturers Output Policy, developed and marketed by the Aetna Insurance Company, illustrates one basic means of opposing change. This was an all risk type policy combining some coverages previously written as inland marine coupled with property insurance not coming within the Marine Definition.

Aetna filed in New York, and shortly thereafter a special committee of the Joint Committee of Interpretation summoned the company to a hearing which it did not attend. Thereafter, the committee issued a report concluding, in effect, following *Interpretative Bulletin No. 90* mentioned earlier, that the policy was inland marine in nature and therefore could only be written under that power, if at all, and further that since it did not come within the definition, it could not be written at all. The committee concluded that the changes in the laws had "simply brought about a manner and means of permitting Fire, Marine companies to write additional kinds of insurance. It did not alter the definition of kinds of insurance."[18] The committee ordered the company to cancel its policies and said that if this were not done the committee would seek remedial action from the states, which it did attempt in *Interpretative Bulletin No. 131.*

---

[17] Address of general manager of the Inland Marine Underwriters Association at annual meeting, 1950.

[18] Report of Special Committee of Joint Committee of Interpretation appointed to consider Case No. 1620, January 6, 1950.

Fortunately, Superintendent Dineen of New York did not buy this theory, and the policy was approved. In a subsequent speech commenting on this action, Dineen said:

Without in any way challenging the good faith of the Joint Committee which, we repeat was interpreting a definition of the pre-multiple line era, we must make equally sure that Departmental and Legislative road-blocks are not replaced by roadblocks erected by companies which are unable or unwilling to write all risk coverages themselves and do not wish to see their competitors write it.[19]

Despite this setback and in part because of it, efforts were made to strengthen opposition through the use of the definition; and in 1953 the power structure moved to have the definition brought up to date, strengthened, and reaffirmed by the states. This would have the effect of maintaining the keystone essential to keeping the property and liability portions of the industry from breaking loose through multiple line policies. A hearing for the purpose of secur-ing reaffirmation was held in Chicago in March, 1953. The record of this proceeding is mandatory reading for any student who desires to understand the opposing forces of the day. The principal spokes-man for the industry spoke in favor of a definition which would prevent independent competitive efforts "flying solo," as he called it. He also referred to the "pure virginity" of the joint committee.[20] Independently minded companies, led by Bradford Smith, presently Chairman of the Board of INA, took the position that multiple line contracts should be treated as a new and separate kind of insurance. Mr. Smith said: "In short the effect is to place in the hands of a few employees of insurance companies, the power to hinder, if not control, the lawful exercise of the charter powers of other insurance companies in competition with them."[21]

The reaffirmed definition was adopted and restrictive efforts under it continued for some years with some limited success, but it evolved before too long into an aid to commissioners to determine

---

[19] Address of Superintendent Robert E. Dineen, "The Battle of the Bureaus," at Annual Meeting of New York Association of Insurance Agents, May 8–9, 1950.

[20] Hearing before Committee of Definition and Interpretation of Underwrit-ing Powers of the NAIC, March 20, 1953, Statement of J. Victor Herd, executive vice president, Continental Insurance Co.

[21] *Ibid.,* statement of Bradford Smith, vice president, Insurance Company of North America.

what was inland marine rather than a means of blocking development of new multiple line policies.

In the spring of 1951, Aetna Fire and INA, which by that time had developed the homeowners policy, along with about 10 other companies founded a national multiple line rating bureau for furnishing services to companies in connection with these policies written on an indivisible premium basis and for filing premiums on their behalf.[22] The organization was created completely independent of the power structure; and immediately organizations within that structure such as the IEA, the National Board of Fire Underwriters, the National Bureau of Casualty Underwriters, and the IMUA appeared in open opposition to its licensing. The efforts were unsuccessful in most instances but their effect remains to this day; and even now after the industry position has changed completely, the Multi-Line Insurance Rating Bureau, a successor organization, has faced repeated litigation in order to secure licenses in a number of states, including even some where MPIRO had been licensed previously.

The organization of MPIRO and the industry's failure to successfully oppose it, plus the increasing acceptance particularly of the homeowners policy, impressed on the industry the need for at least a limited reorganization on a multiple line basis. In 1953 the IEA was abandoned and the initial version of the American Insurance Association took its place. This was said publicly to merely furnish a forum for the discussion of problems. However, the executive who appears to have been the chief architect, in commenting on the inability of existing organizations to cope with independent development of new forms, said: "Not the least of the AIA functions in this respect would be its determination of the method and forum for the consideration of new forms and coverage to the end that 'no jurisdiction situations would be subject to complete top control!' "[23]

It is most important to note that while the top level organization became multiple line in nature, the balance of the power structure remained organized on a separate line basis with rating and advisory associations retaining their separate functions. Furthermore, these organizations zealously guarded against any invasion into what they regarded as their jurisdiction. A procedure known as hand-in-hand

---

[22] See "Multiple Line Organization Planned" in *Spectator* (May, 1951), p 16, reporting on organization meeting of MPIRO.

[23] Letter, H. C. Conick to James Donovan, Esq., November 13, 1951.

filing was developed for multiple line filings. This procedure operated under the theory that each rating bureau, fire, casualty and
inland marine, filed the entire form and rates for the policy, as
agreed to with the other bureaus, but that each bureau retained
jurisdiction over its segment of the policy. Under this theory each
bureau could operate as an aggrieved party to oppose independent
filings or deviations. Furthermore, and most important, the particular segment of the policy was said to be of the same class as the
coverage written separately, particularly in the case of fire insurance, and it was argued that a company which subscribed to the
bureau for fire insurance written separately could not file independently for a package. Any such activity, among other things, was said
to involve unfair discrimination.

Many states, to their credit, had approved independent homeowners filings despite this type argument, and by 1957 a substantial
majority had approved independently filed commercial policies and
rates which used the scheduled fire rate determined by the bureau
following examination. However, the critical case developed in
New York in 1957–58 when NYFIRO opposed approval of the
filings of INA and the American Casualty Insurance Company of
Reading.[24]   •

M-1 CONTROVERSY

About the same time the problem was presented to the NAIC,
partly because insurance departments objected to the mountain of
papers created by the hand-in-hand system and partly because once
the problem came before the NAIC the bureau companies sought to
restrain independence by obtaining an NAIC ruling in their favor.
The problem was referred to a subcommittee of the Rates and
Rating Organizations Committee, known as the M-1 Subcommittee,
and the controversy became known as the M-1 Controversy.

An All-Industry Committee was appointed whose membership
was heavily in favor of the bureau companies. This committee met
during the summer and fall of 1958. No meeting of the minds was
possible, and reports were prepared, the two principal ones repre-

---

[24] *Smith* v. *Wikler*, 10 App. Div. 2d 195, 198 N.Y.S.2d 268 (3d Dept.
1960), appeal denied, 11 App. Div. 2d 746, 204 N.Y.S.2d 119 (3d Dept.
1960), appeal denied, 8 N.Y.2d 710 (1960).

senting respectively the independent and bureau points of view.[25] The independent position was strengthened in August, 1958, when the New York Department handed down a decision in favor of INA and American Casualty approving their independent filings.[26]

The NAIC held the matter over for further study at the December, 1958, meeting, but in effect sustained the independent position at the June, 1959, meeting in a report which stated that "where compatible with applicable law, affiliation with a rating organization should not affect the freedom of an insurer to file independently any multiple-line package" and favoring "vigorous lawful competition."[27]

THE DAM BREAKS

About this time the bureau companies awoke to find out that they had manuevered themselves into an impossible competitive position. The hand-in-hand filing procedure had been replaced by the "interline" filing procedure. In effect this meant only that one policy was filed by a bureau acting for the other two bureaus instead of three filings being made. Each bureau, however, retained its jurisdiction over a segment of the policy. Any change required agreement of all.

Early in 1959 one major company shocked the industry by withdrawing as a member from a bureau of which it was the foremost member. It was clear that unless the industry system of controls were relaxed so that bureau members could obtain sufficient flexibility to compete with independents, who had in effect won the basic battle to protect their rights, fragmentation of the bureaus could be expected. Serious arguments erupted among major companies in the dominant trade associations, and major resignations followed. It may be said that the dam broke and many of the most stalwart members of the trade associations changed their

[25] *Proceedings of the National Association of Insurance Commissioners*, Vol. 1 (1959), pp. 301–31. Reprints in full industry reports and statements.

[26] Decision of Arthur F. Lamanda, First Deputy Superintendent of Insurance, New York, dated August 6, 1958, in Matter of Independent Rate Filings for Commercial Property Coverages by North America Companies and the American Casualty Company. (On appeal, the case is known as *Smith* v. *Wikler*, 10 App. Div. 2d 195, 198 N.Y.S.2d 268 (3d Dept.), appeal denied, 11 App. Div. 2d 746, 204 N.Y.S.2d 119 (3d Dept.), appeal denied, 8 N.Y.2d 710 (1960).

[27] *Proceedings of the National Association of Insurance Commissioners*, Vol. 2 (1959), p. 542.

corporate policies in an effort to be more competitive than the independents. One unfortunate effect was that the organized industry drove down the rate levels for multiple line policies such as the homeowners in an effort to compete vigorously with independents at approximately the same time that experience worsened. Resultant inadequate rate levels accentuated the adverse experience of recent years and resulted in substantial underwriting losses.

PERIOD OF OPTIMISM

Nevertheless, the period of time about 1960 was an optimistic one for believers in multiple line insurance. So far as fire and casualty insurance was concerned, the basic right to hold multiple line powers and to issue multiple line policies had been established. There still remained a rather protracted battle of a secondary nature before bureaus were satisfied to collect fair and reasonable assessments for the services they contributed to multiple line policies written by independents, but the basic right of companies to act independently for the multiple line policies while retaining bureau affiliation for the separate coverage seemed well on the way to becoming firmly established. It seemed fair to conclude that within a short time most of the regulatory problems would be resolved.

In a broad sense perhaps it can be argued that this is so, and possibly my introductory remarks were too pessimistic. However, it is frustrating to find no substantial diminution in the number and severity of problems during the past five years.

PRESENT PROBLEMS

There appear to be several major reasons for this state of affairs. In the first place, the power structure from 1947 to 1960 expended a great deal of effort and considerable ingenuity in developing arguments and theories to the effect that multiple line policies should not be treated as a new kind or class of insurance, particularly for rating purposes, and that the rates and forms for a coverage within a multiple line policy should still be related to the rates and forms of the coverage sold separately in order to avoid discrimination or to preserve the rate structure for the separate coverage or to lessen competition. Judgment rating and individual risk underwriting in multiple line policies had been severely criticized. Even though a substantial majority of the states approved the new theories and the policies which followed, some department personnel became imbued with the bureau company position and have maintained it since even after the position of the companies changed.

It seems fair to say also that since the bureau company position changed primarily because of the forces of competition rather than because of a "conversion" respecting principle, there was less effect in some states where more restrictive laws have restricted competition, particularly in the South and South Central states.

The new competition had adverse effect on several industry groups such as the agents and the mutuals who had previously played secondary roles in support generally of the power structure, and they became leading parties in attempting to prevent changes, particularly those leading to competition. By and large, they actively mined the body of arguments and theories previously advanced by the power structure and reemphasized them.

Finally, the unsettled state of the market, with the substantial losses suffered by the companies, caused a number of commissioners to seek stability by restricting rights to compete that had previously been determined to be lawful. This was exemplified in a sincere effort several years ago by Commissioner Knowlton of New Hampshire in presenting to the NAIC what became known as the Knowlton Principles.

The net effect has been a multitude of problems arising throughout the United States, some stemming from broad controversies of the period and many seemingly isolated. One is impressed, however, with the fact that at the heart of almost all of the problems of the recent past, one still finds the same basic differences and theories which were developed and enunciated in the earlier period.

This is the major reason why it is essential to understand how multiple line insurance developed and the nature and essence of the earlier controversies. It is also the reason why the emphasis in this paper is placed on the history of the past rather than the specific problems of the present.

One wishes there were time to review in detail efforts of states to adopt regulations limiting freedom to develop policies, the difficulties in securing approval of new forms like the DIC (Difference in Condition), the controversies over judgment rating encouraged by the very nature of the multiple line policies themselves, the efforts toward greater individual risk underwriting in the commercial and industrial areas, particularly as it related to schedule rating and expense modification, and the Johnson principles.

This is not possible. However, it might illustrate the present situation to mention that right now, as only one attorney for one company, I am working on problems in five states, or 10 percent of the total, which I would characterize as major. These are as follows:

1. In Oregon we are supporting efforts to remove from the law a prohibition against combining more than one kind of insurance in a single policy, thereby removing the last overall prohibition against multiple line policies in any state.[28]
2. In Oklahoma we are attempting to secure the defeat of strongly supported legislation which would require mandatory auditing of multiple line policies by bureaus or independent agencies and, even more important, would permit disapproval of rating plans on the grounds that they could not be audited. Based on our knowledge of the circumstances in that state, we know this legislation is designed to prohibit judgment and individual risk underwriting by companies independent of a rating bureau.
3. In New York we are seeking a hearing to object to the disapproval by the previous superintendent of a policy combining accident and health insurance with liability insurance on the grounds that no provision of law permits such a combination, even though there are no provisions of law permitting the myriad of other approved policies combining kinds of insurance. Illinois takes the same position.
4. In Massachusetts we participated recently in a hearing to review the disapproval of a Manufacturer's Output type policy, approved in most states, where the disapproval was based primarily on the position that it produced premiums different from those established by the fire rating bureau for real estate and that it permitted too great rating flexibility.
5. In Texas we are faced with the disapproval of a policy based on the grounds stated in the letter of disapproval from the department which reads as follows: "The Board has never seen fit to approve any commercial multiple line policy."

---

[28] The Oregon Insurance Code adopted in 1967, subsequent to the presentation of this paper, amended the law to permit multiple line policies for residential property but not for insurance on other types of risks.

As pointed out, there appears to be no reduction in the number or any simplification in the nature of the problems. Perhaps one avenue which could lead to answers can be found in the fact that knowledgeable consumers oppose these types of restrictions and continue to encourage innovations and an open competitive market. One wonders who the regulation is protecting and against what? Personally, I am hopeful that comprehensive studies, particularly of the type now being conducted in Wisconsin, will produce answers in the public interest. We do know that this year the American public will pay over $2 billion in premiums for multiple line policies, which might be characterized as having been only a gleam in Mr. Diemand's eye a short 24 years ago. Perhaps we may yet rival the Phoenicians.

chapter 13

Statistical Agencies

THE FOLLOWING SELECTION discusses the statistical agency, a subject on which the literature of insurance regulation has been almost completely silent.

Most rating laws provide that the insurance regulator may promulgate reasonable rules and statistical plans in order that "the experience of all insurers may be made available at least annually in such form and detail as may be necessary to aid him in determining whether rating systems comply with the [applicable] standards. . . ." The information so provided furnishes an overall industry picture, with more detail than is available from annual statements, and with somewhat less detail than is available from specific rate filings. A ratemaking organization may also serve as a statistical agent, but some statistical agents are not ratemaking organizations.

Proposals for rate regulatory reform often call for more unified and comprehensive systems of collection of loss data. One possibility is a public utility or government agency to collect and disseminate data for the entire industry. Before any reform along these lines is considered, the history, function, and future of the statistical agency should be carefully studied.

STATISTICAL AGENCIES

LeRoy J. Simon
General Manager,
National Insurance Actuarial and Statistical Association

The premium which is charged an insured is determined by a variety of factors. The coverage to be afforded, the characteristics of the risk, the amount of insurance to be provided, and the physical location of the insured subject are the most common variables used in determining the premium. The premium for an automobile liability policy is determined in a relatively straightforward fashion by eliciting this type of information by direct questioning of the insured by his agent. When the questions have all been answered, the agent is in a position to refer to a rating manual and with a minimum amount of arithmetic he can arrive at the premium for the policy. In contrast to this, determining the fire insurance premium for a large manufacturing company involves a complex and highly technical examination of the property in order to describe the relevant characteristics of the risk. The premises are inspected by an employee of the Fire Rating Organization, who is usually an engineer, and a myriad of characteristics are enumerated and evaluated. The rate to be applied is determined by the results of this inspection plus other characteristics of the property such as its location and the degree of external fire protection provided.

RAISON D'ETRE OF STATISTICAL AGENCIES

While these two examples are vastly different in the methodology used to produce the resultant premium for the insured, the results of both approaches are tested retrospectively through the evaluation of premium and loss statistics which are subsequently produced. In using these statistics in modifying the underlying rate structures, the ratemaker also attempts to make a prospective evaluation of what the results will be under revised systems. This prospective evaluation is based in part on statistics developed from the past and in part on actuarial and other techniques used to predict the future. Because of this basic foundation of statistics, statistical agencies exist throughout the industry for property and casualty lines of business.

STATISTICAL INFORMATION SUPPLIED BY AGENCIES

Let us turn for a moment to another facet of the statistical agency picture. The insurance regulator has at his disposal some statistical information from the annual statement. This is prepared each year by each company and covers the transactions occurring during one given calendar year. The most detailed information available to him for his state is a single page exhibit, known as "Page 14," indicating premiums and losses for each of the lines of insurance shown in the annual statement. Thus, for automobile insurance, he knows the earned premium and the incurred losses for his state for a given company during a given year for automobile bodily injury liability. These statistics are often worthless from a ratemaking standpoint because they involve widely divergent classes of risk, may include experience under excess or umbrella policies, or may be grossly distorted by the presence of extreme claims which are not expected on this volume of business (or conversely the absence of extreme losses which normal expectation would have produced in such a volume of business). Furthermore, the annual statement figures ordinarily cannot be used to test or check a rate filing because the ratemaker very frequently uses a basis for ratemaking (such as the policy year, accident year basis) or uses a fiscal period which does not correspond to the calendar year used in the annual statement. In contrast with the annual statement statistics, the regulator has the statistics presented in support of rate filings by the rate filers themselves. These statistics vary widely in quality and content. In some cases a small organization may wish to copy the rate schedules of a larger organization and will merely submit arguments or simplified statistics to demonstrate that its rates will meet the requirements of the statute. At the other extreme, companies or rating organizations may produce statistics which explicitly match each of the variables in their rate structure, thus statistically justifying every aspect of the rating approach. While it is difficult to generalize for all lines of insurance, ordinarily the insurance regulator, if there were no third source of data on hand, would be confronted with either the grossly inadequate statistical basis for ratemaking found in the annual statement or the detailed data presented by the rate filer when a rate filing is made. In the middle ground between these two extremes the All-Industry Bill has provided for the annual reporting of statistics independently of rate filings and has required them of all companies.

Legal Basis for Statistical Agencies

It must also be recalled that the All-Industry Bill was designed to give the insurance business a type of regulation which would exempt it from certain parts of the antitrust and monopoly legislation which applied to interstate commerce, and under the South-Eastern Underwriters case and Public Law 15, it would apply to insurance ratemaking if appropriate state legislation were not passed. Statistical support of rate filings was one of the regulatory aspects considered necessary in the new bill. Since insurance rates and rate schedules are public information (or could be easily obtained even if they were not), considerations of fair play, equity, or absence of "unfair discrimination" must have been part of the reason for requiring all companies to report statistics under the new bill. A further reason for obtaining premium and loss experience annually in addition to the annual statement filing was to assist the commissioner in his regulatory job by supplying him with some additional detail in the data which he used to review the experience in his state. The bill authorized the appointment of statistical agencies to assist in collecting and compiling this information. (See Appendix, sentence [e].) It is interesting to note that the compilation of statistics is not related in any way to the rate filer and, hence, it must be inferred that the statistical agency's compilations are for the purpose of providing a general or overall check on the industry and not an attempt to pinpoint specific rates. Each rate filer must support his own rate filings in the manner prescribed in a separate section of the bill.

Designation of Agency by Commissioner

The All-Industry Bill also provides that the commissioner may designate one or more rating organizations or other agencies to assist him in gathering these statistics. It is in this respect that the statistical agency functions in collecting of data and submitting it to the insurance department.

A number of statistical agencies are in operation in the various lines of insurance. In many cases a ratemaking organization will act also as a statistical agency for the lines of business for which it makes rates. Examples of this type of organization are: Insurance Rating Board (formerly National Bureau of Casualty Underwriters and National Automobile Underwriters Association), Transportation Insurance Rating Bureau, Surety Association of America, Inland Marine Insurance Bureau, and Mutual Insurance Rating Bureau (this latter organization has a separate statistical agency for fire insurance which is operated by the same management as the Bureau). The Independent Statistical Service is the statistical arm of the National Association of Independent Insurers, a trade association, and is an example of a statistical agency which is not affiliated with a rating organization. National Insurance Actuarial and Statistical Association is an example of a statistical agency which is not a rating organization and, further, is not affiliated with a trade association.

In practice, then, the statistical gathering function is performed by agencies of the companies which are recognized by the states as being designated to collect data and submit it to the commissioner. The great advantage in this arrangement is that since most companies write across state lines, it is possible to prepare a countrywide statistical plan and secure its adoption much more easily. It is also apparent that there is an advantage in having the industry directly support the statistics gathering activity as an entirely independent operation rather than having it be part of the insurance department budget. Massachusetts automobile bodily injury liability is an exception in the casualty field. Texas stands as an exception to this rule in the property insurance field. There are no designated statistical agencies under the Texas fire statute. The insurance department is, therefore, obligated to collect the statistics. The vast majority of companies arrange to have these statistics reported to the Texas Insurance Department by the Texas Checking Office, and the remaining companies report the information directly to the department. The result has been that Texas has appeared as a sole exception to statistical plans in the property insurance field. The systems they have used have often not been compatible with the rest of the country, or they have only adopted compatible systems long after they were effective elsewhere. If such a pattern of individual state statistical plans were to exist throughout the United States, it would obviously increase the cost of company operations significantly and would be especially detrimental to the insurer who operated in a number of states.

Voluntary Acceptance of Uniformity

With the indirect control of the statistical plans which has evolved for most states under the All-Industry Bill, the states have individually accepted certain countrywide uniformities in order to obtain the desirable features of cost reduction and regional or countrywide analyses. Hence, it is customary to find a few state exceptions in statistical plans to reflect certain individual requirements. Nevertheless the basic core of the plan is completely uniform throughout the country. When a state requests an individual variation, costs are increased and the risk of error also is enhanced. The coding and processing of data are always more accurate and economical when there are no state exceptions. It should be emphasized, too, that if one state creates an exception, then, in effect, all the other states have, in a sense, become an exception also. The accuracy of the data is jeopardized not only for the exceptional but for the conforming states. The regulatory officials are quite understanding in this area and have seldom insisted on individual variations.

State Variations

I have spoken quite generally of the provisions of the All-Industry Bill which are of direct interest to statistical agencies. As an appendix, the five provisions of particular interest to statistical agencies are quoted together with special wording found in various states.[1]

It is important to note that the act of designating a statistical agency is wholly discretionary on the part of the insurance supervisory official since the typical law does not set up any standards. However, in New York, hearings were held early in 1951, and the department promulgated certain rules effective September 1, 1951, including the following: "The Department will approve as its statistical agents for a company any rating, service or advisory organization designated by the company that have the necessary personnel and equipment to perform the function of a statistical agency, that agree to comply with these rules and that, in any previous service in this capacity, have done so with reasonable accuracy and promptness."[2]

---

[1] This method of presentation was suggested by similar material found in Thomas O. Carlson, "Rate Regulation and the Casualty Actuary," *Proceedings of the Casualty Actuarial Society,* Vol. 38, No. 69 (1951), p. 9. The present compilation is complete through May 18, 1967, and was prepared by the firm of Watters, Donovan, Dorsey, Burke, and Griffin.

[2] New York Insurance Department ruling "Rules as to Statistical Agents for Automobile Insurance and as to Consolidations of Automobile Experience," effective September 1, 1951.

STATISTICAL PLANS VERSUS RATE FILINGS

Until recently the statistical plan used by the statistical agencies in fire insurance has been relatively simple in its detail when compared to other lines of business. The data submitted by rate filers in support of rate revisions was fundamentally identical with the statistical information collected under the statistical plan. The statistical agency, in effect, would give the state and the rate filer all the information that was available under the statistical plan. Beginning with 1966 statistics, this identity has ceased to exist under the new NIASA (National Insurance Actuarial and Statistical Association) Personal Lines Statistical Plan. The primary objective of information supplied to the state regulatory authorities will remain the same; that is, to provide a basis for a general review of the experience. However, additional information will now be collected beyond that needed for preparing the regular statistical compilation. Special studies of this additional data will be made and may be used by the companies in their underwriting or ratemaking.

Supervisory officials are presented with an interesting problem if the statistical agency is different from the rate filer, but the rate filer utilizes the information of the statistical agency in establishing its rates. This situation exists in the property insurance field and with two of the statistical agencies, National Insurance Actuarial and Statistical Association and Independent Statistical Service. The problem arises when a rate filing is before the commissioner and he asks for additional information. If the information is not already available through the statistical plan, the rate filer could have difficulty obtaining the information. He is not in a position to direct the statistical agency to modify the statistical plan because the membership of the two organizations is different. The commissioner is also inhibited from so directing the statistical agency because he might be asking 100 companies to modify their information-gathering systems to meet the needs of a rate filing of a single company.

While this situation presents something of a dilemma, it must be recognized that there are at least three information levels in question. The first is the amount of information necessary for the regulatory officials to test the general rate level in a state which must be provided by the designated statistical agencies to the regulators. This much information must be provided by all agencies equally.

The second level of information is the data collected by the statistical agency which may in some cases exceed the information provided to the regulatory officials. This additional information is equivalent to the output of a research organization and reflects the costs that the companies are willing to incur in the way of research. This level gives us the required complexity of information the companies must submit to the statistical agency; it usually appears in the form of a statistical plan which the agency employs. In most states and lines this is the statistical plan "promulgated" by the insurance commissioner, but it need not necessarily be promulgated by him. In New York, for example, a generalized minimum automobile statistical plan was promulgated in 1951, but the statistical agencies operate on statistical plans that require more information than the minimum plan.

The third level of information gathering which is conducted is that done by the companies themselves. In a number of cases the companies go beyond the requirements of the statistical agency and will introduce research or experimental coding for their own purposes.

An interesting legal and policy question arises at this point because of the discrepancy between what the state actually required the companies to do and what the statistical agency may require them to do. If a company decides that it does not want a statistical plan which goes beyond the minimum state requirement, the question is whether the statistical agency is obligated to accept data from the company utilizing only the minimum requirement plan. The statistical agency's position is definitely that it should not have to accept such data. It uses data processing equipment which requires extensive programming and is geared to accept information only in the form its own statistical plan requires. Companies are required to submit data to the statistical agent in a format and on a punch card or magnetic tape that meets the specifications set out by the agency.[3] The insurance commissioner, however, may reason that he has designated a given agency and has promulgated a statistical plan. Therefore, any company that cares to report to the agency under that statistical plan is entitled to do so. The section of the law reads that the commissioner may designate a statistical agency to assist

---

[3] Certain extremely small companies at times submit a bordereaux to either a service bureau or to the statistical agency and punch cards are prepared in the appropriate format. The companies are then separately charged for the actual cost of doing this work. This, however, is equivalent to requiring the company to comply with the agency's statistical plan.

him in collecting statistics. Fortunately, this has not become a real issue in any known instance. However, with the increasing complexity of statistical plans, we may see more of this problem. One possible solution to this problem has been put forth in the establishment of a Minimum Plan by NIASA in its property insurance statistical programs. As a regular part of the program of the statistical agency, this Minimum Plan has such simple requirements that even the smallest and least sophisticated writer of the business can comply with it. This works well to ease the burden of the very small company. When it exceeds the premium volume maximum for the Minimum Plan, it must then report in the full detail.

There has not been an extensive literature on the concepts of statistical agency operation and its interrelationship with rate filers and regulators because most of the interest in hearings or court cases has centered around the rate filings themselves and the statistical agency functions have been secondary. There are exceptions. During the latter part of 1965 and early 1966 the relationship between the National Bureau of Casualty Underwriters and its "electronics department," the Insurance Data Processing Center, was the subject of discussion at hearings in Vermont and Kentucky.[4] In both cases this subject was secondary to the principal problem of a rate filing. Also, in 1966 the Virginia State Corporation Commission received a report from the firm of Woodward and Fondiller which treated in part the processing systems and techniques of the various statistical agencies operating in automobile lines in that state.[5] It is close cooperation and coordination between the companies, the rate filers, the regulatory officials, and the statistical agencies that has quite satisfactorily kept the statistics gathering function out of the arena of contest in administrative hearings and courts. This is particularly fortunate since everyone has the same fundamental objective—to provide as much information as possible so that insurers may secure and maintain a profitable operating level, so that regulation can insure that premium rates are not "inadequate, excessive nor unfairly discriminatory," and so the buying public will have an ever expanding insurance capacity to meet the growing challenges of the insurance market.

    [4] February 28, 1966, public hearing of the Vermont Insurance Department and December 27, 1965, order of the Kentucky Commissioner of Insurance.

    [5] Commonwealth of Virginia, Report of Actuaries, Case No. 17680—Investigation into Private Passenger Automobile Liability Insurance Rate Making Procedures, Cancellation Provisions and Renewal Practices—August 1, 1966.

APPENDIX

Rate Administration

Recording and Reporting of Loss and Expense Experience
(Comparative Analysis of Each State's Statutes with the Industry's Model Bill)

The five sentences in the model bill drafted by the All-Industry Committee that are of particular interest to statistical agencies are as follows:

(a) "The commissioner shall promulgate reasonable rules and statistical plans, reasonably adapted to each of the rating systems on file with him which may be modified from time to time and which shall be used thereafter by each insurer in the recording and reporting of its loss, and countrywide expense experience, in order that the experience of all insurers may be made available at least annually in such form and detail as may be necessary to aid him in determining whether rating systems comply with the standards set forth in [the Section relating to the making of rates].

(b) "Such rules and plans may also provide for the recording and reporting of expense experience items which are specially applicable to this state and are not susceptible of determination by a prorating of countrywide expense experience.

(c) "In promulgating such rules and plans, the commissioner shall give due consideration to the rating systems on file with him and, in order that such rules and plans may be as uniform as is practicable among the several states, to the rules and to the form of the plans used for such rating systems in other states.

(d) "No insurer shall be required to record or report its loss experience on a classification basis that is inconsistent with the rating system filed by it.

(e) "The commissioner may designate one or more rating organizations or other agencies to assist him in gathering such experience and making compilations thereof, and such compilations shall be made available, subject to reasonable rules promulgated by the commissioner, to insurers and rating organizations."

The basic casualty status and fire status of the above provisions in the various jurisdictions are as follows:

State	(a)	(b)	(c)	(d)	(e)	Other
Alabama............2	2	2	2	2	15	
Alaska..............1	1	1	1	1	1	
Arizona............1	1	1	1	1	40(a)(b)	
Arkansas...........1	1	1	1	1		
California..........2	2	2	2	2	16	
Colorado...........3	1	1	1	11		
Connecticut........1	1	1	1	1	40	
Delaware...........1	1	1	1	11,12		
District of Col.......2	2	2	2	2		
Florida.............41	1	42	43	1	40(a)(b)(d)*	
Georgia............1	1	1	1	1	40	
Hawaii.............1	1	1	1	1	40	
Idaho..............1	1	1	1	1		
Illinois.............1	1	1	10	11,12		
Indiana............1	1	1	1	1	40(b)(c)	
Iowa...............1	1	1	1	1	40	
Kansas.............1	1	1	1	1,39	40	
Kentucky...........1	1	1	1	11,13	40(a)(b)	
Louisiana...........1	1	1	1	1	40	
Maine..............1	1	1	1	1		
Maryland...........1	1	1	1	1	40	
Massachusetts:						
Stat. auto..........2	2	2	2	2	17	
Michigan...........1	1	1	10	11	40(a)(b)	
Minnesota..........1	1	1	1	11		
Mississippi:						
Casualty..........6	2	1	1	1		
Fire..............2	2	2	2	2	26	
Missouri............2	2	2	2	2	27	
Montana............2	2	2	2	2		
Nebraska...........1	1	1	1	11		
Nevada.............1	1	1	1	1	40	
New Hampshire......1	1	1	1	1	18,40	
New Jersey..........2	2	2	2	2	19	
New Mexico.........1	1	1	1	1	40	
New York..........7	1	1	1	28	20	
North Carolina:						
Auto liability......2	2	2	2	2	21	
Other casualty.....2	2	2	2	2	22	
Fire...............2	2	2	2	2	29	
North Dakota........1	1	1	1	1	40	
Ohio:						
Casualty...........5	1	1	1	1	40	
Fire...............2	2	2	2	2		
Oklahoma...........2	2	2	2	2		
Oregon.............1	1	1	1	1	40(a)(b)	
Pennsylvania.........1	1	1	11	1	23,40	
Puerto Rico..........2	2	2	1	2	31,40	
Rhode Island.........1	1	1	1	1	40	
South Carolina.......1	1	1	1	1	40	
South Dakota........32	1	1	1	32	40	

State	(a)	(b)	(c)	(d)	(e)	Other
Tennessee............1	1	1	1	33	40	
Texas:						
Auto liability......4,6,8,9	2	35,36	2	14	24,40	
Other casualty.....4,6,8,34	2	35	2	14	40	
Fire...............2	2	2	2	2		
Utah...............1	1	1	1	1	11	
Vermont...........25	1	1	1	1	40	
Virginia...........1	1	1	37	1	40(a)	
Washington.........1	1	1	1	1	40(c)	
West Virginia.......1	38	1	1	1	40(a)(b)	
Wisconsin..........1	1	1	1	1	40	
Wyoming...........1	1	1	1	1	40(a)(b)(d)*	

Notes to Chart Above

1. Contains provision of model bill.
2. Provision omitted.
3. The commissioner "may promulgate" in lieu of "shall promulgate" in casualty law only.
4. The clause "reasonably adapted to each of the rating system on file with him" is omitted.
5. "The superintendent of insurance shall promulgate rules and statistical plans, reasonably adapted to each of the rating systems on file with him, which may be modified from time to time and which shall be used thereafter by each insurer in the recording and reporting of its loss and countrywide expense experience, in order that the experience of all insurers may be made available at least annually in such form and detail as is necessary to aid the superintendent in determining whether rating systems comply with the standards set forth in section 3935.03 of the Revised Code."
6. Substitute "biennially" for "annually."
7. "Every authorized insurer shall annually file with the rating organization of which it is a member or subscriber, or with such other agency as the superintendent may approve, a statistical report showing a classification schedule of its premiums and losses on all kinds or types of insurance business to which this section is applicable, and such other information as the superintendent may deem necessary or expedient for the administration of the provisions of this article. The superintendent from time to time may prescribe the form of such report including

statistical data conforming to established classifications." "Statistical plans and rules shall be promulgated for the recording and reporting of expense experience on a countrywide basis."

8. Additional: ". . . after due consideration. . . ."
    Substitute: ". . . loss experience and such other data as may be required, in order that the total loss and expense experience. . . ."

9. Substitute throughout: "rates" for "rating systems."

10. Fourth sentence adds that no company shall be required to report its experience on any basis or statistical plan which differs from that regularly employed and used in the usual course of such company's business in casualty law only.

11. In addition, no insurer shall be required to file its experience with an organization of which it is not a member or subscriber (in casualty law only in Kentucky and Michigan).
    Pennsylvania: Additional: "nor shall any insurer be required to report its experience to any agency of which it is not a member or subscriber."
    Utah: Additional: "No insurer shall be required to record or report its experience to any rating organization or agency unless it is a member of such organization or agency."

12. Companies not reporting to a statistical agency "shall report such experience to the Director" in Illinois and "may be required to report such experience to the Commissioner" in Delaware. Such experience shall be deemed confidential but may be included in compilations with other experience.

13. Experience of individual insurers reported directly to the commissioner shall not be revealed by him except by court order although they may be included in consolidations with other experience. All compilations and consolidations shall be open to public rating and qualified advisory organizations (in casualty law only in Kentucky).

14. The board may designate one or more rating organization or other agencies to gather and compile such experience.

15. A statistical report showing premiums and losses on the various kinds of insurance written shall be filed annually on or before July 1st with a statistical agency and with the Alabama Department, "together with such other information as the bureau (i.e., Department) may deem necessary for the proper determination of the reasonableness and adequacy of rates." Such

reports may be consolidated and filed by an agency. "Such data shall be kept and reports made in such manner and on such forms as may be prescribed by the bureau." Such reports to the Alabama Department shall be kept confidential.

16. "Every insurer, rating organization or advisory organization and every group, association or other organization of insurers which engages in joint underwriting or joint reinsurance shall maintain reasonable records, of the type and kind reasonably adapted to its method of operation, of its experience or the experience of its members and of the data, statistics or information collected or used by it in connection with the rates, rating plans, rating systems, underwriting rules, policy or bond forms, surveys or inspections made or used by it so that such records will be available at all reasonable times to enable the commissioner to determine whether such organization, insurer, group or association, and, in the case of an insurer or rating organization, every rate, rating plan and rating system made or used by it, complies with the provisions of this chapter applicable to it. The maintenance of such records in the office of a licensed rating organization of which an insurer is a member or subscriber will be sufficient compliance with this section for any insurer maintaining membership or subscribership in such organization, to the extent that the insurer uses the rates, rating plans, rating systems or underwriting rules of such organization. Such records shall be maintained in an office within this State or shall be made available for examination or inspection within this State by the commissioner at any time upon reasonable notice."

17. "The commissioner may make, and, at any time, alter or amend, reasonable rules and regulations to facilitate the operation of this section and enforce the application of the classifications and premium charges fixed and established by him, and to govern hearings and investigations under this section. He may at any time require any company to file with him such data, statistics, schedules or information he may deem proper or necessary to enable him to fix and establish or secure and maintain fair and reasonable classifications of risks and adequate, just, reasonable and non-discriminatory premium charges for such policies or bonds. He may issue such orders as he finds proper, expedient or necessary to enforce and adminis-

ter the provisions of this section, to secure compliance with any rules or regulations made thereunder, and to enforce adherence to the classifications and premium charges fixed and established by him. . . ."

18. With respect to automobile liability insurance, "every insurance company . . . shall file with the insurance commissioner, individually or in collaboration with others, in such form as he may prescribe, its classification of risks and premium rates applicable thereto, together with a schedule or rating to be in use and such other statistical information as the commissioner may require."

19. "Every insurer shall file annually with the rating organization of which it is a member or subscriber, or with such other agency as the commissioner may approve at the request of such rating organization, or with the commissioner, if such insurer is not a member or a subscriber of a rating organization, a statistical report showing a classification schedule of its premiums and its losses on all kinds of insurance to which this act is applicable, together with such other information as the commissioner may deem necessary for the proper determination of the reasonableness and adequacy of rates."

20. Additional: "The superintendent shall have power, in his discretion, to prescribe by regulation, uniform classifications of accounts to be observed, and statistics to be reported by insurers and other organizations which are subject to the provisions of this article. He may also in his discretion prescribe by regulation, forms of reporting such data by insurers and such other organizations. Such classifications of accounts, and statistics to be reported and forms of reporting shall be reasonable and may vary with the kind or type of insurer or organization. No such regulation or amendment thereto shall be promulgated by the superintendent except upon notice and after hearing to all insurers and organizations affected thereby. Any regulation or amendment thereto shall be promulgated by the superintendent at least six months before the beginning of the calendar year in which the same shall take effect. Any regulation or order of the superintendent made under this section shall be subject to judicial review by any insurer or organization aggrieved thereby."

21. ". . . the commissioner of insurance is hereby authorized to

compel the production of all books, data, papers and records and any other data necessary to compile statistics for the purpose of determining the pure cost and expense loading of automobile bodily injury and property damage insurance in North Carolina. . . ." ". . . . On or before July 1 of each calendar year the North Carolina Automobile Rate Administrative Office shall submit to the Commissioner the data hereinabove referred to for bodily injury and property damage insurance on private passenger vehicles and a rate review based on such data."

22. "Every insurer shall annually on or before October 1, file with the rating bureau of which it is a member or subscriber, or with such other agency as the commissioner of Insurance may approve or designate, a statistical report showing a classification schedule of its premiums and losses on all classes of insurance to which this article is applicable, and such other information as the commissioner may deem necessary or expedient for the administration of the provisions of this article."

23. Additional: "Such rules and plans shall not place an unreasonable burden of expense on any insurer."

24. "The Commissioner is hereby authorized and empowered to require sworn statements from any insurer affected by this Act, showing its experience on any classification or classifications of risks and such other information which may be necessary or helpful in determining proper classification and rates, or other duties or authority imposed by law. The Commissioner shall prescribe the necessary forms for such statements and reports, having due regard to the rules, methods and forms in use in other states for similar purposes in order that uniformity of statistics may not be disturbed."

25. The Commissioner "may promulgate" in lieu of "shall promulgate". Add after "each insurer," "unless exempted in writing by the commissioner."

26. Statistical reports. Every insurer shall on such forms as may be prescribed by the commission file annually with the insurance commission or, at its option, with a designated agency approved by the commission and representative of either stock, nonstock, or mutual insurers, its loss experience in this state in accordance with classifications approved by the commission. The experience filed with the designated agency selected shall be consoli-

dated by the Mississippi State Rating Bureau and a copy of the consolidated result shall be filed with the insurance commission.

27. In fire law: 1. The superintendent of insurance is hereby authorized and empowered to order any company or insurer to compile and file with the insurance division, or with the bureau of which it is a member and by such bureau filed with the insurance division, at such times as he may designate, the net amount of insurance in force and written, net premiums received and net losses paid for each class within each state, and whenever required, each rating bureau shall make a compilation showing the totals for each class for each state for all its members and file the same with the insurance division. 2. Such reports shall be formulated and maintained according to a uniform schedule and classification, insofar as may be found practicable.

28. First phrase replaced by: Such statistical reports shall be consolidated in accordance with regulations prescribed by the superintendent.

29. "Every insurer shall file annually with the rating bureau or at its option, with a common agency approved by the Commissioner and representative of either stock or nonstock insurers, its underwriting experience in this State in accordance with classifications approved by the Commissioner. The experience filed with the common agency selected shall be consolidated by such agency and a copy of the consolidated result shall be filed with the rating bureau; provided such insurers shall, if directed by the Commissioner, file their individual underwriting experience with such rating bureau. Such data shall be kept and reports made in such manner and on such forms as may be prescribed by the Commissioner."

30. Period after "thereof" continuing as follows: "Such compilations shall be made available to insurers and rating organizations, subject to reasonable procedures and allocation of costs thereof, under rules promulgated by the commissioner."

31. "Every authorized insurer shall annually file with the rating organization of which it is a member or subscriber, or with such other agency as the Commissioner may approve, a statistical report showing a classification schedule of its premiums and losses on all kinds or types of insurance business to

which this section is applicable and such other information as the Commissioner may deem necessary or expedient for the administration of the provisions of this chapter. The Commissioner may from time to time prescribe the form of such report including statistical data conforming to established classifications. Such statistical reports shall be consolidated in accordance with regulations prescribed by the Commissioner.

"Statistical plans and rules may be promulgated for the recording and reporting of expense experience as to items which are specially applicable to Puerto Rico and are not susceptible of determination by a prorating of expense experience elsewhere.

"In the promulgation of statistical plans and rules, the Commissioner shall give consideration to the rating systems on file with him and, in order that such rules and plans may be as uniform as is practicable with those of the several states of the United States, to the rules and to the form of the plans in such states."

32. The word "reasonable" omitted.
33. Additional: "Reasonable rules and plans may be promulgated by the commissioner for the interchange of data necessary for the application of rating plans."
34. Substitute throughout: "rating plans" for "rating systems."
35. "In promulgating such rules and plans, the Board shall have due regard for the rating plans approved by it, and in order that such rules and plans may be as uniform as is practicable, to the rules and to the form of the plans used in other states."
36. Same as 35 above except "rates" for "rating plans."
37. Additional: "or on its behalf."
38. "Such rules and plans may also provide for the recording and reporting of loss and expense experience items which are specially applicable to this State and are not susceptible of determination by a prorating of countrywide experience."
39. Additional: "Provided, That nothing in this act shall be construed to require, nor shall the commissioner adopt any rule to require, any insurer to record or report its loss or expense experience on any basis or statistical plan not consistent with the rating system filed by it."
40. Additional provisions affecting rate administration:
    a) Interchange of Rating Plan Data. Reasonable rules and plans may be promulgated by the commissioner for the

interchange of data necessary for the application of rating plans.

b) Consultation with Other States. In order to further uniform administration of rate regulatory laws, the commissioner and every insurer and rating organization may exchange information and experience data with insurance supervisory officials, insurers and rating organizations in other states and may consult with them with respect to rate making and the application of rating systems.

c) Rules and Regulations. The commissioner may make reasonable rules and regulations necessary to effect the purposes of this Act (chapter).

*d) Cooperation among rating organizations or among rating organizations and insurers in rate-making or in other matters within the scope of this chapter is hereby authorized, provided the filings resulting from such cooperation are subject to all the provisions of this chapter which are applicable to filings generally. The commissioner may review such cooperative activities and practices and if, after a hearing, he finds that any such activity or practice is unfair or unreasonable or otherwise inconsistent with the provisions of this chapter, he may issue a written order specifying in what respects such activity or practice is unfair or unreasonable or otherwise inconsistent with the provisions of this chapter, and requiring the discontinuance of such activity or practice.

41. "The commissioner shall promulgate and may modify reasonable rules and statistical plans, reasonably adapted to each of the rating systems used, and which shall thereafter be used by each insurer in the recording and reporting of its loss and country-wide expense experience, in order that the experience of all insurers may be made available at least annually in such form and detail as may be necessary to aid him in determining whether rates comply with the applicable standards of this part I."

42. "In use in this state" in lieu of "on file with him."

43. Substitute "used" for "filed."

---

* Florida and Wyoming only.

PART V

Nonadmitted and Unauthorized Insurance

chapter 14

The Regulation of Placement of Nonadmitted Insurance

NONADMITTED INSURERS, both alien and domestic, are essential suppliers in the American insurance market, both for direct and reinsurance placements. The following selection critically evaluates present regulatory controls over the nonadmitted market, with special emphasis on the problems of alien insurers.

NONADMITTED ALIEN INSURERS AND INSURANCE REGULATION

Keith Brown
Attorney, LeBoeuf, Lamb, Leiby and McCrae
New York, New York

It has become the tritest commonplace that the regulation of insurance by the states is going through a prolonged period of agonizing reappraisal, a long season of ferment. Friendly as well as hostile critics charge it with a heterogeneous group of alleged inadequacies and, less frequently, offer reasoned schemes for improvement. But the attention devoted to them by outsiders is no more intense than the continuing searching, fundamental self-analysis being conducted by the intellectual leaders among the regulators, the insurance commissioners, both as individuals and through their organization, the National Association of Insurance Commissioners. Animated by the specter of increased or perhaps total federal regulation they are not only critically evaluating their performance but earnestly trying to rethink their underlying rationale, the congeries of related concepts within which they live, move, and have their being.

Although most state insurance codes as originally drafted have a superficial internal consistency, and, in broad outline, present a schematic, articulated scheme of regulation, the pragmatic lessons of experience have engrafted changes which fit but awkwardly onto the original regulatory plan. New legislation, often in other fields, regulations, and, more subtly and pervasively, insurance department practices and attitudes evolve as responses to felt needs, the revelation of questionable practices and attempts to "plug loopholes." A realization of the evolutionary, Heraclitean character of insurance regulatory philosophy probably emerges nowhere more forcefully than from a consideration of the history of regulatory laws and practices with respect to insurance coverages placed with alien nonadmitted insurers and the impact the existence of such coverages has had on regulatory thinking, if not philosophy. A review of some of the current problems and dilemmas in this area may not only be of intrinsic interest but, because they are somewhat atypical, also furnish some oblique insights which will be helpful in a reevaluation of the whole plan of 20th century insurance regulation in this country and its inherent limitations.

However this may be, what I have to say will be principally exposition; it will mostly tell the tale and only occasionally and gingerly attempt to draw the moral. This is not because of any reluctance to criticize but because in areas which call for new ideas, even a new synthesis, I do not have the answers.

I shall try to describe briefly the web of laws and regulations, interpretations, and understandings which govern the placement of insurance coverages with alien nonadmitted insurers. For brevity's sake, when reference is made to the laws of a particular state, not only its legislation but also its regulations are included. Some of what I have to say about surplus line laws may be familiar, but I have found that while the nature of such laws is fairly well understood, the details of how they work are not and it is in their application that they are tested and their problems and inconsistencies found.

SURPLUS LINES LAWS

Insurance of an insured in this country by alien nonadmitted insurers may be either (1) direct, primary coverage or (2) reinsurance of admitted insurers. The placement of primary coverages is governed by what are usually referred to as surplus or excess line laws, regulations and glosses on such laws and regulations. Surplus line laws, which are as old as 1890, are now in effect in 49 states,[1] the District of Columbia, and Puerto Rico; and a brief summary of each of them is included in Appendix A of this chapter.

Although no two states have identical surplus line laws, there is a remarkable underlying similarity in the scheme of all of them. They usually provide that if he is to place surplus line business, a local broker or agent must have a special license as a surplus line broker or agent which usually entails the payment of an additional license fee and the posting of a bond. Most states do not make provision for the licensing of nonresident surplus line brokers.

Diligent Effort Requirements

With respect to each surplus line placement the surplus line broker, less often the producing agent who deals with the surplus line broker and sometimes also the potential insured, must execute an affidavit that the desired insurance cannot be procured after "diligent effort" from insurers authorized to do business in the state. "Diligent effort," or some equivalent phrase, is often further defined by regulation (less often by statute) as refusal of the proffered insurance by a specified number of admitted insurance carriers. The surplus line broker's affidavit is generally in a prescribed form giving more or less detailed information as to the declinations.

Most states require that the executed affidavits be filed periodically with the state's insurance department or, less typically, held in the surplus line broker's files for review by department examiners. In some states a copy of the policy or other evidence of coverage must also be filed with the insurance department.

A few states, such as North Carolina, require the filing of the affidavit, which is then really an application, with the insurance department in advance of placement and that permission to effect the placement be obtained from the department.

Taxation

All states have a premium tax on surplus line insurance which is as great as, and in most cases greater than, the tax on admitted insurance. It is as high as 6 percent of the premium in Oklahoma. This is in addition, of course, to the 4 percent federal excise tax on

---

[1] South Carolina does not have surplus line statutes, but there are recognized, approved procedures for placing insurance with nonadmitted insurers.

nonadmitted alien insurance.[2] In all states, a surplus line broker must place coverages only with solvent, reputable nonadmitted insurers.

Trust Funds

An increasing number of states, by statute or regulation, further specify that an acceptable nonadmitted insurer must meet certain requirements, the most usual of which is the maintenance in this country of a trust fund in a designated minimum amount for the protection of United States policyholders and beneficiaries.

The value of a trust fund to a United States policyholder or beneficiary derives from the fact that the policies or other evidences of insurance coverage of reputable nonadmitted insurers contain what is commonly referred to as a "Service of Suit Clause" whereby the insurer consents to be sued in any court of otherwise competent jurisdiction in this country and to abide by the laws and practice of such court. Service may be made either on nominees designated in the Service of Suit Clause or, at the option of the policyholder or beneficiary, on the appropriate public official, usually the insurance commissioner, provided in the unauthorized insurers service of process statute of the particular state. If a judgment, including a judgment by default, should be obtained against the insurer and a certified copy deposited with the trustee, the trustee is unconditionally required to pay the amount of the judgment after a specified number of days. The policyholder or beneficiary may thus sue and collect from the alien nonadmitted insurer in this country and does not have to pursue his remedy in a distant forum.

"White Lists" and Related Approaches

Some states maintain so-called "white lists" of those nonadmitted insurers with which surplus line placements may be made. Pennsylvania is an example, as is the new Delaware Code. Others, among them New York, do not do this and leave it to the surplus line broker to satisfy himself that a nonadmitted insurer meets eligibility requirements.

A few states, e.g., New Jersey and Florida, permit a risk to be placed or completed with nonadmitted insurers which do not meet "white list" eligibility requirements if the entire coverage cannot

---

[2] One percent on life and sickness and health insurance.

be effected with admitted insurers and nonadmitted insurers which do meet such requirements.

NAIC Information Office

In 1963 the National Association of Insurance Commissioners established the Non-Admitted Insurers Information Office, which receives, analyzes, and disseminates information about nonadmitted insurers. It has been administered by Joseph Humphreys, former Massachusetts insurance commissioner, and is increasingly relied on by commissioners and others as perhaps the best source of reliable up-to-date information upon which to judge such insurers.

Evaluation of Surplus Line Placement Requirements

This once-over-lightly account has passed over some of the most persistent sources of perplexity in both the theory and application of surplus line laws. Many such laws (or regulations) state that if a part of a risk can be placed with admitted insurance carriers, only the remainder or "excess" (an unfortunate, misleading term in this context) may be placed with nonadmitted insurers. An obvious purpose is to prevent the placing of coverages on a surplus line basis by making meaningless or even frivolous changes: for instance, a masonry building in southern Florida may not be insured on a surplus line basis with nonadmitted insurers by the addition of a provision for indemnification for collapse caused by snow; and, of course, if coverage of, say, $1,500,000 is desired and $1,000,000 can be placed with admitted insurers, the entire amount cannot be placed with nonadmitted insurers but only the remaining $500,000. But when confronted with legitimate requests for complicated coverages, the honest, conscientious surplus line broker soon finds himself embarked on uncharted seas.

Most, although not all, surplus line laws forbid the placement of surplus line insurance with a nonadmitted insurer at a more favorable rate or premium than would be charged by an admitted insurer. This is unrealistic, for many surplus line contracts are either "tailor-made" or are of the blanket or omnibus type, perhaps written as excesses of substantial deductibles or self-retentions by the insured, which have no close parallels among the mass market contracts offered by admitted insurers. In apparent half-hearted recognition of this unreality, some recent surplus line laws have made the rate limitation a more general and hence subjective one:

the insurance may not be placed with a nonadmitted insurer or insurers for the purpose of obtaining a more favorable rate.

Fewer, but still probably a majority, of surplus line laws ostensibly mandate the use of forms similar, if not identical, to those in use by admitted insurers. This is even more unrealistic. In its usual connotation, the very term "form" is misleading. As we have seen, surplus line insurances tend to be "tailor-made" comprehensive insurance contracts adapted to what the insured believes to be its individual insurance requirements in relation to its other insurance, its self-insured retentions, and its general business philosophy. Such a contract almost certainly is not the sum of and cannot be embodied in any combination of forms filed by admitted insurers.

IMPACT OF LAWS

In short, as Wilkins Micawber used to say, despite many differences there is a pervasive underlying similarity in the surplus line laws of all states. It is strange that this should be so. What do these laws do?

1. They forbid a broker or agent to place insurance with a nonadmitted insurer with whom an insured wishes it placed.
2. They require the broker to place the insurance with any admitted insurer willing to write it even though the insurer may be unacceptable to the insured and perhaps may have assets a fraction of those of the insured.
3. They prevent the insured from buying insurance at lower cost. Even when it has been found that the risk cannot be placed in the admitted market, the premium charged may not be less than would have been charged by admitted insurers even though the nonadmitted insurer would accept less.
4. They seemingly forbid the use of a "form," i.e., an insurance contract, desired by the insured and particularly suited to his needs.

The result is that the insured cannot buy through a resident surplus line broker, cheaper, better insurance from a more substantial insurer. Nor are these laws limited to protection of the small and ignorant from exploitation by the great, distant nonadmitted insurer. With few exceptions, all surplus line placements are subject to these procedures and strictures. The most persistent critics of what they believe to be the unduly restrictive character of surplus line laws are those knowledgeable executives who as insurance buyers have the responsibility for obtaining the best necessary insurance protection at the lowest cost for their principals. You are familiar with the American Society of Insurance Management, made up of the insurance buying executives of 1600 of the largest corporations, universities, municipal and state governments, religious organizations, cooperatives, etc., in this country. These executives, who often possess sophistication equal to the underwriters with whom they deal, desire freedom of access to nonadmitted insurance markets and are resentful of what seems to them bungling, unwanted "protection."

This is a severe indictment of surplus line laws—it suggests that they are inept and probably hypocritical formulations. But this is an incomplete, one-sided view and, to the extent that it may imply anything invidious, is unfair. Insurance regulation by the states has historically rested upon supervision by each state of insurers organized in the state or admitted, i.e., licensed, to do business therein. The insurer submitted itself to regulation by the state, including the regulation of rates of some classes of insurance and the obligation of filing financial and other reports on prescribed forms and was amenable to compulsory process to enforce regulatory rules. The insurer was under the jurisdiction of the insurance commissioner who could within the limits of the authority granted him tell it what to do. The nonadmitted insurer is not licensed in the state and has not placed itself under the commissioner's authority. The United States Supreme Court has held that a resident of a state may not be forbidden to place his insurance with a nonadmitted insurer.[3] The state's power to regulate and supervise the placement of insurance with nonadmitted insurers consequently rests primarily upon its power to regulate the surplus line broker who puts his license and his sureties in jeopardy and may become liable to even more serious penalties if he does not comply with the state's law.

Surplus line insurance therefore does not fit easily into the underlying pattern of regulation. It is recognized as a fact of life, but like other facts of life, it is sometimes thought to be not quite nice. The nonadmitted insurer does not and cannot submit its rates for the review and approval of the state. It does not and if it is an

---

[3] *State Board of Insurance* v. *Todd Shipyards Corp.*, 370 U.S. 451 (1962). See also *Allgeyer* v. *Louisiana*, 165 U.S. 578 (1897); *St. Louis Cotton Compress Company* v. *Arkansas;* 260 U.S. 346 (1922); *Compania De Tabacos* v. *Collector*, 275 U.S. 87 (1927); *Connecticut General Life Insurance Co.* v. *Johnson*, 303 U.S. 77 (1938).

alien insurer operating under officially mandated accounting rules of another country cannot maintain and submit its accounts on the prescribed Convention Statement basis. Because it is not under the direct supervision of the state insurance regulatory officials and has not the burden that admitted companies do of complying with the state's manifold regulatory requirements, it has traditionally been thought that it would not only be unsafe but in a sense unfair to permit brokers to place insurance with it if such insurance is obtainable from admitted insurers.

POSSIBLE SOLUTIONS TO PRESENT REGULATORY PROBLEM

It is an area of conflicting social values and concepts of equity and fairness, and I do not propose a solution acceptable to all interested parties. It seems evident, however, that today's surplus line laws represent an uneasy and perhaps ultimately unworkable compromise. For an industrial, commercial, or professional concern, insurance is bought to protect capital values and the continuity of income production; the risk of certain contingencies which could cause their impairment is assumed by the insurer for a fee. To what extent such an insured wishes to retain some risks for itself and how large a fee it is willing to pay to have some of them assumed by an insurer are matters of individual business judgment, and because of their differing circumstances, it is unlikely that exactly the same decision will be arrived at by any two insureds. Each will decide what hazards are to be considered part of the ordinarily foreseeable vicissitudes of doing business which can be absorbed and for which it is economically desirable to pay a fee to protect values and income against catastrophes or unprovided for or unusually severe contingencies. Such an insured may wish omnibus, blanket coverage of a sort related to its individual circumstances. This often is not available at an acceptable fee from among the filed forms of admitted insurers, even when such modern, flexible insurances as umbrella and difference-in-conditions policies are considered.

It is beside the point to suggest that theoretically all such insurance coverage could be provided by domestic admitted insurers. The fact is that it has not been. The alien nonadmitted insurance market has long been a source of much of such specialized insurance protection, and there is nothing to indicate that its facilities will not continue to be necessary for as far as the future can be seen, particularly for the increasing number of American insureds with both multistate and international commitments.

The surplus line area urgently needs the infusion of new ideas. But the subject is not an easy one. Careful consideration should be given to recasting the limitations that rating laws impose on the acceptance of so-called "surplus line" coverages by admitted insurers without doing undue violence to the effectiveness of whatever rating philosophy a state may have. There is surely no justification for a state imposing restrictions on admitted insurers merely for the sake of statutory and regulatory consistency and neatness.

Similarly, informed insureds must be permitted free access to the nonadmitted market when this best serves their needs, and such access should be by procedures based on reality rather than fictions.

REINSURANCE WITH ALIEN INSURERS

Insurance is placed with alien nonadmitted insurers not only by primary insureds but by admitted insurance companies themselves who reinsure, or cede, a portion of their portfolio of risks to nonadmitted insurers. This may be by way of facultative reinsurance whereby the ceding company reinsures a fractional portion of a risk or class of risks with a nonadmitted reinsurer; excess reinsurance whereby the ceding company reinsures all or a percentage of a risk or class of risks above a certain amount; or catastrophe reinsurance, a kind of excess insurance, whereby the ceding company reinsures all or a portion of a class or classes of risks above a specified aggregate loss, all up to the limits of the reinsurance. The predominant social consideration here is the effect of the reinsurance on the security behind the primary ceding insurer's undertaking to indemnify its policyholders—on the "solidity" of the enterprise.

It is of value to the ceding insurer to be able to take "credit" for its reinsurance in its financial statements. It wishes to take credit with respect to (1) its loss reserves and (2) its unearned premium reserves.

If the ceding insurer has outstanding losses of $1,000,000 reinsured 75 percent facultatively, such losses reduce its policyholders' surplus by $1,000,000 if it cannot take credit for its reinsurance and by $250,000 if it can take credit for its receivable from its nonadmitted reinsurance. The difference of $750,000 is often referred to as the "penalty" to policyholders' surplus resulting from denial of credit for its nonadmitted reinsurance.

The penalty to policyholders' surplus with respect to unearned premium reserves may be even more severe. If an insurer receives an advance premium for a five-year policy, it earns 1/60th of such premium each month. Oversimplifying somewhat, it must maintain an unearned premium reserve at the end of the first month of 59/60ths with which to reimburse the policyholder should the coverage be terminated at that time. But this does not truly reflect the extent of the unearned premium reserve requirement. The primary insurer does not receive 100 cents of the premium dollar paid by the insured but only the net after commissions and premium taxes, perhaps 70 cents or less, which comes to it 60 days or more after the coverage becomes effective. Its unearned premium reserve obligation and reserve is measured by its liability to repay the unearned portion of the entire premium. It is apparent that the obligation to maintain an unearned premium reserve is particularly severe for a company writing an increasing rather than a level or decreasing volume of business. It follows that it is of value to the ceding company to be able to take credit for its reinsurance in relation to its unearned premium reserve obligation in order that its policyholders' surplus and capacity to do business not be penalized.

It is an important part of the examination process to which states subject admitted insurance companies that their reinsurance, just as their investments, be evaluated in order that their ability to fulfill their obligations may be measured. An admitted reinsurer is subject to examination by its domiciliary and other states just as the primary insurer is. A nonadmitted insurer is not. The states therefore have detailed rules as to what reinsurance a primary insurer may and may not claim credit for.

Simplicity would be served if credit could not be claimed for reinsurance with other than admitted reinsurers. But circumstances have compelled, and increasingly compel, a different rule. Reinsurance is international. The magnitude and number of risks underwritten in this post-Betsy hurricane loss era of civil disorders require that this be so. Admitted reinsurers, including even the so-called professional reinsurers, have reinsurance abroad with nonadmitted insurers. The need for nonadmitted reinsurance is intensified when the capacity of admitted reinsurers to accept reinsurance business is lessened by the effect on their surplus of the decline in the values of the securities in their investment portfolios, as occurred in 1966.

Reinsurance is not written at filed or predetermined rates, but the cost of a ceding company's reinsurance is arrived at as the result of bargaining, usually annual bargaining. A reinsured company which does not have available to it the alternative of placing its reinsurance or a portion of it with reputable solvent nonadmitted reinsurers finds itself in a weaker bargaining position in dealing with the admitted reinsurers with which it is then compelled to contract.

The result has been that 48 states and the District of Columbia now permit a ceding company to take credit for reinsurance with a few nonadmitted reinsurers. The rules vary from state to state, but the test is generally that the nonadmitted reinsurer be solvent and satisfactory to the commissioner and in some jurisdictions that it be admitted in at least one state. A few states impose an additional requirement of the maintenance of a large trust fund for the benefit of policyholders in this country. Only Underwriters at Lloyd's, London, meet the requirements everywhere at this time.

To alleviate the penalty to loss reserves but not that to unearned premium reserves, it has been the practice for many years for substantial alien reinsurers to make dollar advances against their share of the reserves set up by reinsured companies for outstanding claims. These Outstanding Claims Advances, commonly called "OCA's," are held in trust by the reinsured company in separate or segregated bank accounts which may be drawn upon only to reimburse the reinsured company for the reinsurers' share of losses when paid. A form of the simple trust agreement utilized is contained in Appendix B.

Some of these Outstanding Claims Advances have continued in existence for as much as 25 years; for instance with relation to workmen's compensation claims and because commercial bank accounts are usually noninterest bearing, the practice has recently grown up of using dollar Letters of Credit as an alternative to OCA's if this is desired by both the reinsured and the reinsurer. These Letters of Credit, which have been approved by all states and the District of Columbia, are wholly unconditional, unqualified, irrevocable undertakings by the bank issuing the Letter of Credit to honor and pay drafts drawn on it by the reinsured company up to the face amount of the Letter of Credit. Although the reinsured company undertakes in a supplementary agreement similar to the OCA trust agreement to draw against the Letter of Credit only to reimburse itself for the reinsurers' share of claim payments, there is no such limitation in the Letter of Credit itself, and in fact there is no legal inhibition against the reinsured company drawing down the entire sum immediately after it receives it. A copy of a typical Letter of Credit and the form of draft given the reinsured company for its use are included as Appendix C, and a copy of the agreement entered into by the reinsured company receiving a Letter of Credit is found in Appendix D.

To protect the bank issuing the Letter of Credit, a dollar Cash Collateral Account with the bank is established by the alien reinsurer from which the bank may reimburse itself as drafts are drawn on it by the reinsured company. These Cash Collateral Accounts earn interest, which, after the deduction of a small service fee by the bank, inures to the reinsurer. Usually the reinsurer puts the bank in funds to cover payments by the bank in order to preserve the income producing account intact.

Because banking institutions, or at least their lawyers, believe that letters of credit should not be issued for an indefinite term, they are for a term of two years, but the accompanying trust agreement permits the entire sum to be drawn down by the reinsured company during the last 10 days before expiration of the Letter of Credit even though it has not paid claims in the full amount. Although the original Letter of Credit is for a two-year term, in practice it is generally rewritten annually so that the Letter of Credit in the hands of the reinsured company always has an unexpired term of between 12 and 24 months. A copy of a typical Letter of Credit used for extending the term or changing the amount of an outstanding letter is included as Appendix E.

The amount of Letters of Credit now outstanding is said to exceed $130,000,000.

INADEQUACIES OF LAWS RELATING TO ALIEN INSURERS

A slow and hesitant evolution of state insurance laws and practices has produced usually workable but cumbersome and fictional procedures for dealing with the anomalous insistence of insureds on placing business with alien nonadmitted insurers. Theory has trailed practice.

This may be the result, in part, of two fallacies implicit in the laws of most states. The first is that the nonadmitted insurer seeks out the primary insured or reinsured company and that the latter must be protected from the wiles of the former. A corollary underlying assumption is that such insureds are uninformed. This has never been true for reinsurance and is no longer true, if it ever was, with respect to contemporary sophisticated industrial, commerical, and professional insureds. Competition today is between such insureds for markets and capacity for the coverages they believe they require rather than between alien insurers for their business.

The second fallacy is that coverages considered indivisible by both the insured and the nonadmitted insurer may be arbitrarily fragmented (*a*) into separable component parts and types and (*b*) geographically for purposes of regulation and taxation. This might be termed the fallacy of unrealistic localization.

Needless difficulties remain, in other words, because of the persistence of an outmoded conceptualism. When this is recognized, there would seem to be no insoluble problems in evolving adequate, yet realistic, rules with respect to both primary insurance and reinsurance with alien nonadmitted insurers. Consideration of the laws and regulatory practices of other, smaller countries having as their purpose the protection of nationals insured abroad should be fruitful. I have referred to the Non-Admitted Insurers Information Office of the National Association of Insurance Commissioners as a source of current realistic factual information on alien insurers.

But certainly the greatest, as well as the most obvious, source of potential enlightenment and help in fitting state laws and practices into a broader frame without sacrificing essential local interests are those sophisticated insurance consumers, both primary insureds and reinsured domestic companies, who purchase and believe they require coverages abroad by discovering their practices and needs and how they foresee the future. Relevant knowledge and insights may be gained to aid regulators and legislators in making archaic concepts and ponderous practices consonant with today's and tomorrow's realities.

APPENDIX A

Summary of Surplus Line Laws

Alabama [7 *Code of Alabama, Title 28, Ch. 16A, §§ 417(1) to 417(22) (1963)*]. A licensed surplus line broker may procure insurance from unauthorized insurers, if the insurance is not fully procurable after diligent effort, from among authorized insurers actually transacting that kind and class of insurance. The surplus line insurance must not be procured solely for the purpose of securing a lower premium rate than would be accepted by an authorized insurer. (§417(7))

ALASKA   [*Alaska Statutes, Title 21, §§21.33.080 to 21.33.330 (1966)*].   A licensed surplus line broker may procure insurance in unadmitted insurers, if the insurance is not procurable, after diligent effort, from among a majority of authorized insurers. The surplus line insurance must not be for the purpose of securing a lower premium rate than would be accepted by an authorized insurer. The surplus line broker must file an affidavit with the Department setting out these facts within 30 days after obtaining insurance. (§21–33.090)

ARIZONA   [*7 Arizona Rev. Stats. Anno., Title 20, Ch. 2, §§20–407 to 20–422 (1956); §20–408 (filing of affidavit revised in 1961); §20–413 (trust fund revised in 1961)*].   A licensed surplus line broker may procure needed insurance in unauthorized insurers, if the coverage is not procurable, after diligent effort, from among a substantial number of admitted insurers, and the surplus line insurance is not for the purpose of securing advantages in rate or policy terms. (§20–407)

ARKANSAS   [*6 Arkansas Stats. 1947 Annot., Cum., Supp., Title 66, §§66–2908 to 66–2925 (1959)*].   The resident, licensed surplus line broker may procure insurance from unauthorized insurers if the required insurance is not procurable, after diligent effort, from among the majority of authorized insurers. The surplus line insurance must not be for securing advantages either as to rates or policy terms. A broker's affidavit attesting to the above must be filed with the Commissioner within 30 days after the insurance is procured. (§§66–2910, 66–2911)

CALIFORNIA   [*42 West's Annot. California Codes (Insurance Code, §§1760 to 1780 (1967 Cum. Supp.)*]   A licensed surplus line broker may place insurance with non-admitted insurers only if such insurance cannot be procured from a majority of admitted insurers. The insurance must not be for the purpose of procuring a lower rate than the lowest rate which will be accepted by an admitted insurer. A presumption of a lower rate will be inferred unless the surplus line broker files an affidavit with the Commissioner. (§1763)

COLORADO   [*4 Colorado Revised Statutes (1963), Ch. 72, §§72–13–1 to 72–13–17 (1967 Cum. Supp.)*].   A resident, licensed surplus line broker may procure required insurance from unauthorized insurers if the insurance is not procurable, after diligent effort, from among a majority of authorized insurers. The surplus line insurance must not be for the purpose of securing a lower rate. The surplus line broker must file an affidavit with the Commissioner within 30 days after the insurance is procured. (§72–13–2)

CONNECTICUT   [17 *Connecticut General Statutes Annot.* (1958), *Title 38, §§38–78 to 38–86* (1953, *as amended*) *and §38–90a* (1963)]. Both the resident excess line broker and the insured must execute affidavits, when the excess line policy is procured, that both were unable, after diligent effort, to procure the required insurance from any authorized insurer or insurers, and that the excess line insurance is only the excess of the amount so procurable from authorized insurers. (The excess line broker may only place risks in those non-admitted insurers which are set forth in the list of authorized non-admitted insurers published by the Department of insurance). The resident excess line broker must file the affidavit with the Commissioner within 30 days after such policies have been procured. (§37–81)

DELAWARE   [10 *Delaware Code Anno., Title 18, §514* (*b*) (1953)]. The statute expressly authorizes an insured to deal directly with an unauthorized insurer. This is apparently a codification of the prior case law. In *Atlas Mutual Ins. Co.* v. *Fisheries Co.*, 22 Del. 256, 68 Atl. 4 (1907), the court relied upon *Allgeyer* v. *Louisiana* (165 U.S. 576), and held that the laws of Delaware could not deprive a citizen of his right, in good faith, to make a contract of insurance out of the State upon his property situated within Delaware.

DISTRICT OF COLUMBIA   [2 *District of Columbia Code, Title 35, §35–1344* (1944)]. A licensed agent or broker may procure policies from unauthorized insurers if the agent or broker is, after diligent effort, unable to procure the policies from authorized insurers. The policy must not have "abnormal provisions," nor be based on rate-cutting. Monthly affidavits must be filed with Supertendent.

FLORIDA   [18A *Florida Stats. Anno., Title 35 Insurance, Secs. 626.0510 to 626.0534* (1967 *Cum. Supp.*); *Department of Insurance Regulations, Ch. 5–16* (1967)]. The licensed surplus line agent may procure insurance from an eligible surplus line insurer if the full amount of the insurance cannot be procured, after diligent effort, from among the authorized insurers actually writing the line, except that the Commissioner may authorize certain classes as immediately procurable in the surplus line market. The Department has ruled that it shall furnish any surplus line agent with information on file concerning markets for any rates which the agent may have difficulty in placing. Within 60 days after securing the insurance the surplus line agent must file an affidavit with the Commissioner. (§6y6.0517, Reg. Ch. 5–16).

GEORGIA   [17 *Georgia Code Anno., Title 56, Ch. 56–6, §§56–613 to 56–628* (1960); *§56–618* (*revised in 1965*)]. A licensed resident surplus line broker may procure insurance from unauthorized insurers if the full amount of insurance cannot be obtained from licensed insurers, to the extent of the surplus amount, after diligent effort to secure such insurance from among the insurers who are authorized to transact and are actually writing the particular kind and class of insurance in this state. Submission of the risk to not less than three such authorized insurers shall be deemed to be diligent effort. The surplus line broker or the originating broker or agent is to file an affidavit within 60 days after the insurance is procured, and such affidavit shall be open to public inspection.

HAWAII [*Revised Laws of Hawaii, Title 23, Ch. 181, §§181–324 to 181–336 (1955, as amended)*]. A licensed surplus line broker may place required insurance in an unauthorized insurer if, after diligent search in good faith, the insurance cannot be procured from a substantial number of authorized insurers. The surplus lines insurance may not be procured at a lower rate than the lowest rate set by a substantial number of authorized insurers. No affidavit is required to be executed or filed. (§181–325)

IDAHO [*7A Idaho Code Title 41, Ch. 12, §§41–1211 to 41–1232 (1961)*]. A licensed surplus line broker may procure insurance in unauthorized insurers if the required insurance is not procurable, after diligent effort, from among a majority of authorized insurers actually writing that kind and class of insurance in this state, and the amount of insurance exported shall be only the excess over the amount procurable from authorized insurers. The insurance may not be exported for the purpose of securing advantages either as to a lower premium rate or terms of the insurance contract. The surplus line broker must execute an affidavit at the time of effecting the surplus line insurance, and must file the affidavit within 30 days after the insurance is procured with the Surplus Lines Association of Idaho which forwards it to the Commissioner (§§41–1214, 41–1215; Regulation of March 1, 1962)

ILLINOIS [*Illinois Rev. Stats. (1959), Ch. 73, §§1057, 1057.1; Smith-Hurd Illinois Anno. Stats., Ch. 73, §§1057, 1057.1; (1966 Cum. Supp.); Rules & Regulations of Illinois Insurance Dept., Rule 28.01 (1951)*]. A licensed surplus line agent may place insurance in unauthorized insurers if, after diligent effort, he is unable to procure the required insurance from authorized insurers. "Diligent effort" shall be deemed to have been exercised if the surplus line agent or the referring broker "shall cause the risk to be published in its Bulletin by the Chicago Board of Underwriters, or shall, in a bona fide manner, submit each such risk to *three* or more companies, each of whom shall be duly authorized to transact in Illinois insurance business of the kind or kinds involved in the particular requests for coverage. "Surplus line agents must file an affidavit with the Insurance Department on or before the 20th day of each month covering the transactions of the previous calendar month.

INDIANA   [8 *Burns Anno. Indiana Stats.* (*1965 Replacement Volume*), *Title 39, Ch. 45, §39–4509* (*1955, as amended*)]. The licensed surplus line agent or broker may procure insurance in unauthorized insurers if, after diligent effort, the desired insurance is not procurable from any authorized insurer or insurers, and the insurance is not for the purpose of obtaining a lower premium rate than would be accepted by an authorized insurer. The agent or broker must file monthly affidavits with the Insurance Department.

IOWA   [30 *Iowa Code Anno., Ch. 515, §§515.147 to 515.150* (*1966 Cum. Supp.*); *Iowa Insurance Department, Regulation T-4, eff. September 1, 1963*]. The licensed resident agent may place insurance in non-admitted insurers if he has exhausted all the insurance obtainable from admitted insurers. The agent must file an affidavit with the Commissioner within 30 days subsequent ot the effective date of coverage, and must maintain a separate bank account for taxes on unauthorized premiums.

KANSAS   [3 *Kansas Stats. Anno.* (*1964*), *§§40–246b to 40–246d* (*1965, as amended*); *Insurance Department Rule and Regulation 40–8–1 to 40–8–13, as amended* (*1967*)]. The licensed excess agent may procure insurance from non-admitted insurers, provided he has been unable, after diligent effort, to procure the required insurance in regularly admitted companies. No risk may be placed in non-admitted carriers to obtain advantages in rates or terms. The excess agent must file affidavits or exportability each year on or before the 10th of January.

KENTUCKY   [*Kentucky Rev. Stats.* (*1962*) *Ch. 136, §136.360; Ch. 304, §§304.586 to 304.598* (*1950, as amended*)]. The licensed surplus line broker may procure the required insurance from unauthorized insurers if the insurance cannot be procured from authorized insurers. The surplus line insurance must not be for the purpose of securing advantages with respect to rates or policy conditions. The surplus line broker must file an affidavit within 30 days after the insurance is procured. (§304.586)

LOUISIANA   [*West's Louisiana Rev. Stats. Anno.* (*1959*), *Title 22, §§22:1257 to 22:1270* (*1967 Cum. Supp.*); *Louisiana Insurance Department Regulations, Directive No. 6, eff. December 1, 1965*]. If desired insurance cannot be procured from authorized insurers, a written request must be filed by the insured (or producer) with the licensed, resident surplus line broker, stating that, after diligent effort, the insurance has not been procurable from authorized insurers. Within 30 days after procurement, the surplus line broker files an affidavit that he has received the request and that the insurance was not procurable from authorized insurers. (§1257)

MAINE   [13 Maine Rev. Stats. Anno. (1965), Title 24, Ch. 21, §§2504(12), 2515 (1966 Cum. Supp.); Bulletin No. 72 of the Commissioner of Insurance (1956)]. The licensed surplus line broker must make written application to the Commissioner stating his reasons for desiring to insure a particular risk with an unauthorized insurer. The Commissioner shall thereupon grant permission if the insurance is necessary, may be written under the laws of Maine but is not available from an authorized insurer, and the insurer is responsible and financially sound. The surplus line broker must also give the Commissioner written notice within 5 days of the placing of such insurance and also must file a monthly report of all business transacted. [§2515 (1) and (2)]

MARYLAND   [Maryland Stats. Anno. (1964), Art. 48A, §§41, 171, 183 to 200 (1963); Maryland Insurance Department, Regulation 64–24 (1964)]. The licensed, resident surplus line broker may procure insurance in unauthorized insurers if he is unable to procure the required insurance in admitted insurers. The broker must file an affidavit with the Commissioner within 30 days after the insurance is placed. Under Regulation 64–24(IV) the Commissioner issued a list of coverages eligible for export on form 600. The surplus line broker may not place a risk in any unauthorized insurer which has not previously, in writing, appointed the Commissioner agent for the acceptance of service of process. (§§184, 185)

MASSACHUSETTS   [28 Massachusetts Gen. Laws Anno. Ch. 175, §168 (1966 Cum. Supp.)]. The special license insurance broker may procure that portion of insurance in unauthorized insurers which he is unable to procure in admitted insurers. After procurement the broker must execute an affidavit which must be filed within 5 days with the Commissioner.

MICHIGAN   [28 Michigan Consol. Laws Anno., Ch. 500 (Insurance Code of 1956, as amended), §§500.440, 500.1840 to 500.1864 (1967 Cum. Supp.)]. After the resident surplus lines agent has procured the full amount which admitted insurers are willing to write, and within 30 days after surplus lines insurance is procured, the surplus lines agent must file an affidavit with the Commissioner that he is unable to procure, after diligent effort, the necessary insurance in admitted insurers. (§500.1849).

MINNESOTA   [Minnesota Laws of 1967, Ch. 395 (Insurance Code of 1967), Art. 1, §20 (60A.20)]. A licensed surplus lines agent may procure insurance from unauthorized insurers if the required insurance cannot be procured from authorized insurers after diligent effort, and the excess over the amount procurable in the state is not procured for the purpose of securing advantages, either as to a lower premium rate or terms of the insurance contract. The surplus lines agent must file an affidavit with the Commissioner within thirty days after the insurance contract is placed.

MISSISSIPPI [*4A Mississippi Code (1942) Anno., Title 22, Art. 10, §5705–02, as amended (1967)*]. Both the licensed surplus line agent and the insured must execute an affidavit that the insured was unable, after diligent effort, to procure the required insurance from any licensed company or companies. The surplus line agent must file these affidavits with the Commissioner within 30 days from the first of January and July of each year, together with the tax reports.

MISSOURI [*1967 Laws of Missouri (H.C.S. H.B. 262), §§375.031, 375.036 (1967) Missouri Insurance Department, Regulations Nos. 46 and 52 (revised, 1965)*]. The licensed resident agent may place insurance in non-admitted insurers if he has exhausted all the insurance obtainable from admitted insurers. Before he placed such insurance, the agent must file an affidavit with the Superintendent supported by the letters of rejection from authorized companies, and the Superintendent must approve such placement. (Reg. No. 52). The requirement that three letters of rejection be appended to the affidavit, however, may be waived upon request to the Superintendent.

MONTANA [*Revised Code of Montana (1947), Title 40, Ch. 34, §§40–3409 to 40–3426; Ch. 27, §40–2726; Ch. 28, §40–2821 (1967 Cum. Supp.)*]. The licensed, resident surplus line agent may procure insurance in unauthorized insurers if, after diligent effort, the required insurance is not procurable from among a majority of authorized insurers. The surplus line insurance must not be for the purpose of securing advantages either as to rates or policy terms. The surplus line agent must file an affidavit with the Commissioner at the time the insurance is procured. (§§40–3410, 40–3411)

NEBRASKA [*Revised Stats. of Nebraska (1943), §§44–142 to 44–147; §77–908; §81–523 (1966 Cum. Supp.)*]. The licensed agent and the insured (or his authorized agent) must execute an affidavit that the insured is, after diligent effort, unable to procure the required insurance from authorized insurers. The affidavit must be filed within 30 days after procuring the insurance. (§44–144)

NEVADA   [*Nevada Rev. Stats., Title 57, Ch. 686. & 686.280 to 686.380; § 686.010 (1955, as amended)*; *Nevada Insurance Department, Regulation 27, eff. January 1, 1968; Bulletin No. 20 (1964)*]. The licensed, resident surplus line broker may procure insurance in unauthorized insurers. Both the surplus line broker and the insured (or his authorized agent) must execute affidavits that the insured (or his authorized agent) is, after diligent effort, unable to procure the insurance from a majority of authorized insurers. The surplus line insurance must not be for the purpose of securing advantages either as to rates or policy terms. The affidavit must be filed within 30 days after procuring the insurance, and under Regulation 27 (revised November 30, 1967) the affidavit "will be filed" with the Nevada Surplus Line Association. (§ 686.320)

NEW HAMPSHIRE   [*4 New Hampshire Rev. Stats. Anno. (1955), Ch. 405, §§405:24 to 405:31 (1967 Cum. Supp.)*; *New Hampshire Insurance Department, Regulation VII (1963)*]. The licensed resident agent may place insurance in a non-admitted insurer which is admitted in one state, if the agent has first satisfied the Insurance Commissioner that he cannot procure the insurance in an admitted insurer. Monthly statements must be filed with the Insurance Department.

NEW JERSEY   [*17 New Jersey Stats. Anno., §§17:22–6.37 to 17:22–6.69 (1960, as amended)*]. The resident licensed surplus lines agent may export insurance to an eligible surplus line insurer if the full amount of the required insurance is not procurable, after diligent effort, from authorized insurers; except, that the Commissioner may authorize certain classes generally exportable to the surplus line market. Bulletin No. 9 (dated June 1, 1965) lists 23 classes of insurance eligible for export generally. The surplus line policy must not be for the purpose of rate or policy advantages. Within 21 days after the surplus line policy is effected the surplus lines agent and the producing broker must file affidavits, except that no affidavits are required for generally exportable classes, together with a copy of the binder, cover note, certificate, policy or other confirmation of insurance. If a policy is not available upon placement, the surplus lines agent, in no event later than 60 days after placement, shall procure from the insurer its policy and deliver the policy to the insured. (6.50). Immediately upon issuance, the surplus lines agent shall file with the Commissioner an exact copy of the policy (6.51).

NEW MEXICO   [*8 New Mexico Stats. (1953), Ch. 58, Art. 5, §§58–5–31 to 58–5–47; §58–5–1; Art. 18, §58–18–24 (1966 Cum. Supp.)*; *New Mexico Administration Rules and Regulations Code,*

Art. 5, Rule 2 (1949) and Rule 4, §5–4–15 (1966)]. Surplus line broker's licenses are issued to licensed resident agents. Surplus line brokers may place insurance with non-admitted insurers only if such insurance cannot be procured from a *majority* of admitted insurers, and not for the purpose of procuring lower rates. If the insurance is placed at a lower premium than that obtainable from an admitted insurer, violation of the statute is conclusively presumed, *unless* (1) a statement is filed with the Superintendent at the time the insurance attaches describing the insurance and nearest procurable rates, and (2) the Superintendent does not, within 5 days of filing, notify the broker that such insurance violates the statute. (§58–5–32)

NEW YORK [*New York Insurance Law §122, 46, 112 (1967 Cum. Supp.*); *11 New York Code of Rules and Regulations, Parts 21 and 27 (as of 1967)*]. Only certain kinds of insurance (as listed below) are eligible for the surplus line market. Both the resident licensed excess line broker and the insured must execute separate affidavits that they were unable after diligent effort, to procure all or part of the required insurance from at least five authorized insurers. The excess line broker must file the affidavits with the Superintendent of Insurance within 30 days after the policy has been procured.

NORTH CAROLINA [*2B General Stats. of North Carolina, Ch. 58, §58.53.1 (1899, as amended)*]. Before a citizen can obtain a license to procure policies of insurance in foreign or alien companies on risks in the state, he must first execute and file with the Commissioner an affidavit that he is unable to procure the necessary insurance in admitted insurers. He may only procure from non-admitted companies that portion rejected by the admitted companies.

NORTH DAKOTA [*4 North Dakota Centure Code, Anno., Title 26, §§26–09B–01 to 26–09B–13, §26–01–11, §26–17–02, §26–17–06 (1960, as amended)*]. Before the licensed surplus line agent may place a risk in a non-admitted insurer, the surplus line agent must execute an affidavit that the insured is unable, after diligent search, to procure the desired insurance from an authorized insurer. If the Commissioner concurs he may authorize the procuring of the insurance from the non-admitted insurer. (§§26–09B–02, 26–09B–04)

OHIO [*Page's Ohio Rev. Code Anno., Title 39, Ch. 3905, §§3905.30 to 3905.35 (1959, as amended)*; *Ohio Insurance Department, Rule IN–5–01 (1966)*]. The licensed surplus line broker may procure insurance from unauthorized insurers if the required insurance cannot, after due diligence, be procured from an authorized insurer. The surplus line broker and the insured must file affidavits with the Commissioner within 15 days from the time the insurance is bound, and the producer must sign the affidavit. (§3905.33)

OKLAHOMA   [*Oklahoma Stats. Anno., Title 36, §§1106 to 1119 (1967 Cum. Supp.); Oklahoma Insurance Commissioner, Rule 11–1 (March 1964)*]. The licensed surplus line broker may procure required insurance from unauthorized insurers if the insurance is not procurable, after diligent effort, from a majority of authorized insurers. The purpose of insurance with an unauthorized insurer must not be for the purpose of securing advantages either as to premium rate or terms of the insurance contract. The Commissioner, after a hearing, will designate certain coverages as surplus lines, for which the surplus line broker need not execute an affidavit. However, if a coverage has not been so designated, the surplus line broker, before procuring the insurance from a non-admitted insurer, must file an affidavit (Form SL-2) with the Commissioner, and the Commissioner will thereupon rule whether the coverage may be procured from unauthorized insurers.

OREGON   [*Oregon Rev. Stats., Title 56, Ch. 744, §§744.305 to 744.405, Ch. 731, §§731.816, 731.820 (1967)*]. Before the agent holding a surplus line license may procure insurance from an unauthorized insurer, he must file with the Commissioner an affidavit that the insured is unable to procure the required insurance in a majority of authorized insurers. The surplus line insurance must not be at a lower rate than the fair and equitable rate filed with the Commissioner by an authorized rating organization. (There is no statutory requirement that the Commissioner must concur with the affidavit before the risk may be exported.) (§744.345)

PENNSYLVANIA   [*Purdon's Pennsylvania Stats. Anno., Title 40, §§1006.4 to 1006.19 (1966)*]. A licensed resident surplus lines agent may place insurance with an unlicensed insurer if the producing broker has, after diligent effort, been unable to procure such coverage from licensed insurers and the surplus lines agent is not aware of a licensed insurer "satisfactory to the insured" from which the desired coverage may be procured. The premium rate may not be lower than the lowest published rate approved by the Commissioner for licensed insurers and the policy form must, unless unique, be similar to Pennsylvania forms. "Diligent effort" is viewed as a minimum of three refusals. Affidavits attesting to the above must be executed by the producing broker and surplus lines agent and filed with the Commissioner within 21 days after the insurance has become effective. (§§1006.4, 1006.6)

PUERTO RICO   [5B Laws of Puerto Rico Anno., Title 26, Ch. 10, §§1007 to 1018 (1966 Cum. Supp.); Puerto Rico Insurance Department, Regulations 204–1901 to 204–1910 (as amended to 1960)].   At the time of procuring the surplus line coverage, the licensed surplus line broker must file with the Commissioner an affidavit setting forth facts from which it may be determined that the insurance cannot be procured from authorized insurers and that the unauthorized insurance is not sought for the purpose of taking advantage of lower rates. Regulations 204–1901 and 204–1902 require the broker to offer, by mail, (Form O) the coverage that he proposes to procure as surplus lines insurance to all authorized insurers or their representatives in Puerto Rico; the offer is deemed to have been rejected if the broker receives no answer within 5 days. (§§1007, 1008)

RHODE ISLAND   [5 General Laws of Rhode Island (1956), Title 27, Ch. 3, §§27–3–38 to 27–3–42 (1966 Cum. Supp.); Insurance Department of Rhode Island, Regulation XI (1964)].   Both the insured and the licensed surplus line broker must execute separate affidavits showing that the insured and surplus line broker were unable, after diligent effort, to procure the required insurance from any authorized insurer or insurers. The purpose of the surplus line policy must not be for either rate or policy advantages. The affidavits shall be filed by the licensed surplus line broker within 30 days after the policies have been procured. (§27–3–38)

SOUTH CAROLINA   [8 Code of Laws of South Carolina (1962), Title 37, §§37–203, 37–210 (1967 Cum. Supp.)].   There is no explicit surplus line law. However, the statutes provide that a broker, "with the written approval of the Commissioner," may place insurance with non-admitted insurers, upon payment of an "additional license fee" §37–203(3).

SOUTH DAKOTA   [South Dakota Code, Title 31, Ch. 2, §31–2–27; Ch. 11, §§31–11–1 to 31–11–24 (1966, as amended); Title 57, Ch. 57.35A, §§57.34A01(4), 57.35A02(2) (1967 Cum. Supp.)].   Within 30 days after the insurance has been procured by a licensed surplus line broker from an unauthorized insurer, the surplus line broker must file an affidavit with the Commissioner stating that the insured has been unable, after diligent effort has been made to do so, to procure the desired insurance from an authorized insurer. The surplus line insurance must not be placed for the purpose of securing advantageous rates or terms. (§31–11–4)

TENNESSEE   [10 Tennessee Code Anno., Title 56, Ch. 7, §56–707; Ch. 4, §§56–408, 56–411 (1967 Cum. Supp.)].   Any licensed resident agent of the state or any licensed broker may place insurance in unauthorized insurers if, after diligent effort, he has either exhausted the capacity of all authorized insurers or been unable to obtain the desired insurance from licensed insurers. Reports are to be filed with the Commissioner annually before March 1.

TEXAS   [14 Vernon's Civil Statutes of Texas (Insurance Code) Art. 1. 14-2 (Laws of 1967); Texas Insurance Department, Board Order 8165 (1966)]. A specially licensed agent, who also regularly represents an admitted insurer, may place insurance with unauthorized insurers. The agent, before the policy is procured, must execute an affidavit that the insured was unable, after diligent effort, to procure the required insurance from licensed insurers. If the annual premiums paid by the insured are in excess of $25,000, the insured may execute the affidavit in lieu of the agent. Within 60 days of procurement, an exact copy of the policy must be filed with the Secretary of State.

UTAH   [4 Utah Code Anno., (1953), Title 31, Ch. 15, §§31–15–1 to 31–15–16, §31–15–19 (1967 Cum. Supp.); Utah Insurance Department, Regulation 64.3 eff. January 23, 1964]. Surplus line broker's licenses are issued to licensed resident agents. Surplus line brokers may place insurance with non-admitted insurers only if such insurance cannot be procured from a *majority* of admitted insurers, and not for the purpose of procuring lower rates. If the insurance is placed at a lower premium than the lowest premium obtainable from an admitted insurer, violation of the statute is conclusively presumed, unless (1) a statement is filed with the Commissioner at the time the insurance attaches describing the insurance and nearest procurable rates, and (2) the Commissioner does not within 5 days of filing, notify the broker that such insurance violates the statute. Regulation 64–3 (effective January 23, 1964) the required filing may be made with the Stamping Office of the Utah Surplus Line Association. (§31–15–2)

VERMONT   [2 Vermont Stats. Anno., Title 8, Part 3, Ch. 127, §§4800, 4801 (1967 Cum. Supp.)]. A licensed resident of Vermont, pursuant to the Commissioners regulations, may procure insurance from alien non-admitted insurers. Licensees are to file quarterly reports with the Commissioner. The application for a license contains the statement that the licensee "will not attempt to place any insurance . . . until I am satisfied that I am unable to place the coverage requested in a company authorized to do business in Vermont."

VIRGINIA   [6 Virginia Code Anno. (1950), Title 38, Ch. 7, §§38.1–314.1 to 38.1–314.16 (1960, as amended); §38.1–291; §§38.1–5 to 38.1–16; §§38.1–21 to 38.1–24; Title 58, Ch. 11, §§489 to 490

(*1966 Cum. Supp.*)]. A surplus line broker may procure certain classes of insurance (listed in the "special provisions" below) from unauthorized insurers. Insurance may be procured from approved surplus line insurers if both the resident surplus lines broker and the insured are unable, after diligent effort, to procure the required insurance from authorized insurers. The surplus line insurance must not be for the purpose of securing advantages either for premiums or terms. The affidavit of the surplus line broker and the insured must be filed (a) within 15 days after the insurance was procured and (b) within 15 days prior to remitting the premium. (§§38.1–314.1, 38.1–314.7)

WASHINGTON [*Rev. Code of Washington, Title 48, Ch. 48.15 §§48.15.040 to 48.15.170; Ch. 48.14, §48.14.020 (1961, as amended); Manual of the Surplus Line Association of Washington (1967 Reprint)*]. A resident surplus line broker may procure insurance in unauthorized insurers, if the insurance is not procurable after diligent effort among a majority of authorized insurers. The surplus line must not be for the purpose of securing a lower premium. At placement, the surplus line broker must execute an affidavit and file it with the Commissioner within 30 days from procurement date. (§§48.15–040)

WEST VIRGINIA [*10 West Virginia Code of 1966 Anno., Ch. 33, §§33–12–10 to 33–12–18, §33–12–22 (1967 Cum. Supp.)*]. A licensed excess line broker may procure insurance in unlicensed insurers if the coverage is not procurable, after diligent effort, from licensed insurers, and the placing of the excess line is not for the purpose of securing advantages as to rates or terms. An affidavit must be filed with the Commissioner at the time of procuring the excess line insurance. (§§33–12–10, 33–12–11)

WISCONSIN [*25 Wisconsin Stats. Anno., (1957), Title 17, Ch. 201, §201.63, §201.04 (1967 Cum. Supp.)*]. Certain classes of insurance are eligible for the surplus line market, and these classes are listed in a special provision below. Before a licensed surplus lines agent procures insurance in a non-admitted insurer, he must file an affidavit with the Commissioner that he is after diligent effort unable to procure, from any licensed insurer or insurers, the full amount of required insurance.

WYOMING [*1967 Session Laws of Wyoming, Ch. 136, §§208 to 228, eff. Jan. 1, 1968*]. A licensed surplus line broker may procure insurance from unauthorized insurers if the full amount of insurance required is not procurable, after diligent effort, from authorized insurers and the placing of such insurance is not for the purpose of securing advantages as to rates or terms. An affidavit must be filed with the Commissioner within 30 days after the insurance has been procured. (§§211, 212)

APPENDIX B

TRUST AGREEMENT

RECEIVED from   , LONDON ENGLAND (hereinafter called "Reinsuring Underwriters"), subscribing Contract

(hereinafter called "the Company"), the sum of

for securing payment and paying to the Company Reinsuring Underwriters' several shares (up to the respective amounts indicated in Exhibit A attached hereto for the individual claims therein listed) of any loss sustained by the Company in connection with its claims listed in said Exhibit A; said funds to be held in trust upon the following terms and conditions:

1. The Company shall not mingle said funds with its general assets but shall maintain such trust fund in a separate account in the name of the Company in

2. The trust fund so deposited shall be withdrawn by the Company or its successors in interest for the following purposes only:

   a. To pay Reinsuring Underwriters' several respective shares of claims listed in Exhibit A, without diminution because of any insolvency on the part of the Company.

   b. To reimburse the Company for Reinsuring Underwriters' several respective shares of the fixed liability of the Company with respect to claims listed in Exhibit A, without diminution because of any insolvency of the Company.

   c. To make repayment to   , as representatives of said Reinsuring Underwriters, of any sum which is in excess of the actual amount required to pay Reinsuring Underwriters' several respective shares of losses arising out of the claims above mentioned.

The depositary shall have no responsibility in connection with the funds deposited or the disposition of same, except to see that the funds are withdrawn only upon the order of the properly authorized representatives of the Company.

Dated this   day of

By_____

REINSURING UNDERWRITERS,

By   , Their Attorneys

APPENDIX C

LETTER OF CREDIT

---

main street national bank

101 MAIN STREET, NEW YORK, N.Y. 10022

SPECIMEN

RE: Our Clean Irrevocable Credit No. CKL–

Gentlemen:

We have established the above mentioned Credit in your favor, for

If we receive here at our office on or before your sight draft on us, mentioning our reference No. CKL–   , for all or any part of this Credit, we will promptly honor the draft. Except as stated herein this undertaking is not subject to any condition or qualification whatsoever.

Should you have any occasion to communicate with us regarding this Credit, kindly direct your communication to the attention of our Letter of Credit Department, making specific reference to our No. CKL–

Very truly yours,

SPECIMEN

Authorized Signature

```
                                                                    1-8
                                                                    210
                    PLACE & DATE_____    $_____
ON DEMAND
PAY TO
THE ORDER OF_____

_____ DOLLARS

DRAWN UNDER MAIN STREET NATIONAL BANK

CREDIT NO. CKL—_____ DATED _____

TO: MAIN STREET NATIONAL BANK
    101 MAIN STREET
    NEW YORK, N.Y. 10022                   SPECIMEN
    LETTER OF CREDIT DEPARTMENT      BY _____

        ⑈0210⑈0008⑈   0315230 9⑈
```

APPENDIX D

AGREEMENT

WHEREAS,   , LONDON, ENGLAND
(hereinafter called "Reinsuring Underwriters"), subscribing Con-
tract_____in favor of_____
(hereinafter called "the Company") have applied for and secured delivery to the Company of Main Street National Bank's Clean Irrevocable
Credit No._____, dated_____in the sum of_____
expiring on_____for securing payment and paying to the Company Reinsuring Underwriters' several shares (up to the respective
amounts indicated in Exhibit A attached hereto for the individual
claims therein listed) of any loss sustained by the Company in connection with its claims listed in said Exhibit A;

NOW, THEREFORE, in consideration of Reinsuring Underwriters
having so applied for and secured delivery, which is hereby acknowledged by the Company, of said Credit, the Company undertakes to use
and apply any amounts which it may draw upon such Credit for the
following purposes only:

a. To pay Reinsuring Underwriters' several respective shares of
   claims listed in Exhibit A, without diminution because of any
   insolvency on the part of the Company.

b. To reimburse the Company for Reinsuring Underwriters' several
   respective shares of the fixed liability of the Company with respect to claims listed in Exhibit A, without diminution because
   of any insolvency of the Company.

c. To make payment to   , as representatives of said Reinsuring Underwriters, of any balance of said Credit in excess of the
   actual amount required to pay Reinsuring Underwriters' several

respective shares of losses arising out of the claims above mentioned.

d. Where said Underwriters' shares of losses remain unliquidated and undischarged ten days prior to said expiry date and withdrawal of balance of credit is made by the Company within such period, to deposit the amount so withdrawn in a separate account in the name of the Company in any bank or trust company and apart from its general assets, in trust nevertheless, for such uses and purposes specified in a., b., and c. above as may remain executory after such withdrawal and for any period after such expiry date.

In the event of a determination by the Company to withdraw pursuant to d. above, it agrees to notify   of its intention to withdraw prior to or simultaneously with acting thereon, such notice being understood as intended for the purpose of allowing Reinsuring Underwriters an opportunity to offer to secure renewal or extension of the Credit beyond such expiry date; but this undertaking shall not be construed as a limitation upon the Company in acting in its own interests in order to secure Reinsuring Underwriters' said shares of losses.

It is further agreed as between the parties hereto that said Main Street National Bank of New York, with or without notice of the existence of this agreement, shall have no responsibility whatsoever in connection with its execution or, without limiting the generality of the foregoing, with the propriety of withdrawals made by the Company or the disposition of funds withdrawn, except to see that withdrawals are made only upon the order of properly authorized representatives of the Company; and it is understood that the Company shall incur no obligation to said Bank in acting upon said Credit, other than as appears in the express terms thereof.

Dated this   day of

         By_____

         REINSURING UNDERWRITERS,

                        , Their Attorneys

         By_____

APPENDIX E

---

main street national bank

101 MAIN STREET, NEW YORK, N.Y. 10022

SPECIMEN

RE: Our Clean Irrevocable Credit No. CKL–

Gentlemen:

We refer to our captioned Credit which we established in your favor under date of

Please note that effective our captioned Credit is hereby

All other terms and conditions remain unchanged.

Kindly acknowledge your receipt and agreement to the foregoing by signing and returning to us a copy of this letter.

Should you have any occasion to communicate with us regarding this Credit, kindly direct your communication to the attention of our Letter of Credit Department, making specific reference to our No. CKL–

Very truly yours,

SPECIMEN

Authorized Signature

chapter 15

The Special Problem of Mail-Order Insurance: The Wisconsin Experience in Historical Perspective

STATE REGULATION of mail-order insurance faces special problems in a federal system. The following selection discusses the evolution of the controversial, celebrated, and pioneering Wisconsin solution to this problem.

The following selection can be read as history at several levels —it is the history of the substantive problem of legal control over nonadmitted and mail-order insurance; it is a history of the style of operation of the National Association of Insurance Commissioners; it is a history of the state-federal tug-of-war and the resulting interaction between federal power and state policy. Though it is but the story of a single problem and thus is not necessarily representative of all developments in insurance regulation, the resulting historical picture is highly suggestive.

CONTROL OF UNAUTHORIZED INSURANCE: THE MINISTERS LIFE CASE IN HISTORICAL AND LEGISLATIVE PERSPECTIVE

Robert D. Haase
Commissioner of Insurance
State of Wisconsin

The Wisconsin case of *Ministers Life and Casualty Union* v. *Haase,*[1] upholding the constitutionality of the state's 1961 unau-

---

[1] 30 Wis. 2d 339, 141 N.W. 2d 287, appeal dismissed, 385 U.S. 205 (1966).

thorized insurance statute,[2] has excited the attention of scholars in the field of constitutional law because of its novel implications respecting the supposed power of the several states to regulate mail-order insurance. Many doubt, even today, that the extent of this power is commensurate with the responsibility mandated to the states under the provisions of the McCarran Act.[3] They believe, and it may be true, that the Supreme Court's refusal to review the Ministers case amounted to mere temporizing; that the court felt the time was not yet propitious, or the controversy sufficiently delineated, to settle the issues definitively. These are interesting questions, and doubtless there will be other opportunities for the court to speak as the regulators and the regulated continue to spar and probe. However, they are better left to legal scholars and others professing an intimacy with the arcane workings of our highest court.

THE ANOMALY OF STATE REGULATION

It is a classic anomaly of our federal system that an industrial giant whose veritable lifeblood flows in interstate commerce should be given over to regulation by 50 individual states, each with sovereign power over insurance transactions within its borders. On the face of it, there is little reason in logic why this regulatory system should have been permitted to develop or why it should be perpetuated.[4] The roots of the dilemma, of course, are buried deep in traditional 19th century concepts of laissez faire, given vitality by the decision of the Supreme Court in *Paul* v. *Virginia*[5] that the business of insurance was not interstate commerce.

In 1868, the industry was hardly of more importance than the

---

[2] Ch. 397 (1961), Wis. Laws 368.

[3] Act of March 9, 1945, 59 Stat. 33, as amended, 15 U.S.C. secs. 1011–15 (1964).

[4] "It is unfortunate that the Supreme Court of the United States declared that insurance was not commerce and not the subject of federal control and legislation. If it is not, it should be." From remarks of Fred W. Potter, insurance superintendent of Illinois and president of the National Convention of Insurance Commissioners, delivered to the convention meeting at Milwaukee August 22, 1911. *Proceedings of the National Association of Insurance Commissioners* (1911), p. 92.

[5] 75 U.S. (8 Wall.) 168 (1868).

corner apothecary shop or the village smithy. While a few large mutual life companies were operating on a national scale, the insurance business of the mid-19th century was largely confined to fire insurance carried on principally by local companies insuring local risks. Casualty insurance was in its infancy, the multiplicity of exposures to be engendered by an evolving industrial society lay in the undreamed of future. So *Paul* v. *Virginia* was in harmony with the times and state regulation flowered.

CHANGING ENVIRONMENT OF STATE REGULATION

As the wealth of the nation increased, however, so also did the market for insurance and the capacity of the industry to serve that market. The larger fire and casualty companies expanded until their operations touched many states. Generally speaking, most of the sound and reputable companies subjected themselves to regulation by the authorities of those states in which their activities were regularly carried on. Many others, however, did not. Some companies, operating fraudulently or at best on the fringes of respectability, sold their policies exclusively through the mails, soliciting business through public advertising. As to these, it was the almost universal belief of many regulatory authorities at the time that only the domiciliary state had any power to exercise regulatory control. Some even doubted that any effective control was possible. From these factors emerged the problem posed by unauthorized insurance —how best to impose and exercise control over the operations of insurance companies not domiciled in the state yet, without subjecting themselves to the control of such state, writing insurance on risks whose situs was in the state.

Paralleling this was another problem, created paradoxically by the very considerable success of the state regulators in discharging their responsibilities. Strict control had bred a formalistic approach on the part of both insurance companies and regulators, to the point where one or the other, or both, were often unable to respond in an adequate and timely fashion to the changing market demands of a rapidly industrializing society. Risks for which locally admitted capacity was inadequate or unavailable were obliged to procure all or a portion of the required coverage from companies willing to commit themselves in new or extraordinary situations. Often, the only sources for the unusual coverages were the freewheeling Lloyds organizations, whose bold and imaginative entrepreneurs operated in a climate virtually free of regulation. Although coverage through the Lloyds underwriters was generally regarded as an unauthorized form of insurance, Lloyds' coverages were almost universally tolerated by state regulators as a necessary evil—an evil nevertheless with which one day they would have to deal.

It can be said in defense of some companies that in the early period operated on a nonadmitted basis in states other than their domicile, that such action may not have been motivated wholly out of a desire to escape competent and evenhanded regulation. But regulatory authority having been handed to the states, as it were, on a silver platter by the grace of the supreme court before the economic impact of insurance upon society and industry practices requiring regulation had had sufficient time to make themselves felt, it is small wonder that development of state laws and regulatory practices proceeded along diverse, and often contradictory, courses.[6] And since the industry was not under the protection of the commerce clause, the regulatory statutes of many states often discriminated against out-of-state companies or were arbitrarily applied by administrators to effect a similar result. Although the National Convention of Insurance Commissioners was inaugurated in 1871, it is interesting and perhaps illuminating to note that of the states then members of the union, almost half vested regulatory responsibility in some state official (usually the auditor, secretary of state or treasurer) whose primary public responsibilities lay elsewhere. As might be expected, competent regulation tended to be spotty, and it is hard to criticize the negative attitude toward regulation which tended to develop on the part of some company officials.

Nevertheless, as the industry grew and inadequacies, both statutory and regulatory, became increasingly apparent, the cooperative spirit which had manifested itself in the establishment of the Na-

---

[6] "State sovereignty does not, it seems to me, demand that contracts made by insurance corporations with citizens of all the states should be subject, first, to the laws of the State where the corporation is domesticated, and then to 47 other regulations, many of which are of necessity in conflict with each other." *Proceedings of the National Association of Insurance Commissioners, supra* n. 4, p. 92.

tional Convention began to evolve into a willingness to consider common approaches to common problems.[7] The *sine qua non* of effective regulation in the field of insurance as well as in the case of any other line of endeavor subject to public regulation has always been an underlying framework of statute law, soundly conceived and well articulated. So it was that in the case of unauthorized insurance the National Convention, almost from the first, began communally to explore ways and means of dealing with the problem on an effective, statutory basis.

This paper will undertake to examine and to comment upon the efforts of the commissioners as they assembled in convention and association to discover and effectuate means to control unauthorized insurance. It will explore also the evolution of Wisconsin law to that end and the pioneer efforts of the Wisconsin Insurance Department in influencing and directing the development of new laws which ultimately may prove to have pointed the way toward redemption of the trust reposed by the Congress in the efficacy of the regulation of the business of insurance by the several states.

THE COMMISSIONERS OF INSURANCE: SEARCH FOR THE MORE PERFECT LAW

In recounting the travails of the commissioners as they persevered in their search for the more perfect law, it would be well to keep in mind the magnitude of the odds against the attainment of their goal. In the first place, unanimity of agreement among the commissioners themselves, each of whom was a virtual sovereign in his own right and a jealous advocate of his own point of view, as to the proper approach to pursue was almost impossible to obtain. Secondly, the final arbiters were necessarily the legislatures of the several states whose individual imprimaturs would have to be placed on any convention-endorsed reform measures. Thirdly, and in many respects most important, industry would have to be persuaded to endorse, or at least to acquiesce in, any important legislative proposal.

Domestic companies in many states were becoming giants. As

---

[7] "Until the Supreme Court of the United States changes its mind and reverses its decision in *Paul* v. *Virginia,* this association can engage in no better work and make no effort of greater importance to the public we serve, than to direct our attention to uniform legislation." *Ibid.*

their accumulations of capital increased, so also did the political sophistication of their managers. It often happened, in consequence, that the insurance interests in some states were able to flex more political muscle than the commissioner himself in deciding which bills should pass and which rejected.

First NCIC Action: 1888

The first action on the part of the National Convention to assert control over unauthorized insurance was taken in 1888 when the Committee on Legislation (later, the Committee on Laws and Legislation) undertook to study the feasibility of drafting proposals for uniform legislation to that end.[8] Later, a special Committee on Unauthorized Insurance (called the Committee on Underground Insurance until 1893) was established. It took up first the resolution passed earlier by the Committee on Legislation, but soon referred the matter to the Committee on Codification of Insurance Laws.[9] However, at a meeting held the following year the committee on its own behalf called for legislation declaring all contracts of unlicensed companies to be void.[10]

Shortly thereafter, the Committee on Unauthorized Insurance expanded its activities to include the investigation of the activities of Lloyds companies in the United States, and for the first time it began to consider means of eliminating the menace of the wildcat companies.[11] "Wildcat" was a term applied to fire companies operating completely free of any regulation or control. Organized under the general corporation law, they did no insurance business in their state of domicile, and so avoided all contact with that state's insurance commissioner. Their operations consisted in the solicitation of fire insurance business in other states exclusively by mail. They employed no agents in those states in which solicitations were carried on. Needless to say, they operated without authority and paid no taxes in such states. It seems to have been generally

---

[8] *Proceedings of the National Association of Insurance Commissioners* (1888), p. 32.

[9] *Ibid.* (1892), p. 66.

[10] *Ibid.* (1893), p. 21.

[11] *Ibid.* (1895), p. 21.

regarded by the commissioners that these firms "as a rule, [were] totally irresponsible, and their policies . . . of no value. . . ."[12]

But the operations of the wildcat companies were insignificant compared with those of legitimate companies which simply engaged in multistate operations without benefit of qualification. This was a major concern of the commissioners, not alone out of regard for the regulatory aspect but also because of the consequent loss to their states of tax revenues. In 1898, the Committee on Unauthorized Insurance advanced a proposal for uniform legislation to prohibit the payment of commissions to agents in any state in which the company was not properly admitted and to prohibit reinsurance of risks except in companies authorized to do business in the state where the primary risk was located.[13]

The 1902 Attack

A new attack was launched in 1902 upon the mail-order fire insurance companies. In that year, the Committee on Unauthorized Insurance was directed by the Executive Committee to prepare a memorial on behalf of the convention to the Postmaster General of the United States requesting him to deny the use of the mails to companies not authorized by their home state to engage in the business of insurance, and further providing for presentation of a

---

[12] *Ibid.* (1902), p. 40.

[13] *Ibid.* (1898), p. 80. Upon delivery of the resolution to the convention, Commissioner Will Stone of Kentucky moved that the report be referred to the Committee on Laws and Legislation. The motion unanimously carried. Then Committee Chairman Elmer Dearth of Minnesota apparently had second thoughts.

"I would like to know," he inquired, "what the Committee on Laws and Legislation will do with it? I should like the sentiment of the convention to know whether they will adopt it. The purpose is to prevent the transaction of unauthorized insurance. As the laws are in the various states, the party soliciting the business is the one upon whom the penalty shall be imposed. You cannot get at the company. This report simply covers a proposition for the enactment of a law that in case it is discovered that business is being written in a state by a company that is unauthorized, that by filing the necessary information with the Commissioner of the State under the laws of which such company may be operating, he has power to bring the proper action to impose a penalty. In that way you can do away in a measure with the unauthorized transactions of such companies." After a series of parliamentary maneuvers, Commissioner Dearth succeeded in procuring immediate adoption of his committee's resolution by the Convention. *Ibid.,* p. 81.

memorial to the national congress for the passage of necessary legislation should it be determined by the postmaster general that he was powerless to act.[14]

The committee responded as requested, and the memorials were adopted by the convention[15] with the further proviso that a list of alleged wildcat companies (containing the names of approximately 86 companies—40 of which operated out of Chicago)[16] be attached to each memorial.[17]

In consequence of its failure to obtain passage of remedial legislation in the 1903 session of Congress, a copy of the 1902 memorial was sent to each member of Congress, along with a special message pleading for the adoption of a law to give it effect. In addition, a special committee[18] was formed to lobby the legislation through Congress.[19]

Meanwhile, the campaign to publicize the activities of the wildcat fire companies was vigorously pressed by the National Convention and by the individual commissioners. Unsuccessful in its efforts to procure passage of remedial legislation by the Congress,[20] the committee was able to report to the convention two years later that efforts to suppress the wildcat companies through publicity cam-

---

[14] *Proceedings of the National Association of Insurance Commissioners* (1902), p. 39.

[15] *Ibid.,* p. 59.

[16] To the credit of the Illinois Insurance Department, it appears that promptly upon the release of the list of wildcat companies, the department initiated legal proceedings against some 20 of the Illinois-based companies. The trial disclosed that none of the companies proceeded against had a separate bank account, all monies going into a common fund in the name of an agent. Other than the fund itself, no tangible assets were ever found. The report of the Committee on Unauthorized Insurance to the 1903 convention stated that courts in Illinois and Ohio had held the issuance of policies in the state covering only risks located outside the state constituted doing business in the state of issuance. *Ibid.* (1903), p. 134.

[17] The committee proceeded apace with the discharge of the duties entrusted to it. As a result of its efforts, a bill was drafted and introduced in the House of Representatives, where it died in a subcommittee. *Ibid.* (1903), p. 140.

[18] The Committee on Legislation before Congress. *Ibid.* (1905), p. 143.

[19] *Ibid.* (1903), p. 142.

[20] The Special Committee on Legislation before Congress reported that its efforts to lobby the convention-supported bill had been soft-pedaled because of the introduction of other bills calling for federal regulation of insurance business conducted interstate. The committee apparently felt, at least in this instance, that circumspection should be the order of the day. *Ibid.* (1905), pp. 143–44.

paigns and through prosecution in the courts had "to a satisfactory degree, accomplished the objects sought by the National Convention. . . ."[21]

Problem Resolved

Although the convention had failed to obtain legislative relief, it appears that the lobby committee had been successful in procuring the effective cooperation of the postmaster general in denying the wildcat companies access to the mails in cases where active fraud could be established. Moreover, the widespread publicity campaign and the unremitting attention to the problem by the individual commissioners, coupled with revocation of state charters in appropriate cases, enabled the Committee on Unauthorized Insurance to declare in its 1907 report that the problem had been largely resolved.[22]

Nevertheless, the Committee on Unauthorized Insurance continued to press the search for effective solutions to the many facets of the problem. In its 1908 report to the convention it recommended the adoption of laws to reach every company domiciled in a state which did or pretended to do an insurance business, whether or not such business was actually conducted within the domiciliary state. It also recommended again the adoption of laws to prohibit domestic companies from violating laws of sister states by conducting unauthorized operations in such states and the passage of federal law to forbid the use of the mails on the part of unauthorized companies. The committee, also, for the first time, brought out a proposal for the enactment by the states of a uniform law regulating surplus lines to include a provision for the payment of taxes by the insured rather than by the company.[23]

Commissioner James Young of South Carolina, who gave the committee report, stated that he had written to the postmaster general in an effort to persuade him to rule that any company found to be operating in any state in which it was not licensed should be regarded as prima facie insolvent and as conducting its operations

---

[21] *Ibid.,* p. 103.
[22] *Ibid.* (1907), p. 95.
[23] *Ibid.* (1908), p. 93.

fraudulently. He stated that he believed the post office department would go that far, but that he did not think the department would agree to bar the use of the mails to an unlicensed company.[24]

The Movement Stalls

Although the Committee on Unauthorized Insurance had strongly urged action on several fronts in 1908 and reiterated its recommendations at the 1910 meeting,[25] the movement seems to have stalled. Having disposed of the problems generated by wildcat operations to everyone's reasonable satisfaction, the momentum of the movement to institute really effective control over unauthorized insurance seems to have dissipated.

The committee did, however, recommend that it be continued permanently in order that it might continue to receive complaints and reports and coordinate its work with the insurance departments of the states involved.[26] It also offered new proposals in the same year recommending that each state seek legislation to impose on local companies a tax on premiums which had not been subjected to tax in other states and that a premium tax of at least 5 percent be imposed on all premiums paid to unauthorized insurers, the tax to be levied upon and paid by the insured.[27]

There was another effort by the committee in 1915 to revive its earlier proposals for a uniform law to prohibit domestic companies from transacting business in other states without authority, but nothing seems to have come of it.[28]

The Struggle Revived

Following this unsuccessful attempt to deal with unauthorized insurance by striking at the source, nothing of any consequence was attempted by the commissioners until the midwinter meeting of 1922 when the struggle was revived by Commissioner McMahan of South Carolina. Commissioner McMahan placed two resolutions before the convention; the first, to put the convention on record,

---

[24] *Ibid.*

[25] *Ibid.* (1910), p. 265.

[26] *Ibid.* (1913), p. 94.

[27] *Ibid.*, p. 95.

[28] *Ibid.* (1915), pp. 33–34.

again, as favoring legislation by the national Congress to prevent the use of the mails and other means of interstate and foreign commerce by insurers seeking to place business in states in which they were not admitted. Undaunted by the two previous failures, Commissioner McMahan also offered a resolution proposing adoption of uniform legislation authorizing revocation of the license of any domestic fire insurance company which insured property in any other state in which it was not licensed.[29]

In the debate that followed on the first resolution, the fear was expressed by some that such a sweeping law might be unconstitutional.[30] Commissioner Joseph Button of Virginia, secretary-treasurer of the convention and dean of the convention in point of service, rose to commend Commissioner McMahan for his efforts. He recalled that in his early days the convention had appointed a committee to "wait upon" the postmaster general, that all sorts of laws had been suggested, but that always the question of constitutionality had been interposed. "It is a problem that we have been wrestling with ever since I have been a member of this Convention, and it looks as if we are never going to enact any law that is going to stick."[31]

On the second resolution, calling for state laws to bar domestic fire companies from doing unauthorized business in other states, the question whether the resolution should be broadened to apply to all lines of insurance was heatedly debated. Some of the commissioners felt that such a law might cripple the activities of life insurance companies in servicing move-in business.[32] Others felt that it ought to be applied on a reciprocal basis to forestall the possibility, apparently clearly foreseen, that a few states might become sanctuaries for wildcat companies.

Both resolutions were finally referred to the Committee on Laws

---

[29] Ibid. (1923), p. 35.

[30] Deputy Commissioner Burlingame of Rhode Island thought that such a law "would almost nullify the Federal Constitution; it is very drastic legislation. . . ." He moved for referral of the resolution to the Committee on Laws and Legislation. Ibid.

[31] Ibid., p. 38.

[32] The term "move-in business" refers to policies of insurance issued to policyholders in states where the company is authorized to engage in business, and where the policyholder subsequently moves to a state in which the company is not so authorized and where the policyholder continues the policy in force by periodic premium remittances.

and Legislation,[33] which later issued a report condemning wildcat operations as "contrary to public policy and highly objectionable. . . ."[34] It recommended that legislation to control the use of the mails be enacted, whereupon the committee was authorized to draft and submit appropriate legislation for consideration by the several states and by the Congress.[35]

For some unexplained reason, Commissioner McMahan's resolution proposing the extension of state control over unauthorized activities of domestic companies was taken from the Committee on Laws and Legislation and referred to the Executive Committee, where it languished for three years.

In the interim, Commissioner Button resurrected the subject of surplus lines insurance. At the 1924 meeting of the convention, he offered a resolution favoring tighter laws and uniform enforcement practices, but recognizing "that the time has arrived when the needs of reinsurance, particularly as they effect (sic) casualty and surety lines, as distinct from primary or direct insurance, should be recognized."[36]

The Executive Committee, having received the 1922 resolution proposing a national law to bar the use of the mails to wildcat companies and other unauthorized insurers, decided in December, 1925, to refer the matter to the Committee on Unauthorized Insurance.[37] This latter committee, however, after considering the proposal, reported that it was unable to make a recommendation because it was felt that such a law would be unconstitutional.[38] It also declined to make a recommendation respecting the proposal for uniform state laws to curb unauthorized operations of domestic companies for the reason that the resolution did not include the subject of reinsurance within its ambit.[39]

Proponents of measures to control unauthorized insurance were not completely *hors de combat,* however. Indeed, the subject was regarded by some as the most serious and difficult problem facing

---

[33] *Ibid.,* p. 41.

[34] *Ibid.,* p. 50.

[35] *Ibid.,* p. 50.

[36] *Ibid.* (1924), p. 197.

[37] *Ibid.* (1926), p. 21.

[38] *Ibid.,* p. 22.

[39] *Ibid.,* p. 21.

the insurance regulators.[40] Taking a slightly different tack, the Committee on Unauthorized Insurance called in 1928 for the enactment in each state of a uniform law which would limit the corporate powers of all domestic insurance companies to the issuance of policies insuring persons, property, or other hazards only in the domiciliary state and in other states in which they were duly admitted.[41]

The redoubling of efforts on the part of proponents of tighter controls by the domiciliary states is perhaps indicative of a reawakened awareness among the commissioners of abuses practiced by insurers operating free of regulatory restraints. Perhaps this awareness was accompanied by a sense of urgency—even of foreboding—over the consequences which might attend their inability or failure to control the rapidly maturing industrial giant in their charge.

A New Emphasis

The emphasis was now no longer primarily on the elimination of wildcat operations. A new-found concern with the needs of the market as reflected in the lively surplus lines business and with the burgeoning mail-order companies, suddenly grown financially powerful and clutching at respectability, was now uppermost in the minds of many commissioners.[42] There was still division of opinion, however, as to whether the challenge could be met without the aid of new and tailor-made legislation.[43]

Yet it was becoming increasingly clear that a law which did no more than prevent a domestic company from operating in other states on a nonadmitted basis was no longer adequate to deal with the problem, which had become intensified as a result of rising literacy standards and the increasing participation of citizens in a truly national existence. Mail-order insurers, particularly those deal-

---

[40] Remarks by Commissioner M. A. Freedy of Wisconsin in an address to the Convention. *Ibid.* (1928), p. 163.

[41] *Ibid.*, p. 134. The report was adopted and the resolution referred to the Committee on Laws and Legislation. *Ibid.*, p. 135.

[42] "Unauthorized Insurance a Growing Problem," address by Commissioner M. A. Freedy of Wisconsin, *Ibid.*, p. 163.

[43] See remarks of Commissioner R. C. Clark of Vermont. *Ibid.*, p. 105. See also discussion among Commissioners Gentry (Ark.), Vanschaick (N.Y.), Gough (N.J.), Brown (Mass.), Clark (Iowa), O'Malley (Mo.) and Foster (Providence of Ontario). *Ibid.* (1934), pp. 48, *et seq.*

ing in accident and health policies, were turning to radio advertising and the newly founded mass circulation media. The immediate need pointed to a reexamination of traditional concepts of doing an insurance business.

The Attack Expands

Recognizing that the new complexities of the problem were rapidly outstripping the available powers of the commissioners to deal effectively with unauthorized insurance, the Committee on Laws and Legislation decided in 1934 to mount an expanded attack. It called upon the commissioners to seek uniform state laws which would define in a comprehensive way precisely what types of conduct should be construed to constitute doing an insurance business and precisely where such conduct should be declared to have its impact.[44]

One may suppose, also, that there was a growing recognition by some that the business of insurance had attained such a stature and had reached such a point in time that the wisdom of permitting the continued regulation of the business by the states was about to be questioned. In much the same way as their predecessors in the case of the 1905 postal regulation bill, the commissioners in 1935 were divided on the question as to whether the convention ought to advocate the passage of any bill[45] which would give the federal government a foot in the regulatory door.[46] But differences of opinion were finally reconciled, and thus it was that in the final year

---

[44] *Ibid.*, p. 142.

[45] By this time the earlier labors of the Committee on Laws and Legislation had borne fruit in the form of a bill, H.R. 8206, introduced in the House of Representatives by Congressman Hobbs of Alabama to deny the use of the mails to nonadmitted insurers.

[46] "I have about myself, personally, reached the conclusion that we ought to say to them, 'Let us alone, absolutely,' notwithstanding that I proposed at the last Convention that it might be well to ask Congress to supplement our state laws to help us handle unauthorized insurance, because I see in this Convention a tendency, if you please, to not only legislate about matters of unauthorized insurance, but it is quite a coincidence that in this Convention two measures are proposed and suggested to this Convention whereby Congress enters the insurance field; and it may be and, so far as I am concerned, I have been getting a little bit of the opinion that it would be, an entering wedge. If this Convention suggests to Congress the enactment of federal legislation, they may finally supplant the Commissioners of the respective states entirely. That, I do not want to see." Remarks in debate by Commissioner Gentry of Arkansas. *Proceedings of the National Association of Insurance Commissioners* (1935), p. 100.

of the convention[47] the commissioners took their stance in opposition to federal legislation pertaining to insurance in any manner and in favor of solutions to industry problems through the mechanism of uniform state laws and the cooperation of the commissioners of the respective states.[48]

Others, also, were interested in devising means of subjecting unauthorized insurance practices to effective state control. Much of the concern at this time centered over the rise of certain accident and health and benevolent societies whose advertisements and mail solicitations were directed principally to the elderly and seemed to offer benefits which were grossly disproportionate to the small premiums charged. Of course, the seeming benefits were often illusory. Moreover, many of these companies simply refused to pay legitimate claims. In 1937, a Uniform Unauthorized Insurers Service of Process Act, prepared by the Section on Insurance Law of the American Bar Association, was presented to the National Association and assigned for study to the Committee on Unauthorized Insurance.[49]

The reaction of the committee after studying the ABA proposal was, on the whole, negative. It was felt that the proposal, directed at the illegal transaction of the business of insurance, did not reach the evils which had become manifest in the mail-order operations of many of the benevolent societies.[50] In point of fact, the problem was felt to be not so much the illegality of their operations—most of the

---

[47] The National Convention of Insurance Commissioners became the National Association of Insurance Commissioners in 1936.

[48] *Proceedings of the National Association of Insurance Commissioners* (1935), p. 107.

[49] *Ibid.* (1937), p. 173.

[50] "We regret to report that we do not believe the proposed Bar Association Bill adequately meets the issue. It apparently applies only where the insurer is illegally transacting business. The evil is much greater than that. It is that these companies may be legally transacting business but nevertheless are acting without any adequate supervision and no real control by anyone. Most of the business done by such organizations is through the medium of the mails and consequently there is often no illegal transaction of business in the state whose citizens and residents are solicited.

"In the opinion of your Committee, the proposed legislation of the Bar Association while inadequate, is in line with the purpose of this Convention (*sic*), and it is our thought that the Committee on Unauthorized Insurance and the American Bar Association cooperate together and prepare the best possible legislation looking to the control and elimination of this evil through state enactment." Report of the Committee on Unauthorized Insurance. *Proceedings of the National Association of Insurance Commissioners* (1938), p. 26.

offenders were operating within the letter of the law, as the fact that their methods of operation under obsolete and poorly designed state laws made effective regulation of their activities impossible.[51] At all events, nothing came of the proposal,[52] and the matter was given into the charge of the Committee on Laws and Legislation.

Uniform Law Proposal Revived

The Committee on Laws and Legislation deliberated until the summer of 1941, when it again resurrected the proposal for a uniform law providing for revocation of the license of any domestic company doing or attempting to do business in any state in which it was not authorized to do so.[53] In doing so the committee went further than its predecessors and attempted to provide language in form specific enough to strike at mail-order operations: "The term 'transacting business,' as used herein, shall be defined to include in addition to its usual interpretation, advertising locally in any foreign jurisdiction in which an insurer is not licensed or circularizing in any such jurisdiction without regard for the source of such circularization whenever such advertising locally or such circularization is for the purpose of solicitation of insurance business."[54]

The Committee on Unauthorized Insurance supported the model bill proposed by the Committee on Laws and Legislation. It urged its adoption by the states, although at least one of its members seemed to feel "that there isn't much unauthorized insurance at this time that the National Association might be interested in."[55] The

---

[51] *Ibid.*, p. 27.

[52] "Mr. Chairman, the Committee on Unauthorized Insurance held a meeting that was well attended, with lots of interest exhibited, and we wish to report progress." The report of the Committee on Unauthorized Insurance to the Executive Committee of the Association, June, 1938. *Ibid.*, p. 104.

[53] This proposal, unlike the uniform law drafted by the American Bar Association, attempted specifically to deal with the problems created by mail-order solicitation, although in 1941 such an attempt was considered by many to be treading on exceedingly dangerous ground.

[54] From the report of the Committee on Laws and Legislation. *Proceedings of the National Association of Insurance Commissioners* (1941), p. 148.

[55] Chairman Homer C. Parker, Georgia, reporting for the committee. *Ibid.* (1945), p. 210. Superintendent Robert Dineen of New York rose to state that his department had received 544 inquiries during the previous year on unauthorized insurance activities in his state. "I am not prepared to concur . . . that the transacting of unauthorized insurance creates no problem, although the solution . . . to it is a horse of another color." *Ibid.*, p. 210.

committee retained jurisdiction of the matter, however, and at the 1947 midwinter meeting it appointed a subcommittee to give further study to the mail-order problem.[56] In June of the following year, the subcommittee recommended adoption by the states of the parent committee's 1941 uniform law proposal. In addition, it suggested that each commissioner lend all aid and assistance to federal authorities in the prosecution of fraudulent mail-order insurance companies.[57] But Commissioner James McCormick of Tennessee, doubtless with thoughts of SEUA and the McCarran Act uppermost in his mind, voting in favor of the adoption of the report placed himself on record "as not favoring any federal legislation pertaining to the regulation or taxation of the insurance business.[58]

The McCarran Act

With the passage of the McCarran Act and a clear mandate from Congress to structure a system of regulation and control for all facets of the insurance business, the NAIC finally settled down in earnest to find ways to cope with the problem of unauthorized insurance. In 1943, the Executive Committee had appointed a special three-member Committee on Federal Legislation to keep abreast of pending or proposed federal activities and legislation.[59] Following SEUA the subject of federal legislation became of paramount importance to the commissioners, and the scope of the committee's responsibilities was broadened commensurately. After the passage of the McCarran Act, the responsibility for preparing the legislative proposals for consideration by the states was assigned to a drafting subcommittee. In December, 1948, the subcommittee, under the chairmanship of Superintendent Dineen of New York, met with the Committee on Unauthorized Insurance. Out of this meeting came the proposal for, and the text of, the Uniform Unauthorized Insurers Process Act, which was incorporated into the report of the Committee on Federal Legislation and adopted at the 1948 midwinter meeting of the association.[60] The proposed law, although patterned upon (perhaps inspired by) the uniform act

---

[56] *Ibid.* (1948), p. 179.

[57] *Ibid.*, p. 472.

[58] *Ibid.*, p. 473.

[59] *Ibid.* (1944), p. 43.

[60] *Ibid.* (1949), p. 132.

promulgated 10 years earlier by the American Bar Association, was a remarkable piece of work by any standard; more so when considered from the point of view that the commissioners had up to that point grappled with the unauthorized insurance problem for more than half a century with results which could hardly be described as satisfactory. Moreover, as Superintendent Dineen noted in the subcommittee report, the proposal was based upon the realities of the business and was keyed to the modern and more realistic concept of "doing business" as established in the more recent decisions of the United States Supreme Court.[61] Following the lead of the Committee on Federal Legislation, the Committee on Unauthorized Insurance likewise recommended the proposal for adoption by the several states.[62]

It was not to be expected that the mail-order insurance industry would sit idly by in mute witness to the attempts by the regulators to institute an effective system of controls over what hitherto had been its private preserve. The big guns descended upon Galveston in December, 1949, where the Committee on Unauthorized Insurance met—Wendel Berge, counsel for the Association of Insurance Advertisers, Moses G. Hubbard, of the International Federation of Commercial Travelers Insurance Organizations; C. O. Pauley, of the Health and Accident Underwriters Conference.[63] After considerable discussion and exchange of views, the committee agreed to recommend that the Association of Insurance Advertisers be invited to become a participating member in the All-Industry Committee, lately formed to assist the NAIC in an advisory capacity.[64]

Travelers Health Association v. Virginia

Following approval by the NAIC, the All-Industry Committee appointed a subcommittee on unauthorized insurance with instructions to explore the whole subject and to reexamine the Unauthorized Insurers Process Act in the light of recent Supreme Court decisions. At the June, 1950, meeting the Unauthorized Insurance Committee was directed to cooperate actively with the all-industry

---

[61] *Ibid.*, p. 127.
[62] *Ibid.*, p. 316.
[63] *Ibid.* (1950), p. 109.
[64] *Ibid.*, p. 110.

subcommittee to explore and develop ways in which the states ought properly to proceed with regulation of mail-order insurers.[65] However, immediate considerations were stalled pending the handing down of the Supreme Court's decisions in the case of *Travelers Health Association* v. *Virginia*.[66]

The Travelers Health Association, a Nebraska company with sole offices at Omaha but which solicited and sold its policies through the mails in almost all other states, including Virginia, had been enjoined by the Commonwealth of Virginia from selling or offering its certificates for sale there. Service upon the association had been obtained under provisions of Virginia's Blue Sky Law (applicable to insurance) authorizing substituted service upon the Virginia Secretary of State and providing for transmission of a copy of the process to the offender by registered mail. The association had appealed to the United States Supreme Court raising constitutional questions of due process as to the applicability to it of Virginia law. In the decision handed down on June 5, 1950, the majority of the court held that the association had properly been subjected to Virginia's jurisdiction, noting that there were other significant contacts between the association and Virginia citizens.[67] Justice Douglas, in a concurring opinion, went further, stating that even isolated solicitations by mail would themselves have been sufficient to confer jurisdiction for the award of injunctive relief.

By December, 1950, the Unauthorized Insurers Process Act had been adopted in 18 states,[68] and many felt that the *Travelers Health* case had resolved most of the questions raised as to its constitutionality.[69] The committee at its midwinter meeting that year took up next consideration of a bill to deal with false advertising.[70] The Unauthorized Insurers False Advertising Process Act had

---

[65] *Ibid.*, p. 548.

[66] *Ibid.*, p. 548. 339 U.S. 643 (1950). *Proceedings of the National Association of Insurance Commissioners* (1950), p. 548.

[67] The association systematically solicited new members, through the unpaid activities of Virginia residents who were already members, and investigated benefit claims within the commonwealth.

[68] By June 1951, 22 states had adopted the model act; four others had previously adopted laws providing for service of process on unauthorized insurers. *Proceedings of the National Association of Insurance Commissioners* (1951), p. 515.

[69] *Ibid.*, p. 165.

[70] *Ibid.*, p. 169.

already been studied by the All-Industry Subcommittee, which had declined to recommend its passage. However, the Committee on Unauthorized Insurance resolved to retain consideration of this bill on its agenda for further joint study with the All-Industry Subcommittee, with the view to exploring the advisability of recommending the proposal to the NAIC.[71]

But the problem of uncontrolled mail-order insurance had been permitted to exist too long. Public clamor had reached such a pitch as to convince the planners in Washington that the time had come to take a look at the problem and at the efficacy of state regulation in general. Senator William Langer, chairman of the Senate Committee on the Judiciary, scheduled hearings beginning December 2, 1953, before his committee to inquire into practices in connection with the sale of health and accident, hospitalization, medical protection, and life insurance through the mails. Hugh L. Tollack, then assistant secretary of the association, was personally invited to testify.[72] The committee invited testimony concerning the nature of the practices complained of and whether adequate remedies could better be afforded through federal or through state laws. It pointedly included in its hearing agenda a request for comments on the ineffectiveness of the practices and policies of some state insurance departments in attempting to control mail-order solicitation.[73]

The effect of this development upon the NAIC and upon the Committee on Unauthorized Insurance in particular was immediate and positive. Commissioner Donald F. Dickey of Oklahoma proposed that the committee initiate its own comprehensive investigation into the practices and develop its own plan to attack the problem.[74] The committee itself, meeting the day before the senate hearings were scheduled to commence, recommended that the association appoint a special committee to canvass the association membership and to represent the association in giving testimony before the judiciary committee. It further recommended that all interested segments of industry be invited to furnish their suggestions and recommendations as to how to proceed.[75]

---

[71] *Ibid.*, p. 165.
[72] *Ibid.* (1954), p. 155.
[73] *Ibid.*, p. 156.
[74] *Ibid.*, p. 60.
[75] *Ibid.*, p. 151.

NAIC Committee Action

A special committee "On Mail-Order Insurance in Connection with U.S. Senate Judiciary Matter" was duly appointed in accordance with the committee's recommendation. Under the chairmanship of Commissioner W. Ellery Allyn of Connecticut, it met in Washington on February 25, 1954.[76] Commissioner Allyn, together with Commissioners Maloney of California and Murphy of South Carolina (who was president of the Association that year), appeared the following day before the senate committee. Commissioner Allyn gave the principal testimony on behalf of the association. He pointed out that the NAIC had been working on the problem for many years and that with the help of the Federal Trade Commission and the Post Office Department the situation had been brought under reasonable control. He pointed to the passage of the Unauthorized Insurance Process Act in about 40 of the states and the self-policing efforts on the part of the great majority of mail-order companies. He indicated that while the association committee felt that federal legislation to strengthen the supervisory powers of the states to control mail-order operations might be consistent with the system of state regulation, the NAIC was "unalterably opposed to federal regulation of insurance."[77]

Advocates of state regulation carried the day, and at its meeting in Detroit the following June, the Committee on Unauthorized Insurance was able to report that the power to regulate mail-order insurance was, for the nonce, still in the hands of the states.[78] The special committee passed out of existence without ever rendering a final report. It was not reappointed at the June, 1955, meeting.[79]

Efforts to deal effectively with the problem now proceeded in earnest. Since much of the concern of the Senate committee had centered about practices in the accident and health field, with regard particularly for companies operating largely through the mails, the Committee on Accident and Health, at its meeting that June, resolved to conduct its own investigation into mail order industry meth-

---

[76] *Ibid.*, p. 345.
[77] *Ibid.*, p. 345.
[78] *Ibid.*, p. 343.
[79] *Ibid.* (1956), p. 178.

ods and practices.[80] It called first for the states to enact adequate unfair trade practice acts and reciprocal unauthorized insurers acts.[81] Then it enlisted the aid of the All-Industry Subcommittee on Regulation and Self-Regulation in the Accident and Health Field (newly formed earlier in the year) and proceeded with its appointed task.

At the December meeting the committee was able to report that by far the greater number of complaints received by individual state departments on industry practices in the accident and health field related to provisions in the policies themselves, particularly provisions relating to exclusions for preexisting conditions and renewability.[82] However, no attempt had been made to relate these findings to the problem of control over mail-order operators, since the investigation covered these as well as the agency companies. Indeed, 32 percent of the complaints considered attributed the difficulty complained of to the agent or adjuster.[83] The committee also reiterated the recommendations contained in its report of the previous June that the states enact adequate laws to control trade practices and unauthorized insurance. However, the All-Industry Subcommittee, which had been working with the committee, indicated that it was of opinion that the primary remedy lay in the administrative area, particularly in the joint efforts of the companies involved and the various insurance departments. It saw little need for new laws.[84]

NAIC Focuses on Surplus Lines

At about the same time, renewed attention was being given to another major, but long neglected, facet of unauthorized insurance —the surplus lines problem. A subcommittee of the Laws and Legislation Committee, comprising association members and indus-

---

[80] *Ibid.* (1954), p. 249.

[81] *Ibid.,* p. 252.

[82] *Ibid.* (1955), p. 81.

[83] *Ibid.,* p. 79.

[84] *Ibid.,* p. 86. The subcommittee included among its members Millard Bartels, John P. Hanna, Moses G. Hubbard, John W. Joanis, H. Clay Johnson, and V. J. Skutt. At the June, 1955, meeting of the Committee on Accident and Health Insurance, the All-Industry Subcommittee reported that the Unfair Trade Practices Act had been enacted in five states during 1955, was pending in five more (for a potential total of 41 enacting jurisdictions), and that the Unauthorized Insurers Process Act had been enacted in eight states in the same year and was pending in three more (for a potential total of 40 enacting jurisdictions). *Ibid.,* p. 269.

try representatives, was appointed to study and report to the June, 1956, meeting concerning existing surplus lines legislation and the desirability of adopting a uniform surplus lines law.[85] Its report the following June was inconclusive. It indicated, however, that it planned to invite representatives of the surplus line associations to submit suggestions, while at the same time it was awaiting a survey report from representatives of the All-Industry Committee.[86]

A year's delay ensued, during which the subcommittee studied and deliberated. In June, 1957, it reported that substantial differences of opinion had developed among the industry members of the subcommittee concerning the need for, and the nature of, any uniform surplus lines law which might be recommended.[87] Nevertheless, it was decided to recommit the question for further study and for recommendations as to important features which should be a part of any surplus lines law.[88]

In accordance with its mandate, the subcommittee returned the following December with a recommendation that any state considering the adoption or revision of a surplus lines law should incorporate in such law or revision the following guiding principles:

1. Provide for the placing of surplus lines business only through licensed resident agents or brokers;
2. Require all surplus lines business to be placed in a company licensed in at least one state of the United States;
3. Require that the nonadmitted carrier be subjected to service of process in and the jurisdiction of the host state;
4. Require the surplus lines agent or broker to verify that the risk could not be placed in the admitted market, and require a description of the insurance placed in such detail as to enable the commissioner to determine if the line was eligible for export;
5. Require the surplus lines agent or broker to advise the insured that the risk had been placed in the surplus market;
6. Require the surplus lines agent or broker to file annual returns and to pay taxes on the net premiums;
7. Require payment of a premium tax on such business at a rate to be decided by the host state;

---

[85] *Ibid.* (1956), p. 124.
[86] *Ibid.,* p. 338.
[87] *Ibid.* (1957), p. 383.
[88] *Ibid.,* p. 382.

8. Give the commissioner investigatory powers and authority to examine and audit the books of surplus lines agents and brokers;

9. Provide penalties for noncompliance with state law;

10. Provide that no surplus lines insurance be placed for the purpose of obtaining lower rates than those applicable on insurance placed through admitted carriers.[89]

Although industry representatives of surplus lines organizations objected to certain features of the principles as set out in the subcommittee report, the report was adopted in executive session and the subcommittee discharged.[90]

New Study of Mail-Order Problem

Following the demise of the Special Committee on Mail-Order Insurance, which had been appointed to deal with the immediate problems raised by the Senate mail-order insurance hearings in 1953 and 1954, the responsibility for continuing study and action on the mail-order problem devolved entirely upon the Committee on Laws and Legislation. In June of 1957, at the instance of Commissioner Joseph A. Navarre of Michigan, the committee recommended the establishment of a special subcommittee to undertake a new study and review of the problem and to recommend laws deemed necessary to perfect the system of state regulation.[91] The work of this subcommittee was carried out largely through facilities and personnel of the New York Insurance Department; and the Committee on Laws and Legislation, in receiving the subcommittee report at its June, 1958, meeting, took the occasion to commend Superintendent Wikler upon the excellence of the report.[92] Due to the length and complexity of this report, time was needed for dissemination and study. It was, therefore, not until the December meeting that the report was adopted as the sense of the association.[93]

While comprehensive in its treatment of all major regulatory problems respecting the control of the business of insurance, the

---

[89] *Ibid.* (1958), p. 174.

[90] *Ibid.* p. 172.

[91] *Ibid.* (1957), p. 383.

[92] *Ibid.* (1958), p. 356.

[93] *Ibid.* (1959), pp. 135, 179.

report dealt in particular detail with those problems incident to the transaction of business in interstate commerce. Prior to the passage by the majority of states of the NAIC-sponsored Unauthorized Insurance Process Act, it had generally been necessary for a citizen of a state in which a carrier was not admitted to sue on legitimate claims in the jurisdiction in which the carrier was domiciled or in which it could be found. The prohibitive distance and the cost of such litigation often effectively dissuaded such litigants from pursuing their claims. By providing a method of service of process, the uniform act made it possible for such suits in most cases to be brought in the state of residence of the policyholder. The report noted with satisfaction that all doubt as to the constitutionality of the uniform act had been removed by the decision of the Supreme Court in *McGee* v. *International Life Insurance Co. of Texas.*[94] It was recommended, however, since the uniform act applied only to suits brought by policyholders or beneficiaries under policies, that the scope of the act be expanded to include provision for actions by insurance regulatory authorities to exact penalties for the transaction of unauthorized insurance or to issue cease-and-desist orders.

On the question of control of insurers doing business in interstate commerce, the report commented upon several possible approaches. The most satisfactory method would, it noted, be control by the domiciliary state over the out-of-state activities of its domestic insurers, theorizing that such state has an obligation to protect not only the resident policyholders but all of the policyholders of a domestic insurer wherever located.[95] Since the NAIC-sponsored Uniform Unfair Trade Practices Act was limited to insurance company practices "in this state," it was suggested that the model act be amended to apply to acts of domestic insurers outside the borders of the domiciliary state.

Another suggested avenue of approach was the enactment of a requirement that a domestic insurer be licensed in any state in which it solicited, negotiated, or delivered any contract of insurance. It was noted, however, that a reciprocal provision seemed appropriate and, in fact, was found to have been included in the laws of some of the states which had adopted this approach.

The suggested alternative to inadequate control of interstate

---

[94] 355 U.S. 220 (1957).

[95] The case of *FTC* v. *Travelers Health Association*, 362 U.S. 293 (1960), had yet to be decided. See Note 99, *infra,* and accompanying text.

insurers by the domiciliary state would require more effective regulation of such insurers by the other states in which their operations were carried on. Then, in a significant observation, the report pointed the way:

A state could require licensing by all out-of-state insurers, including many now believed exempt, by redefining "doing business" to include the activities outlined in the uniform Unauthorized Insurers Service of Process Act which the Supreme Court in the *McGee* case held sufficient to confer jurisdiction. The holdings in the *Hoopeston* case, *The Travelers Health Association* case, and the *Robertson* v. *California* case also support this conclusion [citations omitted].

As an illustration, the report suggested the following:

"Transacting" or "doing" an insurance business includes any of the following:
    (1) The solicitation, negotiation or effectuation of any contract of insurance with residents of this state or any inducement to effectuate any contract of insurance with residents of this state.
    (2) The issuance, delivery or transmittal by mail or otherwise, of any policy or certificate of renewal thereof to residents of this state.
    (3) The transaction of any matter subsequent to the effectuation of the contract and arising out of it.
This section shall not apply to contracts of insurance procured as surplus line coverage from unauthorized insurers in accordance with the provisions of this law.[96]

Although hindsight demonstrates that the approach to regulation of authorized insurance through the redefinition of acts constituting "doing business," as suggested in the report, was essentially the correct one, the idea was not without its critics. At a meeting of the subcommittee in April, 1959, at which members of the All-Industry Committee were present, Moses G. Hubbard of the International Federation of Commercial Travelers Insurance and Alvis Layne of the Association of Insurance Advertisers objected strongly to any legislation which would require insurers to be licensed in any state in which they solicited business by mail or advertising. As to any amendment of the uniform Unfair Trade Practices Act to control out-of-state practices of domestic insurers, Mr. Hubbard commented

---

[96] *Proceedings of the National Association of Insurance Commissioners,* Vol. 1 (1959), p. 154.

that such legislation in his opinion was unnecessary. It confessed, he argued, the inadequacy of state regulation and invited federal intervention. Mr. Layne opposed it on the ground that it would destroy a method of doing business.[97] In view of the opposition of these and other industry spokesmen, the subcommittee voted in executive session to give the matter further study after receipt of a promised report from its All-Industry Advisory Committee members.[98] However, the All-Industry Committee was not as yet prepared to submit a formal report, preferring to wait until the pending case of *Federal Trade Commission* v. *Travelers Health Association*[99] was decided by the Supreme Court.[100]

Federal Trade Commission *v.* Travelers Health Association

Travelers Health Association, a leader in the mail-order insurance industry, had been ordered by the Federal Trade Commission to cease and desist from uttering and publishing allegedly misleading statements in its circular letters and advertising. Although forced by Virginia in 1950 to secure a license in that state, the association had continued its unlicensed operations countrywide through the mails from its office in Omaha. The association had appealed the FTC order to the eighth Circuit Court of Appeals, arguing that Nebraska law prohibited unfair or deceptive practices in the business of insurance by domestic companies not only in Nebraska but "in any other state."[101] The Court of Appeals agreed and had reversed FTC, being of opinion that "[w]ith every activity of the [Association], in the conduct of its business, subject to the supervision and control of the Director of Insurance of Nebraska, we think that the [Association's] practices in the solicitation of insurance by mail in Nebraska or elsewhere reasonably and realistically cannot be held to be unregulated by State law."[102]

The Supreme Court, however, reversed. It held that "regulation" by state law, as contemplated by and specified in the McCarran Act

[97] *Ibid.*, p. 515.

[98] *Ibid.*, p. 517.

[99] 362 U.S. 293 (1960).

[100] *Proceedings of the National Association of Insurance Commissioners,* Vol. 1 (1960), p. 189.

[101] Neb. Rev. Stat. sec. 44–1503 (1960).

[102] 262 F. 2d 241, 244 (8th Cir. 1959).

and upon the absence of which turned the question of the existence of regulatory authority in the FTC meant regulation under the law of the state in which the conduct of the insurer had its impact. Thus, the fact that Nebraska law attempted to proscribe certain conduct outside its borders was not effective to oust FTC from jurisdiction and authority to regulate conduct otherwise within its competence. Moreover, as the court observed, the motivating purpose behind the passage of the McCarran Act—to leave regulation of the business of insurance in the hands of the states, which as the political entities closest to the people were in a better position than the federal government to regulate the business, would hardly be served by delegating to any one state sole legislative and administrative control over the practices of an insurance company affecting the residents of every other state in the union.[103]

NAIC Report of 1959

Having had an opportunity to study the *FTC* decision, the Industry Advisory Committee prepared and submitted its formal report to the subcommittee in time for consideration at the December meeting.[104] As many had expected, the report advocated the adoption by the NAIC of a uniform Unauthorized Insurers False Advertising Process Act. It also suggested that the association make no recommendation for amendment of the various state statutes defining "doing an insurance business" as a means of attempting to solve the problem of direct-mail advertising, such as had been suggested earlier in the Wikler report. Industry opposition to pursuit of a solution via the "doing business" concept was not without foundation. It was felt, first of all, that such an approach would be ineffective because of a belief in the legal proposition that the Supreme Court had abandoned "doing business" as an acceptable standard for jurisdictional purposes, and hence as a standard for measuring the extent of state judicial power over foreign corporations. Second, certain undesirable consequences of substance were

---

[103] The court pointedly refused to decide the constitutional question which might arise as to the applicability of the Nebraska statute to misrepresentations made by a domestic company to residents of other states.

[104] *Proceedings of the National Association of Insurance Commissioners,* Vol. 2 (1960), p. 489.

postulated. One of these was the fact that a large percentage of mail-order business was carried on by specialized assessment-type organizations chartered under statutes similar to Article IX-B of the New York Insurance Law, which forbade the licensing of any new companies so structured and of any similar foreign companies. The retaliatory laws of the other states would, it was thought, prevent such companies from securing licenses in such other states, and these companies would, therefore, virtually be forced out of business. Another involved "orphan" or "move-in" business, particularly the status of life insurance or noncancellable accident and health contracts, where such policyholders had moved from a state where the insurer was licensed to a state where the insurer was not licensed.[105]

NAIC 1960 Recommendations

When the subcommittee met again in November of 1960, it decided to recommend adoption of the proposed Unauthorized Insurers False Advertising Service of Process Act as the best currently available approach to the problems before the subcommittee.[106] The model bill had been presented in rough form for consideration at the midwinter meeting of the Regulation of Advertising subcommittee of the Committee on Accident and Health Insurance. No action was taken at that time on the proposal.[107] However, the proposal was picked up and polished by an industry subcommittee working with the Association subcommittee to Review State Insurance Laws and submitted as a part of the Advisory Committee report.[108]

Nor had the All-Industry Advisory Committee itself been idle following the June meeting. It prepared and submitted a second comprehensive report to the subcommittee for Review of State Insurance Laws in which it reiterated its recommendation that the uniform law which it had proposed be adopted. In addition, it argued against the broadening of the proposal to cover any unfair

---

[105] *Ibid.* (1959), p. 497.
[106] *Ibid.* (1961), p. 309.
[107] *Ibid.* (1960), p. 149.
[108] *Ibid.* p. 507.

trade practices other than false advertising or to afford equitable relief in addition to legal damages, as had been proposed by some critics.[109] It also opposed any resort to a system of interstate compacts, pointing out that the compact device would result in a partial surrender of the sovereignty of the individual states over the regulation of insurance within their boundaries; and further that Congress might regard such arrangements as inconsistent with the states' position that they were capable of regulating insurance without the intervention of the national government.[110]

Committee on Unauthorized Insurance

In the meantime, the Committee on Unauthorized Insurance had been reactivated in April of that year. It held a public session in New York, industry representatives participating, which resulted in proposals to draft a uniform Surplus Lines Law. Sessions at the annual meeting in May, 1960, resulted in a proposed model draft for submission to the National Association for consideration.[111] It was decided, however, that an opportunity should be afforded to the insurance industry and to the commissioners to study the proposal and to submit, if desired, suggestions for amendments, deletions, or omissions of some of the provisions. October 1, 1960, was set as the time limit for the receipt of any suggestions. The questions and suggestions were many; in fact a completely revised draft was submitted and adopted at a meeting of the committee in November.[112] At the midwinter meeting the committee reported that it planned a further meeting in April, 1961, and would not be able to render a definitive report prior to the annual meeting to be held the following June.[113]

Such, then, was the state of affairs in the deliberations of the National Association of Insurance Commissioners on means to control unauthorized insurance as the time approached when the newly elected members of the 1961 Wisconsin Legislature would take their seats.

---

[109] *Ibid.* (1961), p. 311.
[110] *Ibid.,* p. 316.
[111] *Ibid.* (1960), p. 663.
[112] *Ibid.* (1961), p. 356.
[113] *Ibid.,* p. 356.

PRE-1961 WISCONSIN LAW:
19TH CENTURY CONTROLS FOR A 20TH CENTURY MACHINE

Little of the good which the NAIC had sought over the years to accomplish with regard to enactment of modern and uniform state laws was ever reflected in Wisconsin law. The law was geared to the suppression and control of unauthorized insurance as conducted through the American agency system. It was fragmented, threadbare, and in some respects contradictory. Moreover, as was the case with the law in most of the states, it was never sufficiently particularized to deal effectively with the principal problem which had faced regulators almost from the very first—how to control insurance solicited and written through the mails.

The 1850 Wisconsin Law

Wisconsin's first insurance law[114] dealt casually with unauthorized insurance. Directed primarily at the agent, the law forbade the solicitation or placement of insurance in any foreign company until the local agent had secured from such company a sworn statement from its president and secretary respecting its capital structure and investment portfolio, filed it with the secretary of state, and obtained from that officer a license to solicit and accept such risks.[115] Provision was also made for the licensing of foreign companies. However, resort to this procedure was seldom had inasmuch as a foreign company was required to deposit securities with the secretary of state equal in value to the minimum capital required for the formation of a similar domestic company.[116]

It was not until after the absolute power of the legislature over insurance transactions carried on in the state was established by the state supreme court in *Fire Department of Milwaukee* v. *Helfenstein*[117] that suppression of transactions through unauthorized insurance companies was essayed in earnest.

---

[114] Ch. 232 (1850), Wis. Laws 186.
[115] *Ibid.*, sec. 7, p. 187.
[116] *Ibid.*
[117] 16 Wis. 142 (1862).

Later Amendment

An 1871 law[118] prohibited the placement by a domestic agent of any local fire risk in an unlicensed company, as well as the writing of any local fire risk by a foreign company not lawfully admitted in Wisconsin. The requirement that foreign companies deposit securities with the secretary of state was dropped; qualification on the part of a foreign fire company was accomplished by appointment of the secretary of state as its process agent and by satisfying statutory requirements applicable to local companies respecting minimum capital and surplus.[119] In addition, all companies, both domestic and foreign, were specifically forbidden to do any insurance business, either in the state or with any resident of the state, except in accordance with applicable provisions of state law.

Ultimately, this law was refined through recodification and amendment to provide that no foreign insurance company should directly or indirectly transact any insurance business in the state except upon compliance with all applicable requirements of state law.[120] Until the passage of the Unauthorized Insurance Act of 1961, this section provided the principal weapon in the armory of the department in its battle to suppress unauthorized insurance. Such a regulatory scheme was largely impotent so far as concerned the suppression of insurance transactions effected directly through the mails and without benefit of participation by any locally licensed agent. Its principal utility in that regard lay in preventing such insurers from resorting to the state courts for the collection of premiums and assessments from policyholders residing in the state.[121]

Wisconsin, along with many other states, never felt constrained to prohibit its own companies from doing the business in other states without benefit of compliance with the laws of such states. Perhaps, this neglect was due to apprehension that a few sister states

---

[118] Ch. 13 (1871), Wis. Laws 19.

[119] The secretary of state was commissioner of insurance ex officio. Ch. 56, sec. 32 (1870), Wis. Laws 97. The commissioner of insurance was substituted as process agent upon creation of that office in 1878. Ch. 214 (1878), Wis. Laws 426.

[120] Wis. Stat. sec. 201.32 (1965).

[121] *Presbyterian Ministers Fund* v. *Thomas,* 126 Wis. 281, 105 N.W. 801 (1905).

by omitting to pass such a law would become havens for those companies for which unauthorized operations were becoming a way of life. Perhaps, on the other hand, it was felt that such a law would curtail similar profitable operations by Wisconsin companies.

Penalties Provided

But while Wisconsin never yielded to pressures to prohibit its domestic insurers from engaging in activities in states where not authorized to do so, it very early enacted laws severely penalizing local agents who assisted unauthorized insurers from other states in the transaction of local business.

An 1899 law[122] provided for a mandatory suspension of license for at least 90 days in the case of any agent found guilty of soliciting or aiding in the placement of unauthorized fire insurance. In addition, it provided for personal liability on the part of the agent, should the unauthorized insurer fail for any reason to discharge its liability in the event of a loss payable under the policy. The same law imposed for the first time a requirement that all policies covering local fire risks be locally countersigned,[123] and it limited the right to reinsure local fire risks to placement in licensed companies only. Two years later the law was expanded to include casualty and surety risks within its ambit.[124]

Besides the penalties of revocation of license and personal liability imposed upon agents who aided in unauthorized insurance transactions, severe criminal penalties were provided under a law enacted in 1913.[125] Unauthorized insurers were liable to a fine of up to $5,000, and agents who assisted in any way in the placement of such insurance were subject to a fine and possible imprisonment. A provision making an unauthorized contract of insurance unenforceable by either party was enacted in the same law.[126] However, it was later realized that by providing for unenforceability at the suit of

---

[122] Ch. 190, sec. 6 (1899), Wis. Laws 289.

[123] *Ibid.* The requirement that insurance on risks in the state be written in authorized companies only was made inapplicable to property in the possession of common carriers.

[124] Ch. 227 (1901), Wis. Laws 282.

[125] Ch. 366, sec. 1 (1913), Wis. Laws 404. A similar provision was enacted with respect to life insurance in 1949 when for the first time it was made unlawful to solicit or procure applications for life insurance with any other company. Ch. 399, sec. 4 (1949), Wis. Laws 365.

[126] Ch. 366, sec. 2 (1913), Wis. Laws 404.

either party to the transaction the earlier provision making the participating agent personally liable[127] was to some extent compromised. Accordingly, the statute was amended in 1933[128] to provide merely that such contracts were unenforceable at the suit of the insurer.

The difficulty experienced under the statute imposing criminal sanctions on persons engaging in acts of unauthorized insurance was that its sanctions did not reach the traffic which most needed suppression and control. In the first place, no one was exactly sure what particular conduct was violative of the law. In the second place, it was widely, if not universally, supposed that transactions carried out solely through the mails were beyond the power of the commissioners to control, as witness the abortive attempts of the National Association to procure enactment of a federal law to bar the use of the mails to mail-order insurers. But more importantly, the statute simply didn't work. For in 1915, just two years after its enactment, the attorney general of the state ruled that a foreign insurance company, even though openly doing business in the state, could not be prosecuted under the statute unless service could first be obtained upon an agent of the company within the state.[129] Thus, a considerable amount of unauthorized insurance continued to be placed in the state due in large part to the fact that service of process on the offending companies proved in most cases to be impossible—their contracts having been effectuated entirely by mail.

First Surplus Lines Law

Shortly after the National Convention of Insurance Commissioners had pointed to the need,[130] the Wisconsin legislature enacted the state's first surplus lines law in 1911.[131] Although adequate to the

---

127 *Presbyterian Ministers Fund* v. *Thomas,* 126 Wis. 281, 105 N.W. 801 (1905).

128 Ch. 487, sec. 89 (1933), Wis. Laws 1084.

129 4 *Op. Wis. Att'y. Gen.* 1024 (1915).

130 Though originally contained in the 1908 report of the Committee on Unauthorized Insurance, the subject was reproposed in the 1910 report of the committee. *Proceedings of the National Association of Insurance Commissioners* (1910), p. 265.

131 Ch. 87 (1911), Wis. Laws 90.

times, the law was limited in scope, applying to the export of fire insurance only. It provided for the issuance of a special annual surplus line agent's license and required the agent to file an affidavit with the commissioner as to each risk placed in the surplus market declaring his inability to place the amount of insurance required by the risk in admitted companies.

This law survived periodic recodifications of the statutes substantially unchanged in form until 1949 when it was repealed.[132] It was replaced by a new surplus lines law which, while permitting the export of marine, liability, sprinkler leakage, and automobile lines in addition to fire insurance, restricted the exportable amount to the excess only of the amount required and not obtainable through admitted carriers.[133]

As often happens under comprehensive regulatory systems developed piecemeal, inconsistencies and contradictions were introduced into the laws enacted to control unauthorized insurance. For example, the 1899 law which imposed personal liability upon the agent for placing fire insurance risks in an unauthorized company was not amended when the first surplus lines law was passed in 1911 permitting properly licensed agents to procure fire insurance through unauthorized companies in certain cases. Thus, it was not at all certain whether or not an agent who lawfully procured a surplus lines fire policy would be personally liable to the insured in the event the insurer became insolvent or otherwise refused to pay a proper claim. This question was not finally resolved until the case of *Ferm* v. *Moore*[134] was decided in 1930, making life easier and a little less uncertain for the surplus lines agent.

Success of Regulation

From the earliest times, history can probably be said to demonstrate that the commissioner of insurance was successful in suppressing the attempts of unauthorized companies operating along conventional lines (i.e., through agents who personally solicited business from local insureds) to do business in the state. To a lesser extent, perhaps, similar success was realized in suppressing such

---

[132] Ch. 436, sec. 6 (1949), Wis. Laws 406.

[133] *Ibid.,* sec. 5, p. 406.

[134] 201 Wis. 2d 273, 229 N.W. 77 (1930).

business through control over local agents already licensed by the department and subject to penalties for doing unauthorized business through unlicensed companies. There remained, however, one other avenue of approach, and this was motivated not so much by a desire to control and suppress unauthorized transactions as by a desire to recoup tax revenues lost on premiums paid to those with no duty to account to the state for their receipt.

Even before the passage of the fire surplus lines law, the legislature had provided for the collection of premium taxes upon the local business of unauthorized fire companies, and in default of collection from that source the tax was collectible from the insured property owner.[135] Under the terms of the original law, a delinquency penalty of one tenth per month of the amount of tax due was imposed. This law was expanded in 1949 at the time of the enactment of the comprehensive surplus lines law to cover all transactions by unlicensed companies. At the same time, the delinquency penalty was increased to 25 percent, with an additional 1 percent of the tax for each month of continued delinquency.[136] Also, the basic tax was set at 3 percent of the premium in lieu of all other taxes and fire department dues. (This same approach was continued in the provisions of the 1961 Unauthorized Insurance Act, both as to unauthorized insurance itself[137] and surplus lines insurance,[138] although the new surplus lines law omits the penalty provisions and the provisional liability of the insured for the tax.)

Property owners were required to report instances in which their properties were insured for fire in unauthorized companies[139] so that the tax could be computed and collected.[140] As an illuminating aside, it should be observed that the law required even self-insured property owners to report and to pay a tax equal to 2 percent of the premium otherwise payable had the property been insured, in lieu of fire department duties.[141]

---

[135] Ch. 259 (1909), Wis. Laws 276.

[136] Ch. 436, sec. 1 (1949), Wis. Laws 405.

[137] Ch. 397, sec. 3 (11) (1961), Wis. Laws 373.

[138] *Ibid.*, sec. 5 (12), p. 379.

[139] Wis. Stat. sec. 201.62 (1) (1961).

[140] This provision was also retained in the 1961 law. Ch. 397, sec. 4, Wis. Laws 375.

[141] Fire department dues are collected from the companies out of fire insurance premiums and paid to cities and towns for the maintenance of fire protection equipment and for other related purposes. Wis. Stat. sec. 200.17 (1965).

Wisconsin Regulation Compared to Other States

So Wisconsin law in mid-20th century was, on the whole, neither better nor worse than the laws of its sister states with regard to the conferring of powers upon the regulatory authority for the control of unauthorized insurance. The difficulty was that such powers were, or were thought by many to be, limited under familiar theories of contract law to applicability only in the jurisdiction of the place of contract. And everyone knew that the place of contract in the case of mail-order insurance was the state of domicile of the insurer, wherein the policy was issued and deposited in the mail. Moreover, the Supreme Court of the United States had only recently decided that for purposes of satisfying the McCarran Act, no state law sufficiently controlled acts having their impacts in states other than the enacting jurisdiction.[142]

The uniform acts proposed by the NAIC and adopted in many states provided a partial answer to egregious abuses practiced by mail-order insurers, but they fell short of solving the real problem, which remained, simply, whether a state could lawfully sanction and control the terms of a mail-order insurance transaction affecting persons or property within its borders, as well as the conditions under which it would permit the contract to be written.

WISCONSIN INTO THE BREACH: THE SEARCH CONCLUDED

The 1952 Senate hearings on mail-order insurance abuses had served, at least, to call attention to practices which not only menaced the insurance-buying public but also planted the seeds of doubt in the minds of many in influential circles of government as to the wisdom of continuing the experiment in state regulation of insurance. The abuses undoubtedly were there, and while the NAIC was laboring to effect a solution, it appeared to some that its efforts, protracted as they were and had been, would produce too little too late.

The Wisconsin Problem

While many mail-order companies, particularly the larger benevolent and fraternal societies, conducted their operations in a con-

[142] *FTC* v. *Travelers Health Association,* 362 U.S. 293 (1960).

servative and reputable manner, others were single-mindedly set on exploiting the public through the use of loopholes in the state regulatory systems. Almost without exception, these companies were characterized by an extremely high volume of premiums in relation to capital and surplus, minuscule loss ratios and high expense ratios. One such company, for example, received premium income in one year of $1,400,432, out of which it paid losses of $38,475—a return to policyholders of less than 3 cents out of every premium dollar. Another collected premiums of $1,069,781 and paid out $211,646. Loss ratios of 25 to 30 percent were not uncommon, in fact they were the rule among the pirate companies.

Such was the clamor for reform that the Wisconsin Insurance Department felt it could no longer afford to wait upon the action of the NAIC but should pursue an independent course. Though by no means resolved, the general climate of opinion in the NAIC after the midwinter meeting of 1959 favored attacking the problem principally through the uniform Unauthorized Insurers Process Act proposed for adoption by the states in 1949, and the uniform Unauthorized Insurers False Advertising Process Act similarly proposed in 1960. Although "guidelines" for an acceptable surplus lines law had been formulated, no model bill proposal had been developed up to that point.

Wisconsin View on Model Act

The Unauthorized Insurers Process Act had achieved wide acceptance. Industry generally supported it, and all but three or four states had adopted it. The Wisconsin department felt, however, that the model act did not go far enough. It applied only to insurers and thus even though it purported to control the issuance, delivery, and solicitation of contracts and collection of premiums by mail or otherwise, it omitted to provide a means of control over the acts of independent operators and others through whose agency such acts could be accomplished with impunity. Moreover, by limiting applicability specifically to acts constituting solicitation, issuance, and delivery of insurance contracts and collection of premiums thereon, its general applicability to the business of insurance was to that extent limited. While it was true that the act purported to apply to "any other transaction of business," it was felt that the better course would be to procure an enactment which would specify with particularity those other acts which would constitute a transaction of insurance business. As for the model False Advertising Process Act, the fact that it conferred jurisdiction only in cases where the advertising or promotional literature was alleged to be misrepresentative of the financial condition of the offender, or of the terms of its contracts or the benefits afforded thereunder, was felt to be a serious weakness. The problem, after all, as the *Travelers Health* case had demonstrated, was the lack of control over *all* insurance contracts and *all* advertising and promotional materials on the part of those states in which the materials had their impact.

The stumbling block and the keystone of the industry's position was the legal concept which taught that the place of the making of the mail-order insurance contract was the state of the insurer's domicile, where the policy was issued, became effective and was mailed. Such a concept, however, failed to take into account that such contracts had been solicited by mail, were deliverable to Wisconsin residents, and afforded coverage on Wisconsin risks. Was such a position consistent with the tort rule learned by every first-year law student, as exemplified in the case of the bullet fired from state A and striking its victim in state B, that the state where the impact occurred can take jurisdiction for redress of the tort? To many in the department, including the commissioner, the analogy was appealing, if inapposite.

Administrative Rules Proposed and Adopted

With corrective legislation as its ultimate goal, the department, early in 1960, proposed the adoption of administrative rules, implementing existing statutes, to put its theories to work while the staff labored to ready a sweeping legislative proposal for presentation to the next legislative session, which would meet in January, 1961.

Two administrative rules were proposed: one dealing with unauthorized insurance[143] and the other with surplus lines.[144]

With little in the law of a specific nature to work with, each rule extended the scope of administrative interpretation to the limits of permissibility, and, as some thought, even beyond.

The unauthorized insurance rule, as proposed, prohibited any

---

[143] Wis. Admin. Code sec. Ins. 6.06 (effective April 1, 1960).
[144] *Ibid.*, sec. Ins. 6.07 (effective June 1, 1960).

unauthorized insurer or agent from taking or receiving applications for insurance or collecting or receiving premiums on such insurance. However, this prohibition was of necessity limited in its effect to transactions performed in the state. More importantly, however, the rule prohibited any person from acting in Wisconsin, directly or indirectly, as an agent for or otherwise aiding or representing any unauthorized insurer in the solicitation, negotiation, procurement, or effectuation of insurance; from disseminating information respecting coverage or rates; from forwarding applications, delivery of policies, or collection of premiums; from inspection of risks, fixing rates, investigation or adjustment of claims and losses; or from representing or assisting such an insurer or in any other manner aiding in the transaction of insurance within the state. Transactions involving surplus lines, reinsurance, and move-in business only were excepted.

The enabling statutes on which this rule was based[145] were aimed at the regulation of unauthorized insurers and their agents. The proposed rule, however, included within its ambit the activities in aid of unauthorized insurance by persons who were not agents. Since the Wisconsin Supreme Court had earlier held that certificates issued under group master contracts were themselves contracts, or parts of contracts, of insurance,[146] the conduct of persons and corporations nominally insured under group master life or accident and health contracts written in other states but unauthorized in Wisconsin was subject to question in cases where certificates were issued under the master contracts to Wisconsin residents. Representatives of powerful insurance interests were quick to point this out.[147] In addition, it was argued that the proscription of conduct in sweeping terms was grounded on language found in statutes dealing only with fire insurance or life insurance and hence could not properly be applied to conduct respecting the solicitation or sale of accident and health insurance.

Although these arguments were not without merit, the proposed rule had an administrative hearing on February 11, 1960, and with

---

[145] In part: Wis. Stat. secs. 203.07; 206.41 (2); 209.15 (1959).

[146] *Jensen* v. *John Hancock Mut. Life Ins. Co.*, 266 Wis. 595, 600, 64 N.W. 2d 183, 185 (1954); see 47 *Op. Wis. Att'y Gen.* (Wis.) 184 (1958).

[147] Supplemental statement of Health Insurance Association of America, annexed to transcript of hearing on adoption of Wis. Admin. Code sec. 6.06, (February 11, 1960), p. 5.

minor technical changes was adopted to become effective on April 1, 1960.[148]

The proposed surplus lines rule proved to be considerably less controversial. It did, however, contain a number of the guiding principles, without benefit of statutory sanction, which had been suggested earlier in the 1957 report of the joint NAIC All-Industry Surplus Lines Subcommittee.[149] These included provision for exercise of visitorial and investigatory powers by the commissioner, the prohibition against placement of surplus lines insurance solely for the purpose of obtaining lower rates or preferential treatment, and the requirement that all surplus lines contracts contain provision for appointment of a local process agent and that insureds be advised that their coverages had been placed in the surplus lines market. No substantial opposition having been voiced to the proposal, the rule was adopted and became effective on June 1, 1960.[150]

Little more than a year elapsed between the adoption of the unauthorized insurance and surplus lines rules and the passage of the Wisconsin Unauthorized Insurance Act of 1961. And while the department, in view of questions as to the validity of the unauthorized insurance rule as applied in certain areas, moved gingerly in its attempts to enforce the provisions against mail-order accident and health operators, and policyholders under unauthorized group insurance, the rule nevertheless served notice that the department intended to seek a permanent solution to the problem of uncontrolled insurance operations within the borders of Wisconsin. The department had withstood the attacks and cajolings of the industry; now it remained to be seen whether the state lawmakers, soon to be confronted with a revolutionary proposal, could be prevailed upon to do the same.[151]

Administrative and technical personnel of the Wisconsin department had, of course, attended meetings of the National Association for many years along with their commissioner. Deputy Commissioner Charles Timbers, moreover, had participated in deliberations

---

[148] Cr. *Register,* March 1960, No. 51.

[149] *Proceedings of the National Association of Insurance Commissioners,* Vol. 1 (1958), p. 174.

[150] Cr. *Register,* May, 1960, No. 53.

[151] Wis. Admin. Code secs. Ins. 6.06, 6.07 were rescinded effective May 1, 1964, having been rendered obsolete by the passage of the Unauthorized Insurance Act of 1961, ch. 397 (1961), Wis. Laws 368.

and studies of unauthorized insurance problems conducted by technicians from many state departments. Almost everyone was agreed that really effective and enforceable legislation was needed to control mail-order and surplus lines insurance practices if state regulation were to survive. Equally obvious was the fact that certain segments of the insurance industry, rich and politically powerful, were prepared to block any attempt by the association to devise practical means of asserting the needed controls—and if unsuccessful in the NAIC, then in the caucus rooms of the state legislatures.

The NAIC itself, that is to say, the several commissioners, being apprised of the intentions of the Wisconsin department and furnished with various proposed drafts of the bill intended for submission to the legislature, manifested indifference bordering unconcern. The conviction was widespread that such a bill could never achieve passage. In point of fact, at the December meeting of the NAIC following passage of the Wisconsin law, the commissioner of one of the most important insurance states—a recognized leader in the field of insurance regulation, verbally chastised the Wisconsin commissioner for procuring the enactment of a law which if it were to be found unconstitutional would leave the states completely without power to regulate mail-order insurance and would force the commissioners to petition congress for a liberalizing amendment to the McCarran Act.

Some of the principal writers for the trade publications, too, were less than kind in their observations regarding the soundness of the philosophy behind the bill, although shortly after the Supreme Court refused to hear the *Ministers* appeal one of them was already proclaiming that the decision simply represented a logical step in the post–SEUA development of the state regulatory system.

Department Sets Out to Prepare Bill

Taking their cue from the Wikler report and the report of the Surplus Lines Subcommittee, the department staff had set out to devise a bill which would (1) synthesize all of the useful laws for the control and suppression of unauthorized insurance already on the books, (2) formulate new language to apply those laws to the modern practices which demanded control, and (3) draft new laws to regulate surplus lines insurance in order to insure its availability in all proper cases, to subject it to its fair share of the tax burden, and to protect the regulated lines against unfair competitive advantage.

As they sat down to their task, the first order of business was to devise a workable definition of unauthorized insurance which could be applied to and encompass all of the practices employed by operators to evade the existing regulatory laws. Department Actuary Stanley C. Du Rose, Jr., later to succeed Charles Timbers as deputy commissioner, was assigned full time to the work of drafting the bill. As to the companies themselves, it was decided to include all corporations, associations, partnerships, and individuals, including interinsurance exchanges and mutual benefit societies, engaged as principals in the business of insurance. "Doing an insurance business," whether effected by mail or otherwise, was declared to be the making or proposing of an insurance contract or a contract of guaranty or suretyship (other than one incident to noninsurance activities of the guarantor or surety), the taking or receiving of any application for insurance, the issuance or delivery of a contract of insurance to a resident of the state or to a person authorized to do business in the state, and the receipt or collection of any premium, commission, membership fee, assessment, dues, or other consideration for any insurance contract. Of prime importance was the additional provision that the venue of any of the described acts consummated through the mails lay in the jurisdiction where the matter transmitted by mail was delivered and took effect.

Also included in the definition were the controversial provisions applying to agents and other persons assisting in or abetting the transaction of an insurance business by insurers, which had been included in the unauthorized insurance rule adopted earlier.[152] As if these were not comprehensive enough, the definition also comprised the doing or proposing of any business "in substance equivalent to any of the foregoing in a manner designed to evade the provisions of the statutes . . . ," and "[a]ny other transactions of business in this state by an insurer."

The only exceptions incorporated in the original bill were for authorized surplus lines, reinsurance, and move-in business.[153]

---

[152] Wis. Admin. Code sec. Ins. 6.06 (1960).

[153] Other exceptions for independently procured insurance, insurance-related activities of attorneys at law in the practice of their profession and for the Teachers Insurance Annuity Association were added by the state senate during consideration of the bill. See text *infra*.

Added along with the definition sections were other sections incorporating relevant provisions of existing statutes relating to disclosure, reporting, taxation, and penalties. Provision was also made for appointment of the commissioner of insurance as the agent of any unauthorized insurer for service of process and for the similar appointment of the secretary of state in proceedings instituted by the commissioner of insurance or by the state.

The original bill proposal also contained a provision, long advocated by the NAIC, to make unlawful the knowing solicitation or effectuation of insurance by a domestic insurer in any reciprocating state in which such domestic insurer was not licensed. However, the provision did not survive to become law, suffering death by amendment procured by the domestic companies.[154]

Finally, provision was made for insurance independently procured by insureds on property or risks located in the state but effected through negotiations directly with an insurer, carried on outside the state without the intercession or assistance of a locally licensed agent. Although originally comprehended within the definition of unauthorized insurance, a senate amendment later excluded insurance procured in this manner from the definition. The bill, however, incorporated the existing provision[155] exacting a tax of 3 percent payable by the insured ($\frac{1}{2}$ percent in the case of marine insurance) in lieu of all other taxes and dues, and continued the 25 percent penalty provided in case of delinquency in payment. Independently procured individual life and individual disability contracts were excluded from the operation of the premium tax section.

In the matter of control and regulation of surplus lines insurance, the department staff had merely to expand upon the already existing statute enacted in 1949 by incorporating in it the additional features suggested in the 1957 report of the NAIC Surplus Lines Subcommittee. First, however, experience had demonstrated the desirability of authorizing the export of other additional lines of insurance. Accordingly, it was decided to provide for the export of all the existing lines classified under Wisconsin law with the exception of title insurance, workmen's compensation, and supplementary medical payments insurance. The provisions in the recently promul-

---

[154] See text *infra*.

[155] Wis. Stat. sec. 76.33 (1959).

gated administrative rule governing surplus lines insurance[156] were incorporated in their entirety, except that specific provision was made for the maintenance of suits directly against the surplus lines insurer upon any cause of action arising out of a contract issued by it or by its agent in the state. The subcommittee report had recommended the requirement that an authorized surplus lines carrier be licensed in at least one state of the United States. The department was not convinced, however, that such a requirement would be effective to guarantee that an insurer so licensed would be acceptable as a surplus lines carrier. So the department bill, instead, contained provisions placing responsibility upon the licensed surplus lines agent to ascertain the financial condition of the selected carrier, its underwriting and claims practices, and the competency of its management.

Department Begins Educational Campaign for Bill

By December of 1960 the job of preliminary drafting was complete. Commissioner Charles Manson and his staff were now confronted with the task of educating and persuading state legislators and others in positions of influence whose support would be needed to assure passage of the bill. While bitter opposition from some quarters was expected as a matter of course, it soon developed that the department was not without friends and supporters. First and foremost among the bill's supporters were the trade association groups of the American agency system. Anxious to support any proposal which would stem the flow of illegal business out of the state, with the resultant loss to their members of commission income, they lent the support of their powerful lobby. So, also, did many local insurance companies and trade associations, and for similar reasons. It should be remarked parenthetically that the support of local industry was not obtained without price. The provision in the bill which would have prohibited unauthorized transactions in other states by domestic companies was quietly dropped with but token opposition on the part of Commissioner Manson.[157] Surprisingly, the Wisconsin Chapter of the American Society of Insurance Management, whose national organization was

---

[156] Wis. Admin. Code sec. Ins. 6.07 (1960).

[157] Statement of Commissioner Manson, *Hearing on S. 245 before the Senate Committee on Labor, Taxation, Insurance and Banking* (March 28, 1961).

unremittingly opposed even to the adoption of the NAIC-sponsored uniform acts, offered support for the department's proposal in return for the inclusion of an exception for independently procured insurance on which, however, the 3 percent tax would be reported and paid.

The Legislative Battle Begins

By February, 1961, alliances had been concluded and the battle lines drawn. Although desperate last-minute attempts had been made by the mail-order trade associations to dissuade Commissioner Manson from having the proposal introduced, the carefully structured product of 18 months of work by the department staff was placed in the legislative hopper on Washington's birthday, to begin life as Senate Bill 245.

The workings of the legislative process are indeed strange and wonderful to behold. No circumstance renders this more apparent than the confrontation of irreconcilable forces in a life-or-death struggle over the fate of a controversial bill. In such a struggle no holds are barred, and legislators are regarded as pawns in the hands of expert players, to be manipulated according to the skill and experience of the mover. And S245 was a controversial bill. Although influential members of both parties were on each side, the department was on the defensive from the beginning as the mail-order interests entered the lists with the most skillful lobbyists obtainable. But Commissioner Manson and Deputy Timbers were not without allies in the senate, nor were they loathe to engage, themselves, in a little friendly persuasion. On more than one occasion, the deputy commissioner was bitterly assailed from the senate floor by opponents of the bill for allegedly engaging in lobbying activities in connection with the bill.[158]

First Hearing

A hearing was quickly scheduled for March 28th before the Senate Committee on Labor, Taxation, Insurance and Banking whose chairman, be it noted, was one of those unalterably opposed

---

[158] Lobbying activities by state employees are actively discouraged in the state legislature except at the specific invitation of a member. Moreover, such activity may possibly be in violation of law. See Wis. Stat. secs. 13.70 (1), 16.30 (1965).

to the bill. Commissioner Manson, the bill's chief proponent, devoted his efforts at the hearing principally to a discussion of the undesirable practices by unauthorized companies, the obligation of the state to discharge the mandate of Congress implicit in the McCarran Act, and the overriding need for the control measures proposed in the bill. Opposing forces, on the other hand, led by an *ad hoc* coalition comprising the American Life Convention, the Life Insurance Association of America, and the Health Insurance Association of America, paid scant heed to such matters. Forgetting that one of the principal purposes of the bill was to establish the *fact* of regulatory authority in the commissioner over *all* of the insurance business transacted in the state, they argued that since less than 1 percent of the total health insurance transacted by mail was unethically conducted, it made no sense to subject the entire mail-order industry to burdensome and unnecessary regulation. They pointed to the NAIC model bills which provided for service of process on unauthorized insurers in certain cases, and the False Advertising Process Act which covered misrepresentative advertising, as the preferable alternative.

All the old arguments which for years had hamstrung effective action by the NAIC were put forth: unconstitutional interference with the free use of the mails, violation of the free speech and equal protection amendments, multiple tax impact, license restrictions and retaliatory legislation by sister states, among others. Constitutional arguments there were, in profusion. But a favorite to which opponents kept returning time and again throughout the course of the legislative process (and even in preliminary skirmishes in the *Ministers* case itself) was the fact that Stanley C. Du Rose, the department actuary who drafted the bill, was not a lawyer and that this circumstance alone raised grave doubts as to the bill's constitutionality.

Turning to public policy, they argued that it would be unfair to deny to Wisconsin residents the benefits of insurance through certificates issued under group policies in other states merely because the issuing company was not admitted in Wisconsin or the provisions of the master policy were not acceptable under Wisconsin law. Again, they ignored the more persuasive argument that Wisconsin laws were enacted to benefit Wisconsin citizens and that its citizens were entitled to have enforced the minimum protections afforded thereunder.

Realizing that it would be unwise simply to oppose the bill

without at the same time offering an acceptable alternative, the opposition forces mustered behind a substitute bill,[159] containing essentially the provisions of the NAIC Unauthorized Insurers and False Advertising Process Acts, and the 10-point proposal authored by the NAIC Surplus Lines Subcommittee in 1957.

Attempts to Modify Bill

Once presented with an alternative which gave promise of turning down the political heat, some of the legislative proponents of S245 wavered and suggested in strong terms to Commissioner Manson that he modify his position and accept the substitute proposal. The pressure upon him to do so, magnified by the circumstance that his office was appointive and subject to confirmation by the senate, was intense. However, he elected to remain firm and attacked the substitute amendment by pointing to gross deficiencies and errors in the substantive provisions and draftsmanship of the amendment. Indeed, the document showed unmistakable evidence of having been put together during the midnight hours of the day preceding its introduction.[160] By actual count, the amendment contained 29 specific substantive deficiencies and errors in draftsmanship, which required five pages of single-spaced typing to list.[161]

Meanwhile, the Teachers Insurance Annuity Association, a stock insurance corporation domiciled in New York but licensed in no other state, became concerned over its status should S245 become law. Although a private insurance corporation selling both individual and group life and accident and health insurance policies and annuities, it dealt solely with staff members of educational and scientific organizations and specialized in establishing and maintaining staff benefit plans. Powerful educators urged exemption of TIAA, both as a tax saving measure to hold down costs of benefit plans established in Wisconsin schools and colleges and to avoid the necessity of incurring additional expense on the part of TIAA

[159] Substitute Amendment No. 1 to S 245, offered May 24, 1961. *Wisconsin Senate Journal* (1961), p. 1090.

[160] The declared purpose of the substitute amendment bill was to enact "an unauthorized insurance code and a surplus lines insurance code relating to false advertising by insurers not authorized to do business in this state . . . ."

[161] Memorandum on Substitute Amendment 1 to S 245, filed with the Senate Committee on Labor, Taxation, Insurance and Banking by Commissioner Manson.

incident to qualification and licensing in Wisconsin and perhaps in other states. Although privately he entertained serious doubt as to the wisdom of exempting any insurance company from regulatory supervision, Commissioner Manson neither opposed nor advocated the exemption.[162] An amendment affording exempt status to TIAA was, accordingly, offered[163] and achieved passage with the parent bill.

Second Hearing

A second hearing on S245 was held on June 7, 1961, to consider the three amendments to the parent bill[164] and Substitute Amendment 1, after which the committee voted to recommend adoption of the three amendments and to reject the substitute amendment.[165] The real test of strength now faced the antagonists as S245 and the substitute bill were brought onto the floor of the 33-member senate for action. Each vote was crucial. Each side was kept busy, reassuring senators who had previously expressed partiality to its point of view and attempting to erode opposition support.

The Legislative Battle Continues

Three tie votes preceded final passage. This was pure circumstance, however, as individual senators switched sides as the votes were taken. One influential member of the senate had agreed to support S245, but only on the first vote. And his vote practically assured three additional votes from other senators from the same political party who indicated they would follow his lead. In another case, department forces anticipated the support of a senator who was sympathetic to the views of local insurance interests. These interests had originally opposed S245 but changed their position and agreed to support the bill in return for the deletion of the provision prohibiting unauthorized operations by local companies in

---

[162] Hearing, *supra* n. 157, p. 25.

[163] Amendment No. 3 to S 245, offered June 8, 1961. *Wisconsin Senate Journal* (1961), p. 1239.

[164] Two earlier amendments to accomplish technical changes and agreed revisions were offered on May 22nd and June 8th. *Wisconsin Senate Journal* (1961), pp. 1067, 1239.

[165] *Wisconsin Senate Journal* (1961), p. 1390.

sister states. However, no one had thought to inform the senator specifically of this fact and so his support, which would have won the day on the first vote, was lost.

On the occasion of the debate preceding the fourth and final vote, the proceedings were being observed by the deputy commissioner from the visitor's gallery. The motion to pass the bill came to a vote, and the chairman of the Committee on Labor, Taxation, Insurance and Banking, one of the bill's most obdurate opponents, seeking to delay matters with the view to moving for reconsideration later, registered an affirmative vote for passage. The Wisconsin Senate votes by roll call which makes it possible for everyone to know at once how each senator records his vote as his name is called. At that moment a senator who was safely in the department's camp entered the chamber. Instantly he grasped the fact that voting was proceeding on a motion relating to S245 or to the substitute amendment. Hearing that the committee chairman, of whose views he was acutely aware, had voted affirmatively he assumed that the substance of the motion was inimical to the interest of the bill's backers, and so he registered his vote in opposition. So unsettled did Deputy Timbers become at this point that he rushed onto the senate floor and whispered hurriedly to his friend, who was able to change his vote in time to break the tie vote and assure senate passage of the bill.

The center of attention now shifted to the assembly, where the opposition forces rallied and regrouped for a new attack.[166] They cleaned up their substitute bill, which had been defeated in the Senate, and procured its reintroduction in the lower chamber.[167] The emphasis was now switched from attacks on the bill's constitutionality to more practical objections. Domestic insurers which still opposed the bill argued that retaliation by other states against Wisconsin-domiciled companies, particularly with regard to group policy operations, would seriously impair their ability to compete for large group cases, which would entail the issuance of certificates

---

[166] In the Assembly, the bill was sent first to the Committee on Insurance and Banking, whose chairman was wont to give preferred attention to bills on or near the top of the pile of bills which his secretary kept on the corner of her desk. Commissioner Manson knew this, and he also knew of the secretary's fondness for chocolates. There was a fresh box of chocolates on her desk each day, and S 245 stayed on top of the pile.

[167] Substitute Amendment No. 1 to S 245, offered July 12, 1961. *Wisconsin Assembly Journal* (1961), p. 1767.

to residents of states in which they were not admitted. Others urged rejection on the ground that the tax features applicable to surplus lines and independently procured insurance would result in serious market problems for local insureds.

Final Passage

By this time, though, legislative sentiment definitely favored passage of the department's bill; legislators had begun asking themselves why, indeed, should not all insurance transactions having effect in the state be regulated by the state insurance commissioner. One final attempt was made to water down the bill by incorporating an exemption for locally issued certificates under master group policies lawfully issued to out-of-state policyholders. However, the amendment was beaten down by a two to one majority.[168] The substitute amendment was also defeated, by a majority of three to one,[169] and S245 thereupon passed the assembly. S245, now representing the will of the legislature, was immediately messaged to the governor for approval. Here, too, the opposition forces sought to snatch victory from defeat by rearguing the constitutional issues for the benefit of the governor and his staff. Although the governor's personal legal counsel was urged to recommend a veto, the commissioner, whose views meanwhile had earned the unofficial support of the attorney general's office, was able to prevail. On August 10, 1961,[170] the Governor of Wisconsin affixed his signature to S245, whereupon it became enrolled as Chapter 397 of the Laws of 1961.

So after 16 years of uncertain but steady toil, the final tools for comprehensive and effective state regulation of the business of insurance were at last forged and ready at hand. To the credit of those who in good faith fought so determinedly against the harness, it may be said that they accepted their defeat, on the whole, gracefully and have cooperated both in observing the law and in the department's efforts to enforce it. Those who feared untoward consequences have, up until this time at least, been proved wrong. No report of any retaliatory action on the part of any sister state against a Wisconsin company on account of any provision in S245

---

[168] Amendment No. 1, offered and defeated July 13, 1961. *Wisconsin Assembly Journal* (1961), p. 1830.

[169] July 13, 1961; *Wisconsin Assembly Journal* (1961), p. 1828.

[170] *Wisconsin Senate Journal* (1961), p. 2082.

has been received by the department in the six years since the bill became law. Nor has the surplus lines market "dried up" as some had predicted. On the other hand, mail-order insurance conducted without sanction of law has virtually ceased. Under proper regulation and control of the Wisconsin department, reputable mail-order companies do a flourishing business with Wisconsin citizens. The others no longer do business at all. And in the intervening years it has become manifest that fair regulation, fairly administered, is of special benefit to no single insurer or group of insurers but rather of general benefit to the industry as a whole and to the public which it endeavors to serve.

PART VI

Federal Interest in
Insurance Regulation

chapter 16

An Overview of Federal Interest in Insurance

A MAJOR life insurer recently reviewed its activities involving the federal government and found that it had been in contact with 65 agencies and departments (page 372).

The genesis and ramifications of this widespread federal interest in all insurers is surveyed and analyzed in the selection that follows.

Special attention is given to recent federal investigations of insurance and to a variety of federal controls exercised through agencies such as the Federal Trade Commission, the Securities and Exchange Commission, and the Internal Revenue Service, and federal involvement in the health care area.

THE DIRECT AND INDIRECT EFFECT OF FEDERAL PROGRAMS AND REGULATIONS ON INSURANCE OPERATIONS AND MARKETS

Glendon E. Johnson
President
Great Southern Life Insurance Company

Over the past three decades, the federal government has enlarged the shape and changed the direction of its influence on insurance operations and markets. In recent years, the impingement of federal regulation on and its competition with the private insurance sector has grown more serious. It is the purpose of this paper to explore some of the reasons for the growth of federal involvement in this area and examine its effect on the business of insurance.

If the Founding Fathers of this unique American Republic could have peered into the future 180 years, what pattern of government would they have framed? Although the Supreme Court wrestles continuously with the intrepretations of the words of the framers of the Constitution and looks backward into their intent, the adaptive machinery of the executive and legislative departments of government has moved rapidly ahead to tack new forms to the shape of federal involvement in providing for the security needs and welfare of the American public.

Our initial government formation was based upon the assumption that America was largely an agrarian society and was characterized by the self-sufficiency that accompanies that kind of a society. Today, we are a highly transient society with vast networks of transportation, communication, commerce, and finance as a result of our great technological advances. A mass society is a dependent society filled with specialists. Its citizens are dependent upon others or upon government for the necessities they cannot produce. And they cannot protect themselves against happenings over which they have no control. Metropolitan centers are influenced not only by the governing forces of traditional cities, towns, and counties but by a wide range of overlapping interests of great complexity.

The pressure of these advances and a bulging population has produced tremendous pressures for services of both a governmental and private nature. Increasingly, massed populations have turned away from slower moving local governing bodies to find the answer to their problems at the federal level. At the same time, it is evident that changes of a demographic, economic, and sociological nature are affecting traditional attitudes of the public toward security.

In this paper, I will attempt to trace the impact of federal response to these pressures on the business of insurance with particular emphasis on life and accident and health insurance. To a great extent, the problems facing the insurance business at the Federal level did not develop from attacks on the business of insurance but arose collaterally from the attempts to find solutions, political or economic, to these broad social problems. Whatever their purpose the workings of government in a fast changing world leave their imprint on the business of insurance, affecting the patterns of ownership, sales and service, products, investments, company formation and structure, administration and the form of the insurance business's relations with government and the general public.

STATE VERSUS FEDERAL REGULATION

A young America welcomed the immigrant principle of insurance with enthusiasm, and in the late 1700's "insurance" was well on its way as a vigorous member of the new nation's economic family. Because it was obviously closely connected with the public welfare, it soon became more and more subject to regulation. This supervision started at the state level, and by 1852 Massachusetts had appointed a Board of Insurance Commissioners.[1] Other states followed this lead, and by the end of the Civil War a lively debate was in progress as to whether "insurance" should be regulated at the federal or state level.[2] In fact, as early as 1865, a group of insurance companies were agitating for a uniform federal regulatory statute patterned after the National Banking Act which had been enacted in 1864. Nothing came of these attempts, however.

Paul v. Virginia

The case of *Paul* v. *Virginia,* decided by the Supreme Court in 1869,[3] arose out of an effort on the part of a number of fire insurance companies to secure a ruling from the courts that insurance was interstate commerce and therefore not subject to what they regarded as burdensome state statutes affecting foreign insurance companies. The Supreme Court upheld the *Virginia* statute and in doing so went on to say that the issuance of a policy of insurance was not a transaction of commerce and secondly that a fire insurance policy was a contract of indemnity and not an article of commerce in the proper meaning of the word. The *Paul* decision was relied on for many years to turn back other attacks on state regulation.[4]

---

[1] J. Maclean, *Life Insurance,* (8th ed., New York: McGraw Hill Co., 1957), p. 451; and D. Knowlton, "Planning for the Future of Insurance Regulation," *Insurance* (May 13, 1967), p. 33.

[2] Manual M. Gorman, "Landmarks of Insurance Regulation . . . A Centennial Review" (Continental Assurance Company Conference, September 28, 1966).

[3] 75 U.S. (8 Wall.) 168 (1869).

[4] *Liverpool Ins. Co.* v. *Massachusetts,* 77 U.S. (10 Wall.) 556 (1870); *Ducat* v. *Chicago,* 77 U.S. (10 Wall.) 410 (1870); *Philadelphia Fire Associa-*

Armstrong Investigation

The Armstrong investigation of 1905–6 marked another important step in the development of insurance regulation. Significantly, it resulted in improved state regulation of insurance rather than a new push for federal control. The investigation focused on a number of questionable practices which had developed in the insurance business. Controversy swirled around the use of "tontine" policies, extravagance on the part of some companies and company officers, rebates, high lapse ratios, nepotism, political activities, and contributions. Charles Evans Hughes was counsel for the Armstrong Committee, and his recommendations, covering a broad gamut of life insurance company operation and practices, were adopted by the state of New York and copied in some measure by a number of other states.

New York Life Insurance Co. *v.* Deer Lodge County

No further serious attempt was made to knock down the decision in *Paul* v. *Virginia* until 1913. The case, *New York Life Insurance Co.* v. *Deer Lodge County,* involved $209.79 plus interest resulting from an assessment under a Montana premium tax. The Supreme Court not only upheld *Paul* v. *Virginia* but extended the *Paul* rationale by saying that the manner in which a company conducted its business did not alter the fact that the issuance of a policy of insurance was not a transaction of commerce.[5]

South-Eastern Underwriters Case

A long period of comparative peace followed the Montana case, undisturbed except for the Temporary National Economic Committee hearings and investigation in 1939–40. However, the whole issue was brought into sharp focus in 1942 by a strange cast of characters which saw Attorney General McKittrick of Missouri

---

tion v. *New York;* 119 U.S. 110 (1886); *Hooper* v. *California,* 155 U.S. 648 (1894); *Noble* v. *Mitchell,* 164 U.S. 367 (1896); *New York Life Insurance Co.* v. *Cravens,* 178 U.S. 389 (1899); and *Nutting* v. *Massachusetts,* 183 U.S. 553 (1901).

[5] *New York Life Ins. Co.* v. *Deer Lodge County,* 231 U.S. 495 (1913).

visiting United States Attorney General Biddle on February 12, 1942, to complain, paradoxically, that his office had been frustrated in prosecuting a group of stock fire companies for violation of the Missouri antitrust laws. He felt the interstate nature of the insurance business left state authority powerless to deal effectively with the abuses which were becoming apparent.[6] McKittrick told Biddle that the best interests of the people in his state and elsewhere required action under the federal antitrust laws. Attorney General Biddle, convinced that insurance was interstate commerce, concluded that *Paul* v. *Virginia* and subsequent cases, although they affirmed the right of the states to regulate the business of insurance, were not authority for the proposition that the business of insurance was beyond the power of Congress to regulate. He instituted a test case in Georgia against the Southeastern Underwriters Association and 198 member companies. The charge was violation of the Sherman Act by conspiring to fix rates on fire insurance in the southeastern states, to monopolize trade and commerce in fire insurance in those states, and conspiring to fix commissions and to boycott nonmembers of the association. The lower court relied on *Paul* v. *Virginia* in throwing out the indictment, and on appeal to the Supreme Court, that body after listening to arguments presented by Attorney General Biddle in person, on June 5, 1944, reduced *Paul* v. *Virginia* to memory by holding that the business of insurance is interstate commerce and subject to the Sherman Act. The court said that it was not the nature of an insurance contract but rather the whole chain of events which determined the nature of the transaction. The court noted, however, that the existence of the federal regulatory power did not deny the state the right to regulate those aspects of the business which were related to local welfare.[7]

The McCarran Act

The turmoil created by the decision resulted in the issue being placed before the Congress. The National Association of Insurance Commissioners and the interested industry groups secured the enactment of Public Law 15, the McCarran Act, which declared that

---

[6] See Gorman, *supra* n. 2.

[7] *U.S.* v. *Southeastern Underwriters Association,* 322 U.S. 533 (1944), rehearing denied, 323 U.S. 811 (1944).

continued regulation and taxation of the business of insurance by the several states is in the public interest, that it should be subject to the laws of the several states, and that no act of Congress shall be "construed to invalidate, impair, or supersede any law enacted by any State for the purpose of regulating the business of insurance, or which imposes a fee or tax upon such business."[8]

The insurance business was also given a moratorium period of adjustment to June 30, 1948, at which time the antitrust laws would again become applicable to the business of insurance, but only to the extent that it is not "regulated by state law."

Senate Investigations

During the 1950's the Senate Judiciary Antitrust Subcommittee led by Senator Joseph C. O'Mahoney (D. Wyoming) considered a number of aspects of state regulation in an attempt to measure the efficacy of state regulation. During the fifties and early sixties, the Federal Trade Commission undertook extensive litigation in connection with the solicitation and sale of mail-order health insurance. In 1967, the FTC conducted another investigation of the mail-order life and accident and health insurance business. The study was initiated by Senator Warren G. Magnuson (D. Washington), chairman of the Senate Commerce Committee. Senator Magnuson's interest grew from an investigation by a Washington State Legislative Committee which raised questions as to the adequacy of state regulation in the area of mail-order solicitation. Several states have made efforts to increase their control over "unauthorized insurers," i.e., companies not licensed by a state but which solicit business in that state by mail. California has proceeded against a number of these companies under its general insurance statutes contending that the companies are "doing business" within the state. Wisconsin has adopted a statute specifically regulating mail-order companies. The validity of the statute was upheld by the Wisconsin Supreme Court, and the U.S. Supreme Court dismissed an appeal from that decision on the ground that no substantial federal question was involved.[9]

---

[8] 15 U.S.C. secs. 1011 *et seq.* (1964).

[9] See Chapter 15 for a detailed discussion of the development of the Wisconsin legislation on which the Supreme Court decision turned. *Ministers Life and Casualty Union* v. *Haase,* 30 Wis. 2d 339, 141 N.W. 2d 287, appeal

In 1965 the Senate Judiciary Antitrust Subcommittee, now chaired by Senator Thomas Dodd (D. Connecticut), held hearings on the difficulties presented to policyholders and third-party claimants from the insolvency of a number of "high-risk" automobile insurers. The investigation has since been expanded to other fronts.

Other Recent Federal Interest

President Johnson in a special message to the Congress in 1967 called for a broad gauge investigation into the abuses in the automobile insurance field. Credit life insurance is claimed to be inadequately regulated at the state level and the Senate Antitrust and Monopoly Subcommittee, now chaired by Senator Philip A. Hart (D. Michigan), held hearings on the subject in May, November, and December of 1967. No other action has been taken by the senate, but it is entirely possible that some remedial legislation may be introduced in the 91st Congress. Collaterally, there has been criticism of weaknesses in the staffing of state insurance departments as well as the difficulty of state regulators in supervising mail-order insurance. In a speech presented at a Continental Assurance Company conference on "Trends in Life Insurance Regulation and Taxation" on September 28, 1966, Dean E. Sharp, assistant counsel of the Senate Subcommittee on Antitrust and Monopoly, pointed out a number of areas where he thought state supervision was inadequate. He said that the time had come when the present regulatory system should not be tinkered into correction but that "fundamental reform is necessary to achieve the objectives of sound insurance regulation."[10] John F. Bolton, Jr., director, Department of Insurance of the State of Illinois, speaking at the same conference, rebutted Sharp by declaring that the "American economy and our modern society has been well served by the delegation of regulatory powers over insurance to the various states."[11] He said to continue to improve state regulation, the state legislatures would have to con-

---

dismissed, 385 U.S. 205 (1966). See *People* v. *United Nat'l Life Ins. Co.,* 53 Col. Rep. 639, 58 Col. R. 607, 427 P. 2d 199 (1967), appeal dismissed, 389 U.S. 330 (1968).

[10] Dean Sharp, "It's Too Late to Defend the 'Status Quo'" (Continental Assurance Company Conference, September 28, 1966).

[11] John F. Bolton, Jr., untitled (Continental Assurance Company Conference, September 28, 1966).

tinue to supply regulators with the tools and finances to perform the task. He underscored the fact that only 4 percent of the funds collected from insurance companies is allocated to regulatory departments and that more adequate finances were necessary to properly staff regulatory departments.

Director Bolton was followed by Robert E. Dineen, then President of Northwestern Mutual Life Insurance Company, himself a past New York Superintendent of Insurance, who admitted there was a need for improvement at the state level but expressed his preference for state regulation on two grounds: (1) it is closer to home; and (2) if federal regulation should come, state regulation would continue, so there would be dual regulation.[12]

There is a great deal of evidence that the NAIC is moving aggressively to overcome deficiencies of coordination. For example, the NAIC is (1) planning improvements of the central office and has already started to augment its staff, (2) creating a central library of technical information, and (3) establishing training seminars for new commissioners and training programs for examiners.[13]

INDIRECT REGULATION AND CONTROL

From the foregoing, it is easy to see that regulation of insurance, at least to the present, lies in the hands of state regulatory bodies. Despite that fact and aside from any fallout from the examination into the efficacy of state regulation, it is also apparent that both the Congress and various federal departments and agencies exert considerable control over the operations and markets of life insurance companies.

One major life insurance company recently reviewed its activities which involved the federal government and found that it had been in contact with 65 agencies and departments.[14]

Government policies in the areas of monetary and fiscal control are of direct concern to the life insurance business. The interest of the business in economic growth, price stability, and employment

---

[12] Robert E. Dineen "State of the Union" (Continental Assurance Company Conference, September 28, 1966).

[13] James L. Bentley, "Revamping of NAIC Seen Stemming Flow toward Federal Rule," *The National Underwriter* (Life ed., April 22, 1967), p. 2.

[14] Institute of Life Insurance, *With an Eye to Tomorrow* (1967), p. 133.

fluctuation is reflected in the close watch the business maintains through its trade organizations on the federal budget and appropriations, federal debt management, fiscal legislation, and Federal Reserve Board policy.

In some areas the federal government is a direct competitor showing increasing activity in direct or guaranteed lending. To mention but a few of the agencies involved in this activity points up how significant they have become: The Federal Housing Administration, Veterans' Administration, Farmers' Home Administration, Federal National Mortgage Association, Small Business Administration, and Federal Land Banks.

Social security, a relative newcomer born in the 1930's, has grown to gigantic proportions, both in the size of its commitments and in the scope of its operations. Because of the developing of their interests, the life insurance business is constantly placed in the position of reassessing its role as social security benefits are liberalized. The latest of these benefit liberalizations raises the taxable wage base to $7,800 and puts a strain on the concept that the social security system should provide a "basic floor-of-protection." Since the average wage in the United States is closer to $6,000 than $7,800 and benefits parallel covered salary in large degree, it is clear that the system is "invading" the area of "adequacy" which has been thought to belong to the private sector in providing supplementary security arrangements to social security benefits.

In some areas, life companies are in partnership with the federal government. The Health Care to the Aged program including Medicare, enacted in 1965, is being administered in part by life and health insurance companies and Blue Cross and Blue Shield, acting as intermediaries in the administration of hospital and medical care. Life companies provide federal employees group life coverage (FEGLI) as well as a portion of the Federal Employees Health Benefits Plan[15] and coverage to United States servicemen (SEGLI).

An insurance company acts as the administrator of a large part of the program providing medical care for dependents of servicemen.

During the last 20 years there has been a dramatic growth in the number of areas in which the federal government has extended its activities with respect to the business of life insurance. As a regulator it exerts authority over the business in many areas.

---

[15] These programs have been in effect since 1954 and 1959 respectively.

Regulation of Trade Practices

The Federal Trade Commission and the Department of Justice exercise jurisdiction over group boycotts, unlawful acquisitions, and false advertising. Jurisdiction over group boycotts was preserved for the federal government by the McCarran Act,[16] and jurisdiction over unlawful acquisitions and false advertising results from either the absence, inadequacy, or impossibility of state regulation.[17] In an address before the Legal Section of the American Life Convention in Dallas, October 24, 1967, Paul Rand Dixon, chairman of the FTC, said that he expected the commission to show much more interest in insurance company mergers and acquisitions than had formerly been the case.[18] At the same time, Chairman Dixon acknowledged that studies have shown that price competition can and does thrive in the life insurance business, that the fear that price competition would produce a rash of company insolvencies has proved groundless, and that studies to date clearly indicated that inadequacies of premium structure have not been responsible for company failures.[19] Despite this, he warned that there were some negative signs. Chief among these is the increased merger rate within the industry coupled with what he described as notable weaknesses in state regulation of mergers. He said these factors pointed to increased federal concern and possible future federal action.[20]

Chairman Dixon said that during the past five years the FTC had received over 700 complaints, the majority of which dealt with mail-order insurance advertising. He cited the *Travelers Health*

---

[16] 15 U.S.C. sec. 1013 (b) (1964).

[17] *Ibid.*, sec. 1012 (b).

[18] Paul R. Dixon, "Federal Antitrust Laws and the Insurance Industry," *Proceedings of the Legal Section, American Life Convention* (1967), p. 251.

[19] Donald P. McHugh, "An Industry Outlook—Casualty Insurance," *Insurance Law Journal* (September, 1963), p. 551.

[20] Dixon, *supra* n. 18. See the decisions in *Maryland Casualty Co.* v. *American General Insurance Co.*, 232 F. Supp. 620 (D.D.C. 1964); and *United States* v. *Chicago Title and Trust Co.*, 242 F. Supp. 56 (N.D., Ill. 1965), which support the conclusion that Section 7 of the amended Clayton Act remains a viable statute for challenging insurance company mergers, irrespective of efforts by the various states to legislate in the area.

Association case[21] as authority for the commission to challenge the advertising practices of a mail-order insurer that is not effectively regulated in the states in which the company's practices have their impact. It is especially hard to see where the jurisdiction ceases when a state statute is present.

In a release dated November 23, 1967, the FTC announced completion of its investigation of alleged misleading and deceptive practices in the mail-order insurance industry. The commission noted that practices of approximately 72 companies had been considered and that the majority "operate in a proper and forthright manner." The FTC stated, however, that many companies involved in the investigation are "not subject to effective state regulation as they are not licensed in the state to which the mailings are sent, nor do they maintain resident agents in these states."

The commission listed a series of eight practices regarded as "misleading and deceptive." At the top of the list was the practice of offering insurance policies to parents of servicemen in a misleading manner due to the implication that the policy is made available through the U.S. government. Also branded as misleading and deceptive were circumstances indicating endorsement by the U.S. government of accident, health or life insurance policies, or that such policies are offered at "government rates." Other complained-of practices referred to advertising relating to renewability, cancellation, preexisting health conditions, and the use of well-known company names in misrepresenting the business status of the soliciting mail-order company.

In describing these and other complaints the FTC issued its first consumer bulletin entitled *Pitfalls to Watch for in Mail Order Insurance Policies* which explains and illustrates the deceptive practices the FTC says it encountered. The commission gave no indication of plans for further study or action in cases where in its judgment it found misleading and deceptive practices to exist.[22]

---

[21] *Travelers Health Association* v. *FTC*, 298 F.2d 820, 824 (8th Cir. 1962). This case was appealed to the Supreme Court. Held: FTC has regulatory authority. The rationale was that the state regulation that Congress provided would displace federal law meant regulation by the state in which the insurer's activity is practiced and has its impact. See *FTC* v. *Travelers Health Association*, 362 U.S. 293 (1960).

[22] FTC Bulletin, *Pitfalls to Watch for in Mail Order Insurance Policies* (November, 1967).

Regulation of Sale of Insurance to Servicemen

The Department of Defense exercises jurisdiction over the solicitation and sale of insurance on all military installations irrespective of where they are located. The department has established a set of regulations affecting both company and agent and collaterally authorizes and regulates the use of military allotments in payment of life insurance premiums.[23]

The insuring company must be accredited by the department before it can solicit on any U.S. military installation in a foreign area. The accreditation is on a year-by-year basis and may be revoked at any time. While the company has a right to appeal accreditation denial, the action taken by the Assistant Secretary of Defense for Manpower on the appeal is final. To secure accreditation to solicit business on a military installation in the United States, a company must be licensed in the state in which the installation is located and submit an application to the commanding officer for his approval. The installation commander may suspend or withdraw the accreditation at any time, and the appeal of any local determination again is decided by the Assistant Secretary of Defense for Manpower. The procedures are generally informal, but the regulation is strict and effective.

Regulation of Labor

The Department of Labor exerts considerable influence upon both the commercial operations of an insurance company and its capacity as an employer.

a) The Bureau of Labor Standards and the Bureau of Labor Statistics and the concomitant wage and hour standards requirements are well known to company personnel officers and lawyers.

b) Under the Welfare and Pension Plan Disclosure Act administered by the newly merged Office of Labor-Management and Welfare-Pension Reports, employers are required to file an initial description of their welfare and pension plans (Form D-1) and file annual reports thereafter on their operation. Insurers of these plans

---

[23] See Department of Defense Directive 1334.1, *Solicitation of Life Insurance on Military Installations* (March 3, 1964); and Department of Defense Directive 7330.1, *Voluntary Military Pay Allotments* (December 12, 1956).

are required to furnish to employers the information necessary to the filing of these descriptions and reports. The Welfare and Pension Plan Disclosure Act has become almost inextricably involved in considerations affecting pensions generally, and hence its future and the regulatory pattern affecting life companies may be linked to such proposals as federal standards for fiduciary responsibility of pension trustees, audits, recommendations relating to plan administration, fulfillment of pension expectations, and expanding pension plans to more workers.[24]

c) The Taft-Hartley Act and amendments to its provisions are of concern to the life insurance business since the act covers employer benefits to trusts established to provide fringe benefits to employees.[25]

The Equal Pay and Equal Employment Opportunity Act was designed to prevent discrimination in connection with employment on the basis of race, creed, religion, national origin, or sex. Insurance companies share with most other employers the responsibility to report annually to the Equal Employment Opportunity Commission the ethnic backgrounds of their employees, the operation of apprentice programs if they exist, as well as other information required by the EEOC Information Report EEO-1. The commission has had under consideration the possibility of discrimination in employer-sponsored programs of insurance which provide different benefits for men and women. Insurers are affected by the act and the implementing regulations issued by the commission, especially as they involve fringe benefit coverages sold by insurers to employers.

During the first session of the 90th Congress the Senate Labor Subcommittee held hearings on measures introduced by Senator Jacob Javits (R. New York) and Senator Ralph Yarborough (D. Texas) designed to prohibit discrimination in employment on the basis of age, except where age is considered a bona fide occupational qualification. Congress accepted the theory presented by the life company trade associations suggesting that employee pension and insurance plans should be exempted from the proposed law.[26] The

---

[24] Glendon E. Johnson, "1967 Report on Federal Legislation and Regulation," *Proceedings of the Legal Section, American Life Convention* (1967), p. 310.

[25] Institute of Life Insurance, *With an Eye to Tomorrow,* Report on the Future Outlook Study (1967), p. 130.

[26] Johnson, *supra* n. 24, p. 312.

insurance testimony emphasized that age and age-related factors were necessary and important factors in designing and underwriting all insurance plans. The Bill (S. 830) became Public Law 90–202 on December 14, 1967. The act notes that the terms of a bona fide seniority system or benefit plan may be observed except that it shall not be used simply as an excuse for failure to hire an individual. Although put to bed for the time being, the continuing dialogue over employment opportunity and discrimination presents an area of concern to insurers that legislation and regulation in these areas, designed to prevent discrimination, could hamstring bona fide attempts to provide useful and meaningful insurance benefits.

Securities Regulation

The Securities and Exchange Commission exerts regulatory control over life insurance companies with respect to the issuance of its own stock, as well as proxy and insider trading regulation of stock insurance companies. It also regulates the issuance of equity-funded contracts such as variable annuities and segregated account group annuity contracts. The SEC continues to be interested in the formation of new life insurance companies, although the rate of new company formation is dramatically reduced compared to the rate of a few years ago.

Under current law, the Securities and Exchange Commission contends that all variable annuity contracts, including segregated account qualified group annuity contracts, are subject to the 1933 Securities Act, the Securities Exchange Act of 1934, and the 1940 Investment Company Act. In 1963 the SEC issued Rule 3 c-3 which exempted certain segregated account group annuity contracts from the Investment Co. Act of 1940 if they (1) provided for fixed-dollar retirement annuities; (2) were issued in connection with qualified pension plans; (3) prohibit the allocation of employee contributions to the segregated account; and (4) have at least 25 employees at the outset. In 1964 the SEC liberalized the first requirement by permitting a variable payout. In August, 1963, the SEC issued Rule 156 which exempted from the registration provisions of the Securities Act of 1933 transactions with respect to these contracts. The SEC followed this administrative exemption policy by issuing certain "no-action" letters under the Investment Company Act of 1940 in the case of certain group annuity contracts for use under employed (H.R. 10) retirement plans.

Despite the enlightened and sympathetic administration of this area by the SEC, life insurance companies remain at a competitive disadvantage with banks because of the limitations of the exemptive rules as compared to the much earlier statutory exemptions permitted the banks.[27] The life company trade associations are currently engaged in discussions with the SEC to secure a position of equality with the banks.[28]

The rapid growth of insurance company interest in the equity-funded area, including both variable annuities and equity-funded segregated accounts, has been characterized by an early bid for judicial exemption from the SEC jurisdiction,[29] and failing in that by a continuing attempt to secure administrative exemptions from provisions of the various securities acts which do not fit the pattern of these products. The life company associations (ALC–LIAA) have presented memoranda to the commission addressed to the specific problem areas and making recommendations for relief.[30] Questions have also arisen in connection with the application of the broker-dealer provisions of the Securities Exchange Act of 1934 to persons involved in the sale of variable annuities. The SEC and the NAIC have collaborated with a good degree of success in working out some of the problems in this area.[31]

The impact of federal regulation on the marketing of an insurance product is clearly exposed by the shock experienced by a number of life companies who received a letter from the SEC in late 1967 questioning the validity of their registration statements on file with the SEC relating to tax-sheltered (IRS Sec. 403[b]) annuities.

The SEC letter stemmed from its concern with Revenue Ruling 67–388, issued by the Internal Revenue Service, which dealt with whether or not contracts were "made available" within the meaning of the Regulations. The SEC letter indicated that the companies

---

[27] Section 3 (c) (13) of the Investment Company Act of 1940 exempts "any employee's stock bonus, pension, or profit-sharing trust which meets the conditions of section 401 of the Internal Revenue Code, relating to the qualification of such plans."

[28] Johnson, *supra* n. 24, p. 294.

[29] *SEC* v. *Variable Annuity Life Ins. Co.,* 359 U.S. 65 (1959); *SEC* v. *Prudential Ins. Co. of America,* 377 U.S. 953 (1966); *SEC* v. *United Benefit Life Ins. Co.,* 387 U.S. 202 (1967).

[30] Johnson, *supra* n. 24, p. 296.

[31] For an excellent discussion of these problems, see Loss, "Symposium on Equities and Life Insurance," *Proceedings of the Legal Section American Life Convention* (1967), p. 57 *et seq.*

might have a false registration statement on file with the SEC because the statements contained a legal opinion to the effect that the annuity to be issued would qualify under Internal Revenue Code Section 403(b). These companies then had to submit a request for ruling to the IRS as to whether or not their contracts were "made available" within the meaning of Revenue Ruling 67–388. Meanwhile, a significant cloud existed on a life insurance product which had been marketed without complaint for many years.

Stock life companies have never been exempted from the Securities Act of 1933, and more than 100 life insurance companies that have made public offerings since 1936 have been meeting the reporting requirements of Sections 13 and 15(d) of the Securities Exchange Act of 1934.

On August 20, 1964, President Johnson signed the Securities Act Amendments of 1964 into law (Public Law 88–467). These amendments, called by the Securities and Exchange Commission the most significant statutory advances in federal securities regulation and investor protection since 1940, affect the obligations of issuers of securities and broker-dealers. During the legislative process, an exemption from the provisions of the act was accorded insurance companies if they meet certain requirements spelled out below.

The legislation was designed to achieve two major objectives. The first is to require issuers of securities which are traded in "over-the-counter" transactions to meet the disclosure requirements required of companies whose securities are listed on an exchange. For this purpose, the registration, periodic reporting, proxy solicitation, and insider reporting and trading provisions of the 1934 Exchange Act were extended to a significant portion of the securities traded in the "over-the-counter" markets. During the course of legislative consideration of the bill, insurance companies were exempted from the new registration and reporting requirements provided the insurance company is regulated by the state of incorporation in certain major areas. The second objective is to strengthen the standard of entrance in the securities business and extend the disciplinary controls of the SEC and self-regulatory rules of the broker-dealer organizations, security brokers and dealer organizations, security brokers and dealers and persons associated with them.

The bill finally approved by the Congress exempted the securities of a stock insurance company if all of three conditions are met.

They are: (1) the insurance company is required to and does file annual reports with a state official or agency substantially in accordance with the requirements prescribed by the National Association of Insurance Commissioners; (2) it is regulated in the solicitation of proxies in accordance with the requirements prescribed by the NAIC; and (3) after July 1, 1966, the purchase and sale of securities issued by the insurance company by beneficial owners, directors, or officers of the company are subject to regulation (including reporting) substantially in the manner provided in Section 16 of the Securities Exchange Act of 1934.

The first requirement is satisfied by the filing of the Annual Statement blank. The NAIC acted quickly to provide the proxy regulation called for in the second requirement. At the December, 1964, meeting of the NAIC, the commissioners prescribed guideline regulations relating to proxies and solicitations as a further spelling out of the information to be supplied stockholders in connection with proxies under the Stockholder Information Supplement adopted earlier by the NAIC. Some states also felt it desirable to make statutory provision for the adoption of the proxy regulations and took steps to enact such legislation.

At the December, 1964, meeting the NAIC distributed to member commissioners a model insider trading bill designed to satisfy the third requirement for exemption when enacted into law by the state prior to July 1, 1966, and when accompanied by appropriate regulation.

The SEC is expected to report to the Congress in the near future that insurance company and state regulator performance has been generally satisfactory and that there is no need for further federal legislation or action.

Tax Regulation

The tax laws, implemented and administered by the Treasury Department and the Internal Revenue Service, have exerted great influence on the life insurance business.

In fact, there is a great deal of evidence that tax law and regulation have not only influenced the competitive structure of the business but have had the effect of channeling the activities of a number of companies into certain product areas. The old saying "the power to tax is the power to destroy" could well be reworded to include growth elements as well. The following examples point up the influence of tax laws and regulation on the business of life insurance:

a) The private pension plan business now covers over half the working force in the United States and has book value assets in excess of $95 billion,[32] but the Revenue Act of 1942 provided the initial incentive for employers to cover their workers.

b) It would be difficult to measure the contribution to the growth of group term life insurance by an Internal Revenue Service ruling in 1920[33] that the premiums paid by an employer were not income to an employee. We are still witnessing both pluses and minuses to the group life business by the 1964 Revenue Act provision placing a limit on the tax-free amount of group life insurance that may be provided an employee by his employer.[34]

Over the past five years the Internal Revenue Service has changed the tax effect on the policyholder of so-called "bank-loan or minimum deposit plans," discount on prepaid insurance premiums, employee group term coverage, split-dollar plans, all of which have had varying effect on the sale of the plans. In a very real sense, the tax rules can determine the nature of life insurance products, and the ability to compete with other "security" products in the marketplace.

The Life Insurance Company Tax Act of 1959, placing companies on a total income approach for the first time since 1921, has thrust upon life companies a myriad of tax problems and new procedures entirely new to them. The problems were sufficiently complex that the Internal Revenue Service suspended the closing of life company audits in 1964, pending resolution of a number of controversial items common to the business. The suspense was in effect for three years and only lifted on May 10, 1967. Considering the fact that the act came into being in 1959 and that regulations had been issued shortly thereafter, it was a long period of time for life companies not to know the full extent of their tax liabilities. Proponents of federal regulation who believe federal regulation would eliminate delay and confusion may well ponder the experi-

---

[32] Johnson, *supra* n. 24, p. 254.

[33] Solicitor's L. Op. 1014, *Cum. Bull. 88* (1920), p. 2.

[34] William B. Harman, Jr., *Life Insurance Company Procedure before the Internal Revenue Service and Other Major Federal Government Agencies.* (The Association of Life Insurance Counsel, May 5, 1964.)

ence of the business with the Revenue Service, which is by deserved reputation, one of the most effective and responsible of federal agencies.

On the horizon looms a reexamination by the Congress of an early review of federal estate and gift tax law. The Treasury is currently continuing its study of the social security integration rules in the pension area. All these and many more are of great concern —both to the operation of life companies, their profit structure, and their competitive stance with other financial institutions.

Merger Regulation

The Department of Justice continues to keep a watchful eye on insurance company mergers. No attempt has been made to block any of the numerous insurance company mergers in recent years with the exception of the *Chicago Title and Trust Company* case.[35] This is probably because the insurance business has a relative lack of concentration with the trend being toward the largest companies writing a lesser share of new business. These factors coupled with the ease of entry into the insurance business diminishes the antitrust threat. Of more concern to federal officials is the recent trend toward holding companies or financial conglomerates. In this area, both state and federal authorities have started to show concern.

In New York, a prestigious committee was appointed to consider the impact of holding company formations on the business and policyholders alike. The committee report issued early in 1968 catalogs a number of problems, suggests some answers, and is an important part of the increasing dialogue taking place between federal and state regulators and some elements of the business.[36]

The interlocking relationships between large corporations, particularly in the financial area, have been a matter of concern to federal officers and the Congress. Congressman Wright Patman (D. Texas) chairman of the House Committee on Banking and Currency, has expressed his concern in this area for a number of years. In 1965, the House Judiciary Committee issued a staff report concluding that insurance company and bank interlocks should be

[35] *United States* v. *Chicago Title & Trust Co.,* 242 F. Supp. 56 (N.D. Ill. 1965).

[36] Report to the New York Superintendent of the Special Committee on Insurance Holding Companies (1968).

subjected to federal controls in order to reduce insurance influence over noninsurance segments of the economy. Evidence that such influence exists to any real degree is small, and legislation (H. R. 11572) introduced in 1965 by Judiciary Committee Chairman Emmanuel Celler (D. New York) designed to prohibit such interlocks on boards of directors was not widely supported.

HEALTH CARE

Perhaps in no other area of insurance has the role of the federal government been expanded more rapidly than in the area of health care. Because of this collision of the expanding goals of the federal government and the health insurance business, it affords the viewer a large-scale picture window through which to view the process.

Within the last six years Congress has approved more than three dozen major pieces of health legislation. A large portion of these measures contain provisions which introduce separate subprojects which multiply the number of actual programs presently operated by the federal government. The sheer volume of health activity by the 89th Congress alone is impressive and has paved the way for federal advances in every area of health.

In addition, health was an important component of other major legislation, i.e., the area redevelopment and poverty programs. The federal government now provides a wide range of health services from vaccines and local health care centers to the construction of research facilities and Medicare.

Viewed separately this activity appears to represent scattered pieces of a very large mosaic. The programs are individual and distinct and yet interlocking to form a kaleidoscope of an evolving all-encompassing federal health care picture. Basically, these programs can be classified into six areas of interest:

1. Programs designed to further research in the solution of disease problems and the advancement of biochemical knowledge.
2. Programs designed to remove financial barriers to medical care.
3. Programs designed to improve the quality and availability of health services.
4. Programs concerning consumer and environmental health protection.

5. Programs to meet manpower and facility requirements for health services.
6. Programs designed to support local, regional and State initiative in public health.

The debate is continuing with respect to defining the federal role in meeting the health care needs of this nation. Medicare is unquestionably the foundation of the federal effort. It has projected the federal government in the health care field to provide health care as a matter of right—instead of a qualified need—to a segment of our population. From Medicare the government derives experience in the financing and administration of health care benefits. It is the federal illustration of its capability to operate a nationwide health care program. It is also the federal guide for other programs of a similar nature with respect to acceptable benefits, standards of care, and reimbursement of costs.

The federal objective: quality health care readily accessible to all people at a reasonable cost. Medicare cannot be examined in a vacuum. It is a part of the whole and must be considered in relation to the total spectrum of health programs under development by the federal government.

The second political issue rapidly approaching maturity is the determination of the responsibility of the federal government in the organization of health care facilities and the quality of the services rendered. Federal standards—either direct or indirect—with respect to the practice of medicine seem unavoidable. This is a simple administrative fact of life. Either the government exercises control over the costs and quality of the service of its programs or it cannot meet its pronounced objectives.

The federal government is most concerned, due in large part to its limited Medicare experience, about containing medical costs and providing access to quality care. It has embarked upon a series of planning and conciliatory conferences with physicians, hospital administrators, public health officials, and insurers searching for a method of control. This it justifies on the basis of consumer interest in quality care and the price paid for it.

The final political issue concerns the decision to use general revenue financing in the federal exercise of health care objectives. Resistance in the private sector is strong, but the controversy remains. The social security system is reaching the limits of its taxable percentage and still the costs of the program are mounting at a phenomenal rate. The federal government must release its health care programs from this financial enclosure or reduce its expansion activities under social security and search for another method of delivery.

All of these federal health care programs are currently in the planning or initial stages of development. Many are to be considered by Congress for funding and extension within the next few years. They have been called a "series of promissory notes" which if they are to be honored by the Department of Health, Education and Welfare, must be manageable and capable of delivering their benefits to the public or else face rejection.

The Department of Health, Education and Welfare realizes that it has reached the edge of an abyss with its health care programs. It cannot justify further expansion without added management ability and skilled personnel. For the next five years this will be its prime target. Programs have been slowed by the absence of an organized, workable delivery mechanism.

The Department of Health, Education and Welfare has over one hundred separate health programs providing assistance to states, local governments, universities, private research organizations, voluntary agencies, and others in the health care field which it must administer. Many of these projects must be tailored to suit individual localities, and it is finding it difficult to prepackage a federal solution and start to impose on communities. The federal government must, instead, supply the communities with the ingredients that can be utilized to form an effective program. This demands federal cooperation at the local level and a vast field organization which requires competent management. "Middle management" is becoming as important to the federal government as it is to private enterprise. This requires modernization and a reorganization of present methods of federal delivery. Since 1964, the federal government has entered an era of cooperation and partnership. This movement is labeled "creative federalism" and features the formation of an administrative network between federal, state, local, and nongovernmental interests in an effort to implement federal programs.

Through the disposition of federal funds, the Department of Health, Education and Welfare attempts to exercise great influence on the characteristics and organization of local health units. Title XIX (Medicaid) is a good example of varying matching fund percentages and federal program requirements which provide the ingredients of the basic program.

Federal health programs are also fragmented among various federal agencies and departments. Local health authorities are forced to go shopping in the "federal market" for various bits and pieces of an overall health program which they are providing. The Department of Health, Education and Welfare is currently in a reorganization process and making an increased effort to obtain general grants and programs from Congress to replace specific categorical financing.

Political reasons compel Congress to legislate in categorical rather than general fashion. First, it is difficult to attain concurrence and agreement on broad general issues. Passage of grants for specific subareas can be more easily accomplished. Second, all general aid programs tend to pass major decision making powers from Congress to other political leaders and possible future opponents in the state organization. A legislator's political future depends upon his ability to please his constituents, and one of the most effective ways for him to prove this is by voting for specific categorical measures. The comprehensive health planning measures are moving away from the categorical approach to provide general grants for a wide range of uses. The exact range of these goals will be determined to a great degree by the quality of the performance of the private sector. There is little evidence that the federal answers will not be forthcoming if there is significant default by the providers of private insurance mechanisms.

CONCLUSION

The government is large and getting larger. The business of insurance and the federal government share a common goal in helping to provide for the security needs of American citizens. Hopefully, a more clear delineation of responsibility vis-à-vis the federal government, state government, and the private sector is in the process of being determined. Where the line will be drawn and how long it remains intact will depend in large measure on the quality and the nature of the response of private institutions to the challenges posed by the federal government.

With respect to regulation it appears that the states will continue to exercise jurisdiction through their regulatory officials. Frequently, the federal government will overlap that jurisdiction or subject the efficacy of state regulation to examination. Federal regulatory bodies will continue to exert an influence on the shape of insurance company products, services, and markets and to a large extent on the nature of the company itself. There seems little doubt that the insurance business has a demonstrated capacity to adapt to these shifting patterns. The very size and continuing growth of the business testifies to its public acceptance and to its capacities.

chapter 17

Federal Regulation of Pensions: A New Approach

THE FOLLOWING SELECTION proposes a new plan for federal regulation of pensions through the tax law. The approach is called "ERITD" (Earned Retirement Income Tax Deferral).

Under the plan, every person would be allowed to defer the taxes on up to perhaps 20 percent of his earned income by placing that percentage of income in an approved retirement program, meeting specified standards relating to vesting, funding, assignability, non-cashability, and other characteristics.

The author argues that this approach would help achieve adequacy of benefits, mobility of human resources, flexibility, needed capital formation, and enhancement of the tripartite partnership of public pensions, private pensions, and personal savings.

PENSIONS ARE FOR PEOPLE

The "ERITD" (Earned Retirement Income Tax Deferral) Approach to Federal Regulation of Pensions

Dr. William C. Greenough
*Chairman, Teachers Insurance and Annuity Association
and College Retirement Equities Fund*

Private pension plans in the United States have now reached the highest level of service to the public and to the economy ever achieved in this or any other country, in this or any other time. And yet their potential for even greater service to this country and its people is just beginning to be realized.

In the last quarter century, the number of people covered by private pension plans has increased from 4 million to 26 million, and the assets supporting prospective benefits have increased from $2.4 billion to $94 billion. By 1980, we should see the number of people covered reaching more than 41 million, representing 44 percent of the working force, and with assets to support benefit payments growing to more than $193 billion.

Or am I blind? Are nongovernmental pensions already on the way out? Are the seeds of their destruction already planted? Will we increase social security benefits so much that there is no room for private pensions? Will we overemphasize regulation and supervision to the point where we hamper imagination and innovation? Will we standardize so severely that we discourage diversity, so demandingly that we halt development of the private pension sector?

The things we do in the next few years will determine whether the coming quarter century will see private pensions make enormous social and economic contributions to the country or see them dwindle and die.

This paper will attempt to ask different questions than those usually posed by lawyers, regulators, and tax experts. It will propose a different solution than those heretofore proposed, and perhaps will arouse some discussion that might lead to worthwhile shifts in approach. In preparation, I have been giving a good deal of thought as to how public action can encourage and reinforce the public service function of private pensions—how it can establish the best "climate."

To begin, let me propose a new priority: PENSIONS ARE FOR PEOPLE. How obvious! Of course!

Perhaps it is obvious, but our regulatory and tax structure, our competitive approach, the type of pensions generally used—group annuities and trust fund plans—and the attitude of many people toward pensions are company oriented, not people oriented. And almost always one-company oriented! Repeatedly it is announced that the purpose of pension plans is "to make possible the retirement of older employees whose efficiency has declined," or "to part in a socially acceptable manner with those whose usefulness has been undermined by age," or "to tie our employees to us during their working years."

As an interim objective, this one-company orientation has served us well. The tax laws have encouraged companies to establish pension plans, the competition for talent has pushed them forward, the design of most pension plans has emphasized one-company responsibility, and in the process a large number of people have indeed been served well during their old age. But isn't it time for a change in emphasis? Time to reorient out thinking *toward the individual?* This doesn't mean we should stop thinking about the needs of the firm; but it does mean we should start thinking more about the needs of the individual.

Many years ago we cast aside the old "charity" concept of pensions as a gratuitous reward for long and faithful service, to be handed out arbitrarily and fitfully. More recently we have been challenging the "leave it to the last employer" concept of responsibility, a concept that avoids the degradations of charity but still results in capricious treatment among individuals according to their choice of a "last employer" and whether they work for one firm or several during their careers. I believe we can now adopt a broader goal than the one-employer approach to pensions. And the timing is right. We are now moving toward the far more appropriate concept of funded pension credits constituting a vested part of current compensation from each of a person's employers during each of his working years.

The acceptance of the *pensions are for people* approach leads clearly to the concept that pension credits are a part of current compensation that is set aside for retirement. And this in turn leads to the conclusion that retirement benefits for each individual in our society should always be fully vested in him, that his pension benefits should be wholly funded and invested productively, that each year's obligation of the employer toward each employee should be discharged that year, and that the level of benefit produced by each year's service should not depend on whether the individual leaves an employer or stays with him until retirement.

If we are to emphasize the "people" element in pensions and move toward the improvements which follow from this change in emphasis, we can now work toward new regulatory, supervisory, and tax approaches that will encourage the right developments. New regulation is coming anyway, and coming fast; the only question now is whether its effect on private pensions will be constructive or depressing.

Later on I shall make a specific proposal as to how we might arrive at a "people pensions" approach. I believe it deserves careful consideration. It might even be the answer. Or criticism of it might lead to a better answer.

FEDERAL REGULATION OF PENSION PLANS

For many years the pension world and to some extent the whole benefit world was an overindulged industry, large parts of it being under no direct supervision whatsoever. Those days are passing. Adequate public regulation of this great sector of our life is absolutely necessary. We need not devote time to discussing whether we *should* have federal regulation of pension plans—we already have it. And, things being what they are, there seems to be no question but that the federal government is going to regulate, supervise, and direct this field of endeavor a good deal more than it does now. I want to emphasize that insured pension plans are now regulated under the state insurance laws by state regulatory authorities, and plans funded with state chartered banks are supervised generally under state banking laws. Other state agencies also have similar functions. Incidentally, the proposal to be presented later is unusual in that it does not disturb these state patterns. But since the federal government is already heavily involved in the field of pension regulation and has served notice that it will be in it a good deal more in the future, this paper will focus on the federal scene. Here, the only real points for decision are: regulation by what agency or agencies of the federal government, according to what guidelines, and toward what objectives.

The following is a brief review of existing regulation at the federal level, so brief a review that it oversimplifies and thereby does not give sufficient credit to the thoughtful and energetic efforts of the federal supervisory agencies and their staff members working in their present gerrymandered spheres of control.

Federal Regulation Now Applicable

Internal Revenue Service. The most powerful instrument of federal supervision is, of course, the Internal Revenue Service. Here a certain kind of regulation of commercial employers' pension plans is brought about through the taxing power. The service reviews each employer's plan to determine whether it meets the criteria for federal qualification, which exempts the pension fund from taxation on earnings, makes corporate pension contributions tax deductible to the employer as a cost of doing business, and makes such contributions tax-deferred to the employee until retirement.[1] A separate section[2] establishes a strict set of limitations on the retirement plans of nonprofit organizations as a substitute for federal qualification. Both of these provisions will be discussed later.

The Labor Department. Through the Welfare and Pension Plans Disclosure Act, the Labor Department endeavors to see that people covered by retirement plans receive adequate information regarding the funding and management of those plans.[3]

Federal Trade Commission. The Federal Trade Commission exerts authority over a number of pension plans that are insured by its limited but significant regulation of mail-order insurance.[4]

Proposed Federal Regulation

Federal Extensions Now under Discussion. Suggestions for extensions of federal regulation of pension plans range far beyond the various items of regulation mentioned above.

We are already familiar with the cabinet-level study *Public Policy and Private Pension Programs* released in January, 1965. Its major recommendations include:

1. Improved and earlier vesting.
2. New minimum standards for funding.
3. Broader coverage by the plans.
4. Further study of a system of transference of pension credits.
5. Protection of employees upon termination of a plan.
6. Full disclosure of relevant facts.

Several congressional committees are also concerning themselves with pension matters. The Joint Economic Committee's Subcommittee on Fiscal Policy, headed by Rep. Martha Griffiths (D., Mich.), has made studies of our old-age income assurance systems, and its report has added to the pressure for pension law changes.

---

[1] INT. REV. CODE OF 1954, Secs. 402, 404.

[2] INT. REV. CODE OF 1954, sec. 403(b).

[3] Welfare and Pension Plans Disclosure Act of 1958, P.L. 85–836, 85th Cong., 2d sess., 72 Stat. 997, amended by Act of March 20, 1962, P.L. 87–420, 87th Cong., 2d sess., 76 Stat. 35.

[4] FTC, *Guides for the Mail Order Insurance Industry* (effective July 14, 1964).

Specific Bills Introduced in Congress in 1967. S. 1103, introduced by Sen. Jacob Javits (R., New York), deals with some of the major problem areas pertaining to private pension plans. The bill would establish in the executive branch of the government a new, independent, SEC-type agency—the United States Pension Commission—which would administer and enforce all aspects of the bill. Its purpose is to consolidate the legal requirements relating to all employee benefit funds, including pension plans, under the commission's jursidiction. The bill would set up criteria for communicating provisions of a plan to employees. It would also establish minimum standards for vesting and funding and require periodic reports from all plans. A federal pension reinsurance program would be created to insure against the failure of a plan to pay vested benefits because the employer went out of business. The reinsurance would be optional, but a plan that was not reinsured would not be considered for qualification under the Internal Revenue Code. The bill would also establish a pension portability program and set forth minimum standards for administration of all employee benefit funds (not just pensions). Furthermore, the commission would have enforcement powers.

S. 1635, introduced by Sen. Vance Hartke (D., Ind.), would establish a federal program of insurance for private qualified plans to protect credits earned by employees from the risk of loss. As under the Javits Bill, participation in this insurance would be required as a condition for deduction of employer contributions from taxable corporate income.

H.R. 5741 and S. 1024, the Perkins-Yarborough Bill, provides for full disclosure by employee welfare and pension plans, expanding greatly on the existing Welfare and Pension Plans Disclosure Act by establishing standards of conduct, responsibility, and obligations binding upon all plan managers and others, and by providing sanctions in the case of a breach of such fiduciary standards.

S. 1255, introduced by Sen. John McClellan (D., Ark.), combines fiduciary standards and sanctions, management, and insurance provisions in one package.

Private-Public Action

In many sectors of our economic life the federal government performs a large and growing "climate-setting function." In the benefit field it not only sets the climate but it also accepts a huge direct responsibility for our peoples' welfare through its poverty programs, Aid to Dependent Children, Old Age Assistance, Unemployment Insurance, and Old-Age, Survivors, and Disability Insurance and Medicare. If the private and the public sectors work effectively together, each encouraged to do that part of the job that it does best, then the public programs, other than the broadly based OASDI and Medicare, should contract substantially over the years as the difficulties they were designed to ameliorate are resolved by a combination of private and public action. The elimination of poverty itself and of the various programs depending on direct or indirect "needs tests" is a conclusion greatly to be desired.

SOCIAL SECURITY

The directions already taken and those to come in social security legislation have profound implications for the amount and the kind of pensions needed in the private sector and for their supervision and regulation. Let me mention one specific area where social security can be taken into account in designing the "climate of regulation" for private pensions.

The Internal Revenue Code has been very much concerned over the years to prevent "discrimination" in favor of higher paid employees. The problem of controlling "discrimination" in a pension plan 20 and 30 years ago was one thing; now, with OASDI providing half of salary or more in retirement benefits for all salary up to nearly the $7,500 a year level, the problem is quite different.

In view of those sizable social security benefits, the Internal Revenue Code and the Internal Revenue Service can shift their primary attention from the question of "discrimination" against lower paid individuals *within a single employer's service* to questions of vesting and funding and disclosure. The real problems of discrimination now perhaps relate more to the differential treatment of individuals from industry to industry and from one employer to another; and the differential treatment of two employees, one of whom works for a single employer all his life and the other who shifts jobs one or more times.

OPPORTUNITIES AND DANGERS

It is clear that there are great opportunities and great dangers as legislative and regulatory agencies take increased interest in private pensions. The opportunities include reinforcement of a climate favorable to the general development of private pensions and conducive to their innovative capacity, diversity, and investment productivity. Broader coverage, earlier vesting, and effective investment of pension funds are all trends to be strongly encouraged, so that the sharing of responsibilities between the private and public sectors can be most effectively accomplished. The dangers mostly lie in the possibility that our efforts to strengthen certain aspects of the private pension world and to control specific abuses or imperfections will result (*a*) in requirements that delay the establishment of new plans or the improvement of existing ones; (*b*) in mandating a particular set of provisions to achieve a particular set of social objectives, wherein we may overlook other objectives just as important and introduce pension rigidities or regressions; and (*c*) in establishing minimum standards that might tend to become maximums as well and so halt the rapid improvements now being made. The stakes are clearly high. Will we maximize the gains for the country and for our people, or will we stultify, homogenize, and constrict the whole private pension development?

I have mentioned that our approach so far to private pensions in this country has been *one-company* oriented, not *people* oriented. Approaching pensions from the context of the separate firm results in particular attitudes and problems that are then reflected in the kind of plan set up, in the treatment of individual participants, and in the type of supervision that evolves. Let us take some examples:

1. The firm itself may oppose vesting of retirement benefits because it takes little interest in the treatment of an employee who leaves before retirement. I happen to believe that this is unenlightened self-interest. In any event, it is contrary to the public interest; for society as a whole, early vesting of retirement benefits is essential.

2. The Internal Revenue Service in "qualifying" a pension plan gives a good deal of attention to whether there is "discriminatory" treatment in favor of the higher paid employees in a particular company. But it has no responsibility, nor does any other regulatory agency, to see that the company's workers are treated fairly compared with employees in similar categories in other companies or compared with the needs of particular employment groups or individuals. For example, a corporation can conceivably qualify a pen-

sion plan for favorable tax treatment even though the plan allows little or no vesting of benefits prior to retirement so long as all participants seem to be treated (or mistreated) consistently.

3. The main funding mechanisms that have developed—group annuities and trust funding—are designed for use primarily by separate employers acting separately, with the group contract or pension trust specifying the individual's rights and lack thereof.

4. The benefit formulas that have developed—unit benefits related to final average salary—are sustained by contributions that are small for the young person and very large indeed for the older, highly paid person. This makes true portability of benefits related directly to current compensation nearly impossible to obtain—in fact, true early vesting is a chimera in this kind of arrangement.

Some transition away from this separate firm orientation and toward the individual person is already occurring. Earlier vesting and greater portability, better funding, and, in some employments, emphasis on "money purchase," that is, "current compensation," plans are all signs of this shift of emphasis. (Perhaps "defined contribution plan" is the better name, and I shall use it later.)

I believe a major shift in emphasis is now needed in our approach to private pensions. This is not because private pensions are doing so badly. Quite the contrary! It is precisely because there has been spectacular growth and, in general, great success in private pension plans that we can now take a giant leap forward. This leap will be toward having the great majority of our workers enjoy retirement income directly related to the fruits of their own labor and of the productivity of our economy through pensions oriented to the *individual's* needs and desires and rights as a concomitant to the social orientation of OASDI benefits.

EARNED RETIREMENT INCOME TAX DEFERRAL "ERITD"

I believe there is a way to encourage the trends that lead in the right direction and to discourage the others. This can be done by a twofold provision:

1. Tax deferral for individuals on a stated percentage of earned income, say up to 20 percent, on amounts set aside for retirement income in approved systems.

2. Full disclosure of all pertinent facts regarding investing, plan provisions, and management of approved programs.

Specifically, each employed or self-employed person would be allowed to defer up to, say, 20 percent of his earned income and the taxes on this income by participating in an approved retirement program. The employer, whether a corporation, a college, a self-employed person, would be required to set up a plan or to participate in a broader pooling in order to qualify plan participants for this Earned Retirement Income Tax Deferral.

To add a little precision to this ERITD suggestion, let me offer for discussion the following more detailed explanation. It can help point up the principles involved and perhaps lead to suggesting revisions and refinements to make this approach viable.

ERITD Through Internal Revenue Code and Regulation

The following code provisions relating to ERITD would be the basis for federal regulation of pensions:

1. Funding requirements for prior service benefits at least as strict as at present.
2. Every person would have an individual ERITD allowance determined each year by the following formula:

   ERITD allowance = 20 percent of his earned income for the current year multiplied by his years of full-time employment through the current year (for any employer, including self-employed) minus sums deferred in previous years.
3. The ERITD allowance would apply to contributions made on behalf of an employee by his employer or by the employee himself (including a self-employed person) to an individual annuity contract or to his account in a group annuity or trusteed pension plan provided that such contributions were:

   a) *Fully vested* in the individual for future payment to him as a life annuity or, in event of his death prior to commencement of annuity payments, to his named beneficiary or estate;

   b) *Nonassignable* by the individual or the employer;

   c) *Noncashable* during the individual's lifetime; that is, payable only as an income involving life contingencies;

 d) Reported on the employee's Forms W-2 and 1040 as currently nontaxable income (the employer contribution reportable under a unit benefit plan would be determined in accordance with procedures similar to those now in the regulations for Section 403[b]);

 e) Part of a formal and fully disclosed plan available on a fair and equitable basis to all full-time employees or if not all at least to those who have been in the full-time employment of the current employer for five or more years and have attained age 30.

4. Contributions that qualify for the employee's ERITD allowance would receive the following tax treatment:

 a) Employer contributions would be deductible by the employer as a business expense, and

 b) Employer and employee contributions would not be taxable currently to the employee, but would be taxable as ordinary income to the employee or his beneficiary when received as part of the annuity payments.

5. Investment earnings realized on contributions that qualify for the employee's ERITD allowance would not be taxable currently to the employer, the employee, or the pension fund but would be taxable as ordinary income to the employee or his beneficiary when received as part of the annuity payments.

Testing ERITD against Objectives

This proposal holds up very well indeed—at least I think so—when it is tested against a list of objectives worthy of encouragement through good legislation and public regulation.

DESIRABLE OBJECTIVES FOR PRIVATE PENSION PLANS

 1. *Adequacy* of benefits.
 2. *Mobility* of human resources.
 3. *Flexibility*.
 4. *Capital* formation.
 5. *Enhancement* of tripartite partnership.

Each of these objectives is important because it serves people, because it helps them achieve their economic aspirations, because it helps them live in financial security in a productive economy. Again, people pensions.

1. *Adequacy of benefits.* Achieving adequacy of retirement benefits is a major endeavor. The life expectancy of a man aged 65 is about 15 years, and of at least one member of a couple, both aged 65, is around 21 years. Most working careers are about 40 to 45 years long. This means that *each two years of work have to support one year of retirement.* I believe the ERITD proposal would encourage employers, unions, self-employed people, government, and nonprofit employers and, of course, people, to strive for real economic security during retirement, for reasons outlined later. This security would result from a tripartite cooperation consisting of (*a*) direct governmental benefits from wage taxes through social security, (*b*) employer-employee participation in retirement plans, and (*c*) individual savings of current income until retirement. With reasonable provisions for benefits related to service prior to the start of ERITD, the 20 percent deferral in addition to social security is sufficient to provide a good level of retirement income at all salaries even in light of the necessity for each two working years to support one year of retirement.

2. *Mobility of human resources.* Probably no society in history ever provided greater voluntary mobility of human and material resources than does ours. In trying to improve still further, we must identify and strengthen those areas where additional mobility for advancement of our people is still needed—through broader educational opportunities, through new job availability in depressed areas, and through elimination of barriers of all kinds to mobility of our human resources.

One of the known rigidities in our society is the lack of immediate full vesting or at least early vesting in all too many of our pension plans. This includes the de facto delayed vesting resulting from the unit benefit formula incorporated in final salary pension arrangements. If a person cannot leave a given job and seek one where his particular abilities would be better used, there is an economic, a social, and a personal loss. If the individual is going to have to forfeit a substantial amount of retirement benefits upon leaving, he is a good deal less free to leave. His present employer has an inappropriate economic hold upon him. If he does decide to leave and forfeit part or all of his accrued pension benefits, he comes to any new employer as a pension liability. As such, he may not be acceptable to a new employer. Underutilization of human resources is the result.

The proposed Earned Retirement Income Tax Deferral arrangement would encourage earlier vesting. Corporations could exclude from taxable income monies paid into a pension plan only if they were allocated to and vested in a specific individual's accumulating retirement account. This would encourage employers actually to make such contributions and would also help the individual to realize better than at present that the retirement plan means little for him until vesting actually occurs.

This would enhance the individual's interest in early vesting and would encourage him to seek it as part of his employment opportunities. But unlike the many current proposals for legislative action, there would be no compulsion and no designation of a specified type, term, or point for vesting. It would not establish a particular minimum, which all too often turns into the "normal" or even the maximum.

Mobility with assured benefits, of course, calls for full funding of the vested benefits, whether they are left in the previous employer's plans until the individual's retirement or shifted over to the new one.

Since neither the individual nor the employer would receive any tax deferred credit until funds were actually paid in and ascribed to the individual's account, the ERITD proposal would lead to increased interest in adequate funding and a prevention of even indirect employer recapture of contributions made. Since the contributions of each individual and the employer would have to be put in individual benefit accounts, the individual immediately would have an inducement to take an interest in the funding mechanism and its effectiveness, which, in turn, would encourage more productive investment of pension funds and engender concomitant advantages for economic development. The ERITD suggestion would not in itself lead to adequate funding of all plans, but it would provide a strong and yet flexible *inducement* to funding. It would help to avoid "Studebaker" situations where persons involuntarily separated from a company or industry in its waning years may now be inadequately protected.

In forwarding these goals, the ERITD proposal can help bring us toward a society in which our people have a greater freedom to develop their talents fully either by staying in one job throughout their careers or by changing from job to job as their own personal development and job opportunities dictate.

Social security provides full mobility without loss of benefits among employments covering 90 percent of Americans. Private pension plans have also been moving rapidly toward earlier vesting. With encouragement, perhaps this objective can now rise to first priority as more and more private pension plans accomplish the initial job of providing retirement benefits for people who originally had no expectations and for whom no savings had been made.

Benefits that are fully and immediately vested in the individual have been working effectively for 50 years in the field of higher education. Now 250,000 educators at 2,000 educational institutions are cooperating in the TIAA–CREF nationwide pooling of benefit plans that give them full ownership of each year's accumulating benefits whether they change jobs several times during their careers or stay at one institution the entire time. And they are being financed by 100-cent dollars; a nonprofit employer receives no tax advantage from having a retirement plan.

There are also retirement systems such as unionwide plans, plans covering ministers of given denominations, and Federal Civil Service where opportunities exist for carving out an effective career within a fairly broad range covered by the given retirement plan. However, professional people frequently complain that the separate employer plans found in industry and business work against mobility of chemists, accountants, engineers, actuaries, economists, lawyers, and many of our most important brain-power resources.

3. *Flexibility.* At the present time there is a great deal of flexibility within pension arrangements. This, of course, may be because pensions are not as strictly regulated as other financial organizations. Savings banks, savings and loan institutions, and commercial banks are strictly and comprehensively regulated by law and by supervisory authorities. And as a result, banks of about the same size look pretty much alike. But in the pension field there is broad diversity. There are funded and unfunded plans; there are fixed benefit and there are defined contribution plans; there are plans based largely on equity investments and plans based solely on fixed-dollar investments; there are different plans for nonprofit groups in the colleges, churches, and welfare agencies; there are insured plans and trust fund plans, and there is a wide variety of retirement ages, eligibility provisions, and contribution levels. Benefit schedules vary widely. So do the vesting provisions and the adequacy of funding.

And diversity is intensely to be desired. There should be flexibility across the economic cycle so that both society and the individual building up retirement benefits can adjust well to periods of full employment when compulsory retirement ages are being relaxed and to periods of unemployment when they are being more strictly applied. Experimentation with various methods of funding is also good—variable annuities, split funding, separate accounts, and the more traditional group annuities and trust fund plans.

The full advantages of diversity and pluralism can be most fully realized by the individual if *he* is the participant, if clearly it is part of *his* current compensation that is being set aside in an annuity vested in and owned by him, if funds are actually being accumulated by him and for him. And this is all part of the new ERITD proposal. It would be a substitute, or alternate, to the currently discussed proposals for federal mandating of specific vesting, portability, funding, and participation requirements—moves that have commendable social objectives but which eliminate flexibility. The greatness of this society of ours is related to the fact that it is innovative, it is diverse, it is pluralistic; let us keep it that way in the pension field, too.

4. *Capital formation.* There have been various great waves of capital utilization in this dynamic country. Our earliest settlers effectively utilized the virgin resources of a richly endowed earth; the opening of the West carried the process forward; this was followed by the Empire Builders, the power revolution, automatic machinery, the electronic innovations. A most impressive source of private savings to generate the next great capital goods revolution is private pension savings. It is estimated that a trillion-dollar economy, which we may reach in terms of constant dollars by the year 1975, will require an additional 500 billion dollars of invested capital in the seven years between now and that time. Pension funds, which had total assets of $2.4 billion in 1940, $12 billion in 1950, $52 billion in 1960, and $94 billion in 1967 can provide a substantial portion of this sum.

In this respect social security provides no capital formation for the economy; it is essentially a transfer system that does not and should not build up large reserves. The funds to pay benefits under social security come directly from the current efforts of currently productive people. Again, this is the way a nationwide governmental plan must be financed, and it is quite proper. But it is also proper, and exceedingly important, to have a substantial amount of our benefits for old age provided through capital formation and savings, giving individual rights and equity ownership for participants in addition to their socially determined benefits. It is in the private sector that this can occur and that individuals and concerns can set aside some part of the productivity of this generation to support the people now working when they arrive at old age.

Capital formation is a crucial function of private pension plans. Because this is so, the suggested ERITD method of taxation with its encouragement of private pensions and its emphasis upon full vesting and full funding can assure the continuation and increase of capital production. By emphasizing the importance and viability of the private pension sector, ERITD can continue to keep this sector strong and healthy and therefore productive of investment resources. By encouraging employers to give the "investment position" to the individual, the individual can take more interest in the source of his retirement income and in supporting a healthy economy. This would include a better balance both for the individual and for business as a whole in equity investments through greater participation in variable annuity plans such as CREF.[5]

The mobility of these capital savings is also important. Some restrictions still limit the range of pension investments. Some public plans must invest fairly heavily in federal government bonds or in tax-free municipal bonds. In some states, trust and life insurance codes contain stringent limitations. Common stocks are still not acceptable everywhere. But in general, capital is free to move, in terms of invested savings, from industry to industry, as higher interest rates and greater productivity beckon. Most of the pension funds are large enough to be invested by professionals, skilled in comparing investment opportunities, and thereby able to shift resources efficiently among mortgages, bonds, and common stocks, from company to company and from one section of the country to another, "wherever the action is."

5. *Enhancement of tripartite partnership.* How would ERITD enhance the tripartite partnership of public pensions, private pen-

---

[5] College Retirement Equities Fund (CREF) provides retirement benefits based on investments in equities. CREF and Teachers Insurance and Annuity Association are companion organizations, working together to provide retirement and other benefit programs for educators. CREF is financially separate from TIAA, with its own portfolio of investments and its own board of trustees. Both organizations have the same limited-eligibility, nonprofit status, and the same officers and staff manage both companies.

sions, and personal savings mentioned earlier? The ERITD taxing arrangement by setting a favorable climate for experimentation and diversity will encourage the continuing vitality of private sector pensions. The voters' liking for social security is well demonstrated. If our people also really like private pensions and the direct opportunity to share in the productivity of the American economy, they will be better able to achieve a reasonable balance between public and private pensions and individual personal savings.

ERITD ENCOURAGEMENT OF GOOD TRENDS

It would perhaps be worthwhile now to analyze other aspects of pension plan operations, present and potential, to see how the proposed ERITD arrangement would affect them.

ERITD would help spread the full advantages of private pension plan participation among larger numbers of Americans, especially among younger workers. Years ago when the initial "qualification" requirements were established by the Bureau of Internal Revenue for private pension plans, the immediate objective was to eliminate the sources of discrimination existing then. The qualification tests helped spread out participation among a substantially larger group of employees of each firm establishing a plan and to assure that the benefit formulas for various salary patterns were in reasonable balance. Since the initial demands upon a new pension plan are to provide benefits for retiring and retired staff members, the initial benefit formulas, participation and vesting provisions, and actualities of coverage nearly always favor the older employees. The first problem for the company is "to part in a socially acceptable manner" with the oldsters. Again, as an interim objective this is fine. But it only touches lightly upon the total potential of private pensions for later generations.

In actual operation, final-salary, deferred-vesting plans result in substantially better treatment for most older highly paid people of whatever length of service, and the preference is especially great for those of long service. The annuity contributions to support a final-salary-related benefit formula for an individual who has risen rapidly in salary can really be large. It should be noted that the Internal Revenue Service does endeavor to eliminate discrimination in operation and tends to look at a company's entire system of qualified plans in determining whether discrimination exists.

Under the ERITD arrangement, a trend toward "defined contribution," or money purchase, pension plans would be encouraged. Since no amount could be put under the tax-deferred arrangement until it was vested and actually funded in the individual's name, employees should take more substantial interest in the actual size of contributions to their own pension account at various ages. Many young employees might be exceedingly interested to find that under their present unit benefit plans little or no money was being set aside for their benefits, even though they were being assured that they were "participating" in the retirement plan; they might be disposed to move toward defined contribution retirement plans providing employer contributions of a reasonably level percentage of salary at all ages. This of course is a salutary move toward the concept that retirement plan contributions are a part of current compensation. And it encourages more equitable allocation of retirement plan contributions among participants of various ages and salaries, again helping to make private pensions mean something for more people.

The ERITD arrangement would encourage the direct participation of the individual's pension savings in the investment experience of the fund, including equity funding and variable annuities. At present a commercial employer can have one set of tax-deferment arrangements for its employees under a pension plan and a separate set under its profit-sharing plan, with still a third set under bonus or stock option plans. Government employees of all levels, federal, state, and local, and the entire nonprofit sector including churches, educational institutions, charitable organizations, and a number of organizations such as mutual savings banks and similar corporations do not have available these other methods of setting aside money for the retirement of their employees. In fact, there is considerable, although unintended, discrimination against the nonprofit and governmental employments solely because of the structure of the employing agency and the resultant unavailability of these other arrangements. Since a good deal of the world's work is done by governments and by the independent nonprofit sector, some better balance in tax treatment for retirement income deferral and increased availability of equity funding with the advantages going to the individual, as is true for college teachers through CREF, would seem to be good. Section 403(b), discussed later, helped to encourage individuals and nonprofit or governmental employments to use good pension funding, including variable annuities, to achieve retirement security. But it could not redress the existing imbalance caused by unavailability of profit-sharing and other such plans.

The total amount of tax shift forward or backward under the ERITD proposal would require most careful study by experts. However, several factors might be mentioned:

a) Much of the tax impact would be a matter of timing, not ultimate amount. This is a tax deferment, not a tax avoidance, program. Annuity taxation of the general kind now in force could continue. Although certainly not a part of this proposal, suggestions being made in some quarters for taxing social security benefits and eliminating the double exemptions for people over 65, would, if enacted, bring in substantial revenues.

b) The individual's own contributions to annuities, now taxed currently to him, would under the ERITD plan be taxed when received as benefits during retirement. The present heavy tax load carried by our younger productive members of society just when they are trying to raise their families would be more equitably distributed over their lifetime.

c) Insofar as the economy itself was strengthened by the saving and investment—capital formation—made available through pension plans, the ERITD proposal would help generate new tax revenues.

d) The proposal's encouragement of financial security for all our people would help reduce the welfare tax load.

The proposal could eliminate otherwise duplicatory regulation and supervision. Adequate public supervision is absolutely essential in the area of staff benefits. Competent, effective, imaginative, and flexible supervision—yes, tough and demanding supervision—is a must. But it is apparent also that the private pension world could be circumscribed and stultified by multifold overlapping regulation in coming years. The adoption of just the one structure of ERITD alone would minimize such a danger while permitting flexibility and encouraging innovation in pension planning.

The current anomaly whereby employee contributions are taxed currently to the individual and employer contributions are not, would be removed by the proposal. The differential tax treatment has, I believe, led to a slower growth of pensions, to lesser vesting, lesser funding, and lesser benefit levels than would have been the case had employer and employee contributions been given equal tax deferral treatment.

As to economic cost, economists can point out that the *real* cost of a pension plan is shifted forward to the consumer, backward to the raw materials producer, over to the employee, on to the employer, or backward or forward in time, according to the economics of the particular competitive situation for labor, capital, materials, and the end product. Differential tax treatment of employer and employee contributions is not economically appropriate and would be eliminated under the proposed plan.

The all-pervading orientation toward the single-employer plan could be greatly reduced under ERITD. The present approach is to consider each pension arrangement solely in terms of the separate employing unit. This, more than anything else, prevents really strong developments toward mobility of pensions among employers. Some markets for talent are national in scope, others are statewide, others are local. The marketplace for certified public accountants is different from that for production line workers, is different from that for chemists, is different from that for construction workers. But a given company, employing 10 or 100 or 100,000 people, nonetheless sets up *a* retirement plan, choosing one among these markets or some kind of a compromise in establishing its plan. This is not always helpful. Under the ERITD arrangements, different employees of one employer could be participating in different plans.

Experience in the Nonprofit Sector

A plan similar in certain respects to the ERITD recommendation has been in effect in nonprofit and some government employments since 1958. In that year, Congress enacted Section 403(b) as a replacement for all that had gone before in the nonprofit world and as a substitute for "qualification."

This alternate deferral-of-tax treatment for employees of nonprofit and governmental institutions is permitted only under the strict limitations of Section 403(b) of the Internal Revenue Code,[6]

---

[6] INT. REV. CODE OF 1954, sec. 403(b) sets up congressional criteria for pension plans of nonprofit organizations and certain governmental units. Annuities purchased under this section must be funded, must contain specified provisions, and must observe a limit on the amount of salary that can be used to purchase an annuity with a deferral of taxation. This "exclusion allowance"

which requires that all annuity contributions by the institution be, among other restrictions: (*a*) kept within a statutory percentage of the employee's salary (the 20 percent rule), (*b*) fully and immediately vested in the employee, and (*c*) fully funded through an annuity contract.

The so-called 20 percent rule, while a more stringent limitation in most respects than "qualification," has, even so, provided a good climate for pension development in the nonprofit sector. As a result, certain nonprofit employments have achieved a level of diversity and innovation essential to their needs but not matched elsewhere. To illustrate, let me describe one area where flexibility has been characteristic—the college world.

The establishment of 403(b) has given colleges and universities a framework within which they can continue existing programs and construct new programs, such as the invention of the variable annuity through CREF, to meet their employment needs. The exclusion allowance approach has made it possible for colleges and universities to tailor a number of plans to accommodate to varying situations. At Cornell University, for example, the central faculty group participates in the Endowed Colleges contributory TIAA–CREF plan, certain other employees are members of the New York State Employee Retirement System, another group, mostly staff and maintenance employees, is covered by a noncontributory retirement

---

limit is 20 percent of current salary times years of service, less any employer contributions which have been excluded in the past.

Government officials and legislators realized from the start that qualification requirements established primarily to control corporate use of tax incentives have little meaning when applied to institutions that meet their pension obligations without the incentive of corporate tax deductions, and therefore in 100-cent dollars. The only question for employment in the not-for-profit educational and charitable sector had to do with the employee's tax status. In the early 1930s, the Bureau of Internal Revenue held that a college's contributions toward annuities for its employees were not currently taxable income to the employee. This treatment was added to the Code in the 1942 amendments and was continued in the 1954 Code. Then in 1958, Congress enacted a specific "substitute for educational, charitable, and religious organizations for the 'qualification' required of industrial plans." This substitute is Section 403(b) of the Code.

The criteria and approach of 403(b) not only meets the needs of these organizations more appropriately than would qualification but might well form the approach for *all* pension plans. It does make sense for the colleges; perhaps, modified appropriately, it might make sense for many or even most other employments. This is in many respects the recommendation for study presented in this paper.

plan, and some older staff members hold contracts issued under a previous plan, while still others participate in the Federal Civil Service Retirement System. Multiplicity? Yes indeed. To meet different needs of various employment groups.

CONCLUSION

We clearly are at one of those points in the history of private and public pensions when important decisions will soon be made determining the future course of security for our older people. As is generally true at such times, the temptation will be to follow the same paths as in the past, erecting additional structures on top of existing ones, without a central objective and without taking full account of the changes that have occurred, both within the private and within the public benefit plan sectors.

It is inconceivable that the ERITD suggestion is the answer to all problems. Furthermore, it is not worked out in enough detail to answer all questions, and some of its aspects unquestionably could be improved on or perhaps scrapped. The purpose of this paper and the extensive presentation of a new proposal, Earned Retirement Income Tax Deferral plan, is to stimulate discussion regarding fundamental issues. It does not matter so much whether an eventual plan might take the ERITD approach or be thought through to a different arrangement, just so that whatever is done reinforces the strengths and avoids the mistakes of the past and produces a salutary climate for the future.

This will permit advancement of a "people-pensions" approach, a pluralism in provisions, a climate for innovation, and diversification in investments that is the true strength of the private pension world. This strength will find expression in the private sector's ability to provide the individual with his own pension rights directly related to his own productive efforts in the economy; its ability to generate his benefits directly from that same productive American economy; its provision for flow-through to the individual of the vitality of our private enterprise system.

chapter 18

State versus Federal Regulation

ONE OF THE MOST enduring issues of insurance regulation is the choice between state and federal jurisdiction. Recent developments, including the holding company and merger mania, the automobile problem, and the recently enacted National Insurance Development Program are adding new complexities and new drama to that issue. The following selection states the case for preservation of the historic responsibility of the states to regulate insurance. A conflicting view has already been seen in Chapter 10.

THE CASE FOR STATE REGULATION OF INSURANCE*

Spencer L. Kimball
Dean and Professor of Law
University of Wisconsin

ROLE OF THE ACADEMIC COMMENTATOR

From time to time, I have been requested, as an academic participant in a meeting such as this, to speculate about the future. Perhaps the assumption behind such requests is that since the academician knows so little about what is now going on he might as well speculate about the future—about which no one else knows either. In any event, with becoming modesty, I reject the suggestion that with or without knowledge of the present state of things I can, within acceptable limits of credibility, prophesy about the patterns that the insurance business or insurance regulation will exhibit very far into the future. Perhaps, however, a few statements can safely be made about some of the aspects of the problem that will loom large in shaping the future.

---

* Address to a meeting of the Association of Life Insurance Counsel, May 6, 1968, The Greenbrier, White Sulphur Springs, W. Va.

Apart from his dictated role as a prophet, a number of things can be said about the shape of the academician's role in a discussion of practical problems in insurance.

First, the academician should provide the perspective that can only be provided by a person who is free from the subjective biases that as practitioners you quite naturally have because you think about things from a particular vantage point. If he is to be true to his trust, the academician must remain free from the influence of special interests when he speaks as an academician. It is his moral duty to be truly objective. He has taken the king's shilling and owes his entire loyalty to the king—the public.

Second, the academician should provide the perspective that one can only have when he looks at a subject from the outside, far enough away to see and sketch the forest instead of the trees—to see it in its true relation to other things on the landscape. A subtle balance must be maintained, nevertheless, for at the same time the observer must remain close enough to the forest to realize that there are, in fact, individual trees and what species they are.

Third, the academician has an obligation to provide the perspective that comes from systematic thought, free from the inherently narrowing effect of customary limitation of one's concern to the solution of the unique problems of the moment.

Fourth, the academician has the obligation to reduce his systematic thoughts to written form so that they are not ephemeral but become a part of the general literature on the subject. This is only a duty if the thoughts are worth recording, but he should stop speaking his piece if he does not have anything to say worth recording, at least some of the time. In the revision of the Wisconsin insurance laws, in which I am now heavily engaged, one of the principal contributions that we believe we as academicians are making to the science, or the art, of insurance regulation is the recording of our thinking in the development of an insurance code. Whatever result we may get in the legislature, our revision should for many years be the baseline from which future revisions will begin if they are good revisions. Substantially all thought about previous revisions has been lost, because it was unrecorded and not preserved for the future. Nothing was left but the bare text of the recommended statute. Our drafts, on the other hand, will have extensive comments which will be readily available as a starting point for development of a code.

Finally, the academician can speak plainly and frankly in a degree that is not always possible to involved participants in the day-to-day discussions about insurance regulation. That some of you recognize your own limitations in this respect was clear in the fact that one of the expressed reasons for inviting me to this gathering was the hope that I could speak more freely than persons with company affiliations. But you are all lawyers, and I must qualify that statement by saying that I have detected very little timidity since I have been here. This is a gratifying discovery for it cannot honestly be said that insurance executives are in general so bold.

If I speak plainly about some things, therefore, I hope that you will not interpret disagreement as an imputation of bad motives. I have recently become painfully aware of a remarkable sensitivity of some insurance executives (I hope not many lawyer executives among them) to even a suggestion that the institution or the company represented may be less than perfect. Indeed, the sensitivity is so great as to blind them to reality, in some instances. When I emerged from the "sheltered" halls of academia to enter the big, bad world, I supposed at first that I had entered a world of tough people, able to take as well as to dish out criticism. But I have learned that I must soften my normal bluntness as a concession to the more sensitive ears of my new auditors. In my native environment plain and even caustic speaking is the accepted order of things. One of my colleagues, commenting recently upon a committee recommendation, sent a memorandum to all the faculty explicitly comparing the members of that committee unfavorably with his 18-month-old grandson. And he meant it! Such caustic criticism occurs frequently enough in the academic world that one does become used to it, amused when someone else is the target and philosophical when he himself is.

This cautionary statement may be justified by the necessity of dealing in this paper with a subject that is apparently so sensitive that few insurance executives are prepared to say frankly what they think about it—the relationship of federal and state regulation. You may have gathered that an academic regards few questions as sensitive and to me this is certainly no sensitive question.

SHOULD NATIONAL REGULATION OF INSURANCE BE PREFERRED TO REGULATION AT THE STATE LEVEL?

The discussion of the preceding panel members has led quite naturally to the question whether national or state regulation of the insurance business is to be preferred. The question is often discussed in these days. More and more insurance executives who formerly were committed to state regulation are openly toying with the thought of regulation at the national level. All such mention of the subject was formerly anathema.

To put the question in this way as if it were a question of one simple system against another is a gross oversimplification, however. The question is impossible to answer in so naive a form. It is like the question whether one should use a driver or a putter on the golf course. The question must first be put with much greater refinement. One must ask what kind of national regulation is contemplated and what kinds of state regulation there are now and may be in the future. He must ask, ultimately, not just whether national regulation is to be preferred to state regulation but rather what combination of an almost infinite number of possible combinations of the two, in what variations of each, would best serve the interests of the public. In a sense, this makes the problem one of impossible complexity.

Nevertheless, in order to deal with the problem in the present context, it will be useful to treat it as if it were simple and to run quickly through some of the asserted advantages and disadvantages of state regulation and of national regulation, even though it is perfectly clear that neither will ever exist to the complete exclusion of the other, that they can be combined in different proportions, and that each system is both almost infinitely flexible and alterable.

ADVANTAGES OF STATE REGULATION

The first asserted—and certainly a real—advantage of state regulation is that it is an established and known system. Its virtues and its weaknesses are familiar. Devices for minimizing the impact of the weaknesses have reached a high level of sophistication. There is much to be said in favor of Hamlet's choice of deciding that fear of the unknown makes it better to "bear the ills we have than fly to others that we know not of." Nothing is so unsure as prediction of the full range of consequences of a major change in a complex organic system.

The second asserted—and clearly real—advantage of state regulation is that it does not require a total commitment. It is not necessary to put all the eggs in a single basket. Historically, there have been some occasions on which insurance companies have in fact withdrawn in numbers from states where there was enacted legislation that was perceived as unreasonable. One recalls, readily enough, the withdrawal of the foreign life insurance companies from Texas *en masse* upon the enactment of the Robertson Law in 1907 and a similar withdrawal from Wisconsin at about the same time, upon enactment of some expense limitations that the industry regarded as improper intervention in management prerogatives.[1] There have been even more cases where withdrawal was threatened, but the threat was not carried out for good and sufficient reasons.

Not only is actual withdrawal an important escape that is available to insurers—the ultimate weapon against unfair regulation— but the threat of withdrawal is even more important as a lever against a state legislature that is proposing unwise legislation. This is not to say that a company or even the whole industry should or can casually use or even threaten use of withdrawal, for each called bluff lessens credibility, and actual withdrawal can be very costly. Moreover, it is always possible for the state to conduct an insurance business of any kind. Insurance may be a difficult business in which to make a profit, but it is not a difficult one to run. It is only to say that the availability of withdrawal helps greatly in the resolution of otherwise difficult controversy. It should be clear that there would be no comparable weapon in the industry arsenal if there were national regulation.

Again, an asserted and real but inadequately exploited advantage of state regulation is the chance it provides for cautious experimentation—for trying new techniques without total commitment. This is closely related to the previous point.

As another asserted advantage of state regulation and certainly an advantage to the industry if not clearly one to the public, it can also be said that the industry has more than enough capacity to deal effectively with most state regulators and most state legislatures. In the first place, the lobbying machinery is operating and well oiled at the state level, and the industry's weight seems heavy to the average state bureaucrat and legislator. It is not so clear that the industry can deal with equal effect under all circumstances with the national bureaucrat or with members of Congress. There is much more

---

[1] On the latter withdrawal, see S. Kimball, *Insurance and Public Policy* (Madison: University of Wisconsin Press, 1960), p. 171.

muscle in Washington, and under certain political circumstances, the representations and interests of the industry can be ignored in a way that is unlikely in any state, even the largest. No matter what the political context, competition among the states provides a kind of leverage totally absent in Washington. Though one speaking for the public interest might be expected to opt for the system where the industry's lobbying weight is less likely to be decisive, I do not. Though I think it unfortunate for it always to prevail, I do believe it is desirable for the industry to have to be listened to.

Moving from these pragmatic considerations in which I have focused on industry desires and powers, I wish to suggest that there is importance to our whole society, altogether transcending and overriding industry interests, of some fundamental political values urging state level regulation. The very basis of our federal system is at issue. Decentralization and dispersion of political power is in itself an important value in a democratic society. Concentrations of power are bad per se, and it is irrelevant whether the concentrations are in government, in labor, or in business.[2] In any case they are in people. For present purposes, however, I am only concerned with powerful government. Undue concentration of power in Washington is unwise from any point of view. Any problems that *can* be dealt with adequately at the state level *should* be handled there in preference to Washington. I assert this generally and categorically. Please understand that I have no ideological objection to public intervention in private business; indeed, in my view private business has a claim to exist only if it serves the public welfare. I am quite relaxed about the prospect of extensive government intervention in any business, whenever good reason can be shown. But I do fear concentration of the power of intervention in one city, or on one river, or in one man, or in one commission. A single controller of insurance companies has altogether too much power. Even the best regulator, state or federal, can have too much power if his reach is too long. You should appreciate this better than anyone else—you who often complain of the undue power of the New York Insur-

---

[2] This is, incidentally, a sufficient reason for fearing the current holding company development. If the present unwise trend continues, increasingly powerful business will eventually meet its nemesis in powerful government. A federal death-sentence bill on insurance holding companies is a possibility if enough fears should be stirred up. Speaking more broadly, the current trend toward greater and greater concentrations of economic power, and not just in insurance, may need to be reversed, and only government can force its reversal.

ance Department over your investments, your marketing arrangements, your management practices, and yet who talk glibly about
putting such power into the hands of a national bureaucrat from
whom you cannot possibly escape.

At this juncture, there seems to some of us to be encouraging
signs of a long-awaited reversal of the long-range tendency toward
a concentration of talent in this country. What was once a centripe-
tal tendency to an extraordinary and undue concentration of ability
in the major centers of the northeast may have been reversed. Not
only has the overwhelming dominance of New York as a financial
center clearly passed but even the dominance of Washington as a
domestic political center may have passed its peak and begun to
decline. There are new foci of power in existence and in course of
development. Whether this judgment is correct or not, I suggest
that statesmen of the insurance industry ought to wish to encourage
such a development to the maximum extent they can. If power and
talent are still moving toward the center, you should be the first to
seek to slow or even reverse the movement.

ADVANTAGES OF NATIONAL REGULATION

It is often suggested as a major advantage of national insurance
regulation that instead of dealing with 50 different state agencies,
insurance companies would only have to deal with one in Washington. This is pure illusion. Not only is it highly likely that if there
were a national insurance commissioner he would have to decentral-
ize his operation and regulate regionally with respect to many
things,[3] but it is surely also the case that "insurance regulation"
would be fragmented among many agencies. If the bar of the
McCarran–Ferguson Act were removed, surely the Securities and
Exchange Commission would aggressively move further into the
field of insurance regulation. Nor is there the slightest prospect that
the Department of Justice or the Federal Trade Commission would
quietly withdraw. There is no doubt that the Internal Revenue
Service will continue its interest in insurance companies no matter
what the regime of regulation may be, and its impact on insurance
accounting, at least, will continue to expand. The interest of HEW,

---

[3] I have been told here that you are getting increasing variation in tax
rulings from the Internal Revenue Service because of decentralization. Surely
this is almost inevitable in an undertaking so complex as insurance regulation.

DOT, and many other agencies is unquestioned. Instead of dealing with 50 state and two or three national agencies, a life insurance company would have to deal with a dozen or more national agencies. The tendency to fragmentation is greater with the more complex government. Moreover, it is not likely that there would be a clean sweep of the state agencies. It will be a long time before you will have seen the last of them. Again, while at the state level reasonable accommodation seems usually to be reached between state agencies of a single state (such as between insurance and securities), and quite often even among the various departments in the several states, life is said to be different in Washington. Internecine warfare among agencies is said to be a law of life. Each seeks to expand its jurisdiction with imperialistic aggressiveness. The life insurance company subject to national regulation may easily become a victim of the feuds that now exist and may develop among the agencies. Overlapping and conflict of jurisdiction is endemic on the Potomac.

It is frequently suggested that better talent would be available for regulation in Washington. Statistically this may be true at the present time—at least it is true if one compares the national civil service with that in the smaller states. It is less clear that it is true when one compares the national civil service with the civil service in the largest and most populous states. Increasingly, able people prefer to stay where they grow up rather than migrate to the banks of the Potomac to live in the much less relaxed atmosphere of the nation's capital. The always dubious attractions of Washington look less glamorous now than recently. Moreover, the quality advantage is only marginally true. One needs only to compare the quality of the best and the worst national agencies to realize that there is no clear and sharp contrast in quality between national and state regulation.

Again, whatever the situation may be now, there is no assurance that over the long pull the attractions of the national civil service will ensure quality regulation there. The attraction of the metropolis in the first half of this century has become less today. At a more mundane level, the German experience since World War II has suggested that a national bureaucracy can in the long run compete no better than a state one for the services of high-quality people. What was formerly a remarkable civil service in Germany seems to face imminent decline under conditions of relatively full employment because what were once high salaries and excellent conditions of work are no longer competitive with private industry. That is a perennial problem of a relatively full-employment economy at the national as well as at the state level. Our national civil service already suffers constant drain of its trained men to private law practice and to business.

Even granting greater competence in Washington, the nature of the power at the center tends to produce a messianic complex, which is not unusual among Washington bureaucrats. An academician listening around in Washington may hear expressions of a viewpoint the company executive is luckily spared. One recent luncheon conversation in Washington shook me, and I am not easily shaken. It was the casual matter-of-factness of the viewpoint that was disconcerting. It was something like this: "Here is the way *we* (i.e., the speaking bureaucrats) are going to restructure the insurance industry to do its proper job, *which it does not now do.*" The speakers, and there were several, had very clear notions of what the insurance industry should (and by God would) look like when they got through. There are many very bright young men—mostly lawyers—who float around in Washington from agency to agency at the medium levels of the national civil service who have learned a great deal about manipulation of institutions but have not yet acquired the wisdom to understand the limitations upon human capacities, and especially upon their own, to deal with complicated problems. They are not reluctant to tamper, with or without understanding.

An often expressed notion when the national versus state regulation choice is discussed is that state regulation must stand or fall according to the quality of the regulation of the weakest state. This familiar "weakest link" argument is pure fallacy. State regulation should be judged in terms of its effectiveness in the protection of policyholders. In 1965 New York licensed companies wrote 79.5 percent of the property and liability insurance business of the country and 66.5 percent of the life insurance business.[4] If New York regulates its licensees effectively, two thirds of the life business and four fifths of the property-liability business of the country is well regulated, and that percentage of policyholders are well protected at least with respect to those matters that New York really regulates. If California and Texas and Wisconsin and Illinois

---

[4] New York Insurance Dept., *Report of the Special Committee on Insurance Holding Companies* (1968), pp. 12–13.

and Massachusetts also regulate their licensees well, the percentage of the business of the country that is well regulated mounts to overwhelming heights.[5] A dozen such overlapping circles would cover most of the country's insurance business. This does not assert that licensees must be regulated as closely as domiciliary companies but only that they be regulated well enough (when necessary because of the weakness of regulation at the domicile) to give reasonable protection to policyholders.

If a few policyholders should remain in states with inadequate regulation who are hurt because they buy from companies not licensed by *any single state with good regulation of its licensees,* that is unfortunate, of course, but its dimensions as a weakness in our social organization should be kept in perspective. Hundred percent protection of all policyholders in the country with equal and complete adequacy is simply not among the most urgent of the problems that face us as a nation. It is far down in the priority list, particularly since the social cost of hundred percent protection may be very high.

Finally, the present lack of uniformity among the states is often cited as an advantage of national over state regulation, on the assumption that uniformity would result from the shift. Several points should be made about this matter. The first is that national regulation would not necessarily be as uniform as is usually assumed, as already indicated. If a policy of decentralization should produce regional offices, a law uniform in the statute book would be differently interpreted and applied in the various regions. Lack of uniformity is inherent in a large and continental economy. Second, and conversely, uniformity has already been achieved by interstate cooperation in such things as the form of annual statement and the actuarial laws of the life insurance business, where it really matters most. Nationwide operation is possible. Such uniformity as is really *essential* can develop despite state level regulation. Third, much more can be done to produce substantial uniformity, and current developments in the National Association of Insurance Commissioners may presage increased uniformity.[6] Again, it is soon enough to worry about uniformity when we have something that is good enough to want it everywhere. Part of the problem of developing

---

[5] Choice of these states is not intended to assert that these particular states do or do not regulate well.

[6] Consider, for example, the recent development of an effective central office of the National Association of Insurance Commissioners.

uniformity is the uncertainty what regulation should be like. We see this as part of the role of the Wisconsin revision—to be a starting point from which something can be developed that is good enough to want everywhere. It may give some comfort for me to emphasize that I see it (i.e., the Wisconsin revision) as the starting and not the ending point.

Finally, I think it can be suggested that uniformity is a much overrated virtue. There are matters with respect to which uniformity would be helpful, but many others as to which it could hardly matter less. Indeed, there is also advantage in diversity—where local conditions vary, or perhaps simply to permit experimentation.

THE VARIETIES OF NATIONAL REGULATORY REGIMES

It does not tell the whole story to say we will or may move to a system of regulation that is primarily national, for there are many varieties of national regulation, and not every one is equally innocuous or advantageous. Moreover, though there might be, there is not likely to be, a clean and sharp shift over to national regulation, with concomitant total elimination of state activity. It is much more likely that there would be some sort of mixed system. Even in Germany, the archetype of comprehensive national insurance regulatory systems, in effect since 1900, not all of the regulation of insurance is concentrated in Berlin. In addition to the national regulatory agency, there are regulatory agencies in each of the constituent states of Germany to regulate companies that are primarily local. In total number the locally regulated companies exceed those that are nationally regulated.

A little more sophistication about the character of legal and institutional history than most commentators seem to have would lead many of those who now speak as if there will be an early and clean and quick shift over to national regulation to be somewhat more restrained in their predictions. Institutional developments are seldom either clear-cut or rapid. Far more commonly a new layer of social institutions is imposed on existing layers that continue to exist and even to flourish. Eventually the superimposed layer may be sufficiently dominant and drive the subordinate layers out of business. But it may not; the subordinate ones may remain indefinitely, as living and interesting and very complicating institutions.

My earlier suggestion that a resurgence of vigor at the state level may be in process or in prospect adds poignancy to the problem of choosing. There is increasing realization that not all problems can best be solved on the Potomac. Many of us here belong to a generation that thought so and has been hugely disillusioned. The continuing importance and now even the increased importance of the state capital as a significant focus of our political and social life is symbolized in many ways. Perhaps there is hope for greatly increased vitality in the federal system in this resurgence.

The most likely form national regulation would take would be based upon formal continuance of adherence to the principle of the McCarran–Ferguson Act—that basically regulation of insurance belongs at the state level—but would be accompanied by increasing abandonment of the principle in fact. There would be continuously increasing national intervention on specific matters of national importance without a formal change of regime. This is the most likely course of development because it is the natural evolutionary and thus historical method. The Securities and Exchange Commission would continue its involvement and gradually expand it. The Department of Justice and the Federal Trade Commission would continue to enlarge their spheres of activity and interest. A national guaranty fund for automobile insurance might eventually become a *de facto* insurance department. The national fisc would continue to intervene in ways that increasingly affected the method of operation of the insurance business and thus forced change in the pattern of state regulation. One illustration is the increasing national pressure on life insurance accounting.[7] This whole pattern of dual and overlapping regulation might better be described as an uneasy truce between national and state regulation. The two would coexist, with state regulation being formally predominant but with national regulation being of increasing importance.

Another form of national regulation could result from the enactment of a statute authorizing the national chartering of insurance companies. National companies would then be regulated by the

---

[7] On the other hand, sometimes the national revenue agent can be overcome—for example, on the catastrophe reserve problem the increased pressure from riot losses on insurance companies and latterly on government may ultimately result in the relaxation of the revenue rules with respect to catastrophe reserves. See, e.g., the recommendations of the *Report of the President's National Advisory Panel on Insurance in Riot-Affected Areas, Meeting the Insurance Crisis of Our Cities* (1968), pp. 105–7. Although they were not adopted, they point to a possible direction of development in the long run.

national commissioner, while state companies would continue to be regulated as at present. This would be analogous to present banking regulation, with the insurance company having the power to choose its course of action and to get the kind of license it wanted to have. Superficially, at least, this is a very attractive pattern. If federal regulation is unduly burdensome, companies new or old could opt for state charters. If state regulation were harrassing and cumbersome, even existing companies might choose to reorganize and operate under the federal regulator. The systems would compete with each other. From the public point of view one serious question is raised, however—whether a variant of Gresham's law would operate. At the turn of the century, when the insurance industry seriously pressed for federal regulation, it was clear that what they wanted was weak regulation. They would then have found that in Washington, but they could hardly count on it now. Of course if the states want the business badly enough in competition with Washington and if they really compete for it, bad state regulation might drive out good federal regulation. We have illustration enough of this pattern in our general corporation law, and it influences, though it does not dominate, the patterns of state insurance regulation. I suspect, however, that this would not be a point of contention between the state and the national regulatory systems. On both sides, regulation would probably be very intensive, and no company would be likely to choose its path merely to escape effective control. In such a competitive system, the state regulatory system might gradually model itself more and more after the national system, whatever that looked like.

Another method of dividing the field between national and state regulation would be on the basis of the scope of operation of the insurance company. Companies operating strictly or largely within a single state would be subject to state regulation, while companies operating on a wider basis would be subject to national control. This would tend to rob state regulation of most of its significance and might ultimately destroy its quality, though that is by no means a foregone conclusion.

Another pattern of division between national and state responsibility would give to the national government certain problems, especially those with which the states have special difficulty, while the states continued to handle what remained. This solution would have much attraction. Some of the questions for which state regulation is difficult are mail-order insurance, mergers, antitrust, and holding company problems. But if the national control went so far as to concern itself with the fundamental question of the solidity of insurers, then the states would have lost most of the interesting problems and would be left to deal only with the minor details. This also would then rob state regulation of its significance.

Predicting which one of these patterns will in fact develop is risky. It could be any of them, or perhaps others not yet mentioned. In any case, choice will result from a variety of pressures—from national imperialists active in the District of Columbia, from state-house political machines with jobs and influence contingent upon the continuance of state regulation, and from the industry. And as you are better aware than I, the pressures from the industry will be split into various components and will not all push in the same direction. Nor should they. You do yourself a great disservice when you seek artificial unity—it makes you look far more like a dangerous monolithic force than the true facts would indicate. The important point that I should like to emphasize here is that the life insurance industry is in no position to blueprint the results, and should not try, although you can and should try to have some influence upon the shape of the outcome. But in all of your thinking about the choices before us it would be most unwise for you to postulate an ideal national system which *you* will design which you then compare with the present state system with all its defects. That is not the choice before you at all. What you will get is a bastard system that is the vector sum of all of the forces that play upon the industry and the various governments. What you get may or may not be an improvement on the present system—in my judgment it would be unlikely to be much better and fairly likely to be far worse.

CAN STATE REGULATION BE SIGNIFICANTLY IMPROVED?

This leads naturally to the question whether it might be possible for state regulation to be improved in ways that will make it much less attractive to contemplate significant changes in basic structure. This requires at least a sketchy look at some of the problems facing state regulation and any possible solutions to them.

The basic question already suggested is whether a sufficient

number of high-quality personnel can be obtained. This arises at
two levels: the quality of the commissioner himself, and the quality
of the permanent civil service. Although the former is a factor of
considerable importance, it should not be overemphasized in any
consideration of alternatives. Whether at the state or national level,
it is inevitable that most commissioners will be of relatively brief
tenure and limited experience. This is true with regulation of all
sorts at both the state and the national level. Political appointments
are the norm in our system, and they will not always (or perhaps
even often) be made either by presidents or by governors on the
basis of either quality or experience, and they will certainly not be
made as career appointments. So far as it is relevant, however, some
recent state appointments have been very encouraging.

Far more crucial and realistic, however, is concern for the level
of competence in the civil service. The national government currently has an advantage over most state governments in the competition for able people. The national government is not without its
problems in getting good people, however, and does not necessarily
have an overwhelming advantage, particularly compared with the
larger states. Moreover, the advantage may loom less large in the
future, for reasons I will only suggest.

It is not clear how far one can emphasize the point, but I think it
is fair to say and is worth saying that the general quality of
education in this country has increased in recent decades in a
striking way. If we can solve our basic problems, some of which are
of horrible proportions, and if the new technology does not put
impossible demands on us, there may be something of an American
renaissance in the making. I know that it is fashionable to decry
the ability of college or even law students in these days—to say that
they cannot express themselves or spell. I think the judgment is
simply erroneous. What is being compared is an elite student
population of an earlier day with half the population today. Everybody now goes to college, and it would be quite natural for the
general cultural level of students to drop. Yet, I doubt very much if
it has dropped. In the law schools, at least, one sees a steady rise in
the quality of the student population—many of us in this room
would now have difficulty in getting into the law schools from
which we graduated. This has been quite visibly true during my
career as a teacher.

A more important fact is that the career choices of students (not only, but including, law students) are changing. There are fewer now than in my generation for whom a successful Wall Street or LaSalle Street law practice is the ultimate in achievement. Increasingly they go to government and to the universities. Others find fulfillment on Main Street, and eventually I think the tendency will be for more highly qualified people to go back to the county seat. Why should this be? I think two factors contribute significantly. The first is that the quality of life is becoming better at the periphery of our society and seems to be deteriorating at the center. Culture is being diffused to the masses. In general it is possible for the lawyer in a small city to live as rich and full a life as he could formerly live in the big city. Second, the increasing affluence of our society has made the attraction of the richest centers and the most profitable jobs decline relatively. Students are more concerned with the social and humane values of their careers. The recent salary increase for beginning lawyers on Wall Street reflects not the strength of Wall Street but its competitive weakness.

I cannot predict the ultimate dimensions of these changes. But if such changes are really taking place, they seriously affect the problems with which we are dealing. More qualified people will be attracted to jobs in which they see social significance rather than to jobs with maximum financial rewards. Beyond a certain point, the marginal utility of money declines rapidly.

There are of course some potentially explosive elements in the picture, too. The increasing alienation of young people from the middle class value system in which you and I were nurtured is hopeful, but it is also frightening. Such alienation could reach the point where a large part of the generation now in high school and college is separated from the mainstream of American life, with incalculable damage to our society. But if the alienation does not go so far and only involves rejection of the emphasis upon "things" and the placing of a larger emphasis upon the meaning and social significance of one's life, it may ultimately enrich American life and most of all outside of the large centers.

In addition to these unmeasurable changes that are taking place in education and in fundamental attitudes in this country, there are hopeful technological developments that may make it possible to improve greatly the quality of state regulation of insurance. The first of these is the explosive development of electronic data processing. Insurance companies have been among the leaders in the use of

EDP, and it is now time for insurance regulators to begin to use it effectively also. One possibility is the development of mechanized examinations, especially for large companies. This is bound to come soon. It is silly to use the same techniques to examine the Crossroads Life Insurance Company of Paw Paw, Nebraska, and the Metropolitan or the Prudential.

Where a company itself has a highly sophisticated computer setup, the examination process in the future could be much simplified. The department computer expert (and he must be a real expert, whether an employee of the department or a consultant) will spend whatever time is needed discussing with the company's computer experts the company's communications systems, with special emphasis on internal controls. Then programs would be developed by the insurance department to be used on the company's own equipment to get out of the company's records the information the department needs. This information could be less comprehensive but more searching than present examination techniques permit. It could also be completely up to date. The possibilities inherent in spot-checking would be emphasized, and the reliability of spot-checking would be enhanced through the development of sophisticated random examination strategies, themselves developed by computers. Eventually, the commissioner could get instantaneously any reasonable information he might want. The information derived in this way would be more reliable than the old-fashioned audit.

Obviously, assuming present examination objectives, there would still be other things to be asked and done, like counting the bonds and checking the complaint files, that could not be done by computer. But much of the work that now is done laboriously by hand may prove to be unimportant enough to be abandoned, and more of it can be simplified and mechanized.

A similar development is the use of outside experts. Department employees may not always be available with the necessary competence to handle these highly sophisticated techniques. Nor is it important that every department have such people. The larger departments will need and want them, but the smaller ones can operate just as successfully if they make appropriate use of consultants. What needs to happen is for the smaller departments to achieve a level of sophistication that will enable them to see when they need to make use of outside experts.

Another technique that needs to be, and can be, learned by the small states is how to rely more heavily on the big states for effectuating their regulation. This also requires enough sophistication to know what one can do effectively and what he cannot do and must rely on experts to do.

Most important, however, in making state regulation adequate to the tasks that it has to face is more realistic selection of what it is that needs most to be done. This is a problem that would have to be solved by national regulation too—it is no inherent problem of state regulation as such. Again I emphasize that it is not desirable to do the same things with the Metropolitan or the Prudential that one does with the Crossroads of Paw Paw. Most of those who were vigorous liberals in the 1930's and had strong hopes that all of the vices and inadequacies of business enterprise could be cured by comprehensive government regulation long ago abandoned the notion. The vices and inadequacies of businesses continue. Regulation is not the panacea it once was thought to be. It tends, even at its best, to be bureaucratic and rigid and unreceptive to new ideas. At its worst, it tends to be either crassly or subtly corrupted by the industry it is supposed to regulate. This makes it important to think carefully about what we should do in regulation and how we should do it.[8]

In this connection I wish to report on what I consider to be a major break-through in thinking about regulatory techniques in insurance. We have been feeling our way toward this notion in the Wisconsin revision over many months and it has only become clarified and focused in our thinking recently. It is best illustrated in the first two drafts of the chapter on investment regulation which were released in April and August, 1968. It should be emphasized that it still needs improvement before we are prepared to recommend it for passage. But I am concerned here with major ideas only.

As we saw the problem that faced us, it was twofold. The first aspect was the unwarranted but prevalent assumption that each insurance department should do fully whatever the statutes either empowered or instructed it to do, so far as time and resources permitted. The second was the feeling that somehow either constitu-

---

[8] There are many regulatory activities with high cost and questionable return. They need reexamination and in some cases abandonment, in others a clearer determination of objectives and careful restructuring. Rate and form regulation are illustrations. There are others.

tional (or general legal) principles about equal protection and the absence of unfair discrimination require that the Metropolitan and the Crossroads be treated in the same way.

The solution to the second aspect of the problem is simple, and we think it raises no constitutional or policy issues. It is to distinguish between restricted and unrestricted companies. An initial and natural adverse reaction needs to be faced at the outset. That is the fear that such a classification will result in invidious distinctions—in second-class citizenship, in a word. The formula used can, however, minimize any stigma that might otherwise attach to special restrictions. The term "restricted companies" does not need to be used. The method is to liberalize the rules generally for all companies but to provide that the commissioner may, by order, subject any company to special restrictions. In the second draft of the investment chapter of the Wisconsin revision, all companies that have had licenses in the state for less than five years would initially be placed in the restricted category. Companies would then be removed from the restricted list either by the mere passage of time or by an order of the commissioner, or after the five years' period might be added to the list by specific order, which under Wisconsin law would be subject to judicial review in accordance with the Wisconsin administrative procedure act.

There are many possible variations on the theme. Companies might be restricted for all matters or for individual subjects—for investments, for example, but not for financing methods, or perhaps the converse.

This approach would make it possible to liberalize and to simplify the rules applicable to insurers generally, thus eliminating a great mass of detailed regulation now religiously carried out. For companies subject to the special restrictions, which would include nearly all the younger companies but only a very few of the older ones, there would not only be a regime of control as intensive as now exists, but there would also be increased individual attention to the problems of the particular company.

In our investment chapter, all insurers would be made subject to a few general and short statutory provisions implemented by a limited number of insurance department rules. Then the small class of restricted insurers would be subject also to (1) prior approval, or (2) subsequent disapproval, or (3) reporting of investments to the commissioner or other procedural restrictions, or (4) special limitations on the categories of permitted investments, all in accordance with the rules or orders of the commissioner.

For unrestricted insurers—i.e., most insurers—permitted investments would include all of the classes now permitted by the law, with fewer detailed earnings tests and other special qualifications now included in the statute. There would continue to be a leeway provision of 5 percent, and opportunity for the commissioner to authorize other investments by rule or order.

Another section of the draft then prohibits certain investments: illegal enterprises and investments that would result in the control of unrelated enterprises. For foreign insurers, the prohibited investments would merely be treated as unadmitted assets if permitted by the domiciliary law, though the license of the foreign insurer would be subject to revocation on a specific finding by the commissioner that particular investments, though permitted by the law of the domicile, were dangerous to the interests of Wisconsin policyholders. The finding would of course be judicially reviewable.

Beyond the flat prohibitions, other limitations would be applicable to domestic insurers, but with less than prohibitory effect. Illustratively, these would limit the holding of common stock (for life insurers), of nonamortizable bonds, of home office real estate, and of income-producing real estate, to a specified percentage of admitted assets or to some relationship to policyholders' surplus. They might similarly limit to some percentage of admitted assets the preferred stock of a single insurer, the common stock of a single insurer, all security issues of a single corporation, or investments in ancillary subsidiaries.[9] An important but fairly obvious suggested innovation would be to measure value at market rather than cost.

We also propose an important change in the sanctions against violating any of the limitations except the prohibitory ones. Characteristically divestment is now required by the laws. The prohibitions have a public policy objective, and violation would continue to lead to compulsory divestment of the asset. Otherwise, however, when only solidity is in question, violation of a rule would not render the investment illegal, nor trigger stringent enforcement measures. Instead, assets invested in violation of the rules would be first treated as leeway and then as assets that could not be used to test financial

---

[9] It should be emphasized that I am not describing a final draft; the specified percentages are merely starting points for discussion.

soundness, with no need to dispose of the assets if there was a sufficient surplus. This point of view is a further development of the notion of "surplus surplus" as it appeared in Appendix One to the Report of the New York Special Committee on Insurance Holding Companies.

This description of our investment chapter is intended only to illustrate an important point in the adaptation of law to reality. There should be a focus on the important things to be done—on the companies that need close supervision and on the kinds of control that meet the legitimate objectives of the law. You will not have to agree with every provision of the investment chapter, I think, to see that it represents a new and important departure from traditional patterns. Its main outlines, we are immodest enough to think, constitute a significant breakthrough in the thinking about insurance regulation.

CONCLUSION

In brief summary a number of points may usefully be made.

First, on the merits, national regulation is unlikely to be strikingly better than state regulation if it should be adopted. Moreover, it is unlikely that we shall have pure national regulation and altogether abandon state regulation for a long time into the future.

Second, on the probabilities, it would be shortsighted for anyone to put all his chips at this moment on the ultimate, and *a fortiori* on the immediate, victory of national over state regulation. Confident predictions of the early arrival of national regulation within three to five years remind one of those old predictions of the end of the world that had to be recalculated as each specified date passed uneventfully. It should be apparent that we are still some distance away from the introduction of pure national regulation, though in truth we have enough of it already to satisfy some who think businessmen should be left quite alone. Wildly optimistic (or pessimistic as the case may be), predictions of early change ignore all the teachings of legal and institutional history. Inertia and tradition are weighty factors in the evolution of human institutions; the cumbersomeness of change from state to national regulation will probably ensure that it will be a slow and inconvenient development, at the very least. There are many forces operative in this field and a shift to national regulation, if one should occur, is likely to be an evolutionary rather than a revolutionary development, and to produuce a mixed and probably very messy system.

Again, on the merits, there are some hopeful signs about the development of new techniques and patterns of insurance regulation, whether it is to be at the state or national level. There are possibilities of change in state regulation that will liberalize the regime by focusing on the important questions and abandoning others, and by relaxing even in important areas the more stringent aspects of the regime for responsible companies. This should eventually make the state regulatory regime a more sufferable and reasonable enterprise, without reducing its effectiveness.

A further word needs to be said about the corruption of the regulatory process. The word "corruption" is too strong but I don't really know a better one for making the point. In the case of insurance, on the whole the "corruption" has been very subtle and unconscious but nonetheless quite pervasive and real. The insurance regulator is conceived by far too many insurance executives, and too often he conceives himself, as a part of the industry, existing to serve the industry. Indeed, I have heard life insurance men express the notion that it would be useful to have a national regulator to "represent" the industry in the executive branch of the national government. Nothing unsavory was intended—whatever else one may say about the insurance business, it is a business run by honorable men. However, the notion that a regulator should "represent" the industry is a subtly corrupted point of view. The industry should represent itself to whatever agencies affect its life. It is entitled to do so with vigor. But the regulatory agency should represent the public and nothing but the public. (The same thing is of course true of educators concerned with insurance.) This is not to say that the agency's mission is the destruction of the industry. Quite the contrary. In general, the preservation of the industry and the protection of its health is essential to the public welfare. But the public welfare should be the object, and nothing else.

In between bureaucratic rigidity and the flexibility of a captive regulatory agency is a different kind of flexibility that comes from susceptibility to sundry political pressures of a less subtle kind. They come sometimes from the industry and sometimes from other elements in the community whose interests are affected. Such pressures are not always of the most savory kind, whether they stem from industry sources or from outside the industry. We have seen enough of this kind of pressure in recent years to be very wary of it. It would help if the industry realized much more clearly what the regulator's role properly is and would help protect him against themselves and against others.

In summary, I think we can look forward with some hope to significant improvements in the quality of regulation, whether it be at the state or national level. This does not necessarily mean less effective regulation. Instead it may mean more effective regulation. What it should mean is reasonable but effective regulation about the things that matter and only the things that matter. The dialogue leading to a more informed and sophisticated kind of regulation is already beginning. Some very important things are being said in academic circles on some of these problems. Unfortunately, the exchange between academicians and practical business executives is not always effective. Both sides are at fault.

This speech is an effort on my part to communicate some of the thinking that is going on in academia on the subject of insurance regulation to the men who are concerned with it daily. But you, as a part of the "reasoning, reasonable element" in the nation, as Maitland called English lawyers of an earlier era, have a special responsibility to participate in that dialogue. I urge you, as Frank Marryott did recently,[10] to get in on the dialogue and to help adjust academic thought to practical reality instead of ignoring it. Will you nill you, some of the things that are being thought and written in the academic world about insurance will become law. The near miss on Keeton-O'Connell last year and its possible success next year should be warning enough that professors cannot safely be ignored.[11] There are important and basic changes in process in this land and the old formulas for predicting what will and will not get through legislatures cannot be relied upon into the indefinite future. I urge you to become an integral part of the insurance dialogue, from its most theoretical and abstruse formulations to its most concrete and specific statements. Otherwise you may, in the end, be left out of the real decision making altogether because it may take place at quite a different level of discourse than in the past. The academician has his responsibility, too, to try to say his piece in media more likely to reach you. That I am trying to do here.

---

[10] Remarks, 1967 Ill. L. F. 387, 395.

[11] The Aponte-Denenberg plan, just enacted into law in Puerto Rico, is another such object lesson (Act No. 138 of June 26, 1968).

Your industry is capable of a high level of statesmanship, as you illustrated by your billion-dollar pledge of investments in the ghettos. Even that was not enough, and it is to be hoped that you will do far more in the future, but it was both an imaginative (and magnificently timed) gesture. The high statesmanship of which you have sometimes proved you are capable is too seldom displayed, however. Your lobbying activities and the discussions that take place in your industry groups tend to be narrowly parochial—to be concerned only with your own short-run interests. The downfall of the automobile manufacturers on the safety issue is an object lesson in the practical consequences of a lack of statesmanship. My plea is that you avoid that kind of catastrophe for yourselves—that you realize that your industry has a great mission to perform and that you reach beyond your ordinary limitations and exhibit always and on all subjects the high statesmanship and the constructive thought that your leading spokesmen have sometimes demonstrated.

PART VII
The Diagnosis and Treatment of Sick Insurers

chapter 19

Wisconsin's New Medical Kit

PATTERSON HAS POINTED out that insurers are regulated from the cradle to the grave. One of the most challenging and difficult tasks facing the regulator is the care and treatment of sick and sometimes dying insurers. The following selection discusses a broad range of problems relating to delinquency proceedings in insurance based on the approach of recently enacted Wisconsin legislation, now beginning to be copied by other jurisdictions.

DELINQUENCY PROCEEDINGS IN INSURANCE: THE INSURERS REHABILITATION AND LIQUIDATION ACT OF WISCONSIN

Spencer L. Kimball
Dean and Professor of Law
University of Wisconsin

Herbert S. Denenberg
Harry J. Loman Professor of Insurance
Wharton School of Finance and Commerce
University of Pennsylvania

"Delinquency proceedings" includes any proceedings commenced against an insurer for the purpose of liquidating, rehabilitating, reorganizing or conserving the insurer. These are devices for handling an insurer in any kind of serious trouble, whether it be in deep insolvency, involved in consistently unfair business practices, or in serious violation of rules, regulations, or statutes. They are not appropriate devices for dealing with ordinary regulatory problems, however.

The term comprehends the bankruptcy of any insurance company. Congress expressly exempted insurance companies from the

Federal Bankruptcy Act[1] in recognition of the fact that they are subject to a complete system of state regulation, which extends to include rules governing insolvency.[2] These rules governing insolvency are one aspect of delinquency proceedings.

This discussion centers on the "Insurers Rehabilitation and Liquidation Act" of Wisconsin, enacted in 1967.[3] That act is the only comprehensive systematic legislative treatment of delinquency proceedings in insurance to date.

There has been little discussion of the subject either on a national level or in Wisconsin, prior to the 1967 revision.[4] Indeed, the rehabilitation and liquidation of insurance companies is a subject rarely discussed and considered, despite its importance as a part of the regulatory framework. There is undoubtedly good reason for this omission. Death and disease, whether of a human being or an insurer, are topics naturally avoided. And when applied to an insurance company, the subject may be avoided not only on psychological grounds but for more compelling statistical reasons: even in the worst of times, the mortality and morbidity tables of insurers have included comparatively few companies, and these tend to be marginal operations that are not well established.

Consequently, the leaders of thought in the insurance business are usually no closer to the problem than is the average citizen unless a rash of insolvencies occurs which seriously threatens the public image of insurance, as has been the case recently in the substandard automobile business. Even under aggravated circumstances, the concern of the industry with the matter tends to be casual. When a series of insolvencies throws a spotlight on the subject, passing attention is given to it, but the crisis is usually over

---

[1] Federal Bankruptcy Act, 11 U.S.C. sec. 22 (1964).

[2] In *Re Supreme Lodge of Masons Annuity,* 286 F. 180, 184 (N.D. Ga. 1923), the court explained the rationale of the exemption as follows: "No reasons for making these exceptions were assigned by the committees of Congress, but they may be surmised to lie in the public or quasi-public nature of the business, involving other interests than those of creditors, in the desirability of unarrested operation, the completeness of state regulation, including provisions for insolvency, and the inappropriateness of bankruptcy machinery to their affairs."

[3] Ch. 89 (1967), Wis. Laws 220.

[4] For a New York point of view, see Bennett, "Liquidation of Insurance Companies," in Center and Heins (eds.), *Insurance and Government* (1962), pp. 197–236; for a Wisconsin point of view, see Boesel and Feldman, "Liquidation of Mutual Insurance Companies in Wisconsin," *Wisconsin Law Review,* May, 1951, pp. 493–517.

before it can get the sustained attention it needs. A few practicing attorneys who have been involved in insurance liquidations develop some ideas about the special problems they have faced, but rarely do they attempt to work out a systematic framework for dealing with them; even more rarely do they publish or even preserve their experience.

In their work for the Insurance Laws Revision Committee of the Legislative Council of the State of Wisconsin, the authors of this essay were required to make a systematic study of the major issues involved in insurance delinquency proceedings in order to formulate a statutory draft. This essay is a report on that study and the resulting statute.[5]

UNSYSTEMATIC NATURE OF PRESENT LAW

Insurance statutes deal with rehabilitation and liquidation of insurance companies in the most fragmentary way, leaving most of the law to be pieced together by borrowing liberally and unsystematically from federal bankruptcy practice and from the doctrine and practice of equity receiverships and paying little or no attention to the special needs of the insurance business. Insurers are explicitly excluded from the Federal Bankruptcy Act for good reasons— among them, that special problems and needs dictate the development of special law for the insurance business and that liquidation of a regulated enterprise is so intimately connected with regulation that it should be handled by regulators. Liquidation is in fact regulation—of the most direct and intensive sort. Comparatively little such special law has developed, however, either by statute or decision. Sporadic and sparse decisional material cannot provide the needed framework. This is especially so when the decisions must be built on an inadequate and skeletal statute. Even statutes have not provided the systematic treatment of the process that could be expected of them. Once statutes are enacted in a leading regulatory state such as New York,[6] they spread from one state to another

---

[5] The authors gratefully acknowledge the support of the Wisconsin legislature that made this comprehensive study possible.

[6] New York has also exercised a great deal of influence over the development of the law and procedures of delinquency, and has long maintained a well-staffed liquidation division. For the New York point of view, by a former head of that division, see Bennett, *op. cit.*, pp. 197–236.

without critical evaluation or appropriate integration. As a result the law, while by no means uniform, has much similarity from jurisdiction to jurisdiction and is especially alike in its uncritical acceptance of patchwork solutions to a difficult and interrelated congeries of problems.

BASIC PROBLEMS

Several major groups of problems can be isolated for consideration in a study of delinquency proceedings in insurance. As they appear in logical sequence they are as follows:

1. The causes of insolvency,
2. The detection of incipient difficulty in the insurance company operation,
3. The devising of ways to induce the insurance commissioner to take early action to correct remediable defects in insurer operation, before the sickness has become serious,
4. The provision of effective procedures for rehabilitation of companies seriously sick but still salvageable,
5. For companies that cannot be saved, the development of efficient, inexpensive, and expeditious procedures for liquidation that will distribute the unavoidable burden fairly, and
6. The complications superimposed on the above problems by the existence of a federal system as the setting for delinquency proceedings.

This discussion deals with all of these groups of problems, though with some much more than with others. The first two are treated only tangentially because they are more closely connected with substantive regulation than with delinquency proceedings. The others are dealt with in succession.

SUMMARY PROCEDURES

Insurance commissioners do not now deal with a financially ailing or otherwise sick insurance company operation, in many instances at least, until long after it is common knowledge in the industry and even in regulatory circles that the company is in serious trouble. Reluctance to take effective action despite adequate knowledge is a fundamental problem of insurance regulation, and the new law attempts to solve the problem by providing new summary procedures.

In order to encourage early action by the commissioner of a more discriminating sort than is possible using traditional methods, very flexible summary procedures were devised. Since the commissioner has previously had available to him only rather gross methods that usually involved the destruction of the company through liquidation or through an ineffective effort to save it by formal and public rehabilitation procedures, he has often been hesitant to take action until all hope was lost. Moreover, when he has merely suspected difficulty he has been unwilling to proceed because he was not sure of his ground for action and because the publicity attendant upon any proceeding was destructive of the company.

It is true that under former sec. 200.09,[7] the commissioner has had summary power to seize an insurance company in an emergency, but he has never used it. That restraint seems wise since the statute was devised to deal with bank insolvencies and is poorly designed for insurance companies. Hence it is necessary to equip the commissioner with a variety of discriminating weapons that will enable him to deal effectively and promptly with incipient difficulty, if he will use them. Unlike traditional regulatory tools, the new procedures are designed to eliminate unnecessary damage to the insurer and needless intervention in the industry.

There should be no reason why the commissioner would not use the new procedures. They are not novel devices; they have counterparts in the Wisconsin banking law[8] and in similar procedures in the California insurance statutes.[9] Nor are they dangerous. They are hedged about with procedural safeguards against arbitrariness by the commissioner, including quick and easy access to judicial review. Moreover, because they can be used with minimum publicity and less massive intervention, they can be used with less risk of destruction and interference with the company and are thus less dangerous than more formal methods.

The chapter creates two kinds of summary procedures, one a simple order, either mandatory or inhibitory, and the other a seizure order. Normally, the former type of order would be obtained after a

---

[7] Unless otherwise indicated, statutory references are to Wisconsin Statutes, 1965. The discussion focuses also on the State of Wisconsin.

[8] Sec. 220.08.

[9] Cal. Ins. Code secs. 1011–12, 1065 (West Supp. 1967).

hearing; in emergency situations the commissioner may issue such an order without hearing but subject to immediate and speedy court control at the instance of the company. The seizure order would normally be issued by a court, and only in an emergency by the commissioner.

These devices will enable the commissioner to deal effectively with single practices that endanger the company solvency or the public interest. Where venal manipulation of assets is feared, he will be able to seize assets and books quickly enough to protect them and to learn what is happening. The prospect of immediate court supervision and the possibility of devastating criticism of his action in the insurance world where he values his reputation highly will suffice to keep the commissioner from abusing this carefully limited power. In addition, a commissioner will not be unaware of possible tort liability if he should act improperly. Indeed, the greater difficulty is to give the commissioner sufficiently discriminating weapons to induce him to act as soon as he should; nearly always he is inclined to do nothing until it is too late. Experience to date indicates no tendency on the part of the commissioner to abuse his right to use summary procedures.

FORMAL PROCEDURES

The summary proceedings just described will not always be appropriate. When difficulties have reached a certain point, more formal action is necessary. Statutes generally distinguish between rehabilitation and liquidation, and this distinction is retained. However, rehabilitation has been conceived heretofore in the same legalistic way as liquidation—the problem is seen erroneously as one of undertaking formalized legal action to save the company—perhaps through merger, consolidation, mutualization, conversion to the stock form, or other reorganization. Occasionally these formal devices may be useful, but the emphasis has been altogether misplaced.

What is needed for rehabilitation of an insurance company is new management with the capacity to see what is wrong and the power to correct it. The chapter, therefore, tries to devise a rehabilitation procedure with a focus on management expertise. The key to success is twofold. Early action is one half, and obtaining a satisfactory rehabilitator the other half. The rehabilitator cannot be the insurance commissioner, except in a formal sense, for the commissioner has too many other things to do and may or may not know how to manage an insurance company, however able he may be as a regulator. He should not be a practicing lawyer, unless he is also management oriented and trained. He should be a manager of talent and experience in the insurance business. It is important to draw from the industry an experienced executive of recognized ability who will regard it both as his public duty and his private opportunity to save the company.

To obtain the "right" person requires help from the industry. If they will, insurance executives can help find the man and can help convince him and his present employer that on the grounds of public service and private career opportunity he must take the job. He should be compensated liberally so that he does not lose financially. He should then be given wide discretion in management, subject only to general court supervision, so that he can take such action as is necessary to revitalize the company. Conceptually he should be treated as new management with especially broad powers, including the power to propose to the court the formal legal reorganizational devices that have heretofore been the focus of rehabilitation but that should normally be subordinated in the future to the larger management task. This change is more one of "tone"—of attitude—than of change in the formally stated rules. But tone or attitude can be a decisive factor in achieving success in a complex undertaking.

GROUNDS FOR FORMAL PROCEEDINGS

Traditionally the grounds upon which action might be instituted against an insurer were the same for rehabilitation as for liquidation, the choice between remedies depending on an estimate of probable success if the former were attempted. The new Wisconsin law retains this notion in part but tries to tailor it to reality. Rehabilitation is not appropriate at a point where a company has been allowed to approach insolvency, unless substantial additional resources are poured into the enterprise *immediately* by contributors of capital funds. A serious error in recent insurance regulation has been the futile hope that insolvent enterprises might yet survive, held long after it was too late. Consequently the grounds are now separate: those that suggest insolvency are grounds for liquidation while those that indicate only difficulty of a different order are now grounds for rehabilitation. Flexibility is preserved (1) by making either procedure *possible* on any ground, though the chapter points the procedure in one direction or the other, depending on the situation, and (2) by permitting conversion from one type of proceeding to the other.

One indication of approach is the elimination of failure to remedy an impairment of capital after a commissioner's order as a ground for liquidation. Insolvency now includes every case of impairment of capital; whenever an order to restore impaired capital is necessary, it is too late and the company should be put into liquidation. Generosity on this matter would be misplaced. The only exception to a rule that such a company should be liquidated immediately is if money is poured into the enterprise so quickly that it is again clearly solvent before the commissioner irreversibly commits the company to the liquidation process. He should not wait to begin to do what is necessary to protect the public while efforts are made to find money.

Insurance codes generally include a substantial list of grounds for rehabilitation and liquidation. New York sec. 511, for example, lists a dozen or more grounds. Wisconsin's former law[10] contained seven grounds. The new Wisconsin law includes all conventional grounds as well as several not found in other codes. One new ground provides for rehabilitation if the control of the insurer, whether by stock ownership or otherwise, is in any person found by the commissioner after notice and hearing to be dishonest or untrustworthy.[11] This ground was inserted because of concern with recent indications that criminal elements are attempting to enter the insurance business.

Another new ground for rehabilitation is failure not only of the insurer but also by any person having executive authority in the insurer to submit for inspection by the commissioner any books, records, accounts, or documents pertaining to the insurer.[12] The

---

[10] Sec. 200.08.
[11] Sec. 645.31 (5).
[12] Sec. 645.31 (7).

provision is novel in reaching those with executive authority as well as the insurer itself.

LIQUIDATIONS

Liquidation is an unfortunate end to an enterprise, to be handled as efficiently and expeditiously and economically as possible and with as equitable as possible an allocation of the inevitable loss.

The influence of the Federal Bankruptcy Act is quite apparent in the sections dealing with liquidation. That act provides a time tested, though not ideal, source for liquidation procedures. But the act has not been blindly followed when the special problems of insurance liquidation and regulation or other considerations urge a departure from the model.

The chapter tries to provide for an orderly and complete procedure; for a technique for the handling of claims, especially third-party claims, in which everyone makes some concessions to the common necessity and no one suffers too much; for a system of priorities in claims that will enable some classes of claims to be paid earlier than they are now and that will ensure that the insurance company comes as close as possible to performing its social function even in its death throes; for powerful and discriminating devices to recover assets improperly dissipated while the patient was in a coma.

The section on priorities establishes a complete system of distribution among unsecured creditors based on relative social and economic importance of the claims likely to be asserted against the insurer. The system is more intricate than any list of priorities provided in any other law. It would have been possible to simplify the system by having fewer categories. This is what the traditional priority system does, for it generally gives priority only to a few kinds of claims—indeed the traditional pattern is no system at all. Its crude simplicity does crude injustice and fails to carry out sound public policy by minimizing the damage done to the insured community when an insurer fails. The insurance enterprise should be made to do its proper job in the social organism so far as that is possible with the limited assets that remain in a liquidation.

High on the new list of priorities are claims for losses in excess of $200.[13] They are followed by claims for losses of $200 or less and claims for unearned premium reserves.

The new Wisconsin statute subordinates government claims, a category traditionally given high priority. There is no justification for giving a high priority to the sovereign because it is sovereign, notwithstanding tradition. The United States, as well as other governmental bodies, should be able to survive without hardship even if given low priority.

The statute also subordinates claims based on judgments. If a claimant files a claim and bases it both on the judgment and the underlying facts, the claim shall be considered by the liquidator who shall give the judgment such weight as he deems appropriate. Thus, the claim if substantiated by proof beyond the mere judgment itself will attain the priority it rightly deserves. Without such proof, the claim will be subordinated. Whether or not recent judgments can be rendered invalid under other provisions of the law, they should always be suspect because of the likelihood of inadequate defense in the last days of an insurer. This priority is an effort to provide additional protection to the estate of the insurer against unwarranted depletion by such inadequately defended suits.

INTERSTATE PROBLEMS

Complicating all of the problems of insolvency is the inevitably complicated federal system. A great deal of attention was paid to the interstate implications of insolvency. One possible solution to interstate problems would be a federal procedure for the liquidation of insurance companies. Though some might argue for federal insurance legislation modeled on the Federal Bankruptcy Act to solve the interstate problems, the Wisconsin draft was based on two assumptions: (1) that such a solution is not necessary to achieve a workable system and (2) that because of widespread acceptance of and emphasis on the advantages of a decentralized governmental system, such a solution would not now be acceptable. More extensive adoption and application of the Uniform Insurers Liquidation Act would help—many interstate problems are solved when all

---

[13] Sec. 645.68 (3) provides that claims under life insurance and annuity policies, whether for death proceeds, annuity proceeds, or investment values, shall be treated as loss claims for purposes of priority determination.

states involved enact and observe that law.[14] Though it needs revision, that act was a cornerstone of the Wisconsin draft's interstate system. Its inclusion reflects recognition of the virtues of uniformity rather than conviction that the act was adequately designed for the present day. Furthermore, it was modified in several respects to strengthen Wisconsin procedures.

The chapter adopts the Uniform Insurers Liquidation Act, formerly ch. 616, in substance and effect. In form, however, the Uniform Act has been broken up and integrated into the fabric of this completely reorganized treatment of delinquency proceedings. Some changes have also been made. By integrating the act in this law, a more logical structure was achieved. At the same time, all benefits of enactment of the Uniform Act's provisions are retained. It is still appropriate to regard this state as a "reciprocal state" within the meaning of the Uniform Act as that term is defined in sec. 645.03 (9) and in the Uniform Act. Although the Uniform Act may be regarded as the cornerstone of the chapter's approach to interstate problems, that act is both modified and extended to assure more efficient regulation of interstate delinquency problems.

The new law gives the Wisconsin liquidator express statutory power to ask for a federal receiver (sec. 645.45). This is an extraordinary remedy and one that should not be used indiscriminately. But it has important advantages in special circumstances. The principal advantage is that federal law (28 U.S.C. sec. 754) gives the federal receiver control of all property throughout the United States, with the right to possession thereof, regardless of local law. Under the Uniform Act, he would have the equivalent of this power in a state receivership in reciprocal states, at least if they cooperate, but not necessarily in nonreciprocal states.

A commissioner might wish to seek a federal receivership if much of the insurer's property was located in nonreciprocal states or uncooperative reciprocal states and if he anticipated difficulty in reducing it to possession. The classic case was the Inland Empire debacle where a federal receiver was appointed by the Federal District Court for Utah on petition of a Utah creditor.[15] He then handled the liquidation of the company, which was domiciled in Utah. Both the Utah and Idaho commissioners supported the appli-

---

[14] Promulgated by the Conference of Commissioners on Uniform State Laws in 1939, and apparently now adopted in 27 states. 9B U.L. Ann. 284 (1966).

[15] *Inland Empire* v. *Freed,* 23 F. 2d 289 (10th Cir. 1956).

cation for a receivership in view of the difficulty in reducing the company property to possession.

Limitations inherent in the federal system may make some of the devices proposed in the draft less useful than they might be otherwise, but they should be considered for enactment for whatever effect they would have. The federal system has its price. The draft assumes that the state wishes to pay that price, but the adequate procedures to solve the interstate problems may reduce the price. This entire area—the interstate implications of the liquidation procedure—is fraught with difficulty.

A NOTE ON PROBLEMS EXCLUDED FROM THE NEW LAW

Not every topic relating to insolvency is treated in the Wisconsin draft. Much of the literature on that subject has focused on the causes of insolvency. As already indicated, the draft does not treat that problem but left it to be dealt with later in connection with substantive problems where it can be more appropriately considered.

Likewise, the draft does not consider security funds for payment of the inevitable losses incident to insolvency and liquidation. Such solutions will be of interest at a later date in the study of other substantive problems of insolvency. But whatever devices are used to lessen the burden of liquidation, there will always be need to rehabilitate and liquidate some insurance companies, and this proposal concentrated on those problems. Though some liquidation problems, for example, determination of priorities, would be lessened or eliminated if security funds were created, the bulk of this law would remain untouched. The recently introduced bill for a Federal Motor Vehicle Guaranty Insurance Corporation[16] is a different matter. If it were enacted in its present form it might spell the end of significant state regulation of insurance and thus could alter the entire field in revolutionary and unpredictable ways. For obvious reasons, no serious consideration could be given in the Wisconsin study to the changes that passage of that bill would necessitate.[17]

---

[16] S. 3919, 89th Cong. 2d sess. (1966); S. 688, 90th Cong., 1st sess. (1967).

[17] In a new bill, introduced into the 1969 legislature as S. 525, the security fund problem was approached by the revision staff by proposing a

One basic proposal contained in a preliminary version of this draft was later excised. It has not been abandoned but rather was postponed for later consideration. It seems important to provide new and better ways to channel all available information on insurer insolvency (and on other problems) from the industry to the insurance department early enough to be of help in regulation, and particularly to make it possible to take effective action to deal with insolvency problems. One possibility is the creation of a defined industry group with specific responsibility to provide a channel for such information. The preliminary draft proposed the creation of a formal advisory committee of insurance executives who would assist the commissioner in many ways, of which this would be one. This committee was originally given other official responsibility also, such as helping to find a good special deputy for rehabilitation. It was hoped that an official connection with the task and a public responsibility to provide information would ensure the full cooperation of the industry in keeping the department systematically informed of industry knowledge about impending insolvencies. This group could also be used on important problems other than delinquency proceedings, and it seemed wise to postpone working out provisions for its creation and governance until the organization, powers, and procedures of the insurance department are considered. Various possibilities would exist. The committee might be named by the commissioner or by the governor, with statutory safeguards to ensure quality and variety of the members. The idea received both enthusiastic endorsement and strong opposition, and there was much disagreement about the way such a body should be formed.

CONCLUSION

The new statute will provide a marked improvement over present delinquency provisions which are unsystematic, incomplete, and generally inadequate by substituting a comprehensive treatment which fully and fairly balances the conflicting interests of policyholders, the public, and insurance company ownership.

---

post hoc assessment procedure to meet the needs created by the deficiencies developed in liquidating either domestic or foreign insurers.

PART VIII
Overview

chapter 20

European Perspectives on American Insurance Regulation

INSURANCE REGULATION, like the insurance technique itself, is a highly pragmatic art. Actual experience, even if abroad, is sometimes more useful than pure theory, even if domestic. One of the most neglected of all sources of thought about insurance regulation is the international insurance arena.

The following selection focuses European insights and regulatory experiences on current American problems.

AMERICAN INSURANCE REGULATION SEEN THROUGH EUROPEAN EYES

Werner Pfennigstorf
University of Hamburg, Germany
Research Associate
University of Michigan

The clearest impression this country makes upon any European visitor is in terms of sizes and numbers. It inevitably takes time to adjust to the dimensions prevailing here, both geographical and economic. Insurance is no exception. Whether it be total premium income or the number of insurance companies operating in the market, the amount of life insurance in force or the total assets held by insurers, the United States ranks at the top of almost every statistic in this field. Even the consolidated figures for the six European Common Market countries do not compare with this gigantic market.

But the market is not only vast, it is also hard to explore, as everyone who tries soon finds out—it can much more appropriately be described as a jungle than as an open prairie. Assistance provided by trade associations leads even farther into the wilderness. There are scores of associations, commonly known and referred to by their initials. The full names are sometimes only slightly more descriptive of the nature and purposes of the particular association, and the foreigner is little comforted to learn that even high government officials are sometimes confused. But the real problem is that each of the associations represents only a small portion of the industry.

None of the many associations speaks for the industry as a whole, which means that there is no table at which a common policy could be formulated, and no office in which authoritative statistics could be assembled on consistent and reliable bases. Special ad hoc committees have so far been the industry's response to particularly serious challenges affecting all or most of the various factions, as, e.g., in the tense situation created by the South-Eastern Underwriters decision of the U.S. Supreme Court. Yet it seems that this method of dealing with problems may be too cumbersome and too slow to anticipate and react properly to more subtle challenges.

In the jungle of the American insurance market a merciless struggle for life seems to be going on, reflected by a huge turnover of insurers entering and leaving the market. Around a solid core of old, established companies, an amazingly large number of new insurers are formed each year, matched by an equally impressive number of mergers and dissolutions. The turnover is greatest among the smaller new companies, indicating that it is relatively easy for new enterprises to gain entrance into the market where they are left to find out for themselves whether they can survive and prosper. The latter, obviously, is not easy.

On the other hand, there are complaints that the market is not adequately served. Inadequate health insurance protection for the aged led to the introduction of Medicare; and the difficulty of finding coverage for certain risks in property and in automobile insurance has subjected insurers to compulsion in various ways and threatens to subject them involuntarily to almost revolutionary change.

All this creates a special degree of curiosity in the foreigner with respect to American insurance regulation. What does a regulatory system look like that can supervise such a gigantic and chaotic industry?

THE SHAKY POSITION OF STATE REGULATION

The first thing a foreigner discovers about American insurance regulation is that it is done by the states. This increases his confusion. While it is clear that in a federal state jurisdiction must be distributed somehow, a European is accustomed to consider the free movement of trade and commercial services as one of the prime responsibilities of the central government in such a federation and the existence of uniform legal rules for large-scale business operations as an essential condition for that free movement. Large-scale operations may not be desirable in all areas of economic life, but they certainly are in the case of insurance. It is a business that performs best if risks can be spread most widely, both over classes of risks and geographically. Consequently, many American insurers operate in more than one state, and the big ones are active everywhere. This is true even though some of the individual states exceed many European countries in size and population.

Actually, state insurance regulation has indeed been felt to be an obstacle to the transaction of insurance on a nationwide basis, as it was in Germany, Switzerland, and Austria, and the present state of affairs is attributable in part to what may properly be called historical accident. In the absence of *Paul* v. *Virginia,* the United States might have had federal insurance regulation or a mixed system as early as the early 1870's.

The observer's curiosity is greatly increased: How do 50 independent jurisdictions with powers limited territorially manage to regulate the activities of organizations which do most of their business elsewhere? And, on the other hand, how do the insurers manage to continue operating effectively on the national level despite competing and possibly conflicting regulation by the various states?

Moreover, while in Austria, Germany, and Switzerland the matter was decided once and for all 80 years ago and is no longer in issue, it appears that in the United States, after 100 years of state regulation, the question is still unsettled, or, more accurately, after it had appeared to be settled for 75 years, the question has been revived and is now as controversial as ever. This is unfortunate; it is a consequence of the fact that the decision to continue state regulation was in supposed involuntary compliance with the Supreme

Court decision in *Paul* v. *Virginia* rather than the result of careful comparative evaluation of the merits of different available systems. Such an evaluation has become meaningful only after the Supreme Court in the South-Eastern Underwriters case opened the way for federal regulation. But today the choice cannot be made as easily on the merits as would have been possible in 1870. State insurance regulation, which was only in its beginnings at that time, has developed into a complex and dynamic institution with strong vested interests. Insurers, likewise, have learned to live with the existing system and show their traditional dislike for any change.

The very fact that the issue is being discussed so vigorously after the states have had such a long time to prove their case indicates that there is less than general satisfaction with the operation of the system. The present uncertainty about the future of state regulation is worse in its effect than the deficiencies of either system, securely established, would be. Basic questions like this should not be left hanging in the air, undecided, for such a long time. The compromise reached in the McCarran Act might have been an appropriate way to keep state insurance regulation from collapsing during the period of adjustment after the South-Eastern Underwriters decision. But the constant, never-ending threat of congressional action does not seem to provide the kind of climate in which state insurance regulation in the true sense of independent, decentralized governmental initiative can thrive. In a sense, in responding to this threat, the states have already abandoned the idea of state regulation and have in fact made a federal matter of it. In order to avoid repeal or revision of the McCarran Act, they watch with the closest attention the mood of Congress or its committees, and whenever actual or alleged deficiencies in the regulatory system seem likely to arouse concern, they tend to move promptly and responsively to remove the cause for the concern. The current strengthening of the National Association of Insurance Commissioners is a necessary step towards making anticipation of, and reaction to, such federal threats more rational and effective. In order to do a good job, the NAIC has been and will be forced to take on more and more of the characteristics of a central federal regulatory agency, although it will never have the powers of such an agency. This, then, will be neither state nor federal regulation, and it may be doubted if such a situation is a desirable compromise. The lack of power in the NAIC and the resulting enforcement gap may well provide the cause for a final federal takeover, and in the meantime, the mood of congressional committees seems to be a basis of questionable solidity for sound regulatory policy. Anticipated, but not yet materialized, federal moves may, indeed, provoke overreaction on the part of the states and lead to unnecessarily strict regulation.

Because of this uncertainty, the issue of state versus federal regulation cannot be considered as an isolated question. Rather, it provides the background for the discussion of almost every regulatory problem that comes up today. Whether it be the performance of automobile insurance or the availability of fire insurance in urban areas, health insurance for senior citizens, or objectionable practices of mail-order insurers, any proposed solution has to pass the additional test of whether it favors the position of state regulation in its fight against federal intervention. The weight of such policy considerations may be so strong as to prevail over considerations of regulatory effectiveness.

THE MANY DIVERSE FACES OF REGULATION

The problem is further complicated by the fact that "regulation of insurance" is a very broad term used to comprehend many different activities. For instance, the direct consequences of the SEUA case were limited to the applicability of existing federal antitrust law. On the other hand, much of the opposition among the states to "federal regulation" seems to be based on the more remote possibility of losing to the federal government the states' income from premium taxes. Between these extremes, there are many aspects of regulation which according to their nature ought to receive separate consideration in the distribution of powers between federal and state governments.

There is a marked difference between, for example, the problem of controlling mergers of large, nationally operating insurers domiciled in different states and the problem of licensing local agents. There is also a significant difference between supervision of the business of insurers operating in several or all of the states and of insurers with operations restricted to a single state.

Another difference exists between regulatory legislation and its administrative enforcement. This crucial difference seems scarcely to be appreciated in the United States but is fully recognized and is of great importance in some European countries. In Germany, for example, the federal insurance regulation law applies to all of the 9,000 insurers operating in Germany, but only 900 of them are supervised by the federal insurance department. The others, mostly small local mutuals, are supervised by state agencies, but according to the provisions of the federal law.

Finally, there is a difference, not sharply delineated in the United States, between the administrative regulation of business operations and the law of the insurance contract. Unlike the American system which assigns to the "insurance code" all statutory enactments relating in any significant sense to insurance, the civil law countries have separate codes for each of the two subjects. This is based on a long tradition of distinguishing strictly and with technical precision between matters of private law (concerning the dealings of private citizens among themselves) and matters of public law (concerning all actions of the state in the exercise of governmental authority). General principles of private law do not apply to public law, and there are even separate court systems to decide controversies. Of course the distinction is not unknown in the United States, but it has not acquired the degree of practical importance it has in Europe.[1] It may well be, however, that with the further development of administrative law and the extension of governmental functions, and especially if there is an establishment of special administrative tribunals in the United States, a similarly strict partition of the law may result.

THE SPECIAL PROBLEMS OF INSURANCE CONTRACT LAW

The present inclusion of contract law provisions in the insurance codes can easily be explained by the fact that in the Anglo-American legal system the rules of contract law in general have traditionally not been a subject of legislation but have been announced and shaped by the courts. Legislatures have usually interfered with this process only when they felt it necessary in order to enforce a specific public policy contrary to existing case law, or where no case law

---

[1] See Kimball and Pfennigstorf, *Legislative and Judicial Control of the Terms of Insurance Contracts: A Comparative Study of American and European Practice,* 39 Ind. L.J. 675, 678–679 (1964) for an explanation of this difference as it applies to the control of insurance contracts.

existed. The conventional dogma still is that statutes constitute an illicit inroad into, and an exception to, the traditional body of case law. Only a few insurance codes try to lay down anything like a general and comprehensive restatement of the rules of insurance contract law. In most codes, the scattered enactments relating to contract law matters are so few, so specific and unrelated that taken out of the general insurance codes, they would not add up to an appreciable, even if disorganized, "insurance contract code" of their own.

At present, of course, almost the entire body of both insurance contract law and insurance regulation law is exclusively at the state level, and thus there is no practical need for separation. But what would be the effect of federalization of regulation? Would it and should it be extended to insurance contract law?

The question is hardly academic, for the present state insurance codes contain many important provisions about insurance contracts, such as nonforfeiture laws, standard fire policies, and elaborate standard provisions for disability and sometimes for life policies. If a federal regulatory code developed, it might well be desirable to take the contract provisions over into the federal insurance code, along with the requirement that policy forms must be filed with and approved by the regulatory agency. It would be impractical for a federal insurance department to consider the statutory and case law of 50 states each time it had to approve a new policy form in order to determine whether the form was "in compliance with the law."

On the other hand, if only existing provisions were included in a federal insurance code, it would only affect the statutory portion of insurance contract law. The bulk of the subject would be case law at the state level. Policies approved by the federal agency would still continue to be subject to interpretation under the common law of different states, and the courts would apply the different ideas of public policy that prevail in the various states. The Erie doctrine tells us there is no federal common law.

Moreover, if a federal code were applicable only to "interstate" insurers, the market and the courts in each of the states would end up with different rules of contract law depending on whether a policy were issued by an insurer operating in one state only or by an insurer operating across state lines. This would be an unfortunate situation, with one more jurisdiction added to the present 50 odd. To avoid this result, a federal insurance contract law would have to be so comprehensive and detailed as to leave no room whatsoever for any conflicting statutory or case law of the states.

Thus it seems that uniformity in the field of insurance contract law would not necessarily be achieved even if "insurance regulation" were to be federalized. Whatever progress can be made here would be more likely to come through voluntary cooperation among the states. There seems, indeed, to be little merit in having different rules with respect to the consequences of concealment or misrepresentation in each of the 50 states. Diversity of legal rules in the field of insurance transactions is no more appropriate than in the sale of goods or in negotiable instruments where the Uniform Commercial Code has recently brought about a considerable degree of uniformity. As a matter of fact, uniformity of contract rules has been an important objective in insurance circles for a long time, and the NAIC in particular has been active with considerable success in preparing and proposing model acts. However, there is a very long way to go before a "Uniform Insurance Contract Code" similar to the Uniform Commercial Code can be written.

A uniform code of this type still would not solve all problems. First, it would have to be adopted substantially intact in all the various jurisdictions, which means that in many states time-honored specific legal rules would have to be sacrificed. Second, the uniformity would have to be protected against subsequent amendments in individual states. A high level of cooperation among the states would have to continue so that any necessary changes could be made in accord. Finally, there is the danger of losing the uniformity of the statutory law as it becomes overgrown by case law. With as many as 50 separate and independent state supreme courts (and numerous federal courts) busy in applying and interpreting the uniform provisions, this process would not take very long. In Germany, the various states forming the "Deutscher Bund" envisaged this problem when they adopted a uniform commercial code in the middle of the 19th century. With the code, they established a central court with supreme authority to decide legal questions arising under the new code. Whether such a tribunal would be feasible under prevailing American constitutional law and institutional practices is doubtful, but it would be the only way to preserve unity in the law, short of comprehensive enactment of a federal insurance contract law.

The discovery that the American system of insurance regulation

consists of 50 independent jurisdictions would discourage the foreigner from further inquiry were it not for the fact that a small
number of states have acquired, over the years, leading positions,
and are, in fact, setting the pace and determining the direction for
the regulatory policy of most of the other states.

THE NATURE OF AMERICAN INSURANCE CODES

Looking for the legal bases of insurance regulation, it is encouraging, at first glance, to find a special "insurance code" in almost
every state. However, it soon appears that these codes belong to an
entirely different species than the codes of the civil law system.
Under the traditions of the civil law system, statutes are not only
the supreme source of law but also the primary source of law. Cases
only aid in the interpretation of statutory provisions and have no
independent authority of their own. All the effort and skill that in
Anglo-American legal practice and legal education goes into the
analysis, comparison, and distinction of cases is in the civil law
countries devoted to the interpretation and analysis of statutes.
European statutes are read more often and more carefully and are
generally considered as far more important than American statutes,
and this attitude affects not only the method of application but also
the method of statutory drafting. Consistency and clarity of language, the careful grammatical construction of sentences, and systematic organization are at the heart of the drafting process.
Amendments are often delayed in order to avoid upsetting the
systematic unity and consistency of a code, and then they are
carefully framed to fit neatly into the existing pattern.

In marked contrast, American insurance codes reflect much more
the pragmatic case-by-case approach of Anglo-American case law.
Legislatures, like courts, deal with one problem at a time, whenever
it becomes sufficiently urgent to be pressed upon them. They do not
worry about the systematic character and conceptual integrity of the
system. The resulting "codes" are therefore, as a rule, not comprehensive and systematic codifications but loose collections of
hundreds of individual enactments, sometimes assembled by a
public official in charge of the official compilation of statutes,
sometimes by a private publisher, but rarely by an expert insurance
lawyer. A distinct advantage of the American method is that it
avoids the danger of legislating too far ahead into the future, before

a problem has fully materialized. It also facilitates, rather than discourages, quick legislative action in case of emergency. The negative aspects of this approach have been summarized by American critics in the terms "piecemeal legislation" or "legislative chaos," and "paste-and-scissors revisions," indicating the danger that in enacting many small statutes for small problems, each based on small-scale studies, some big but less obvious problems are overlooked, or similar problems receive different and inconsistent treatment because their similarity is not recognized, or the same problem is dealt with inconsistently in two different places. As a result, some American insurance codes are so unclear and confusing as seriously to endanger the quality of substantive regulation. It is encouraging to notice, however, that many states have recognized the importance of clear and consistent statutory rules and are presently engaged in revisions of their insurance "codes." Whether they will actually succeed in developing comprehensive, systematic, and consistent treatment of the subject is another question.

THE NATURE OF THE REGULATORY AGENCY

The next important factor in the framework of American insurance regulation is the regulatory agency. Even the best statute can achieve its purposes only if it is effectively enforced by a competent administrative agency. In the United States, the 50 state insurance laws are, of course, enforced by 50 different insurance departments, as different as are the resources, the administrative traditions, and the political constellations in the various states. Some are very big, some only a tiny annex to another agency; some do a good job, some do almost nothing at all, some are said to be captives of the insurance industry, and some are said to harass it. This is not surprising, given the enormous differences that exist among the states.

Noteworthy are the characteristics which these agencies, or most of them, have in common and which distinguish them from their European counterparts. For example, the European observer is amazed to find that only one of the 50 insurance commissioners is appointed for life within the civil service system, while most of the others are either political appointees with limited tenure or are even elected by the public. In Europe, the insurance department is generally regarded as a technical rather than a political department within the structure of government, and the department head is normally a civil servant appointed for life. The difference reflects a general difference of political thinking, with the Americans favoring direct political control, while Europeans tend to rely on the traditions of an unpolitical professional bureaucracy. The fact that the office of the regulator is a political office in the United States has practical consequences, most of them undesirable consequences. One is the high turnover rate among commissioners which greatly reduces the period of time during which they can make intelligent and informed decisions and discourages departments from pursuing long-term developmental projects. Another consequence, much deplored recently in the context of rate regulation, is the responsiveness of regulatory decisions to political considerations or pressures rather than to the merits of the subject.

Basic differences of philosophy have effect upon the operation and performance of American insurance departments in many other ways. A deep and strong suspicion against all kinds of governmental power and governmental activity is part of the American tradition. Only in recent decades have Americans realized, slowly and reluctantly, that they simply cannot run their nation and their states without the services of a large professional bureaucracy. But the adaptation has not yet fully been made. For instance, the general principles of administrative law are still only poorly developed. While in Europe such general rules have existed since the middle of the 19th century, American administrative law and theory is still in its infancy. Different rules on administrative hearings, on the effect of orders, and on judicial review can be found not only for different government departments but even within the insurance codes for different subjects. Great diversity and uncertainty also exist with respect to the enforcement of statutory requirements and administrative orders. Lack of sufficiently flexible and effective enforcement tools sometimes places the insurance commissioner in a position where he can choose only between doing nothing at all and revoking a foreign insurer's license, or liquidating a domestic insurer.

Another relic of the traditional American antigovernment attitude is the lack of prestige and social status of government civil service, and, closely related to it, the inadequate compensation of government employees which is so often cited as the main reason for the generally poor quality of insurance department staff members in some states and for the difficulty of attracting highly qualified experts.

American insurance departments constantly complain about insufficient funding. Although many of them collect more in fees than they expend and although premium taxes for general revenue greatly exceed regulatory costs, they experience great difficulty in getting adequate budgets approved by the legislatures. In most European countries, the costs of insurance regulation are directly assessed in full or in major part among the supervised insurers. Only one of the American insurance departments is financed in this rational way.

THE SUBSTANCE OF REGULATION

The substantive rules of insurance regulation show many more similarities than differences when compared to the European systems. Insurers are closely supervised from cradle to grave. Generally speaking, more aspects of company operation are regulated in the United States than in Europe.

A major difference of some consequence is that many of the rules which are expressly elaborated in American statutes are contained in Europe in rules issued by the departments under more broadly framed general powers. This is true, for example, for investment requirements and trade practices. Also, it is interesting to find the financial requirements to be met by a new insurer specified in exact amounts in American statutes, separately for each line of insurance. This may be a crude way of measuring the financial viability of a new enterprise, but it is easier to apply than, e.g., the test prescribed by the German law under which the insurance department must be satisfied that the new insurer will "continuously be able to meet its obligations." In applying this provision, the German insurance department has developed a rough schedule of minimum capital amounts quite similar to that of American insurance codes, with sufficient flexibility left, however, to evaluate the special situation of each individual applicant.

This difference in methods is another consequence of the different legal philosophies already mentioned: A delegation of powers is meaningful only if it can be expected that the agency has both the competence and the political integrity to exercise the powers in the way the legislature intends. It is noteworthy in this context that modern American statutes show a tendency to delegate more and broader authority to regulatory agencies, indicating an acknowledged need for greater flexibility as well as an increased reliance on the technical knowledge and experience of regulatory officials.

THE ADMISSION OF NEW INSURERS

All regulatory systems face the problem of accommodating insurers existing and operating at the time the system is established, and at the same time providing forms in which insurers may be organized in the future. In most European systems only two forms of organization are available: the stock corporation and the mutual corporation. It is fascinating, therefore, to see that in the United States there are some additional options for the organizer. Most states permit the formation of reciprocals. Some states have groups of private underwriters of the Lloyd's type. Another hybrid form of insurer, halfway between a mutual and a state institution, has emerged in the "Blue Cross" and "Blue Shield" organizations. All this seems to indicate a greater flexibility in the regulatory system and its openness to new ideas. But it is equally easy to draw the opposite conclusion, i.e., that the new special forms of enterprise are evidence of the inability of the system to accommodate these new ideas without having to invent new corporate forms for them. The reciprocals were first recognized by the insurance code because they seemed to offer specific advantages to insureds not available within the framework of a mutual corporation. As time went by, the form became a popular vehicle for launching an insurance enterprise without having to meet the strict capital requirements imposed on stock and mutual corporations while, on the other hand, legislatures, regulators, and the pressure of competition assimilated them more and more to the traditional mutuals in all significant respects. In the case of the "Blue Cross" and "Blue Shield" plans, the motivation was the desire to encourage and promote a scheme which promised medical assistance for large segments of the working population and at the same time provided hospitals with guaranteed payments, all this in a time of general financial hardship and distress. Thus these plans were privileged by exempting them not only from taxation but also from most of insurance regulation. But here, too, time has worked to erase most of the practical differences, and the privileges still enjoyed by the "Blues" are subject to serious challenge as no longer justified.

These observations seem to confirm the earlier remarks on the American method of legislation: legislators are easily convinced that there is a new problem that deserves attention. Rather than making extensive studies about solution of the problem within the existing statutory framework or with minor adaptation, they make an entirely new statute to accommodate the problem and leave it to future litigation, administrative practice, or additional legislation to reconcile any inconsistencies created in the process.

American insurance regulation usually affects an insurance company even before it is organized; most insurance codes contain elaborate provisions for the formation of domestic insurers, substantially deviating from the procedure and requirements prescribed in the general business corporation laws. In contrast, European codes usually have special rules only for mutual corporations and for stocks rely essentially on general corporation law. This difference, however, like many others in the admission process, has no great practical importance; simple considerations of sound management and practical dealing with regulators make it imperative for promoters to seek the insurance department's advice before they launch a new company.

THE TREATMENT OF FOREIGN COMPANIES

The foreigner looks with particular curiosity at the provisions on the admission and control of insurers organized in other states of the United States. For this is a uniquely American problem, created by the fact that the insurance business, although transacted on a national scale, is regulated by the states. For Europeans, the American regulatory pattern became particularly fascinating with the formation of the European Economic Community and the consequent efforts to create a more homogeneous insurance market among the six member countries. The idea in the European Community is, of course, to abandon or to soften for insurers from member countries the additional requirements or barriers that now generally exist with respect to foreign insurers in each of the six countries.

With this objective in mind, the European observer is startled to find that most American insurance codes do not treat "foreign" insurers substantially better than "alien" insurers. The only major difference is that insurers from other states of the Union are allowed to keep any necessary additional deposits required by the law of the state where they want to operate, in their home state, while alien insurers, quite understandably, are required to place a deposit equivalent to the minimum capital and surplus of a domestic insurer within the United States. But once the applicant has furnished the money and complied with the other statutory requirements, which usually do not differ much from those prescribed for domestic insurers, the insurance commissioner's decision follows the same standards of evaluation, whether the applicant is a foreign or an alien company. In some states it seems to be a ministerial decision not different from that to be made in the case of domestic insurers; in others, it is left completely to the discretion of the commissioner who may refuse a license if "in his judgment such refusal will best promote the interests of the people of this state," with no judicial review available.[2]

Such unrestricted discretion whether to approve or to reject is now the rule in most European countries with respect to alien insurers,[3] but it is felt to be incompatible with the idea of a common market within the EEC. It will therefore be replaced by a rule under which insurers from other common market countries *must* be admitted if they meet certain uniform standards of financial solidity,[4] and other applicable requirements of the law. It will no longer be possible, e.g., to deny admission on the ground that the market is already being adequately served.[5]

---

[2] N.Y. Ins. Law sec. 40 (4), (7) (McKinney, 1966).

[3] For an account of the situation in 18 member countries of the Organization for Economic Co-operation and Development as of 1963, see *Supervision of Private Insurance in Europe* (Paris: O.E.C.D., 1963), pp. 14 and 18.

[4] The new rules are contained in a proposal for a "Directive for the Coordination of Legislative and Administrative Provisions concerning the Business of Direct Insurance (other than Life Insurance) according to Article 57 (2) of the Treaty of Rome," pulished in French in 1966, *Journal Officiel des Communautés Européennes 3055,* October 3, 1966. This draft was prepared by the Commission of the E.E.C. and has yet to be acted upon by the Council of Ministers. The crucial provisions are in art. 10–12.

[5] The so-called "need test" will be expressly prohibited under art. 10 (3) of the proposed Common Market Directive. Need tests are now provided in a number of European countries both for domestic and foreign insurers; for details, see *Supervision of Private Insurance in Europe, supra* n. 3, p. 18; Kimball, *The Purpose of Insurance Regulation: A Preliminary Inquiry in the Theory of Insurance Law,* Minn. L. Rev., Vol. 45, No. 471, pp. 514–516 (1961).

Under the American system, insurers operating in more than one state are generally required to comply with the legal provisions of each of these states applicable to like domestic insurers. This rule is indispensable in order to avoid unjustified competitive advantages for foreign insurers. But compliance with different statutes at the same time can be very difficult and may even become impossible if the requirements of the various statutes are inconsistent. Such instances are rare, fortunately, and recent statutes prevent hardship by requiring only compliance "in substance" by foreign insurers. The rules proposed for the European Community try to solve these problems partly by harmonizing the conflicting law and partly by eliminating the possibility of conflicts. For example, rules for the investment of assets will continue to be made by the individual countries, but only with respect to the assets needed to cover actuarial reserves relating to policies written within that country— all assets not thus earmarked for particular reserves will not be subject to any investment restrictions.[6]

It is obvious that the American insurance laws and the state insurance departments do not, in general, recognize the fact that an insurer has been licensed and is being supervised by another state as any greater guaranty of the insurer's financial solidity and lawful management than if it were domiciled and supervised in a far-away foreign country. The insurance codes provide not only for a complete examination of every foreign insurer prior to admission but also for thorough continuing control, including examinations of the insurer's financial affairs at regular intervals. If these examinations were to be conducted on a fully independent basis, they would present an impossible task to all except the two or three largest departments; if they were conducted independently by all departments, the larger insurers would never cease being examined by various departments. Such consequences are avoided, however, partly by the statutes themselves which permit the commissioner to accept the results of an examination conducted by another commissioner instead of conducting one himself, but mostly by the practice of conducting joint "convention examinations" in the framework of the N.A.I.C.

---

[6] This is expressly provided in art. 15 (2) and 18 (1) of the proposed directive for nonlife insurers. European insurers have traditionally been free in the investment of capital and surplus or "uncommitted assets." See *Supervision of Private Insurance in Europe, supra* n. 3, p. 20–21.

THE ARCHAIC TRADITION OF INTERSTATE DISTRUST

For all practical purposes, then, the American system appears to be one in which the basic question of the degree of "faith and credit" to be given the insurance regulation of other states is not decided in general terms by the legislature but is left to the commissioner's discretion—a necessary consequence of the enormous differences in the quality of regulation among the states and the impossibility of any statutory classification. A thorough analysis of the administrative practices and policies of each insurance department could probably produce some kind of rank order of the esteem with which the commissioners regard each other's performance. This mutual evaluation is, of course, subject to constant change due to the ever-changing legal and personnel conditions under which the various departments operate.

The present practice demonstrates that the American insurance commissioners are not indiscriminately satisfied with each other's performance. If each of the 50 insurance departments effectively and adequately supervised domestic insurers, all the other states could rely on that regulation, and there would be no need for the extensive supervision of foreign insurers presently provided for and exercised. All that would be needed would be exchange of information among insurance departments and mutual assistance in the verification of insurers' reports. The present struggle for adequate control of mail-order insurers shows how far away this goal still is.

Nothing illustrates the mutual distrust among the American states and the resulting difficulties for the improvement of insurance regulation better than the archaic principle of retaliation applied by the states against each others' insurers. It allows or even directs the insurance commissioner to do unto the insurers of another state exactly what that state does to the commissioner's domestic insurers. Retaliation is especially important for taxes and fees, but sometimes it extends to every requirement or restriction imposed upon insurers, and the only check against ridiculous results are the difficulties of application. One of the regrettable effects of retaliation is that whenever a state contemplates improvement of its regulatory system, those insurers which operate in other states are likely to object on the ground that the home states of the foreign insurers affected by the proposed change will retaliate in a formalistic and unwarranted manner and thus make it impossible for them to operate there. Most regulators seem to agree that the principle is outdated and should be abolished, but unfortunately, abandonment is only possible if all of the 50 states agree to do so at the same time.

Retaliation of the kind practiced in the United States is not exercised by European countries even with respect to foreign countries. Rather, they practice the positive counterpart of retaliation: reciprocity. Within the framework of the European Economic Community, a much greater degree of mutual reliance is envisaged than exists presently among the various states of the United States. It is proposed that insurers domiciled in a member country wanting to do business in another member country should apply for admission there, and the business they write in the other country should be subject to that country's laws relating to policy forms, rates, reserves, and investments. But the supervision of general management and financial solidity will be the responsibility of the home country, while the insurance departments of the other countries are charged with forwarding information and rendering administrative assistance.[7]

THE HEAVY BURDEN OF RATE REGULATION

Among the main features of the continuing regulation of American insurers, rate regulation is the one that has not only received the most attention by American legislatures in recent years but that also provokes the most interest in a foreign observer because of the heterogeneous policy considerations which compete, largely in unarticulated form, in shaping the principles and rules of control in this field. The most interesting interaction is that between the law of insurance regulation and the general antitrust law which in the United States is further complicated by the fact that the former is state law while the latter is mainly, though not exclusively, federal law. It does not take long, however, to conclude that at the present time it is impossible for a foreigner to analyze, let alone evaluate, the American way of controlling rates. The present diversity and confusion is the consequence less of divergent thinking than of historical accident. American insurers, regulators, and legislators themselves appear to be in complete disagreement not only about

---

[7] General standards and procedures for evaluating the financial solidity of the insurance enterprise as a whole are provided in art. 13–21 of the proposed E.E.C. Directive.

what should be done but even about what is being done now. The only safe conclusion that can be drawn from a look at the present practice of rate regulation[8] and the raging discussion is that most of the criticism voiced by representatives of the insurance industry is not founded on a basic consideration of the function of rate regulation within the total system of insurance regulation and antitrust law but rather on the relatively adventitious fact that the office of an insurance commissioner is a political office and that his decisions on rate increases are therefore inevitably subject to "political" pressures. It is difficult to see how any change in the law short of complete abolition of control over rates could eliminate the particular danger of politically inspired decisions.

Nor can a foolproof solution be offered based on European experience. Present laws and practices differ more among the European countries than they do among the American states. Even the six countries of the European Economic Community have not been able so far to agree on a common policy in this respect. The proposed common market rules leave the matter of rate regulation in the jurisdiction of the individual countries. While in Germany property and liability rates, with the single exception of automobile rates, are completely free and need not even be filed with the insurance department, other Common Market countries like France and Italy provide for rate control to various degrees.[9] And, as could be expected, these powers have in some instances been used by the governments to prevent, for political reasons, rate increases thought to be necessary.[10] Even in these countries, however, the existing statutory powers have been used only sparingly in administrative

---

[8] See, e.g., *Kentucky Legislative Research Commission, Insurance: A Study of the Administration of Kentucky Rating Laws,* Research Report No. 46 (1967); and Kimball and Boyce, *The Adequacy of State Insurance Rate Regulation: The McCarran-Ferguson Act in Historical Perspective,* 56 Mich. L. Rev. 545 (1958).

[9] For a survey of the different forms of rate regulation in European countries, see *Supervision of Private Insurance in Europe, supra* n. 3, pp. 144–45.

[10] In France, e.g., the general rule is that property and liability rates be filed for information only (*Décret du 30 décembre 1938, art. 181 al. 5*); but the minister of finance who is charged with the administration of the insurance laws has a general power to prescribe upper and lower limits for premium rates and commissions (*Ordonnance du 29 septembre 1945, art. 8*). While he has exercised the latter power only exceptionally, he did so in 1964 to order a general "freeze" for automobile rates, admittedly for the sole purpose of enforcing a general price stabilization plan adopted by the government in September, 1963. For details, see Blondel, *Le contrôle français des assurances* (Paris, no year, about 1965), pp. 176–77.

practice, and never to the extent to which they are used in certain American states.

THE LEGAL JUNGLE OF POLICY FORMS

Another aspect of continuing supervision which attracts the foreign observer's attention is the control and approval of policy forms. Like most European insurance codes, the American codes usually provide that policy forms must be filed with the commissioner and must either be affirmatively approved by him or can be disapproved within a certain time. It is not the law that amazes the observer but its practical implementation. The staggering numbers of policy forms processed as shown in occasional surveys put him in awe. He never ceases to wonder how the departments can possibly manage to review these innumerable forms, knowing from his own experience how long it takes a lawyer to read an insurance policy from beginning to end. It is true that many policy forms filed are standard or repetitious and that others need only be reviewed to see whether they contain certain forbidden or statutorily required standard provisions. But elimination of the cases requiring only a mechanical check leaves many independent policies and deviations from standard forms which according to the law must be disapproved if they are "unjust," "unfair," "inequitable," "misleading," or "encourage misrepresentation." These abstract concepts can be applied to an individual policy form only after a careful consideration of their meaning according to the rules of statutory interpretation and close attention to the policy language. The interpretation of the statutory concepts and the subsequent analysis and evaluation of the policy form require the skill and training of a professional lawyer. And yet it is rare to find lawyers involved in the policy examination process in an American insurance department. Occasionally, the attorney general is asked for his opinion whether a particular clause is "more favorable to insureds" than a statutory standard clause, but thousands of forms flow across the desks of American insurance departments without ever being seen by a legally trained person.

Even among the regulators there seems some concern about the superficiality of this control. However, there is little that could be done to improve the situation. Even if the departments had the means to hire, or to train and keep, lawyers sufficiently experienced in the technicalities of insurance law, there would still be more forms than could be adequately analyzed. Permanent improvement seems to be possible only if a much higher degree of uniformity can be achieved, not only in the various state laws but also in the policy forms. A higher degree of standardization, incidentally, would not only help regulators in more meaningful evaluation of forms but also policyholders in comparing the coverages offered by competing insurers. Insurers, too, would benefit, in terms of economics and efficiency as well as through a decreasing risk of litigation and unfavorable court decisions based on real or alleged ambiguities.

THE STRUGGLE AMONG COMPETING PUBLIC POLICY GOALS

In reviewing the impressions gained from a look at American insurance regulation, it seems appropriate and desirable to compare the results and achievements of regulation with its purposes and goals. But what are these goals? The great number of jurisdictions involved and the particular way in which statutes are made in this country make it extremely difficult to identify them. Official statements are scarce and rarely complete. Professor Kimball has examined the contents of the existing insurance codes and distilled an impressive list of diversified goals and policies from them.[11] He has demonstrated that not all of the provisions of an insurance code can be explained directly by the desire to protect policyholders in their inherently weak position vis-à-vis the insurer, although this is the only ground usually cited for the "'public interest" that "affects" the insurance business and justifies government interference with freedom of contract and freedom of management. Indeed, some provisions are based on considerations that are not even indirectly related to the protection of policyholders or insureds. One example is taxation and the provisions designed to help in the collection of taxes. The sole purpose of taxes, including insurance premium taxes, is, of course, to provide revenue for the state, and there is not the slightest benefit for policyholders involved—to the contrary, it is they who are taxed, directly or indirectly. By the same token, the provision, found in most insurance codes, that directs the insurance commissioner to refuse renewal of an insurer's license if the premium tax has not been duly paid, can be explained only as a

---

[11] Kimball, *supra*. n. 5.

tax enforcement measure, not as an element of a system of policy-holder protection.

What makes this group of purposes that are not policyholder-protection oriented so intriguing is that it can be approached from different directions. Professor Kimball's method of description was pragmatic: he looked at the actual duties, requirements, restrictions, and administrative acts to which insurers are subjected by the insurance codes and by the activity of insurance departments and determined the underlying reasons for the various provisions. When he talks of insurance regulation, he means everything that *is* actually being done to insurers by the government, and consequently, he finds many purposes of insurance regulation in addition to the protection of policyholders.

German writers on insurance regulation take a different approach, which might be characterized as analytic. Their point of departure is not what insurance regulation *is* but what it *should be*, i.e., they start with the purpose of regulation as an abstract concept rather than with the complex fabric formed by actual law and practice. The purpose they specify on theoretical grounds is the protection of policyholders—the same goal that appears as the central and paramount purpose of American regulation. These writers realize, of course, that the government or the legislature does or can at any time interfere with the insurance business for many other reasons. But they draw a line between insurance regulation "proper"—i.e., the activities designed to protect the citizens against the inherent dangers of insurance transactions—on the one side, and all other government activities which have the insurance industry as their subject, on the other. These activities are classified according to the objectives they serve, as part of tax administration, antitrust control, securities control, or general economic policy. This attitude is not restricted to academic writing but also permeates the discussion of planned legislation and the discussions and decisions of administrative agencies.

THE IMPORTANCE OF CLEARLY PERCEIVED POLICY GOALS

Why should we care at all about the purposes of insurance regulation? First, an understanding of the purposes of a statute is indispensable for its intelligent and rational interpretation and implementation. Second, the purposes and objectives of a statute are the decisive criteria for its evaluation under constitutional standards. If a "public interest" in the insurance business is created by the inherent need of policyholders for public protection, it is at least doubtful if this same "public interest" can with any justification be cited in support of, e.g., a statute requiring that all insurance contracts be countersigned by a local agent. Rather, such an objective not related to the protection of policyholders should be scrutinized independently and allowed to stand only on its own merits. The plight of policyholders should not be used to provide free admission into the statute books to any measure that has the label "insurance regulation" attached to it. Third, and most important, an inquiry into, and full understanding of, the purposes and goals sought to be achieved by legislative bills can help lawmakers and other interested persons to evaluate more adequately the political as well as the more far-reaching legal, economic, and social implications of a proposed measure, including possible alternative solutions. Ideally, it can lead to a more rational and thus more effective and at the same time more equitable system of regulation.

For an example, let us return to the provisions that make renewal of an insurer's license to transact business dependent on prior payment of the state premium tax (sometimes called a "license fee"). It is obvious that the insurer's tax default does not itself endanger the interests of policyholders. So far as the basic goals of insurance regulation are concerned, licenses could be issued for indefinite terms; the protection of policyholders requires constant surveillance, not review at annual intervals. The default may, of course, indicate that the insurer is in financial trouble, but it may also be due to some disagreement about the proper computation of the tax. On the other hand, loss of the insurer's license is usually detrimental both to the insurer and to its policyholders; even if the insurer is solvent and can pay all current claims, the policyholders are forced to seek new coverage elsewhere, and thereby incur inconvenience and expenses. A look into the tax statutes reveals that the tax collection agencies do not, as a rule, suffer from a lack of enforcement powers. They are in a position to compel payment of taxes due without much difficulty or additional delay. Even insolvency of the insurer usually has little effect on recovery under tax claims because of the high priority these claims enjoy under most bankruptcy laws, compared to the claims of policyholders.

Making tax payment a condition for the renewal of the insurer's license thus does not seem to be indispensable for tax collection. It is an extra, additional club for enforcing timely tax payment, put into the law solely for the taxing government's convenience.

THE DANGERS OF DIVERSION OF POWERS

Is it proper to use the insurance commissioner's licensing power, established in the interest of policyholders' protection, to facilitate the collection of taxes? Is it not rather a *misuse* of governmental power? Imagine a law denying registration as a voter to every citizen who has not paid his income tax exactly on the due date. Or a town administration refusing the issuance of a building permit because the applicant is in arrears with his property tax. These examples illustrate the broader problem: Should a government use powers to pursue purposes not related to the particular power? The danger does not lie in the exercise of governmental power as such but rather in the diversion of powers to uses for which they were not originally intended. A system under which the government was completely free to establish connections and dependencies among all its many functions, and to apply the powers entrusted to it for unrelated and incommensurate ends, would not only violate traditional American ideas but might eventually result in a totalitarian state.

The examples suggest that the problem is mainly one of degree. Practice can fall anywhere on a scale from complete harmony between the power and the objective, through arguable but legitimate judgments on which reasonable men might disagree, to patently arbitrary and capricious acts. I do not suggest that to bar renewal of an insurer's license for nonpayment of taxes is unconstitutional. I only wish to demonstrate the importance of the relationship between governmental powers and their specific objectives, and the dangerous consequences that can result if this relationship is forgotten or is obscured. This is why it is essential to see clearly the objectives of every single statutory provision, and to distinguish clearly between those designed to protect policyholders and those serving other unrelated interests. A legislature acting upon a provision tying together two subjects as little related as insurer licensing and tax collection should at least know clearly what it is doing.

There are many other examples of similar distortions of regulatory power. Rate regulation, for instance, has become a complicated blend of policyholder protection and antitrust elements in the United States. Professor Kimball has demonstrated how little connection there is between actual practice and the basic ideas of regulation.[12] Even under the puristic German philosophy, the regulatory authorities have felt responsible for keeping a watch over rates even in lines where the statutes do not require prior approval. While the insurance department does not concern itself with the adequacy or excessiveness or even with unjustified discriminations in individual cases, it does feel compelled to step in whenever the market forces do not operate properly, either threatening the stability of insurers by excessive competition at inadequate rates, or neglecting the policyholders' interests by restricting competition at excessive rates. The general powers of the insurance department are broad enough to permit rather stiff measures, which, however, so far have not been necessary. The existing power and experience of the insurance department were the reason for treating insurance companies more liberally than other enterprises in the general antitrust law. This law is flexible enough, e.g., to permit price-fixing cartels if the price structure of a market is about to be ruined by extreme competition, as happened recently in the commercial fire insurance business. Such cartels are permitted only as long as they are absolutely necessary to bring rates back to a reasonable level, and during that time they are subject to close and joint supervision by the antitrust and the insurance departments.

THE DANGERS OF CONFUSION AMONG PUBLIC POLICIES

Another rather striking case in point is furnished by the various provisions forcing insurers to join assigned risk plans or underwriting pools, or, more recently, limiting their right to cancel insurance policies in certain lines. The idea that citizens are entitled to have insurance does not belong to the traditional philosophical foundations of insurance regulation.[13] Insurance regulation was established in order to protect citizens within the insurance market, not in order

---

[12] Spencer L. Kimball, "The Goals of Insurance Law: Means versus Ends," *Journal of Insurance*, Vol. 29, No 1 (1962), pp. 19–29.

[13] Cf. Stewart, "The Social Responsibility of Insurance Regulation," *supra*, Chapter 1.

to create that market or to guarantee access to it. As Professor Kimball has pointed out,[14] these provisions are products of a different and evolving political philosophy tending to the "socialization of risk."

This movement to extend or guarantee the availability of insurance coverage, while it is unrelated to the basic goal of insurance regulation as traditionally conceived, is itself the result not of one homogeneous philosophy, but of a number of diverse and quite unrelated public policy considerations, and is also influenced by the various reasons for the shrinking supply provided by the "natural" operation of the market.

For instance, the strong public interest in automobile liability insurance stems mainly from a concern for the victims of automobile accidents. While only three states have enacted compulsory insurance statutes, the financial responsibility laws of the remaining states are designed to indirectly pressure automobile owners into buying liability insurance. Any system of direct or indirect compulsory insurance can, of course, achieve its purpose only if the coverage is actually available. Thus it is quite logical in any such system to provide for insurance in case the ordinary channels of the market fail to provide it. It can be done by restricting the insurers' right to reject an application (Germany), by an assigned risk plan (United States), by a special board authorized to specify individual rates and deductibles for hard-to-place risks (France), by a pool, or by a state insurance institution. All these measures need not necessarily lead to a "socialization of risks," though. All they are supposed to do is to make insurance available, but not to give it away free or at inadequate rates. Every automobile owner, whether insured through ordinary channels or through one of these special devices, continues to pay a premium that corresponds to his risk exposure, so far as possible. However clear and convincing this may be in theory, the actual situation in the United States seems to have been influenced by a feeling among insurers that the rates, as authorized by the state insurance departments, are not adequate, and thus selective underwriting is necessary for them to operate profitably. If this is true, it means nothing else than that the authorized rates are adequate only for the accepted risks while for the rejected risks the rates ought to be higher. If under these circumstances insurers are forced to accept risks they would otherwise reject, without being

---

[14] Kimball, *supra* n. 11, pp. 512–14.

allowed to charge higher rates for them, the result is that a part of the increased total risk exposure has to be borne by the more desirable risks, and that could indeed be called a "socialization" of risk. This effect would be compounded if the idea that everybody must be guaranteed insurance "at a rate he can afford" were to receive general acceptance.

The situation in the field of workmen's compensation is quite similar to that in automobile insurance, so far as the public interest in complete coverage is concerned.

THE CONFLICTING POLICIES INVOLVED IN THE URBAN FIRE PROBLEM

However, as regards the problem of providing adequate fire insurance in urban areas, the public policy considerations are not only different but much more complicated. While it is impossible to deal fully with the subject in this context, it appears that there are, in reality, two problems which are only loosely related to each other. The first of these problems seems to be that the risk exposure with respect to "ordinary" fires and burglary is higher in city core areas than elsewhere. The second is the recent explosive and unexpected increase, and the incalculable potential for further increase, of the risk from civil disorder. It is unfortunate that these two problems are not clearly distinguished in the present discussion of possible solutions, for they seem to be subject to entirely different policy considerations.

Taken alone, the problem of high exposure to ordinary fire and burglary risks in inner core areas could probably be solved if insurers were allowed to exclude coverage for riot damages from ordinary fire policies and were given somewhat greater ratemaking freedom. This would be a logical reaction to the fact that the riot risk, so far negligible, has suddenly turned into a catastrophe risk of incalculable proportions. Elimination, or rather separation, of this risk would seem to be justified as a method of allowing insurers to continue the basic fire coverage on a sound basis. It is true that such separation would require a change in the language of the standard fire insurance policy which now includes coverage for riot-caused fire damage. But statutes will have to be made or amended anyway. The only remaining problem in the field of basic, i.e., nonriot-related, property insurance would then be the accurate evaluation of the individual risks and finding the appropriate premium for each of them. If premiums based on actual risk exposure should turn out to be prohibitively high, it might be necessary to subsidize inner city property owners, e.g., by spreading the extra cost of their coverage among a broader group of policyholders. This problem would not seem to be basically different from closing the automobile insurance coverage gap.

If separated from the ordinary fire policy, the riot risk itself could then be dealt with on its own merits and characteristics which would be more clearly discernible. There is not only the question whether compensation *can* be provided by means of a traditional insurance scheme—a question very similar to that of the feasibility of flood insurance—but also, and more important, whether compensation *should* be provided by traditional insurance, or in other words, how small or how large the group should be among which the cost of riot compensation is to be spread. A traditional or "pure" insurance scheme would spread the risk and resulting losses only among those who are exposed to it, i.e., the owners of inner city property, provided that they are insured. It seems obvious that such a scheme could not operate without being subsidized, either by making more persons share in the costs, or by a commitment of public assistance. Everyone seems to agree that riot damages should not go uncompensated, and that it is the duty of society as a whole to guarantee that compensation, to the extent that it cannot be provided by insurance. Under these circumstances the most logical and at the same time most equitable solution would be to distribute the loss on the broadest possible scale—by paying it out of public funds, so that eventually each taxpayer contributes his share. The idea that society at large is responsible for such damages represents a long tradition, not only in the Anglo-American legal system but on the European continent as well. It would be difficult to justify a system in which compensation for riot losses depended on the existence of a fire insurance contract, especially under present market conditions.

THE SOCIAL RESPONSIBILITIES OF THE INSURANCE INDUSTRY

There is a marked and increasing tendency in the United States today to remind insurers of the duties they owe to society. I do not argue with the reasonableness of these demands; they are partly justified by the simple weight of the capital accumulated by the insurance industry, and can also be explained as a response to the insurers' inability to satisfy some of the most pressing insurance needs. Nor would the implementation of these demands be without precedent elsewhere. The governments of European countries have sometimes used the insurance industry as an instrument of their general social and economic policy, far beyond the original purposes of solidity and policyholder protection.

However, it would be dangerous for the "social responsibilities" of the insurance industry to be mixed up with the traditional goals of insurance regulation. The demands of the larger society should be carefully evaluated to make sure of their compatibility with these basic goals. If without such evaluation insurers were forced to provide coverage to everyone without being allowed to charge a premium commensurate to the risk exposure, the results would ultimately be very disappointing for both policyholders and the public in general.

A SUMMARY VIEW

A summary look shows American insurance regulation to be burdened with a task of discouraging proportions and complexity. A huge and chaotic nationwide market has to be supervised by the divided forces of 50 state agencies, hampered in their effectiveness by bulky, incoherent, sometimes inconsistent, and much too often amended statutes, by inadequate financial and personnel resources, by limited powers that usually end at the state line, and by mutual distrust that precludes the optimum degree of cooperation. These inherent weaknesses account for a number of gaps in the regulatory system, despite serious efforts on the part of the great majority of regulators to improve the situation.

On the other hand, the subject of insurance regulation has almost always been a political subject. In addition to the basic and original goals, policy considerations of various and sometimes doubtful weight and merit have constantly increased the burdens of both the insurance industry and the regulatory agencies. Moreover, direct political pressure has sometimes prevented regulators from making sound and rational decisions.

Whatever the reason or justification, today neither the public nor the regulators themselves are fully satisfied with the state of insurance regulation in the United States.

Specific solutions to the problems mentioned in this paper will be difficult to devise. Any solution should be reached only after there is at all times and at all stages a full and clear understanding about the basic goals of insurance regulation as contrasted to the other goals of social and economic policy that might affect the insurance industry. One excellent method to enhance thinking and discussion about the goals and purposes of statutes is to have every bill accompanied by a comment explaining the objectives sought by the proposed measure. This method has long been practised in Europe where statutory drafting is a carefully cultivated art; it is now being used in the preparation of the new insurance code for the state of Wisconsin.[15] It will, hopefully, have a salutory effect not only on the substance and language of the new code, but also on its future application by the insurance commissioner and by the courts, as well as the drafters of amending statutes. Equally encouraging is the move of the NAIC to reevaluate its purposes, organization and procedures. The increased emphasis on research and planning resulting from this reassessment is likely to make regulators more fully aware of the different weights and natures of the various objectives of government intervention, and to design more discriminating and more rational policies.

---

[15] See, e.g., Comments in ch. 89 (1967), Wis. Laws 223, *et. seq.*, and Chapter 5, *supra*.

Epilogue

Epilogue

WE LIVE in an age of rapid and profound change—change so rapid, indeed, as to appear almost to be a series of discontinuities. But however trite such a statement may be, the triteness disappears when one stands face to face with the problems rapid change presents to an industry that has traditionally been built upon observation and measurement of the past; i.e., upon the assumption that the future will be so much like the past that only the slightest effort at projection of observable trends is necessary to adapt the industry to the needs of the future. Today, however, the insurance industry is facing change rapid enough that it must reverse its direction of observation, from backward to forward.

Insurance regulation, like the industry it regulates, must also deal with change of the same magnitude. The impossibility of comprehending and anticipating fully the alterations taking place in the society around us and, inevitably therefore, in the industry the regulation of which concerns us, must not stop us from trying to anticipate them.

These essays could not hope to present even a backward look at all the developments that are daily changing the face of the industry and its regulatory needs. Many of the most important problems could not even be touched—the impending drastic changes in the underlying law governing compensation for automobile accidents, the staggering problems of the inner city, the unanticipable restructuring of the industry barely adumbrated in the holding company development to date. Of necessity, emphasis has had to be placed on philosophies and techniques of regulation with respect to situations that have already clearly emerged. There has been little speculation about the future in these pages. Our excuse and that of our contributors can only be that there is not yet a systematic literature about the insurance regulation of the past and the present. We do not yet know enough even about what exists to do much in projecting it toward the future. What has been done here can at best provide a start for more ambitious and more innovative thinking about the future course of regulation. Some of the authors represented in this collection will be contributing to that innovative thinking. Hopefully they, and others, will be stimulated by what is contained here to go further afield in their thinking.

The whole fabric of regulation, and perhaps even the direction of society itself (or at least of the insurance industry), will be altered by the determination of some regulatory issues now moving rapidly toward resolution. How far will federal agencies succeed in replacing the state regulators? Will the tort liability system and its insurance superstructure evolve rapidly and satisfactorily enough to survive or will the legal basis of accident compensation be totally rewritten? Will government insurance increasingly supplement and eventually supplant private insurance? Will the holding company movement continue its virtually unrestrained proliferation, reshuffling our economic organization and ultimately calling forth drastically new regulatory and antitrust devices to control the economy?

Fundamental questions of this sort cannot immediately or easily be answered. Yet they affect the whole framework of insurance regulation. At the outset, there are fundamental questions relating to the "validation" of the enterprise. What will be considered "insurance," and thus be legitimate within this part of the economy? Only such activities as are "insurance" will be subject to insurance regulation. Variable annuities fall in the shadowy borderland between insurance and securities. What new forms of "securities" will have to be fitted into a dual regulatory scheme as both insurance *and* securities? Or will the one regulatory system squeeze out the other? What warranties, expanded beyond current concepts, will be subjected to control as "insurance"? How will new and old forms of insurance *stricto sensu* be encouraged, circumscribed, or forbidden by the application of the regulatory machinery? What kinds of insurance, yet to be created, will be sanctioned or prohibited?

As the business evolves, new decisions must be made about its corporate embodiment, its marketing machinery, its underwriting freedom, its premium collection techniques and financing. What new organizational forms and rules will appear, and which disappear? Will Lloyd's of London be admitted as it now exists to all our states? Or will it undergo a transformation? Will reciprocals disappear? Will even mutuals long survive the restructuring of business enterprise? What of those remnants of a simpler society, the fraternals and the town mutuals? What new rules of corporate democracy will be promulgated and what old practices will be condemned?

How should the capital mobilized by the industry be invested and controlled? What broader monetary and social controls will be exercised over these vast pools of highly liquid capital? What demands of the larger society will be imposed on the insurance industry? What is the degree of social responsibility properly to be borne by the insurance industry and how will that responsibility be enforced? That these are no mere fanciful and speculative questions is evident in the recent handling of inner city insurance problems, in the winds of change that are stirring in the automobile field, and in the growing and sometimes irrational fury of the new consumerism.

Finally, how can the most intransigent regulatory problems be solved—the assurance that the accumulated funds are properly used to satisfy their *raison d'être,* the payment of claims? One of the most troubling of all insurance problems is how to assure prompt and equitable settlement of claims, large and small, first and third party.

These and a host of other questions are much more easily asked than answered. They can be asked coldly, in an aseptic and isolated analytical framework. But they must be answered in the real world of men and devils, where all the licit and illicit forces of life—political, social, and economic, pulling and pushing in antagonistic directions—play upon imperfect institutions. The neat outlines and satisfying thought patterns of the study will, one can confidently predict, be grossly distorted by the forces of the real world, where the only certainty is uncertainty, and the only reality complex beyond comprehension.

Despite all the imperfections and distortions one must anticipate and suffer, the solution of the problems before us must begin in the study—in the reflective thought of men acquainted with both the theoretical and the practical dimensions of the subject of insurance and insurance regulation. It is with the hope that it may help in making a true discipline out of the latter that this book was conceived and is offered as a modest contribution to the solution of the staggering problems we face.